Comparing Nations

Comparing Nations

Concepts, Strategies, Substance

Edited by

MATTEI DOGAN

and

ALI KAZANCIGIL

BLACKWELL
Oxford UK & Cambridge USA

Copyright © Basil Blackwell Ltd 1994

First published 1994

Blackwell Publishers
108 Cowley Road
Oxford OX4 1JF, UK

238 Main Street
Cambridge, Massachusetts 02142
USA

British Library Cataloguing in Publication Data
A CIP catalogue record for this book is available from the British Library.

Library of Congress Cataloging-in-Publication Data
Comparing nations: concepts, strategies, substance / edited by Mattei Dogan
  and Ali Kazancigil
        p.   cm.
    Includes bibliographical references and index.
      ISBN 0−631−18644−1 (alk. paper). −ISBN 0−631−18645−X (pbk.: alk. paper)
      1. Comparative government.   I. Dogan, Mattei.   II. Kazancigil, Ali.
  JF51.C622   1994   93−5450
    320.3−dc20   CIP

Typeset in 10½ on 12 pt Baskerville by Apex Products, Singapore
Printed in Great Britain by Page Bros, Norwich

This book is printed on acid-free paper.

Contents

Acknowledgements

This book has been prepared under the auspices of the Social and Human Sciences Sector of UNESCO, Paris, and of the Research Committee on Comparative Sociology of the International Sociological Association.

List of Contributors

Mattei Dogan is Senior Research Director at the French National Centre of Scientific Research, Paris; and Professor of Political Science at the University of California, Los Angeles (UCLA). He is also Chair of the Research Committee on Comparative Sociology, International Sociological Association.

Joshua B. Forrest is Professor of Political Science at the University of Vermont. He has carried out research in several African countries, and is a former scholar at Harvard University's Academy for International and Area Studies.

Ali Kazancigil is Editor of *International Social Science Journal* and Director of the Division for the International Development of Social and Human Sciences, UNESCO, Paris. He has taught political science and international relations at the Middle East Technical University, Ankara.

Seymour Martin Lipset is Professor at George Mason University, Fairfax, Virginia, President of the American Sociological Association, Past President of the American Political Science Association and Senior Fellow at the Hoover Institution. He has taught at the Universities of California (Berkeley), Columbia, Stanford and Toronto.

John D. Martz is Distinguished Professor of Political Science at Pennsylvania State University, and Editor of *Studies in Comparative International Development*. He is also a former editor of *Latin American Research Review*.

Fred W. Riggs is Professor of Political Science at the University of Hawaii and Chairman of the Committee on Conceptual and Terminological Analysis (COCTA), International Social Science Council.

Giovanni Sartori is Albert Schweitzer Professor in the Humanities, Columbia University, New York, and Editor of *Rivista Italiana di Scienza Politica*. He is a former professor at the Universities of Florence and Stanford.

Introduction

Strategies in Comparative Research

Mattei Dogan and Ali Kazancigil

In the literature on comparative politics, there is a vivid contrast between what scholars preach and what most of them do. Periodically during the last decades, the best comparativists have advocated empirical theory, that is theory tested by empirical evidence. In reality too many books and articles claiming to be comparative are either at a level of abstract generalizations, or ideographic. The emphasis in this volume is on an old precept, often forgotten by many scholars: the need to combine theory and data.

Such an emphasis provides a common thread running through all the chapters, despite their varying topics. The chapters are all explicitly comparative or raise comparative issues. They avoid being holistic in approach, comparing not entire political systems but selected segments thereof.

This book discusses eight salient theoretical or methodological issues: the comparative method; the limits to quantification; the conceptual homogenization of a heterogeneous field; the binary analysis; the deviant case and exceptional case; the comparison of similar countries; the diachronic comparison; and the empirical testing of comparative concepts.

As a whole the book weighs more than the sum of its parts. Each chapter should be evaluated according to its own substantive merits, but in addition it provides an illustration of a particular strategy. The diversity of topics included represents a deliberate choice: they were selected for their exemplarity.

Chapter 1: **Compare Why and How** (*Giovanni Sartori*)

There is no such thing as comparative chemistry, only experimental chemistry. Mathematics is universal, but not comparative. In the natural sciences, researchers compare the results of experiments, but they do not claim to be comparativists. The comparative method is adopted exclusively in some fields of the social sciences. From this point of view, Giovanni Sartori is right when he writes that 'comparative politics as a field [is] characterized by a method'.

The scientific method *par excellence* is the experimental one, widely used in the physical and biological sciences. The statistical method is second best, in terms of the requirements of scientific inquiry. Comparisons are less than perfect from the point of view of the latter. Yet the use of the scientifically weaker comparative method is necessary because the particularities of societal phenomena forbid the use of the experimental method. The statistical method, on the other hand, has a wide application to political and social phenomena. It consists in isolating certain parts of the object under study into quantifiable variables and concentrating on their interrelationships. However, when the number of cases from which variables are extracted is small (for example, national political systems), the statistical method rapidly reaches the limits of its usefulness.

Sartori shows that, when all is said and done, comparisons are indispensible in the social sciences because, in many instances, the control function can only be exercised through the comparative method. To him, besides their function of controlling-checking the validity of theoretical propositions, comparisons can have a second purpose: learning from others' experiences.

Comparisons have a wide and varied field of application. Comparative method assumes a probabilistic causality – meaning that a given set of conditions will modify the likelihood of the anticipated outcome – not a deterministic causality, that is, that a given set of conditions will produce the anticipated outcome (Lieberson, 1991).

Sartori returns to an intricate yet central issue in comparative social science: tying individual cases to generalizations. Unless this is done correctly, the results will be disappointing, no matter how good the research techniques used. Sartori's suggestion is to follow the rule of 'upward aggregation' (to render a concept more general it is necessary to limit the number of characteristics mentioned), or 'downward specification' (to make it more specific, increase the number of characteristics), as the case may require.

Chapter 2: Use and Misuse of Statistics in Comparative Research (*Mattei Dogan*)

In comparative research, quantitative data can be used, or not, depending on the nature of the subject, the scope of the research and the strategy adopted. The number of countries included in the comparison largely determines the amount of quantitative data to be used.

In the single case study – which can be highly comparative if the scope of the analysis is the testing of a theory applicable to other countries – the statistical method is not a tool of research, even if statistics are presented. Arendt Lijphart, in his *Politics of Accommodation* (1968), illustrates his discourse by a series of statistical tables concerning a single country; his statistics are not directly comparative, but they are comparable.

In implicit binary analysis, numerical measurements are often assumed to be familiar already and so are not presented. In explicit binary analysis, statistical evidence may help, but since only two countries are included, multivariate analysis is inapplicable. Reinhard Bendix, in his comparison of the samurais and the Junkers, does not provide numerical information. On the other hand, in a binary analysis of electoral cleavages in France and Italy (Dogan, 1967), a variety of statistical data are included. The same is true for the binary analysis of caste and race in India and in the United States by S. Verba, B. Ahmed and A. Bhatt (1971). The recourse to statistics depends, obviously, on the subject analysed. The chapter by S.M. Lipset in this volume is an example of quantitative binary analysis.

If a large number of countries are included in the analysis, the need for statistical data is greater than in a binary comparison. The greater the number of countries, the greater also the need for statistical treatment – in order to demonstrate either analogies or differences, or both.

Where the strategy adopted is the conceptual homogenization of a heterogeneous field, the integrating force is the concept, not the statistical approach (Dogan and Pelassy, 1990, ch. 18).

In contrast, in worldwide holistic comparisons, the statistical method is unavoidable, in spite of all the difficulties encountered. In most strategies of comparative research – case study, binary, comparison of similar countries, comparison of contrasting countries, conceptual homogenization, exceptional cases – recourse to statistics is optional. But in worldwide comparisons statistics are required.

The main methodological problem in the use of statistics in comparative research is the gap between the accuracy of data and the sophistication of the statistical techniques adopted. This chapter deals mainly with this issue.

Chapter 3: Conceptual Homogenization of a Heterogeneous Field (*Fred W. Riggs*)

The ingenious comparativist chooses carefully the countries to be compared. The criterion of choice is not immediately obvious. In all cases, however, the choice must be made according to a clear concept. The comparativist can select countries from the four corners of the world, and find common characteristics to countries apparently dissimilar. It is he who creates a concept capable of homogenizing a heterogeneous series of countries. Some examples will illustrate how this conceptual homogenization is achieved.

The consociational democracy was not understood or recognized until the concept was forged, describing a society segmented into religious, ethnic or cultural communities, but where consensus was institutionalized at the summit. In the same way, the concept of neo-corporatism has allowed meaningful comparisons of some European countries. Another example is the concept of the 'one-dominant-party-system'. In these examples, the explanatory hypothesis pre-existed the selection of countries to be compared.

In the chapter by Fred Riggs several comparisons are super-imiposed. Armed with a concept – presidentialism – he first builds a universe around this concept. The coherence of this universe is strictly conceptual, since it is composed of countries very different from the economic, social and cultural points of view, and spread over five continents.

Many authors have compared presidential regimes and parliamentary regimes. We have learned a lot from this kind of comparison. But Riggs presents an innovative type of comparison by comparing presidential systems to one another. The integrating concept – presidentialism – gives coherence to a heteroclite universe: Brazil, the United States, South Korea, Chile: in total more than 30 countries. This apparently disparate aggregation is conceptually coherent.

At this stage, however, Riggs finds a contrast within this homogeneous universe: between the United States and all other presidential systems. Riggs is the first scholar to try to explain the success of the American presidential system in the light of the failures of such systems in more than 30 countries in Latin America, Africa and Asia: 'We must not reject comparisons between the US and other presidentialist regimes because of the failures of the latter – rather, they provide the information we need in order to explain the relative success of the United States.' Riggs makes a clear distinction between formal constitutional rules and para-political constitutional practices. He arrives at a paradoxical conclusion: 'The more "democratic" a presidentialist regime, the more likely it is to be overthrown and replaced by authoritarianism.' So for him, the United States is an exceptional case: it is the only successful presidential system, if we exclude the particular case of the French system (which is at times superpresidential without countervailing powers, at times simply parliamentarian, but never truly presidential; it is unofficially called semi-presidential).

Riggs uses two strategies of comparative research. First, conceptual homogenization; secondly, the identification of an exceptional case.

The pinpointing of exceptional cases is discussed even more systematically in the following chapter, by S.M. Lipset.

Chapter 4: Binary Comparisons (*Seymour Martin Lipset*)

Lipset's chapter is an example of binary analysis. He discusses the important strategy of revealing exceptional cases through comparisons, but here we are considering his contribution as a binary analysis, reserving the problem of exceptionalism for later discussion.

If the comparativist limits the comparison to two carefully selected countries, he is making a binary comparison. Two kinds of binary comparison can be distinguished: the implicit and the explicit. In implicit comparison, the country of the comparativist serves as reference. Some characteristics of the French society became clear to de Tocqueville through his study of the American society. One knows one's own country better when one learns about other countries.

But the inclusion of the comparativist's native country is not indispensable. He may choose two foreign countries, according to clear hypotheses, for instance basic analogies cutting across major differences. Why is France dominated by a single mega-city, while Italy has 33 regional metropolises? We must look to history for the explanation. Why was the industrialization of Britain so different from that of Germany? One could be interested in the pair Costa Rica–Salvador, or Morocco–Tunisia. Some pairs are interesting and some meaningless.

A binary analysis may have the ambition of covering two countries in their entirety, for instance the process of modernization in Japan and Turkey (Ward and Rustow, 1964). But such an ambitious attempt may result in a series of parallel studies that are not directly comparative. Significantly, there is not a single comprehensive study comparing communism in the Soviet Union and in China.

Even though we may be interested in a hundred countries, it would clearly not be worthwhile to compare each one with all the others. For placing a country in a comparative perspective other strategies would be more appropriate. However, two well chosen countries can become prototypes for a series of countries. Thus binary analysis can be expanded into a comparison of a series of similar or contrasting countries.

In a binary analysis the two countries have to be chosen according to clearly stated criteria, reflecting intriguing hypotheses. There are no comparisons of Brazil and Nigeria because such a pair of countries does not seem to generate interesting questions.

Lipset clearly justifies his choice of Japan and the United States: the 'two foremost examples of industrial success.' But this common characteristic is only one aspect of the binary design. The second is that these two countries have followed 'very different paths' to reach such a position. 'They are the two developed nations that are most different from each other.' In order to test these differences, Lipset analytically 'cuts' each country into many slices: values, tradition, modernity, religion, work ethic, equality, freedom, consensus and conflict, meritocracy, status, gender, family, and so on.

For each of these aspects, Lipset has collected empirical evidence, particularly survey data. This binary analysis is full of empirical data. By breaking down these two exceptional countries into segments, he has demonstrated that in most domains the differences between them are differences of degree. Thus exceptionalism or uniqueness seem to appear only at the global level, as *Gestalt*. We shall return to this important point.

Chapter 5: The Deviant Case in Comparative Analysis
(*Ali Kazancigil*)

The chapter by Ali Kazancigil offers a historical-interpretative analysis of the state and society of Turkey. It is also a 'deviant case' analysis, according to the taxonomy elaborated by Lijphart (1971, pp. 691–3). It shows the historical and institutional conditions, and particularly high stateness, that made the Turkish political system deviate from an established generalization concerning the political systems in Muslim societies, where the general rule is a weakly institutionalized polity, low stateness, chronic instability and authoritarian regimes.

High stateness as a concept covers an apparently heteroclite group of countries, such as France – the classical case – Russia, Japan or Mexico, to name a few. Strong states should not be equated with authoritarianism. Indeed, in developing regions most dictatorial regimes are in countries with a weak state, as shown by Joshua Forrest (chapter 7 in this volume) and by Joel Migdal (1988).

Historically, Turkish polity has proved to be a striking deviance, and the author identifies the following features which explain its deviant character: (a) an autonomous, legitimate political system, dissociated from the religious sphere: (b) high stateness, with a strong, centralized, bureaucratic polity; (c) a civil society based on a market economy; (d) a democratic regime; (e) secularism. In the analysis, features (a) and (b) are considered as independent variables, the other three being dependent ones. Interestingly enough, when the 'experimental group', that is the Turkish case, is set against a 'control group' outside the Muslim political systems, namely Western European high stateness countries, such as France, the deviance is reduced.

If we consider the above-mentioned heteroclite sample of countries, this contribution is also an example of conceptual homogenization of a heterogeneous field. However, if we consider only the set of Muslim countries, it appears as a case of deviance. This chapter can be linked to those by Riggs and Lipset.

Chapter 6: Comparing Similar Countries (*John D. Martz*)

John Martz's chapter elaborates on the category of similar nations. It concerns a region – Latin America – that appears from a distance to be relatively homogeneous. A geographical area can indeed delineate a historically, culturally and economically similar milieu, appropriate for discovering causal relationships, noting similarities and differences between countries, enabling the control of a large number of variables. As a matter of fact, for many decades Latin America has been considered a good illustration of the value of the area concept for comparisons, and numerous comparative studies, many of which are quoted by Martz, have been devoted to this region.

However, the relevance of the geographical area approach for comparative politics is not as straightforward as it may appear at first sight. Similarity is not necessarily linked to contiguity. Geographical proximity in itself is not always meaningful for comparing (Rustow, 1968). There are nations or political systems that belong to the same region, are contiguous, and yet are very different – such is the case, for instance, of the South-east Asian countries.

Martz finds that 'students of Latin American politics remain enduringly frustrated by the problems of diversity', and that none of the broad theories that were applied to Latin America as a whole, such as the *dependencia* (Cardoso and Faletto, 1978), bureaucratic-authoritarianism (O'Donnell, 1973) or the transition theory (O'Donnell et al., 1986; Linz and Stepan 1978; Rustow, 1968) allowed a proper conceptualization of the politics of the region and region-wide comparative studies.

Another problem highlighted by Martz is what he terms the disjunction between monographic area studies and the more generalizing comparative concepts. There are indeed certain risks of confinement that the regional studies conceal when they put the emphasis too heavily on the specificities of the region instead of trying to identify those features that are linked to the particular historical paths of the region.

After a thorough review of the strengths and weaknesses of the literature on Latin American politics, Martz puts forward a number of recommendations to overcome the difficulties of conceptualization and comparability:

- in order to implement a strategy of comparing similar countries and to generate meaningful theories, limit the spatial reach; that is, instead of taking the whole of Latin America, restrict the object of study to carefully selected sub-regions, such as Central America, the Southern Cone or Grancolombia (Venezuala, Ecuador and Colombia);
- rather than looking for macro-theories, aim at middle-range theories, built on multivariate empirical analysis, and situate the analysis at middle-level generalizations;
- practice greater analytical eclecticism, and in particular introduce the cultural variable in the analysis together with the economic and institutional ones:
- in order to escape regional parochialism, link area research to global issues and trends, methodologically, theoretically and substantively.

The strategy of comparing similar countries has recently been criticized by Adam Przeworski:

> I do not know one single study which has successfully applied Mills' cannon of only differences ['most similar systems design' in the Przeworski–Teune, 1970, terminology]. I continue to be persuaded,

indeed, that the 'most similar systems design' is just a bad idea. The assumption is that we can find a pair (or more) of countries which will differ in all but two characteristics and that we will be able to confirm a hypothesis that X is a cause of Y under a natural experiment in which a *ceteris paribus* holds. There are no two countries in the world, however, which differ in only two characteristics and in practice there are always numerous competing hypotheses. (Przeworski, 1987)

Such a criticism is not justified because the similar countries are not chosen on simple characteristics, but on the criteria of basic analogies, such as the sociological context or the socio-economic level. There are many differences among the Latin American countries, but they also share a series of basic analogies.

Chapter 7: Asynchronic Comparisons (*Joshua B. Forrest*)

The contribution by Joshua B. Forrest is an asynchronic comparison between contemporary Africa and mediaeval Europe. Forrest's aim in adopting such a method is to investigate the dynamics of politics in weak states. He does so on the basis of an impressive amount of empirical evidence from contemporary Africa and mediaeval Europe, concerning the following features that characterize weak states: inadequate administrative capacity; low level of state penetration because of strong local powers; the dominance of informal politics, involving personal rule, unbounded power struggles, multiplicity of factions, use of force, military involvement and *coups d'état*, over formal political institutions.

Forrest provides us with an illustration of comparative imagination, well served by rigorous scholarship. The intellectual and contextual circumstances that triggered his imagination as a comparativist are worth exposing:

The idea of comparing post-colonial Africa and medieval Europe came to me while doing fieldwork in Senegal and Guinea-Bissau. Certain images struck me and called forth recollections of my readings of medieval European politics: the relatively tiny 'political class', the leaders consumed with their personal power struggles and divorced from the impoverished masses, political leadership conjoined with military might, reliance on patronage for the construction of centre-local alliances, the relative economic and political disunity of the nation-state despite the geopolitical claims of political elites, the extent to which the vast majority of Africans have absolutely no chance for upward social mobility. These social realities made clear the Africa-

medieval Europe comparison on the human, street-level dimension;
the comparison of political life came to my mind more slowly and
gradually, but no less compellingly. It was by living in rural and
urban Africa month after month that the academically imposed illusion
of 'developing' and 'capitalist' Africa became torn away. The reality
of political life mirrored ever more clearly the political behavior of
the royal families, nobles, knights and lords of medieval Europe.
When I returned to Harvard University, I studied more carefully
and thoroughly the political history of parts of medieval Europe. This
time, the 'recollections' were reversed: rather than my experiences in
the field recalling Europe, my studies of medieval Europe were calling
back the images of 'the field'.   (Forrest, in a letter to the editors)

Forrest's asynchronic comparative analysis illuminates certain
problems of contemporary political systems in Africa. But the author
remains very cautious about the possibility of extending the Africa-
mediaeval Europe comparison to the study of future trends in African
politics. On the contrary, he maintains that there is no certainty
whatsoever that the historical paths of African polities will be similar
to those of the post-mediaeval states of Europe.

The literature concerning the 'weak and reflexive' African state
shares this cautious approach. A basic factor urging prudence in
speculation as to whether the African state today is likely to follow
the course of the post-mediaeval European state is the modern
international system, which interferes economically with the 'peripheral'
African state. In fact, the latter's very survival is attributed by
some scholars not to its innate viability, but rather to the 'juridical'
identity it gains in international law through its recognition and
support by the interstate system (Jackson and Rosberg 1982).

Forrest's contribution is first of all an example of the asynchronic
comparative method. But it also is an illustration of the strategy
of conceptual homogenization of a heterogeneous field, since his
analysis is built on the concept of a 'weak state', bringing together
countries from two continents separated by seven to ten centuries.
From this point of view Forrest's contribution is a valuable com-
panion to the chapter by Riggs. It can also be set against the
chapter by Kazancigil.

Chapter 8: The Pendulum Between Theory and Substance
(*Mattei Dogan*)

In the Weberian typology of legitimacy, the concept of charismatic
leadership plays a crucial role. But if one tries to apply the concept

of charisma to contemporary leaders – without stretching it too far – one finds, through empirical research, only a handful of genuine cases during the last few decades, and even fewer cases of traditional hereditary legitimacy: only three or four, if ceremonial kings deprived of real political power are excluded. Consequently, two of the three 'boxes' of the Weberian typology are almost empty for the contemporary world. The third 'box', legal-rational-bureaucratic rulership, is swollen with about 160 contemporary independent countries, and it is also impure, since it amalgamates a large variety of regimes: Latin American bureaucratic authoritarianism, Scandinavian neo-corporatist democracies, African tyrannical regimes.

The theoretical discomfort becomes even more acute when the empiricist finds that most regimes included in this third 'box' are not even legitimate. Thus the old Weberian typology does not include the majority of contemporary regimes. This classical typology must be updated by adding a fourth type, reserved to semi-legitimate regimes, and a fifth for totally illegitimate rulerships.

Checking again, the researcher finds that these two new types of authority are still too heterogeneous; the choice is then between multiplying the number of types and the distinction of several sub-types.

Remembering that, according to classical theory, legitimacy is not a paragraph in a constitution but a belief to be found in the mind of the people, the researcher needs survey data. He then discovers that the dichotomy legitimacy–illegitimacy is too rigid and that another concept is needed, one that can be operationalized in empirical research by gradual measuring: the notions of confidence and trust. Hence the right questions to ask are: 'How much confidence, by whom, in which domain?' This chapter displays this interplay between theory and empirical testing.

Anomaly, Deviance, Exceptionalism and Uniqueness in Comparative Research

Even in the most imaginative comparative research there remain, in the final analysis, certain irreducible phenomena which reflect the originality of each country. History is the greatest generator of national configurations. The older a country, the more it has been shaped by its history. Two or several countries may have many features in common, but they are never identical, because the attributes are combined differently for each country. We are always facing unique realities that we call China, Switzerland, Egypt, Russia, India or Spain.

In international comparisons we may distinguish anomalies, deviant cases and exceptional cases. It is a matter of degree.

An anomaly is an unexpected position in a ranking, curve or diagram. Statistical eccentricities can be discovered by crossing variables in a scattergram. For instance, life expectancy in Bulgaria is higher than we would expect, considering the other correlates of this country. The number of students per thousand inhabitants in India appears 'abnormal' for a country with such a low standard of living. An anomaly can be revealed only in a comparative light. In comparative sociology it may play the same role as the clinical case in biology or medicine.

The deviant case is less frequent than the anomaly, but it is more significant because it is an entire sector of the society or the political system which appears unusual, abnormal. Deviance can be defined in relation to a set of expectations drawn from a series of countries similar in many ways. As shown in chapter 5, Turkey appears as a deviant case among the Muslim countries.

The exceptional case is a multiple deviant case, an extreme case from many points of view. India, according to certain theories, 'should not' be democratic; it is an enormous exception. The difference between the deviant case and the exceptional case is a difference of degree. Exceptionalism refers to the accumulation of several deviances in systemic or contextual characteristics, forming a configuration, a *Gestalt*. It is in this sense that S.M. Lipset considers Japan and the United States as exceptional cases.

When we decompose the configuration into variables, the distinctiveness tends to be obscured, because we are extracting the variables from their contextual significance. Japan and the United States are exceptional as wholes, but when we 'segment' these configurations, when we isolate variables and indicators, the differences between the two countries become differences of degree. Among the three dozen partial comparisons, and sectoral analyses, Lipset always finds differences of degree; it is never 0 per cent in one case and 100 per cent in the other. The exceptionalism of each of these two countries resides in their national configuration.

The search for deviant and exceptional cases is an alternative strategy to the statistical approach. Instead of high correlations, we are looking for a meaningful clinical test.

Exceptional cases do not limit the potential of international comparisons. On the contrary, the search for exceptions can be a *sui generis* strategy of comparative research, for only by comparing can one say that a country is or is not abnormal, deviant, exceptional.

References

Bendix, R. 1964: *Nation-building and Citizenship*. New York: John Wiley.

Cardoso, F.E. and Faletto, E. 1978: *Dependency and Development in Latin America*. Berkeley, Cal.: University of California Press.

Dogan, M. 1967: 'Political cleavages and social stratification in France and Italy'. In S.M. Lipset and S. Rokkan (eds), *Party Systems and Voter Alignments*, New York: The Free Press.

—— and Pelassy, D. 1990: *How to Compare Nations: strategies in comparative politics*, 2nd edn. Chatham, N.J.: Chatham House.

Jackson, R.H. and Rosberg, C.G. 1982: 'Why Africa's weak states persist: the empirical and the juridical statehood'. *World Politics*, 35(1), October.

Lieberson, S. 1991: 'Small N's and big conclusions: an examination of the reasoning in comparative studies based on a small number of cases'. *Social Forces*, no. 70.

Lijphart, A. 1968: *The Politics of Accomodation, Pluralism and Democracy in the Netherlands*. Berkeley, Cal.: University of California Press.

—— 1971: 'Comparative politics and the comparative method'. *American Political Science Review*, 65(3), 682–93.

Linz, J. and Stepan, A. 1978: *The Breakdown of Democratic Regimes*. Baltimore, Md: Johns Hopkins University Press.

Lipset, S.M. 1977: 'Why no socialism in the United States?'. In S. Bialer and S. Sluzar (eds), *Sources of Contemporary Radicalism*, Boulder, Col.: Westview Press.

Migdal, J.S. 1988: *Strong Societies and Weak States*. Princeton, N.J.: Princeton University Press.

O'Donnell, G. 1973: *Modernization and bureaucratic-authoritarianism: studies on South American politics*. Berkeley, Cal.: University of California Press.

O'Donnell, G., Schmitter, Ph. and Whitehead, L. (eds) 1986: *Transitions from Authoritarian Rule: prospects for democracy*. Baltimore, Md: Johns Hopkins University Press.

Przeworski, A. 1987: 'Methods of coss-national research, 1970–1983: an overview'. In M. Dierkes, H. Weiler and A. Berthoin Antal (eds), *Comparative Policy Research: learning from experience*, Berlin: Wissenschaft Zentrum.

—— and Teune, H. 1970: *The Logic of Comparative Social Inquiry*. New York: John Wiley.

Ragin, C.C. 1987: *The Comparative Method: Moving Beyond qualitative and quantitative strategies*. Berkeley, Cal.: University of California Press.

Rustow, D.A. 1968: 'Modernization and comparative politics: prospects in research and theory'. *Comparative Politics*, no. 1, October.

Sartori, G. 1970: 'Concept misformation in comparative politics'. *American Political Science Review*, 64(3), 1033–53.

Sombart, W. 1976: *Why Is There No Socialism in the United States?* London: Macmillan.

Verba, S., Ahmed, B. and Bhatt, A. 1971: *Caste, Race and Politics: a comparative study of India and the United States*. London: Sage.

Ward, R.E. and Rustow, D.A. 1964: *Political Modernization in Japan and Turkey*. Princeton, N.J.: Princeton University Press.

1

Compare Why and How

Comparing, Miscomparing and the Comparative Method

Giovanni Sartori

It may be the case, as Przeworski contends (1987, p. 34), that 'by the early 1970s the field of comparative methodology had run out of steam'; even so, does anybody remember what that 'steam' was about? Erwin Scheuch (1989, p. 148) makes the similar point that 'in terms of methodology *in abstracto* ... most of all that needed to be said has already been published', but hastens to add that 'methodological discussions are often reinventing what has been forgotten' and that we are endangered by 'collective amnesia in methodology'. I happen to doubt whether all has really been said. But if Scheuch is right, as I believe he is, about our amnesia, then to rediscover the 'forgotten known' is just as important as to discover (anew) an unknown. On this consideration my questions will be (a) why compare? (b) what is comparable? and, (c) compare how?

In the early 1950s, when Roy Macridis blasted (1953, 1955) at the traditional comparative politics of the time, his first and major charge was that it was 'essentially noncomparative'. Much, or indeed more, of the same can be said today, since the field defines itself (in the United States) as studying 'other countries', generally just one. Thus, a scholar who studies only American presidents is an Americanist, whereas a scholar who studies only French presidents is a comparativist. Do not ask me how this makes sense – it does not. As Sigelman and Gadbois (1983, p. 281) nicely put it, 'the traditional distinction between American and comparative politics is ... intellectually indefensible .... Comparison presupposes multiple objects of analysis ... one compares something to or with something else.' The fact none the less remains that a field called comparative politics is densely populated by noncomparativists, by scholars who have no interest, no notion, no training, in comparing. The preliminary point must thus be to establish the distinctiveness of comparative politics as a field characterized by a method.[1]

It is often held that comparisons can be 'implicit' and/or that the scientific approach *per se* is inherently comparative. I certainly grant that a scholar *can be* implicitly comparative without comparing, that is, provided that his one-country or one-unit study *is* embedded in a comparative context and that his concepts, his analytic tools, are *comparable*. But how often is this really the case?[2] I equally grant that, in some sense, the scientific method itself assumes a comparing; but this is a long shot. The short of the matter is that *if* a scholar is implicitly (thought not unwittingly) comparative, this doubtlessly makes him or her a better scholar. But the difference between the implicit and the explicit cannot be slighted to the point of automatically making the 'unconscious comparativist' a comparativist.[3] On this criterion there has never been a behavioural revolution because students of politics have always, implicitly, observed behaviour; there has never been a quantitative revolution because even the simpletons of the past said much, little, greater, lesser, and were thus, implicitly, quantitativists. How absurd – as is attested by the blatant fact that under the 'inevitably comparative' cover-up the social sciences are actually inundated with parochial yardsticks and hypotheses that would founder in a second if ever exposed to comparative checking.

Why Compare

Indeed, comparative *checking*. Have I not already answered my first question, namely, *Why compare?* While I am surely not the first to assert that comparisons *control* – they control (verify or falsify) whether generalizations hold across the cases to which they apply – none the less this is a seemingly forgotten answer. According to Przeworski, a 'consensus exists that comparative research consists *not of comparing but of explaining*. The general purpose of cross-national research is to understand ...' (1987, p. 35).[4] Przeworski appears to be right about the current consensus. In similar fashion Ragin (1987, p. 6) holds that comparative knowledge 'provides the key to understanding, explaining and interpreting'; and Mayer (1989, p. 12) 'redefines' (in his title) comparative politics as a field whose goal is 'the building of empirically falsifiable, explanatory theory'. Well, one can hardly disagree with an intent described as understanding and explaining; for all knowledge, none excluded, is aimed at understanding and all knowledge seeks to explain.[5] But then, why compare? What is the specific reason for being of a comparative route to knowledge? What are comparisons *for*? Against the loss of purpose that appears by now to dominate the field, let a purpose be forcefully reinstated, namely, and to repeat, that *comparing is controlling*. To be sure, one may engage in comparative work for any number of reasons; but one is under no obligation to compare (seriously) unless *the* reason is control.[6]

Take the statements, 'Revolutions are caused by relative deprivation'; or, 'Presidential systems are conducive to effective government, while parliamentary systems result in feeble government'; or, 'Poverty and democracy are inversely related'. True, false, or what? How do we know? We know by looking around, that is, by comparative checking. Granted, comparative control is but *one* method of control. It is not even a strong one. Surely experimental control and, presumably, statistical control, are more powerful 'controllers'.[7] But the experimental method has limited applicability in the social sciences, and the statistical one requires many cases.[8] We are often faced, instead, with the 'many variables, small N' problem, as Lijphart (1971, p. 686) felicitously encapsulates it; and when this is the case our best option is to have recourse to the comparative method of control.[9] The reason for comparing is thus, in its basic simplicity, a compelling one. To this one may sensibly add that comparing is 'learning' from the experience of others and, conversely, that he who knows one country only knows none. Quite so. But an author who engages in cross-country *systematic* comparisons with no 'control purpose' in the forefront of his mind is importantly missing something.[10]

What is Comparable?

Second question, *What is comparable*? We frequently argue that apples and pears are 'incomparable'; but the counterargument inevitably is: How do we know unless we compare them? Actually, with pears and apples the issue is easily solved. But are stones and monkeys comparable? We may still reply that in order to declare them 'incomparables' we have, if for only one second, compared them. None the less, if the entities[11] being compared have nothing in common, there is nothing more to be said, and this is what we mean when we declare that stones and monkeys are not comparable: the comparison is of no interest, it ends where it begins. Returning to pears and apples, are they comparable or not? Yes, they are comparable with respect to some of their properties, that is, the properties they share, and non-comparable with respect to the properties that they do not share. Thus, pears and apples are comparable as fruits, as things that can be eaten, as entities that grow on trees; but incomparable, for example, in their respective shapes. Making the point in general, the question always is: *comparable with respect to which properties or characteristics*, and incomparable (that is, too dissimilar) with respect to which other properties or characteristics?[12]

It will be appreciated that the foregoing establishes that to compare is both to assimilate and to differentiate *to a point*. If two entities are similar in everything, in all their characteristics, then they are a same entity – and that is that. If, on the other hand, two entities are different in every respect, then their comparison is nonsensical – and that is again that. The comparisons in which we sensibly and actually engage are thus those between entities whose attributes are in part shared (similar) and in part non-shared (and thus, we say, incomparable).

Does the above simply push the problem back to the Osgood question, namely, 'When is the same really the same?' and, conversely, 'When is different really different?' (1967, p. 7). Many authors have been struggling without avail with this question, and much research has foundered on its reefs. Yet the question does have a safe answer if we remember that it is answered by classifications and/or by the *per genus et differentiam* mode of analysis.[13] To classify is to order a given universe into classes that are mutually exclusive and jointly exhaustive. Hence, classifications do establish what is same and what is not. 'Same' brings together whatever falls into a given class; 'different' is what falls under other classes.[14] Let it also be underscored that classes do not impute 'real sameness', but *similarity*. The objects that fall into a same class are more similar among themselves – with respect to the criterion of the sorting – than to the objects that fall into other classes. But this leaves us with highly flexible degrees of similarity. As a rule of thumb, the smaller the number of classes yielded by a classification, the higher its intraclass variation (its classes incorporate, so to speak, very different sames). Conversely, the greater the number of the classes, the lesser the intraclass variance. If we divide the world just into monarchies and republics, we have two classes that are, if anything, impossibly large and excessively varied. Still, the example shows that there is no merit in the objection that to classify is to freeze sameness. Any class, no matter how minute, allows for intraclass variations (at least of degree); and it is up to the classifier

to decide how much his classes are to be inclusive (broad) or dis-
criminating (narrow).

The gist is – let it be reiterated – that what is comparable is
established by putting the question in its proper form, which is:
Comparable *in which respect*? Under this formulation, pears and apples
are, in a number of respects (properties), comparable. So are, but
lesser so, men and gorillas (they are, for example, both erect animals
with *prensilis* hands); and so are, at the limit, even men and whales
(both are mammals, and both cannot breath under water). But, of
course, the incomparables grow as we pass from the first to the third
example. When and how is it, then, that we go wrong? I do not
claim that the *only* way of playing the comparative game without
error is to rely on classificatory orderings. Indeed, my claim has
been, above, that it is a 'safe' (not an exclusive) way to go about it.
But since the point has been misconstrued by my critics, it is well
first to counter their attacks.

Let me quote for all Eugene DeFelice (1980, 1986), who finds
'illogical and unscientific' the argument that classification ought to
precede measurement and implies that this view, 'if followed ...
would restrict any particular empirical study to only those countries
classified as similar' (1986, p. 415). Needless to say, this implication
is a *non sequitur* that is only in DeFelice's mind, for I hold just as
much as he does that if 'comparative researchers mistakenly restrict
their causal inferences to hypotheses that can be tested only among
similar countries, they will have needlessly abandoned hypotheses that
can be tested just as well by comparing countries that are different'
(1986, p. 416). Thus far, then, DeFelice attacks a windmill. His
major point, however, is that 'a procedure of measurement not
only determines an amount but also fixes what it is an amount *of*'
(1980, p. 121). This is a quotation from Abraham Kaplan (1964,
p. 177), which entails, in DeFelice's reading, that 'all levels of
measurement share [an] "either–or" function', and therefore that
'since quantitative concepts can express not only the degree of an
attribute's presence but also the fact of its absence', everything can
be handled quantitatively.

But no. Here DeFelice extends his misreading talents to Kaplan
and, by implication, also to Hempel (since he argues that 'Hempel
simply means to say what Kaplan said'). It is quite obvious, as
Kaplan puts it (1964, p. 177), that 'what is measured and how we
measure it are determined jointly'. However, Kaplan's premiss is
that 'whether we can measure something depends ... on how we
have conceptualized it, on our knowledge of it' (ibid., p. 176). And
Kaplan's earlier warning had been that the 'mystique of quantity

is an exaggerated regard for the significance of measurement ...
without regard ... to what has been measured' (ibid., p. 172). So,
conceptualization precedes measurement. As for Hempel, DeFelice's
misreading leads him to ignore that Hempel's 'comparative concepts'
are not quantitative concepts (see Hempel, 1952, pp. 54ff), and therefore do not sustain DeFelice's measurement mystique.[15]

Resuming my thread, let me now look into our 'going wrong' by
way of illustration and by having recourse to the 'cat-dog' imagery,
an imagery that can be made into a story (I hope an amusing one).

Mr Doe is ready for his dissertation, but he must be original and
must have, he is insistently told by his advisers, a hypothesis. His
subject is the cat-dog (one cannot be original, nowadays, just with
cats or just with dogs), and his hypothesis, after much prodding,
is that all cat-dogs emit the sound 'bow wow'. The adviser says,
'interesting', and a foundation gives him $100,000 for a worldwide
research project. Three years later Mr Doe shows up in great dismay
and admits: Many cat-dogs do emit the sound 'bow wow', but many
do not – the hypothesis is disconfirmed. However, he says, I now
have another hypothesis: all cat-dogs emit the noise 'meow meow'.
Another three years go by, another $100,000 are dutifully spent in
researching, and yet, once again, the hypothesis is not sustained: many
cat-dogs do emit the noise 'meow meow' but many do not. In deep
despair Mr Doe visits at dusk the oracle of Delphi, who on that day
has grown tired of making up sibylline responses. My friend, the
oracle says, to you I shall speak the simple truth, which simply is that
the cat-dog *does not exist*. End of story, and back to non-fiction.

How does the cat-dog come about? It is fathered, I submit, by four
mutually sustaining sources: (a) parochialism; (b) misclassification;
(c) degreeism; and (d) conceptual stretching.

Parochialism refers, here, to single-country studies *in vacuo*, that
purely and simply ignore the categories established by general theories
and/or by comparative frameworks of analysis, and thereby un-
ceasingly invent, on the spur of the moment, an *ad hoc*, self-tailored
terminology. For example, a recent article of Sundquist (1988) deals
– the wording of the title – with 'coalition government in the United
States'. Now, throughout the world 'coalition government' stands
for parliamentary systems (not American-type presidential systems)
in which governments are voted into office and supported by parliaments and happen not to be single-party governments. Not one of
these characteristics obtains in what Sundquist calls coalition government. Thus a cat-dog (or, worse, a dog-bat) is born; and as soon
as the misnomer is entered into our computers it is bound to mess
up whatever is correctly known of coalition governments (proper).

In the example above a cat-dog results from a mislabelling which results, in turn, from parochialism. A second source is misclassification, pseudo-classes. Take the one-party category in the literature on political parties, a huge basket that has long included (a) the so-called one-party states in the United States, Japan and, off and on, Sweden, Norway and India; (b) Mexico; (c) the Soviet Union, China and Eastern European countries. The above collapses into one three utterly different animals, and thus is, I submit, a cat-dog-bat.[16] Suppose now that we wish to explain what causes uni-partism. Huntington suggests that 'the social origins of one-party systems are to be found ... in bifurcation', that is to say, 'one-party systems ... tend to be the product of either the cumulation of cleavages ... or the ascendancy in importance of one line of cleavage over the others' (Huntington and More, 1970, p. 11). Right, wrong? We shall never find out. Neither his hypothesis nor any other will ever pass the test of the cat-dog-bat, for no generalization can conceivably hold under the joint assaults of such a three-headed monster. What might apply to cats will apply only in part to dogs, and in almost no respect whatsoever to bats (and vice versa). One may wonder why, here, the culprit is misclassification. Well, because classifications are orderings derived from a single criterion. In the case in point, under a correct classificatory treatment 'one' will include only the polities in which 'second' (more than one) parties neither exist nor are permitted to exist. Under a classificatory treatment, therefore, the United States, Japan, India and so on could not possibly fall into the one-party box. But under a pseudo-class anything goes.

A third producer of cat-dogs and further – in increasing order of teratological messiness – of dog-bats and even fish-birds is, I have suggested, 'degreeism'. By this I mean the abuse (uncritical use) of the maxim that differences in kind are best conceived as differences of degree, and that dichotomous treatments are invariably best replaced by continuous ones. To exemplify, under a continuous, or continuum-based treatment, democracy cannot be separated from non-democracy; rather, democracy is a property that to some (different) degree can be predicated of all political systems and, conversely, non-democracy is always more or less present in any polity. We may thus obtain a worldwide continuum ranging, say, from 80 per cent democracies, across semi-democracies, to 80 per cent non-democracies, whose cut-off points are stipulated arbitrarily and can, therefore, be moved around at whim. This is too good to be right; and is not right, because the exceptions that might cripple a hypothesis generally lie in the vicinity of the cutting points. Thus, in the continuous treatment the exceptions (disconfirmations) can simply be made to disappear by cutting a continuum at astutely doctored points.[17] Along this route we obtain, then, the Cheshire cat-dog – it appears – grins at us, and vanishes before we catch it.

Fourthly, comparative futility and fallacies simply and generally result from definitional sloppiness and 'conceptual stretching' (Sartori, 1970). Take *constitution*. If the term is stretched to mean 'any state form', then the generalization 'constitutions obstruct tyranny' would be crushingly disconfirmed (while it would be confirmed under a narrower meaning). Take *pluralism*. If all societies are declared, in some sense, pluralistic, then the generalization 'pluralism falls and stands with democracy' no longer holds. Another good example is *mobilization*. If the concept is stretched to the point of including both self-motion (participation as a voluntary act) and its obverse, namely, hetero-motion, being coerced into motion (mobilization proper), then we do not only have a perfect cat-dog but we may also end up with a cat-dog fight in which the two components eat up each other. *Ideology* would be a further excellent instance of a concept deprived of all heuristic validity, let alone testability, by having been stretched to a point of meaninglessness. As currently used and abused, the word ideology never ceases to apply (it has no opposite), everything is ideology, and thus a worthy tool of analysis is turned – following up on the dog-cat imagery – into zoology in its entirety, into meaning 'all animals, none barred'.

It may look as though I have already moved from the question, *What is comparable?* to the question, *How compare?* Even so, a number of method-specific issues still lie ahead.

Compare How

There are many possible ways of conceiving the basic, general strategy of scientific inquiry. My favourite is the insightful outline provided by Smelser. The initial picture of any phenomenon that a social scientist attempts to explain, he writes,

> is one of a *multiplicity* of conditions, a *compounding* of their influences on what is to be explained (the dependent variable) and an *indeterminacy* regarding the effect of any one condition or several conditions in combination. The corresponding problems facing the investigator are to *reduce* the number of conditions, to *isolate* one condition from another, and therefore to *make precise* the role of each condition ... How does he do that? (1976, pp. 152–3).

He does that in two major ways: (a) by organizing the conditions into independent, intervening and dependent variables, and (b) by treating some causal conditions as *parameters*, parametric constants or givens (as when we invoke the *ceteris paribus* clause) that are assumed not to vary, and treating other conditions as *operative variables* that are instead allowed to vary in order to assess their influence upon the dependent variable(s) (pp. 153–4). To be sure, no variable is inherently independent or dependent, and 'What is treated as a parameter in one investigation may become the operative variable in another' (p. 154).[18]

Another general point bears on research designs. By and large, 'at times comparativists will emphasize similarities, at times differences. They will tend to look for differences in contexts that are roughly similar, or . . . will try to find analogies in contrasting political systems' (Dogan and Pelassy, 1984, p. 127). But shifts in emphasis can also become distinct research methodologies. Most comparativists adopt a 'most similar system' design; but, as Teune and Przeworski (1970, pp. 31ff) point out, one can also abide by a 'most different system' design. In the most similar system strategy, the researcher brings together systems that are as similar as possible in as many features (properties) as possible, thus allowing a large number of variables to be ignored (under the assumption that they are equal). Simply put, a most similar strategy (as with area studies, Anglo-American countries and the like) assumes that the factors that are common to relatively homogeneous countries are irrelevant in explaining their differences. The recommendation thus is: choose entities that are similar, if possible, in all variables, with the exception of the phenomenon to be investigated. Sure. But the reverse way of attacking the problem is to choose the most different systems, that is, systems that differ as much as possible and yet do not differ on the phenomenon under investigation. In the example of Przeworski and Teune, if rates of suicide are the same among the Zuni, the Swedes and the Russians (indeed utterly different systems), then systemic factors are irrelevant for the explanation of suicide and can be disregarded (1970, p. 35). Again, fine.[19]

Entering more troubled waters, an issue that recurs without convincing answers is when and to what extent exceptions kill a rule, that is to say, law-like generalizations endowed with explanatory power. Of course, if we assume that a law is 'deterministic', just one exception suffices to kill it. But far more often than not we declare our law-like generalizations 'probabilistic', and this appears to get us off the hook. Does it? Note, first, that the argument is not reserved to statistical laws, for which it is impeccable, but extended to any law-like explanation. If so, what does probabilistic mean when no mathematical power is attached to the notion? It can only mean, I believe, that we are dealing with 'tendency laws' with respect to which one or a few exceptions do not entail rejection. Even so, exceptions are disconfirming; but it is too easy to leave the point at that.

Assume that our laws are given the *if . . . then* form – a formulation conducive to condition analysis; and let it be stipulated, for the purpose at hand, that the 'if' consists of the necessary conditions, the conditions without which a law does not apply. Thus, the spelling out of necessary conditions specifies when a law is, or is not, applicable; and the addition of further necessary conditions restricts the ambit of its applicability. For the issue at hand this means that exceptions are handled (reduced) by reducing the range of application of a rule on the basis of its necessary conditions. For instance, Galileo's law of falling bodies was bound to be experimentally disconfirmed unless the necessary condition 'falling in a vacuum' was entered. There is, however, another way of handling the problem, which is to reformulate a law in such a way as to incorporate its exceptions.[20] And it is only when both strategies have been pursued to their reasonable point of exhaustion that a rule may be retained (if at a low level of confidence) by explaining away its exceptions on *ad hoc* grounds.[21] But it is impermissible, I submit, to declare a law 'deterministic . . . with the exceptions noted' (Riker, 1982, p. 761).

Another unsettled issue bears on how case studies – especially of the 'heuristic' and the 'crucial' variety[22] – relate to the comparative method. I must insist that as a 'one-case' investigation the case study cannot be subsumed under the comparative *method* (though it may have comparative *merit*). On the other hand, comparison and case study can well be mutually reinforcing and complementary undertakings.[23] My sense is that case studies hinged on comparable concepts are most valuable as hypothesis-generating inquiries. They cannot confirm a generalization (one confirmation adds confidence, but cannot add up to a confirming test), and they can only disconfirm a regularity to a limited degree. But heuristic case studies do provide ideal – perhaps the best – soil for the conceiving of generalizations. If so, however, case studies are first and foremost part and parcel of theory-building (as Eckstein underscores), not of theory-controlling.[24]

We are ready for the most crucial and, at the same time, most unsettled issue of the lot. Let us go back, in order to confront it squarely, to the knock-down question: Is the comparative enterprise at all possible? All along there have been many ways of formulating this fundamental objection. A more recent one rallies the negators under the banner of a so called 'incommensurability of concepts'. In my understanding, 'incommensurable' basically conveys that we have no measure, or no common measure, for something. If so, what I have been saying is hardly affected by an incommensurability indictment. However, 'incommensurability' is currently brandished in a strong sense that implies that all our concepts are context-embedded to the point of being inescapably idiosyncratic.[25] This is an overkill: if anything, concepts are generalizations in disguise, mental containers that amalgamate an endless flow of discrete perceptions and conceptions. But to dismiss incommensurability in its extreme claim is not to dismiss the one-century-old distinction, put forward by Rickert and Dilthey, between idiographic and nomothetic sciences. In their understanding (which preceded the *Annales* school) historians addressed the unique, thus coming on the side of what we call a configurative, context-embedded focus. Conversely, the natural sciences were nomothetic, sought laws, and thus dissolved singularity into generality. Here, then, we do not have inescapable prisons of closed incommensurables, but an alternative that allows for trade-offs between gains and losses. On balance, case studies sacrifice generality to depth and thickness of understanding, indeed to *Verstehen*: one knows more and better about less (less in extension). Conversely, comparative studies sacrifice understanding-in-context – and of context – to inclusiveness: one knows less about more.

Is there no way of bridging this gap? In theory, that is, methodologically speaking, we do have to chose between alternative strategies of inquiry. In practice, that is, in our actual proceedings, the comparativist is required to draw on the information provided by single-country, configurative studies; and, conversely, the single-country specialist who ignores comparative findings harms his own endeavour. Along parallel lines Lipset (1963, pp. 9–10) puts it very well:

> The analyst of societies must choose between a primarily historical or a primarily comparative approach. ... But ... he cannot ignore the other. Without examining social relations in *different* countries it is impossible to know to what extent a given factor actually has the effect attributed to it in a *single* country.

Take, to illustrate, the topic of corruption. To the contextualist, corruption in, say, Egypt is only corruption in Egypt, and is not, furthermore, corruption at all, since 'paying for a service' is not perceived as Westerners perceive it: an illicit and harmful social practice. Right. The finding of the comparativist will be, instead, that corruption is 'normal' (and quasi-universal) in the Middle East, Asia, Africa; 'endemic', though deprecated, in Latin America and other parts of the world; and counteracted with some (different) modicum of success in, say, some 20 to 30 Western-type countries. Wrong? No, because his point is to assess the extent to which, across the world, bureaucrats, politicians and eventually judges provide their services on the basis of payments or gifts. The context-ignorant comparativist is likely to be wrong, however, in the interpretation and, in its wake, in the explanation. What he observes – his common denominator – is *a particular class of exchanges*, not corruption as bribery, not the sub-class 'illicit exchanges'. Should we leave this at saying that the contextualist and the comparativist both discover half-truths? Certainly not. But we now need a theoretical framework that accommodates the two halves. In such a framework the general category would be exchange, its subsets 'economic' versus 'extra-economic' exchanges, and the explanation (leading, in its refinements, to a causal argument) might roughly be that extra-economic exchanges become dysfunctional, illicit and morally wicked when polities reach the stage of structural differentiation that provides – in Max Weber's terminology – for a 'rational-legal' bureaucracy. It is only when a civil service is paid for its services by the state (that is, by tax revenues), only when judges become civil servants (on a payroll), and when, in turn, politics is no longer conceived of as a wealth-making resource, it is only at this point that the citizen comes to expect services in exchange for nothing and that corruption and bribery are perceived as wrongdoings.[26] Note, incidentally, that this framework not only endows the comparativist with the amount of contextual understanding that he needs; it also suggests that the Egypt-only specialist might be wrong in overstressing Egypt's uniqueness.

The methodological point remains, to be sure, that we *are* confronted with an alternative between individualizing and generalizing. Even so, the alternative is not intractable and bridges do exist that help us to switch from generalization to context, and vice versa. In a much-quoted passage Sidney Verba makes this convergence appear as a self-defeating sort of vortex, as an entanglement that ends in strangulation (of comparative politics). The passage reads as follows:

> To be comparative, we are told, we must look for generalizations or covering laws that apply to all cases of a particular type. ... But where are the general laws? Generalizations fade when we look at the

particular cases. We add intervening variable after intervening variable. Since the cases are few in number, we end with an explanation tailored to each case. The result begins to sound quite idiographic or configurative. ... As we bring more and more variables back into our analysis in order to arrive at any generalizations that hold up across a series of political systems, we bring back so much that we have a 'unique' case in its configurative whole.   (1967, p. 113)

The foregoing may be a truthful account of how we have been messing things up, but should not be taken as a recipe for making headway. 'Where are the general laws?' Well, nowhere – for even if we were capable of formulating them (and we are not: see Sartori, 1986) the cat-dog would kill them. 'Adding intervening variable after intervening variable' certainly is a wrong way of proceeding. My suggestion has long been (Sartori, 1970, pp. 1040–5; Sartori et al., 1975, pp. 16–19; Sartori, 1984, pp. 44–6) that an orderly way – indeed, method – of relating universals to particulars is to organize our categories along a *ladder of abstraction* whose basic rule of transformation (upward aggregation and, conversely, downward specification) is that the connotation (intension) and denotation (extension) of concepts are inversely related. Thus, in order to make a concept more general, namely, to increase its travelling capability, we must reduce its characteristics or properties. Conversely, in order to make a concept more specific (contextually adequate), we must increase its properties or characteristics. As I was saying, the problem is not intractable.[27] But some routes are more difficult to travel than others. The one that I propose admittedly requires painstaking thinking, while it is infinitely easier to behead problems by invoking incommensurability or by letting computers do our work while we relax.[28]

Conclusions

Vis-à-vis the high hopes of three decades ago, comparative politics is, to say the least, a disappointment. In the early 1960s the survey of Somit and Tanenhaus (1964, pp. 55–7) indicated that comparative politics was seen as the field in which 'most significant work was being done'. But three years later Verba already asked himself: 'why has there been so much movement and so little movement forward?' (1967, p. 113). In part, he replied, 'the answer is in the toughness of the problem' (ibid.). Quite. The other part of the answer is, however, that a discipline without logical, methodological and linguistic *discipline* cannot solve, but only aggravate, problems for itself. In the last 40 years or so, we have enjoyed moving from one 'revolution' to another: behavioural, paradigmatic, 'critical', postpositivist, hermeneutic, and so on. But revolutions (in science) just leave us with a new beginning – they have to be followed up and made to bear fruits. We have, instead, just allowed them to fade away, as ever-new beginnings hold ever-new promises which remain, in turn, ever unfulfilled. In the process the simple basics that I have been addressing in this chapter have been lost. David Collier (1991) has provided an assessment of the issues of comparative method debated in the last 20 years. Since Collier's coverage is indeed excellent, it is highly telling that the control purpose of comparing is nowhere covered. Yes, our sophistication has grown – but at the expense of an increasingly missing core: a missing core that allows growing numbers of comparativists (in name) who never compare anything, not even 'implicitly', thus forsaking standardized labels, common yardsticks and shared parameters.

Bluntly put, the normal science is not doing well.[29] A field defined by its method – comparing – cannot prosper without a core method. My critique does not imply, to be sure, that good, even excellent, comparative work is no longer under way. But even the current good comparative work underachieves. When everything is in place for coming to the framing and testing of hypotheses, we cease to deliver. This attests, I submit, to loss of focus, to our having lost sight of what comparing is distinctively *for*. Panebianco argues that the decline of comparative politics goes all the way back to a fundamental disagreement 'as to what constitutes an acceptable explanation' (in Sartori and Morlino, 1991, p. 151). But why should this disagreement affect the *control function* of comparisons? All social science explanation – whether law-like, functional-like or other – involves generalization; and, in turn, all generalization is amenable to some (appropriate) kind of comparative testing. Granted that we do disagree on 'explanation', still the major single reason for our failings is, it seems to me, logical illiteracy.

Notes

I am indebted to Jean Lecas, S.M. Lipset, Joseph LaPalombara and Arend Lijphart for their critical responses to an early draft of this essay. A short version of this article has appeared in the *Journal of Theoretical Politics*, 3(3), July 1991.

  1. Indeed, comparative politics is the one field of political science that defines itself by 'a methodological instead of substantive label' (Lijphart,

1971, p. 682). Similarly, in Holt and Turner (1970, p. 5): 'the common-sense meaning of the term *comparative* ... refers to a method of study and not to a body of substantive knowledge'.

2. Not often, as one can easily infer from a skimming of the biblio-graphies. Most single nation studies plainly and wholeheartedly ignore the comparative frameworks and literature that bear on their topics. As Richard Rose (1991, p. 449) correctly indicates, 'The presence or absence of concepts applicable to a multiplicity of countries is the test of whether a study can be considered comparative. More often than not, single-country studies are cast in idiographic ... terms .... The result is a jumble ....'

3. Indeed, it is precisely because everybody in some sense and to some extent compares, that Marradi (1985, p. 298) forcefully recommends that 'the term comparison should indicate only *explicit* and *conscious* comparisons'.

4. My emphasis; but the assertion that the comparative craft does not con-sist of comparing is startling enough to warrant underlining. Przeworski's assertion cannot be read as a mere stock-taking of the current state of the field; it also endorses it.

5. Note that even 'explanations' appears too strong a requirement to Cantori. In his appraisal, 'comparative politics is more inclined towards interpretation than explanation', the difference between the two, being that explanation 'seeks to *demonstrate* the validity of its conclusion', whereas interpretation 'seeks to *convince* only by means of persuasion' (Cantori and Ziegler, 1988, p. 418).

6. It should be understood that the point bears on the normal science. In authors of the stature of Tocqueville, Durkheim or Max Weber, the comparative component of their work is part and parcel of the richness of their thinking. As all my examples indicate, I am not speaking to 'grand schemes' but to the single generalizations (causal-like hypotheses) that authors would 'normally' formulate in pursuing a topic. True, 'comparison starts from the logic of a matrix' (Rose, 1991, 453). But I am particularly worried by discrete generalizations that are not construed in matrix form and that truly smuggle, therefore, 'false universalisms'.

7. I say 'presumably' to account for the counterarguments of Frendreis (1983, p. 258), and especially of Ragin (1987, pp. 15–16), who con-tends that 'the comparative method is superior to the statistical method in several important respects'. Still, as Jackman (1985, p. 179) sensibly argues, 'statistical analysis can be a powerful aide to causal inference'.

8. Lijphart and Smelser take a different view as to whether the experi-mental, statistical and comparative methods are distinct methods (Lijphart), or simply different implementations of a same comparative logic (Smelser 1976, p. 158). Since the methods in question are not equivalent, in my opinion their distinctiveness matters more than their similarity. As Morlino judiciously points out, even if the only difference

between statistical and comparative methods was in the 'few cases' of the latter, 'that difference alone carries deep implications ... for the procedures and intents of empirical research' (Sartori and Morlino, 1991, p. 12).

9. Of course, in some instances one may control both across a relatively small and a relatively large number of cases, that is, statistically. Let the hypothesis be: party cohesion is a direct function of the degree of interparty competition (and, thus, the lesser the competition, the higher the degree of intraparty fractionism). Here a comparative checking will help refine the hypothesis, so that a statistical control may subsequently become correctly applicable.

10. Reference to 'cross-country' comparisons does not exclude, to be sure, within-country and/or multi-level systematic comparisons. But the full case – with all its complexities – is more fully confronted across countries. Note, on the other hand, that cross-country is not 'whole country'. (Rose, 1991, p. 454) makes the point neatly: 'The subject is not countries *per se* but analytic attributes common to many countries.'

11. Entity stands here for whole systems, sub-systemic 'segments' (vigorously upheld by LaPalombara, 1970, pp. 123ff), processes, or even, at the limit, for a single property or characteristic of a universe.

12. Marradi (1985, p. 294) refines the point by noting that we do not actually compare 'properties' but 'states of properties'. I certainly agree; and this entails that comparisons also investigate different states of a same property.

13. This is a 'safe answer' to the Osgood question but does not entail in the least – as Jackman assumes (1985, p. 168) – that the items being compared *must* be of the same class. Of course not. Comparisons, I say all along, bear on attributes and characteristics. Jackman equally misreads me when he writes that for both Kalleberg and myself 'comparison involves ranking and quantification' (ibid.). This is a view of Kalleberg which baffles me (note below).

14. The point is made by Kalleberg (1966, pp. 77–8) as follows: 'Truly comparative concepts ... can only be developed after classification has been completed. Classification is a matter of "either–or"; comparison is a matter of more or less.' But why *must* comparisons be a matter of more-or-less? Possibly Kalleberg has in mind, here, intraclass (not interclass) comparing.

15. My methodological views are well upheld by O'Kane (1993), whose conclusion – to which I very much subscribe – is that 'comparative analysis must not be done for the sake of technique at the expense of conceptual logic'.

16. To specify, the first group of countries are predominant party systems that belong to a competitive setting (Sartori, 1976, pp. 192–201); Mexico is a hegemonic party polity that 'licenses' a limited competition (ibid., pp. 230–8); and the third group is (was) one-party proper, in that it impedes competition and any other party (ibid., pp. 221–30).

17. For instance, Douglas Rae avoids conceiving two-partism as a class
    or a type, and speaks instead of 'two-party competition' defined as
    the occurrences 'in which the first party holds less than 70% of the
    legislative seats, and the first two parties together hold at least 90% of
    the seats' (1971, p. 93). But why 90 instead of, say, 89 per cent? Indeed,
    89 per cent would include Germany in 1980 (not a two-party system
    and thus a disconfirming instance). And why should the first party
    have less than 70 per cent? This value already permits more exceptions
    than Rae knows of (it allows for the inclusion of Turkey in 1957 and
    Greece in 1981); and still more would follow under a ceiling of, say,
    68 per cent. Be that as it may, the point is that the evidence can be
    'gerrymandered' just by juggling the cut-offs.
18. While I quote from Smelser's more recent writing, one should also
    look into Smelser 1966 and 1967, *passim*. Concerning the terminology,
    variables that are held constant are generally said to be 'controlled'
    and called 'control variables'. This is very different from saying that
    comparisons are a method of control.
19. Whether the most different systems design differs from the most similar
    one in that the former consists of multilevel analysis and must observe
    'behavior at a level lower than that of systems' (as its proponents
    hold, Przeworski and Teune, 1970, p. 34) is a differentiation open to
    question. The point remains that seeking contrast and seeking similarity
    are different approaches.
20. Both strategies are discussed and illustrated in Sartori (1986, pp. 48–50
    and *passim*). Take the 'rule' that says: 'a plurality system will produce
    ... a two-party system ... under two conditions: first, when the party
    system is structured, and, second, if the electorate which is refractory
    to whatever pressure of the electoral system happens to be dispersed
    in below-plurality proportions throughout the constituencies' (p. 59).
    Here, the first condition enters a necessary condition, and the second
    one actually incorporates in the law the exceptions resulting from
    above-plurality or above-quotient distributions of incoercible minorities.
21. My argument is confined to 'rule disconfirmation'. Generally, and
    in principle, a theory T is falsified, and thus rejected, 'if and only if
    another theory T^1 has been proposed with the following characteristics:
    (1) T^1 has excess empirical content over T ... (2) T^1 explains the pre-
    vious success of T ... and (3) some of the excess content of T^1 is
    corroborated' (Lakatos, 1970, p. 116).
22. These are the labels employed by Eckstein (1975, pp. 80ff). Lijphart
    (1971, pp. 691–3) also discusses the various uses and types of case
    studies. By combining the wordings of the two authors, one can dis-
    tinguish among the following five kinds of case study: (a) configurative-
    idiographic (Eckstein); (b) interpretative (Lijphart); (c) hypothesis-
    generating (Lijphart); (d) crucial (Eckstein), that is, theory-confirming
    or disconfirming (Lijphart); (e) deviant (Lijphart). An outstanding
    instance of the latter is Lipset et al.'s *Union Democracy* (1956), in which

the International Typographical Union is systematically studied as a 'deviation' from Michels' iron law of oligarchy.

23. See, notably, George (1979).

24. Note that my distinction between case study and comparison does not imply in the least that the latter is a superior form of inquiry. If, as Eckstein (1975, p. 88) holds, 'The quintessential end of theorizing is to arrive at *statements of regularity*', then the distinctive claim of the comparative method is not the discovery of 'rulefulness' but its testing. There are many paths, not only the comparative one, that lead to discovery of law-like regularities.

25. This extreme view is drawn from Feyerabend (1975), whose epistemological stance is that (a) theory determines concepts, and that (b) data themselves are a function of theory, so that data described in terms of theory A cannot be 'compared' to data stated in terms of theory B. For a rebuttal, to which I subscribe, see Lane (1987).

26. This is born out by the history of language. *Munus* in Latin, *doron* in Greek, *shohadh* in ancient Hebrew, applied indifferently to gift and to what we call bribe. So everything was gift, nothing was bribe.

27. Even so, it cannot be handled, I believe, by assuming as Przeworski and Teune (1970, p. 12) do, that 'most problems of uniqueness versus universality can be redefined as problems of measurement'.

28. This last remark must be left at that, except for noting that many current failings of comparative politics are not of the method itself but result from shaky data. The more massive the information, and the larger the number of countries from which it is drawn, the less the person at the computer is in control of the evidence. How accurate and valid is it? One cannot be sure. But what is quite certain is that much of the data that was aggregated is ill-compared, in that under a same label the slicings (even from researcher to researcher) of the real world under scrutiny are different. Sometimes cats are only cats; sometimes they are cat-dogs; sometimes they are only white cats; and they may also be cat-fishes. Printout giants are easily erected, but over a marsh.

29. Indeed, 'dismal' is how the state of the field generally looks to the practitioner that Verba surveys (1985, p. 28). Verba himself disagrees. His assessment is that 'things are in fact getting better ... but ... one never has enough of ... progress, and progress brings new problems and frustrations'. So, 'comparative politics is and has been disappointing ... but in comparison to past ... hopes, not ... in terms of its accomplishments' (ibid., p. 29). My own reading is, instead, that comparative politics is disappointing (and largely downsliding, albeit with important exceptions) precisely in its accomplishments.

References

Bendix, Reinhart 1977: *Nation-building and Citizenship*. Berkeley, Cal.: University of California Press.

Cantori, J.L. and Ziegler, A.H. (eds) 1988: *Comparative Politics in the Post-behavioral Era*. Boulder, Col.: Lynne Rienner.

Collier, David 1991: 'The comparative method: two decades of change'. In D.A. Rustow and K.P. Erickson (eds), *Comparative Political Dynamics: global research perspectives*, New York: Harper & Row.

DeFelice, Eugene 1980: 'Comparison misconceived: common nonsense in comparative politics'. *Comparative Politics*, 13: 119–26.

—— 1986: 'Causal inference and comparative methods'. *Comparative Political Studies*, 19: 415–37.

Dogan, Mattei and Pelassy, Dominique 1984: *How to Compare Nations: strategies in comparative politics*. Chatham, N.J.: Chatham House (2nd edn published 1990).

Eckstein, Harry 1975: 'Case study and theory in political science'. In F.I. Greenstein and N.W. Polsby (eds), *Handbook of Political Science*, Reading: Addison-Wesley, vol. 7, ch. 3.

Feyerabend, Paul 1975. *Against Method*. London: Verso.

Frendreis, John P. 1983: 'Explanation of variation and detection of co-variation: the purpose and logic of comparative analysis'. *Comparative Political Studies*, 16: 255–72.

George, Alexander L. 1979: 'Case studies, and theory development: the method of structured, focussed comparison'. In Paul G. Lauren (ed.), *Diplomacy: new approaches in history, theory and policy*. New York: Free Press.

Hempel, Carl K. 1952: *Fundamentals of Concept Formation in Empirical Science*. Chicago, Ill.: University of Chicago Press.

Holt, Robert T. and Turner, John E. (eds) 1970: *The Methodology of Comparative Research*. New York: Free Press.

Huntington, S.P. and More, C.H. (eds) 1970: *Authoritarian Politics in Modern Society*. New York: Basic Books.

Jackman, Robert W. 1985: 'Cross national statistical research and the study of comparative politics'. *American Journal of Political Science*, 29: 1.

Kalleberg, A.L. 1966: 'The logic of comparison: a methodological note on the comparative study of political systems'. *World Politics*, 19: 69–82.

Kaplan, Abraham 1964: *The Conduct of Inquiry*. San Francisco, Cal.: Chandler.

Lakatos, Imre 1970: 'Falsification and the methodology of scientific research programmes'. In Lakatos and Alan Musgrave (eds), *Criticism and the Growth of Knowledge*, London: Cambridge University Press.

Lane, Jan-Erik 1987: 'Against theoreticism'. *International Review of Sociology*, 3: 149–85.

LaPalombara, Joseph 1970: 'Parsimony and empiricism in comparative politics'. In Holt and Turner (eds).

Lijphart, Arend 1971: 'Comparative politics and the comparative method'. *American Political Science Review*, 65: 682–93.

—— 1975: 'The comparable-cases strategy in comparative research'. *Comparative Political Studies*, (8): 158–77.

Lipset, S.M. 1963: *The First New Nation: the United States in historical and comparative perspective*. New York: W.W. Norton.

—, Trow, M. and Coleman, J.S. 1956: *Union Democracy*. Glencoe, Ill.: Free Press.

Macridis, Roy C. 1953: 'Research in comparative politics' [Report of the Social Science Seminar on Comparative Politics]. *American Political Science Review*, 47: 641–75.

—— 1955: *The Study of Comparative Government*. New York: Random House.

Marradi, Alberto 1985: 'Natura, forma e scopi della comparazione: un bilancio'. In D. Fisichella (ed.), *Metodo Scientifico e Ricerca Politica*, Florence: La Nuova Italia.

Mayer, Lawrence C. 1989: *Redefining Comparative Politics*. Newbury Park, Cal.: Sage.

O'Kane, Rosemary H.T. 1993: 'The ladder of abstraction, the purpose of comparison and African coups d'état'. *Journal of Theoretical Politics*, 5: 2.

Osgood, C.E. 1967: 'On the strategy of cross-national research into subjective culture'. *Social Science Information*, 6: 7.

Przeworski, Adam 1987: 'Methods of cross-national research, 1970–83: an overview'. In M. Dierkes et al. (eds), *Comparative Policy Research: learning from experience*, Aldershot: Gower.

—— and Henry Teune 1970: *The Logic of Comparative Social Inquiry*. New York: John Wiley.

Rae, Douglas W. 1971: *The Political Consequences of Electoral Laws*. New Haven, Conn.: Yale University Press.

Ragin, Charles C. 1987: *The Comparative Method: moving beyond qualitative and quantitative strategies*. Berkeley, Cal.: University of California Press.

Riker, W.H. 1982: 'Two-party system and Duverger's Law'. *American Political Science Review*, 76: 753–66.

Rose, Richard 1991: 'Comparing forms of comparative analysis'. *Political Studies*, 39: 446–62.

Sartori, Giovanni 1970: 'Concept misformation in comparative politics'. *American Political Science Review*, 64: 1033–53.

—— 1976: *Parties and Party Systems: a framework for analysis*. New York: Cambridge University Press.

—— 1984: 'Guidelines for concept analysis'. In Sartori (ed.), *Social Science Concepts: a systematic analysis*, Beverly Hills, Cal.: Sage.

—— 1986: 'The influence of electoral systems: faulty laws or faulty method?' In B. Grofman and A. Lijphart (eds), *Electoral Laws and their Political Consequences*, New York: Agathon Press.

—— and Morlino, Leonardo (eds) 1991: *La Comparazione nelle Scienze Sociali*. Bologna: Il Mulino.

—, Riggs, Fred W. and Teune, Henry 1975: *Tower of Babel: on the definition and analysis of concepts in the social sciences*. Pittsburgh, Pa: International Studies Association.

Scheuch, Erwin 1989: 'Theoretical implications of comparative survey research: why the wheel of cross-cultural methodology keeps on being reinvented'. *International Sociology*, 2: 147–67.

Sigelman, Lee and Gadbois, G.H. 1983: 'Contemporary comparative politics: an inventory and assessment'. *Comparative Political Studies*, October: 275–305.

Smelser, Neil J. 1966: 'Notes on the methodology of comparative analysis of economic activity'. In *Transactions of the Sixth World Congress of Sociology*, Evian: International Sociological Association, vol. 2, pp. 101–17.

—— 1967: 'Sociology and the other social sciences'. In P.F. Lazarsfeld et al. (eds), *The Uses of Sociology*. New York: Basic Books.

—— 1976: *Comparative Methods in the Social Sciences*. Englewood Cliffs, N.J.: Prentice-Hall.

Somit A. and Tanenhaus, J. 1964: *American Political Science: Profile of a Discipline*. New York: Atherton.

Sundquist, J.L. 1988: 'Needed: a political theory for the new era of coalition government in the United States'. *Political Science Quarterly*, 103: 613–35.

Verba, Sidney 1967: 'Some dilemmas in comparative research'. *World Politics*, 20: 112–27.

—— 1985: 'Comparative politics: where have we been, where are we going?' In Wiarda (ed.)

Wiarda, Howard J. (ed.) 1985: *New Directions in Comparative Politics*. Boulder, Col.: Westview Press.

2

Use and Misuse of Statistics in Comparative Research

Limits to Quantification in Comparative Politics: The Gap between Substance and Method

MATTEI DOGAN

The chariot of science is trailed by three horses: theory, data and method. If the three horses do not run at the same speed the chariot may lose its equilibrium. Such a maladjustment has happened in the field of comparative politics. During the last three decades the horse flying the flag of methodology has run faster than the horse carrying empirical data, and the theoretical horse has repeatedly tried to unleash himself. There is today in the field of comparative politics a serious gap between substance and method, particularly in the arena of quantitative research.

The horse of methodology, raised and educated in statistics, algebra, economics, social psychology and computer science, has been enthusiastically adopted by some political comparativists. But this skilful horse is not, in his new field, at ease with the second horse, the draught-horse conveying rough statistical material. The third horse, the theoretical one, is a racer, and very individualistic. He does not like statistical hay, he prefers concepts.

How to match theory, data and method is an old issue. Comparativists admire the natural scientist who can change the conditions of experiments. But as Claude Bernard observed long ago, comparative observations can replace direct experiments by altering the circumstances of a series of observations. Through quantification the comparative method can become a substitute for the experimental method. The method of concomitant variations described by J.S. Mill contained the logic of statistical correlations and multiple regressions that social scientists use today.

After a third of a century of progress in quantitative comparative politics, an up-dated and comprehensive evaluation is needed. Among the many issues that could be raised I have selected twelve to discuss briefly. I shall not look at the entire field of comparative politics, only at efforts of quantification and at the limits of the statistical method. I shall not consider the counterbalancing weight of non-quantitative comparative politics, and consequently many great comparativists will not be cited here, particularly those belonging to the tradition of historical sociology (see Rueschemeyer, 1991) and to the school of 'political development' (see Riggs, 1981). A short comment on this school would be appropriate. The eight volumes of the Princeton series on political development, written by 80 scholars, total some 4500 pages, but include fewer than 100 small and simple statistical tables and no regression analyses. These comparativists have not made a *tabula rasa* of previous work. They have given priority to empirical evidence as well as to theoretical frameworks, but have neglected statistical methods. It is true that six of the eight volumes are characterized by parallelism, rather than cross-national analysis – despite Almond's manifesto and Coleman's research agenda presented in the fist volume. Perhaps this group has committed the sin of insufficient quantification.

I shall refrain from commenting on the other end of the comparative spectrum – the castles of grand theories. I shall leave aside the literature on mathematical modelling, because few studies of this kind have been published in comparative politics: they are more often practised in other fields, for instance in international relations. Nor shall I discuss the another important gap, that between method and theory. It raises enormous problems that are analysed by Giovanni Sartori in this volume (see also the interpretation of Stefan Nowak, 1989).

What is Meant by Overquantification?

There has been a tremendous fascination with statistical technique in some fields of political science. Statistical data have lured some researchers into a false sense of security and prevented them from seeing the real problems. 'Reducing social systems to a set of equations has the merit of elegance, but only rarely that of relevance' (Uphoff and Ilchman, 1972, p. 494).

The most virulent critics of cross-national quantitative research are some of the practitioners themselves. In 1970 Richard Merritt admitted that time and again the reader of empirical political studies will find that the indicator used by the researcher is inadequate, invalid, or downright irrelevant ... He will leave such studies with a feeling of dissatisfaction – a feeling that the researcher has tried to do something akin to analyzing measles by counting the red spots on the body, a feeling that the researcher has missed politically relevant points because of his concern solely with mindless quantification and statistical analysis within a narrowly conceived conceptual framework. Much of this disappointment is justified. (Merritt, 1970, p. 15)

In the last two decades an important advance has been achieved in statistical methodology that has not been matched by equivalent progress in data collection and retrieval. Today, most criticism focuses on the increasing gulf between data and method. After decades of methodological improvements in comparative research we are today in a situation of imbalance between the level of accurate quantitative data and the technological capacity of statistical treatment. We have arrived at a stage where the available statistical information simply does not match the methodological sophistication achieved.

Some comparativists show more devotion to their skills in statistical analysis than to the logic of comparative inquiry. The facilities offered by the computer have generated practitioners of what could be called statistical fishing expeditions. In a few great universities graduate students in political science and sociology receive more training in statistics than in comparative social science; as a result they do not perceive clearly enough the imbalance between the quality of data and conceptualization on one side and methodological sophistication on the other. Too often statistical exercises serve as a substitute for critical judgement and for the lack of clear understanding of the politics involved. 'The esteem for mathematics has resulted in a neglect of another instrument for stating relationships, namely, the effective use of language' (Bernhard, 1972, p. 503). Underspecification may result in grossly simplistic models.

Measurement and statistical evidence are obviously needed in all social sciences. The limits to quantification appear when there is a gap between the amount and quality of data available and the statistical technique adopted for its treatment. In other words, overquantification consists in the treatment of soft data by very sophisticated statistical techniques. Some sophisticated methodologists bravely quantify the unquantifiable or, failing that, quantify the irrelevant as a proxy for the unquantifiable; they try to transmute poor data into gold. The result is counterfeit coinage. Others are simply too enthusiastic and imprudent. Producers of data, such as the United Nations or the World Bank may alert readers of their publications to the fact that certain statistical tables are based on estimations and not on hard data. Statisticians, considering that soft data do not satisfy the assumptions of statistical techniques, may advise against the use of powerful statistical methods in the social sciences (Freedman, 1987). But these premonitions do not discourage some enthusiastic comparativists, who behave like alchemists. Of course, the problem is not the nature of evidence but its uncritical use. Most comparativists are aware of the fact that the quality of data lags far behind methodological sophistication. They are more interested in substance than in method. They behave as true comparativists, not as narrow-minded quantifiers.

I shall not try to explain why so many scholars get caught in overquantification. This would require a long discussion. I simply note that I found suggestive what Charles Ragin calls 'the configurational character' of the comparative method: 'Typically, the explanations of comparative sociology do not cite single causes; they cite convergent causal conditions' (Ragin, 1981, p. 110). Such multiple causality opens the door to multivariate analysis, and this can be a wise and productive approach. The problem is to avoid the pitfalls of overquantification at the very moment of 'operationalization', when the researcher elaborates the 'statistical design', an obligatory step in many studies.

The relationship between data collection and theory-building is another important issue. As Giovanni Sartori writes in this volume: 'concept formation stands prior to quantification'. His point is that a model should not be chosen because it is amenable to quantification. Such a choice would ignore the purpose of research, which is to explore the complexities of the real world. We should make a clear distinction between 'data analysis' and 'statistical theory'. (Uphoff and Ilchman, 1972, p. 480). Data analysis refers to a search of quantified data for evidence and clues for theory-building.

The Heroic Years of Quantitative Comparisons

In the history of comparative politics, the 15 years between 1958 and 1972 remain the golden years of 'correlates of democracy'. This period of intensive and imaginative research witnessed the convergence of several trends. First, the access to independence of some 50 former colonies (25 French colonies gained independence all at the same moment in 1958). Secondly, the rapid diffusion of the computer and its increasing capacity to process vast amounts of data. Thirdly, the collection, standardization and publication by international organizations, particularly the statistical branch of the United Nations, of a wide variety of statistics. At the same time, big American foundations gave priority, and maintained it for more than a decade, to research on the Third World, sending several thousands scholars – mostly political scientists and sociologists – to Africa, Asia and Latin America. This was also a time when American politicians believed generously and naively in the possibility of exporting democracy everywhere.

From the many books and articles published during this period emerge two or three dozen publications which shared three important characteristics: comparison by quantification, an interdisciplinary approach, and cumulative knowledge. Such a rich combination had never previously been achieved in the history of political science.

The theme 'correlates of democracy' was from the beginning eminently interdisciplinary. At that moment new perspectives were opened up to political science in the directions of sociology, economics, anthropology. It is not by accident that many of the most famous 'correlators' were hybrid scholars, part political scientists, part sociologists, economists, anthropologists or statisticians. Most of the variables they used were demographic, economic, cultural, ethnic and more generally sociological. Relatively few were strictly political. For instance, in their *World Handbook*, B. Russett et al. (1964) presented 75 variables, of which only 12 were strictly political and eight others were economico-political. In the second *World Handbook* Taylor and Hudson (1972) made a serious effort to add data on political protest, but there were only six other purely political variables.

Looking back on the literature on 'correlates of democracy' one is impressed by its cumulative character. Each new study has built on previous ones, like the construction of a high rise building, floor after floor. Almost all empirical comparativists started their analysis with direct reference to previous work. Some 40 or 50 publications from this period constitute a cumulative chain. Another important characteristic of the literature on 'correlates of democracy' is the use of statistical evidence, or the effort to scale variables. I am referring particularly to a series of studies that focus on quantitative comparisons: D. Lerner (1958); S.M. Lipset (1959); K.W. Deutsch (1960); K.W. Deutsch (1961); Ph. Cutright (1963); A. Banks and R. Textor (1963); B. Russett et al. (1964); H. Alker (1965); R. Marsh and W. Parish (1965); R. Merritt and S. Rokkan (1966); D.E. Neubauer (1967); L. Adelman and C. Taft Morris (1971); R. Putnam (1967); M.E. Olsen (1968); S. Rokkan (1968); M. Needler (1968); M. Dogan and S. Rokkan (1969); A.K. Smith (1969); G.R. Winham

(1970); J.V. Gillespie and B.A. Nesvold (1971); C. Taylor and M. Hudson (1972).

All these authors, except the first, have cited Lipset's seminal article published in 1959, and most of them cite Deutsch's and Cutright's articles. A latecomer, Kenneth A. Bollen, reconsidered the issue in 1980. He proposed a new index of political democracy, tested with a sophisticated method, the so called confirmatory factor analysis. Another latecomer, Tatu Vanhanen, related democratization to socio-economic variables for 147 states in the period 1980–5 by regression analyses in order to disclose a general pattern: 'Four of my six explanatory variables are the same as those used by Lipset, Lerner, Deutsch and others who have tested modernization theory by empirical evidence ... for me the causal factor behind democratization is the level of resource distribution' (Vanhanen, 1989, p. 120), in which small farm ownership appears for the first time as a key indicator. Between Lipset in 1959 and Lipset et al. in 1993 three dozen scholars have accumulated over three decades an impressive body of knowledge in comparative politics. This has been a royal road, starting with great ideas and a weak methodology and ending with the confirmation of old ideas by a more rigorous methodology.

In the early 1970s comparative politics started to move from the nation as an object to the nation as a context, from whole societies to sectoral comparisons, from 'correlates of democracy' to political economy, to survey research, without communicating with the school of 'grand theories' in the tradition of Parsons or Easton.

Most publications on 'correlates of democracy' are also relevant to what could be called worldwide statistical analysis.

Worldwide Statistical Comparisons

'The principal problems facing the comparative method can be succinctly stated as: many variables, small number of cases', wrote A. Lijphart in 1971. 'There is, consequently, no clear dividing line between the statistical and comparative methods; the difference depends entirely on the number of cases.' More than two decades later, looking back on progress in comparative politics, such a statement remains convincing only for certain types of comparisons. With 180 independent nations (in 1992), the number of cases does not look so small. In the last two decades many insignificant variables have been abandoned and other indicators, because of their interchangeability, have been combined in indices.

The literature on comparative politics can be divided into several categories: case studies in comparative perspective; binary analyses; comparisons of similar countries; comparisons of contrasting countries; the conceptual homogenization of a heterogeneous field (Dogan and Pelassy, 1990); and worldwide correlational analyses. Of these six strategies, only the last is eminently statistical. Worldwide analysis, called by Raoul Naroll (1972) 'holonational' (adapted from the anthropological term hologeistic) consists of the study of whole societies, counts each country as one case, computes formal mathematical measures of relationships among variables and uses these measures to test general theories (Naroll, 1972, 212–13). The larger the number of countries included in the comparison, the greater the need for quantitative data.

Worldwide correlational analysis has experienced a period of stagnation and today is out of breath, a saturated form of research. The main reason for this decline is the discrepancy between the quality of statistical data for the advanced countries and for the developing ones. Scholars became aware that in comparing the two sets of countries they were dealing with material of unequal accuracy. It became clear that the lower the level of development, the lower is also the validity of quantitative data. The difficulties encountered in worldwide correlational analyses mark one of the limits to statistical approaches in comparative politics. The weakness of worldwide statistical comparison can also be explained by the fact that it is based on national averages.

National Averages and Intra-national Diversities

With very few exceptions, cross-national comparisons use national averages. But we all know that when on the Gauss curve the distance between average, mean and mode is great, an average is not a significant statistical value. In a distribution the average does not reflect skewness. In other words, the skewness of a distribution differently affects the mean, mode and average.

The assumption is that the internal diversity of countries is less significant than the differences between them. But in reality most countries are characterized by important internal diversity, either regional, or vertical in terms of social strata. Some of the most significant characteristics are distributed unevenly. Internal diversities can be ethnic, linguistic, religious, social, economic. Almost all countries could be ranked according to their degree of homogeneity–heterogeneity. In some matters, such as pluralism, internal diversity is an essential dimension.

The internal diversity of countries is not necessarily related to their size. Some small countries are very heterogeneous and some large countries relatively homogeneous. Regional diversities are visible in all European countries except, perhaps, Denmark. There are three Belgiums, four Italys, eight Spains (Linz, 1969). In Finland there are old regional contrasts. Yugoslavia has exploded into six pieces, and instead of a single national average for the entire Soviet colossus, there are today 15 independent nation-states and as many national averages.

Geographical diversity may be expressed in survey research by the notion of social context. When these contexts are taken into consideration, the risk of the individualistic fallacy (Scheuch, 1966) is seriously reduced, particularly in ethnically diverse countries. 'Cross-national comparison may be most fruitful when based upon within-nation comparison' (Verba, 1971, p. 309).

For the analysis of intra-national diversities statisticians and geographers long ago elaborated adequate indices, such as the Gini index of inequality, translated into Lorenz curves and coefficients of dispersion. We have the appropriate tools but the standardized statistical data on internal diversity were, until recently, scarce. An important indicator of internal diversity is the degree of linguistic homogeneity, which has been quantified by Laponce (1987) for a large number of countries.

Many political phenomena cannot be explained by national averages. Take, for instance, the level of poverty. People do not revolt against poverty as such, they revolt against injustice; they do not revolt against the national average of poverty. In statistical terms social inequalities may be expressed in standard deviations.

In some countries, governments have been reluctant to collect and publish data on regional, ethnic or social inequalities. Nevertheless, the World Bank has published data on income inequality for about 80 countries (Jain, 1975), and so has the OECD for 15 Western countries. Regional disparities have been studied in many fields, including voting behaviour. Disparities among social strata – and their changes – have so far received but little systematic comparative attention, except for Western Europe.

Today we can do better. We have more data on many more countries and we know much more about the diversity within these countries. It is very likely that in the future more attention will be given to intra-national disparities because, for many significant variables, within-nation differences are larger than between-country differences. In this way it will be possible to explain a larger part of the variance.

The Shadow Economy

Inaccurate statistics used in comparative politics often originate from the shadow economy, also called the underground economy, the black market, the submerged economy, clandestine work, the parallel economy, the concealed, informal, hidden, illicit, unobserved, dual economy.

The official Gross National Product includes all economic activities which are paid for in money, pass through some sort of market, are reported to the government, supervised and taxed by it and form the basis of all conventional economic indicators. Yet these indicators understate the volume of economically significant activities. They omit the self-consumption of households in agriculture, the unpaid work of housewives, goods and services exchanged informally through barter, and goods and services exchanged in informal transactions not reported to the authorities.

In some advanced countries, the consumption by peasant households of their own produce is partially included in official estimates of the social product. This is done by estimating the portions of agricultural output. Housewives' work and barter are often mentioned but rarely estimated, and so far no good indicators for them are available for comparative studies.

An important part of the shadow economy is monetary transactions concealed from the government and therefore missing in its statistics. With regard to goods, these are usually referred to as being on the 'black market'. In regard to labour and services, one now most often speaks of the 'black economy'. The total of the two varies greatly from country to country and from time to time. It has been estimated at 12 per cent for Britain, a little less for Japan, as high as 30 per cent for Italy and nearly 50 per cent for India. Without estimates of the extent of the black economy the GNP is a deceptive measure.

Higher taxes and extensive governmental controls are likely to drive more economic transactions underground. Increased levels of unemployment tend to have similar effects; so does the lag in the incomes of workers and low-level civil servants behind the cost of living, which impels them to seek second jobs. Compulsory health and welfare contributions motivate employers to offer jobs at lower rates or lower side costs. They are not reported to the authorities. The problem is illustrated by a remark by President Mitterrand in 1984, to the effect that the higher the level of taxation the less income the state can extract from it. (perceived as a criticism of the policy adopted by his own government in 1981–3).

The implications for comparative analysis are obvious. In OECD statistics, Britons are on average still richer than Italians. In reality it may well be that the standard of living in Italy, except in the deep South and Sardinia, is higher than it is in Britain. How much does the vigorous Italian black economy contribute to the outcome? Tuscany and Emilia, where it may produce one third of the local GNP, are in reality much richer than figures in the official statistics suggest. In general, the black economy reflects the activities of artisans and small businessmen, and the production of agriculture and food. Much of the latter stays within the country. According to the wise beliefs of certain Italian politicians, as long as the government tolerates the black economy people may be more willing to tolerate the government.

Clearly, better estimates and new indicators are needed here for studies both of developing and highly industrialized countries. Family and household surveys, such as India's annual 25,000 family survey, may offer useful starting points. Without estimates of the size of the black economy, real economic growth or decline is hard to assess.

The black economy limits the potential of quantification: how can one quantify accurately what is by definition clandestine? Obviously the black economy has a direct impact on the calculation of the gross national product per capita, but this impact is too often neglected in quantitative comparative analysis. We should not worship this golden calf fabricated by economists for their own needs.

A King to be Dethroned: GNP per Capita

GNP is one of the most frequently used indicators in comparative analysis. It has been defined by economists as the market value of all final goods and services produced by the economy during a given year. It does not measure the standard of living, but rather the commercial value of goods and services produced. It is a valid indicator in economic comparisons. When applied to comparative politics it loses a large part of its validity, for several reasons. The proportion of goods that are commercialized varies according to the level of industrialization. Agricultural production is undervalued. As already mentioned, the status of women is another source of distortion in international GNP per capita statistics, for instance as between Muslim and Western countries. If a housewife goes out to work and hires a maid, she increases the GNP by two incomes where there were none before. Baking bread at home does not raise the GNP, but buying it in the a shop does. The GNP per capita can theoretically be weighted according to the importance of the agricultural sector and the proportion of women in the workforce, but such a correction has rarely been attempted.

As M.D. Morris puts it, 'the less developed a society, the smaller the proportion of goods and services that are produced for, and exchanged in the market. The GNP is an appropriate measure of output, but not a very satisfactory measure of welfare. As a measure of welfare, GNP is fundamentally flawed' (Morris, 1979, p. 13).

Moreover, by convention GNP is calculated in US dollars, into which monetary statistics are converted. The fluctuation of the dollar can modify the difference between the USA and most other countries. This distortion was recognized long ago: 'The result of exchange rates is that the poverty of the underdeveloped countries is exaggerated, perhaps by a factor of as much as four for the least developed areas' (Russett et al., 1964, p. 150). The distortion has been noted, but conversion into dollars continues. It has been demonstrated that the resulting underestimation could range from 10 per cent to 300 per cent. The lower the GNP per capita, the higher the underestimation.

The distortion is of such an amplitude that it defies common sense. When the GNP per capita is evaluated at $300 for India and at $9000 for Canada, it has to be taken in its narrow commercial sense. In reality the gap cannot be so enormous. One need only calculate in local currency by various sociological methods the minimum subsistence level for survival to conclude that in comparative politics GNP per capita has much less meaning than in monetary economics, and consequently should not be taken as an accurate indicator.

Further, the statistical comparisons based on GNP per capita between advanced and developing countries are misleading because of a well known statistical artefact, too often forgotten. In growth percentage terms, an increase from $10,000 to $11,000 per capita is equivalent to a change from $200 to $220 per capita, that is 10 per cent. Statistical evidence is indispensable in comparative research, but we should always remember that equal increases in percentages can mean a greater gap in absolute terms.

GNP tends to become an instrument of measurement in international relations. For instance, in 1992 at the Rio Earth Summit it was proposed that every country should allocate 0.7 per cent of its GNP to the United Nations Fund for Environment. Because of the size of its economy, but also because the American GNP is comparatively inflated, the United States would have to contribute to such a Fund as much as about 80 of the smaller or poorer countries.

For several decades, GNP per capita has been a privileged indicator in dozens of studies on development. But in recent years it has been severely criticized, even by economists. To replace it, several composite indices have been proposed, by D.M. Morris among others.

The OECD's *Purchasing Power Parities* (PPP), intended to replace the classical GNP, is an improvement. For instance, calculated in GNP per capita, the standard of living appears 40 times higher in France than in India ($300 compared with $12,790 in 1987). Calculated in purchasing power parity, the distortion is diminished to 13 times ($1,050 as against $13,960) (United Nations Development Programme, 1990, pp. 130–1). But for political comparisons the PPP remains a deception. First, because it is limited to OECD countries, whereas the underestimation of standard of living is heavier for the poor countries (fortunately, data for India are available). Secondly, it covers only currency conversion, eliminating the differences in price levels between countries, but does not evaluate the real differences in national production and consumption. As its title indicates, the objective is the monetary purchasing capacity. The field of quantitative comparative politics is still deprived of an appropriate tool for measuring the wealth of nations.

The impact of some indicators may be immediate. Other indicators suggest staggered consequences. GNP per capita and school enrolment, for instance, have different time dimensions.

The Temporal Dimension: Causal Relationships Are Staggered Over Time

The time dimension is important for understanding political processes and effects. Rates of change are essential for the analysis of political development. Rapid changes may have different effects from slow ones. Comparisons of rates of change may reveal important differences.

Nevertheless, most comparative research over the last quarter-century has used synchronic data, often because they seemed to be the only ones available. For a long time most survey data were synchronic; only recently have comparative time-series become available. Synchronic political analysis was an important step, but often it could only explain a fraction of the variance. This is one reason why many findings reach only minimal results, and often are not even published.

Time lags are crucial in understanding causality or probabilistic influence. Everything in politics takes time, and so do all changes in society. No social change is instantaneous. Even if communications take place with electronic speed, the social impact of political decisions takes time. Even revolutions need time to engender social consequences.

A technical means for dealing with the time-consuming aspects of human communication and response is the use of lagged variables. If we assume for theoretical reasons, or from experience, that a change in variable A will have an impact on variable B, we must still ask how much later this impact will take place and have observable results. We must compare variables A and B not at the same time, but variable A at a certain moment and B at some later time. This delay may be quite long. The historian William L. Langer points out that the introduction of compulsory primary education in several Western countries around the 1860s was followed by the rise of the 'yellow press' in the 1890s. The historian Daniel Vernet has demonstrated that in France, during the eighteenth century, revolutionary ideas and behaviour spread in the countryside two decades after the rise of radical ideas in the main cities.

Other time lags may be short, depending on the scale of the processes involved, but some lag is always to be expected. For instance, the attainment of power by social democratic or similarly welfare-orientated parties – often in the form of coalitions – has been linked by several authors to the enactment of additional social welfare legislation and to an actual rise in welfare benefits. Many of these studies, however, have not given enough weight to time lags, and hence have underestimated the actual impact that occurred. The time lags involved include the time between the formation of the government, enactment of specific legislation, its promulgation, its effective implementation at the administrative level, and the time it takes the public to learn to make full use of the opportunities under the new laws. The rise in the number of social security beneficiaries partly illustrates this process. In all Western democracies social expenditures has changed slowly, by an incremental trend (see Flora and Heidenheimer, 1981; Flora, 1987; Taylor, 1983). A phalange of comparativists have tried to ascertain the importance of social democratic parties in the growth of government, but because they neglected the time dimension and the delayed, incremental social consequences of the participation of social democrats in power, they have succeeded in explaining only a small part of the variance (Dogan, 1988, pp. 247–9).

The vexed question of economic development and the prerequisites for the establishment of stable democratic regimes also involves considerable time lags too often neglected. Causal relationships in contemporary demographic trends in the Third World would emerge more clearly if urbanization and literacy were considered at a certain moment and birth rates and infant mortality one generation later. Such staggering does not require sophisticated statistical techniques.

The neglect of the temporal dimension has long limited the explanation of variance. Its inclusion in research designs could enhance the potential for comparative quantitative analysis.

From Isolated Indicators to Composite Indices

Single isolated indicators are often misleading. When a researcher relies on only one or two indicators to measure a complex phenomenon, these are likely to be invalid measures. An example: some still use the number of radios per 1000 population as an indicator of the development of the entire communications network of a nation. While such extrapolation may have been valid several decades ago for many nations, there are today cases where this indicator is invalid. In radios per 1000 inhabitants a relatively poor country could rank as high as a relatively rich country. At the same moment the rich country could rank very high on television sets and daily newspaper circulation per 1000. Except for comparisons between the 50 or 60 poorest countries the indicator 'radios per 1000' could today be abandoned.

The same problem is evident in many other areas where there are complementary items, as in the transportation network. Cars, trains, buses, boats and aircraft all fulfil similar functions. The relative frequency in the use of one or more of these modes of transport is influenced by geography, average distances, cost and cultural preferences. In Europe the rail system is more developed than in the US, there being shorter distances to cover and higher population densities. The train is not seen as a lowly form of transport in Europe, as it is in the US. It would be misleading, then, to use air traffic as an indicator of the development of the transportation system. While many social scientists have assumed that the number of cars per thousand inhabitants is a valid indicator of development, they may not have recognized the importance of the fact that there are alternatives available.

Energy consumption per capita is another variable which needs an index to help integrate various energy data. The consumption of energy can reflect many social indicators; industrialization, mechanization and even mass communication. Forms of energy include oil, electricity, coal, gasoline and nuclear energy. For purposes of international standardization, the index of energy expresses data in coal equivalents to oil, natural gas and electrical energy.

Another aspect of the relevance of indicators is whether certain variables can meaningfully be quantified. It is not enough to assign numbers to events. The second edition of the *World Handbook* (Taylor and Hudson, 1972) contains quantified data on indicators of political protest. Aside from problems of accuracy, these data are of questionable validity: do they really measure unrest in a society? Even if we grant that demonstrations, riots, armed attacks, deaths from domestic violence and governmental sanctions can be quantified accurately, it is still questionable whether we can assume that these categories represent the true level of unrest in a society. Discontent may not appear without a spark to bring it into the open. Even more fundamentally, the indicators of unrest fail to acknowledge the role of suppression in affecting the statistics. Dictatorial governments around the world suppress the expression of unrest. The existence of this underlying level of unrest was demonstrated by the crises in East Germany, Czechoslovakia, Poland and Hungary in 1989–90.

By compounding various indicators in an index, the sociological significance of statistical data could be enhanced. Too often, isolated indicators are still treated by complex methods, even when a simple statistical treatment of indices would be sufficient. But in some cases the components of a composite indicator may obscure more than they illuminate.

We now possess quantified indicators difficult or impossible to obtain in the 1970s for a large number of countries; for instance, for life expectancy, access to safe water, number of people per hospital bed and school enrolment at age 10–12. By combining isolated indicators into indices, quantitative comparative analysis would be facilitated, because the number of variables would be reduced and their explanatory power enhanced.

Certain indicators do not need to be combined into indices, because their explanatory power is sufficient, as attested by numerous empirical analyses. Among these privileged indicators is infant mortality. One does not need sophisticated factor analysis to understand why, sociologically, infant mortality is one of the best indicators in comparative research.

Ecological Indicators

We need data on geographic and socio-ecological conditions for economic and political development. Some older sociological schools of thought, particularly that of Ellsworth Huntington, overstressed geographical determinism; as a reaction (see Sorokin), geographical conditions were neglected for a generation; but most recently the evolution of the ecological sciences has greatly increased the possibilities for analysing the environment.

Some writers, such as Andrew M. Kamarck of the World Bank have spoken of tropical societies as distinct from those in the temperate zones. Three-quarters of Africa is in the tropics. The well-known fact that the vast majority of the world's poor people live in the tropical or semi-tropical zones is highlighted by the 'North–South' categorization.

Human behaviour depends not only on temperature and humidity, but also on the rarity or prevalence of morbidity and debilitation. The frequency of infection by parasites and chronic malnutrition not only reinforce each other, but they also interact in feedback cycles with economic productivity and growth, speed or slowness of behaviour, human energy and capacity to work and the gap between thoughts and feelings on one side and effective action on the other. Large cohorts of tropical populations are not sick enough to die but sick enough to remain poor. Epidemics or widespread tropical diseases may not destroy governments but the population may lack the energy to wipe them out. Malaria and sleeping sickness have been driven back but not eliminated. Hook-worm, bilharzia and trachoma still blight the lives of hundreds of millions. Chronic malnutrition has been estimated to account for about two-thirds of morbidity and child mortality in Africa, South Asia and tropical Latin America. Trypanosomiasis kills horses and cattle and makes it difficult to get to the interior from the coast using animal transport. 'The transport obstacle alone was quite sufficient to postpone for centuries any appreciable economic development in tropical Africa' (Kamarck, 1976, p. 19).

Comparativists have not yet asked this difficult question: How far is the low level of development in most of Africa and in some Asian countries to be explained by their tropical environments? Such an interrogation is completely absent even in the best recent books on Africa (see, for example, Shaw and Aluko, 1985).

In the southern regions of the United States and in Northern Australia similar conditions of heat and humidity prevail but the economic handicaps have been overcome. Before the coming of modern hygiene in the eighteenth and nineteenth centuries, major ecological handicaps also prevailed among the poorer strata in the temperate zones. Rats and lice spread plague; epidemics of cholera, typhus and tuberculosis were frequent and often endemic, and so were rickets and other diseases due to deficient nutrition. The mass availability of industrially produced soap and cotton underwear increased as early as the eighteenth century. Clean drinking water, free of epidemic germs, is not available everywhere. The spread of tea in parts of Asia, but not in Africa, meant that drinking water was boiled. Desinfectants came later, used first in hospitals and later in homes. Malaria was wiped out in the south of Italy only about 50 years ago.

The experience of Western countries, temperate or hot, suggests that social and economic conditions can contribute substantially to reducing morbidity and mortality. It is the same for the highest strata in tropical countries: the Latin American upper classes have for centuries been healthier than the poor.

A set of additional quantified new indicators, highlighting these conditions, could lead to significant revisions of many received theories of economic and political underdevelopment. They might even lead to a revision of the received and often ethnocentric notions about easy self-help by tropical nations.

In the advanced countries the ecological problem is reappearing at a higher level in concerns for the 'quality of life'. Access to green spaces, to woods and meadows, is becoming rarer and more difficult. Water and air are polluted, less often by germs and parasites and more often by industrial effluents. Smog burdens eyes and lungs. Along with such conditions new political movements and parties have arisen in European countries. Indicators for these ecological problems are available at least for urban areas in many countries, but they are difficult to integrate as international statistical series. This is why comparative researchers have been slow to use them and to relate them systematically to social and political issues. But these problems will not go away; they will grow. And political scientists will have to catch up with them.

The ecological dimension may require nominal indicators as well as quantified ones.

Mini-states and Mega-cities

There were in 1992 214 countries and territories, 187 of them independent. Of these 214, only 132 have a population of over one million and only 122 over two million. One-quarter of the countries represented at the United Nations have together a population equivalent to that of Colombia, which ranks thirtieth among nations in demographic terms. At the same time, half the world's population lives in four countries: China, India, the USA and Russia.

For many comparative purposes, such disparity creates no difficulties. In a typology of political systems the size of the country does not matter. One can compare social mobility in a series of countries without taking their size into consideration. The political systems of Denmark and Costa Rica can be compared with those of India and Nigeria. It is appropriate to compare the presidential system of France and of Sri Lanka even if one country is six times larger than the other. But under some circumstances, size may have an impact on the functioning of a democratic regime (see Dahl and Tufte, 1973). Size always has an impact in international relations: we cannot evaluate the role of Ghana and of Brazil in the international arena if we ignore their sizes.

When the analytical approach is basically statistical, the number of cases and the diversity of their size can be an essential dimension. When it is remembered that Norway is not much more populous than Connecticut, there is a feeling of unease about a comparison of electoral behaviour in the United States and in Norway. A sample of 2000 individuals in each country might be statistically justified, but one cannot avoid certain doubts about the choice of this pair of countries.

One remedy would be to weight the countries according to their demographic size. This is already done in some comparisons of European countries and in studies which consider the continent as a whole. In such analyses, France counts sixteen times more than Finland.

The problem of the size of nations is aggravated when we contrast small states with giant cities. Considering only independent countries (leaving aside the territories), 95 out of 187 had in 1992 less than four million inhabitants. At the same moment there were nearly sixty mega-cities of over four million people, many in middle-sized countries.

During the 1950s, urbanists defined cities as agglomerations of 5000 and, for some world regions, of 10,000 inhabitants. Later they adopted a criterion of 20,000 people, and still later of 100,000 people per agglomeration. Comparative political researchers followed these definitions, since they depended on the data made available to them. These changes in definition seemed to reflect reality, since urban centres evidently grew. But in part the new definitions were adopted for reasons of convenience rather than of insight. Giant cities of more than one million are a new category. They are of crucial importance in the politics of the countries in which they exist. In 1950, there were about 50 such cities; in 1982 there were 278; in 1992, about 330.

Statistical data on giant cities are not easily rendered comparable. Some include only the population in the city itself, administratively defined; others include the suburbs or the entire urbanized area gravitating to the central city. The United Nations has made a serious effort to standardize these criteria, but in many cases it is still necessary to evaluate rather than to count.

It is the metropolises of several millions that should attract our attention. These giant cities require separate treatment. Their number in a country makes a difference to its political system. If there is only one, it is apt to dominate the country and make it 'monocephalic' (singleheaded), usually with a star-shaped system of internal communication, as in France, Britain, Austria, Peru, or the Republic of Korea. Some 30 or more countries, from Hungary to Mexico, Argentina and Thailand, are in this condition. Other countries are 'polycephalic': they have several giant cities, none dominating the others, with a grid-shaped system of transport and communications. Here we find some of the largest countries in the world – China, India, Russia and the United States – but also middle-sized countries, such as Germany, Italy, Canada, Spain, Australia, Poland, Morocco, and also a number of small countries such as Switzerland, The Netherlands and Belgium. Some countries are bicephalic or double-headed, such as Turkey, Syria and Vietnam.

For certain comparisons of European countries it is useful to take into consideration the system of cities. All else being equal, the fact that France, Austria, Denmark, Ireland and Finland are 'macro-cephalic' countries, and, on the contrary, that Germany, Italy and The Netherlands are 'polycephalic', makes an important difference in many political domains. If Yugoslavia had a single powerful mega-city instead of six important regional cities, the dismemberment of the federation would probably have taken a different course. The link between a network of old major cities, born of history, and federalism is obvious.

Comparing large American and European cities, one should take into consideration the public transportation system, particularly the underground infrastructure. The metros in Paris, London, Moscow or Tokyo represent an investment that Los Angeles would need more than 20 or 30 years to build. The cost of the Parisian metro is perhaps equivalent to the cost of the entire production of automobiles in the United States over two or three years. Such a comparison cannot remain at the statistical level.

The metropolitan areas of Mexico City, Buenos Aires, São Paolo, Cairo, Bombay, Calcutta, Seoul and other mega-cities had in 1990 a larger population than each of the 120 smaller independent nations.

In some countries, the primate city accommodates a significant part of the population (Athens and Santiago about 40 per cent, Montevideo almost half, Beirut about three-quarters) and includes the lion's share of economic, financial, cultural, educational, scientific, artistic and political activities of the country. A *World of Giant Cities* (Dogan and Kasarda, 1988) is replacing progressively the world of territorial nations.

In his *Political Order in Changing Societies*, Samuel Huntington asked in 1968, 'What groups are most likely to be revolutionary in the city?'. In the last two decades it has been necessary to explain why the urban *lumpenproletariat* did not revolt despite the continuing growth of shantytowns, *favelas* (Brazil), *poblaciones* (Chili), *barriadas* (Lima), *ciudades esperidida* (Mexico), *Kutcha* (Calcutta) and other slums and *bidonvilles* at the peripheries of mega-cities from Casablanca to Bogota and from Bombay to Lagos. It may be that tomorrow many comparativists will have to give priority to political unrest in the giant cities of the Third World; they will then need new indicators to replace older ones. Lerner's model (urbanization → literacy → communication → participation) had a nice run in comparative politics but, for the study of primate cities in Asia, Latin America and Africa and their *lumpenproletariat* and troglodytes, it appears obsolete today.

Some 40 quantified indicators are available for a large number of cities, not all standardized. There is an important monographic literature on mega-cities, but very few comparative studies. As the number of giant metropolises will inevitably continue to grow, there is a need for systematic comparison not only of metropolises, but also between small countries and giant cities; for instance, the budget of the municipality of New York or of the Metropolitan District of Mexico is higher than the national budget of dozens of small countries.

Scoring and Scaling as a Substitute for Formal Statistics

Many of the most significant aspects of political life cannot be treated in statistical terms. The alternative is scaling by experts. The recourse to judgemental rankings and to scoring finds a justification in a statement by the mathematician Tukey: 'Far better an approximate answer to a right question, than an exact answer to the wrong question, which can always be made precise' (cited by Banks and Textor, 1963, p. 7).

The translation of qualitative aspects into measurable variables requires scaling by judges. The involvement of judges raises the question of coder reliability: how likely are two or several judges to rate the same situation in the same manner? If an expert says that country A is more democratic than country B, and this last more than country C, he must admit also that A is more democratic than C. The reliability of an expert can be tested by the consistency of his rankings. To show the potential of scoring and judgemental rankings, I have selected four examples from the literature.

The first one is from Phillips Cutright's 'National political development: its measurement and social correlates'. This article is one of the most cited in the literature on comparative politics and one of the few still relevant today of those published three decades ago. With the help of experts, Cutright constructed an index of political development. He allocated for each country two points for each year in which a parliament existed and where the minority party had at least 30 per cent of the seats. He allocated only one point when the minority party was weaker, and no points for each year when no parliament existed. He did the same scoring for the executive branch. Over a period of 22 years a country could accumulate 66 points. Cutright used a simple but pertinent index.

The validity of his scoring can be tested retrospectively. He found for 1963 an imbalance for Chile, the Philippines, Indonesia, Nicaragua and Guatemala: political development was higher than socio-economic development. In the following years the façade of democracy in these countries collapsed. The opposite was 'predicted' for Spain, Portugal, Czechoslovakia and Poland. These countries were supposedly ripe for democracy. Cutright's analysis based on scores and a simple statistical model should be compared with many other articles published at roughly the same time which disappeared from the literature despite the mountains of statistics on which they were built. Cutright's method of scores could be applied today to Eastern Europe: the implosion in 1989–90 can be explained by the gap between the relatively high socio-economic level (education, health, urbanization, industrialization) and the low level of political development.

A second example of scoring as a substitute for formal statistics is the voluminous book by Banks and Textor, *A Cross-polity Survey* (1963). They proposed a series of 57 dichotomized variables, most of which were directly political: interest articulation and aggregation, leadership charisma, freedom of group opposition, freedom of the press, role of the police, character of the bureaucracy, *personalismo*, westernization and others. The authors preferred significant aspects of political life to quantified but unimportant variables, even if their dichotomization was uncertain. They gave approximate answers to good questions.

Another codification of variables which are not directly quantifiable was adopted by Irma Adelman and Cynthia Taft Morris in their *Society, Politics and Economic Development: a quantitative approach* (1967). This book has been severely criticized by some scholars (Kingsley Davis, among others) and appreciated by others. These contrasting evaluations can be explained by the fact that it consists of two parts. The first (pp. 1–129) contains an interesting discussion of 41 variables, most of which were and remain not directly quantifiable. The second part consists of a confusing factor analysis. I mention this book for its first part. I use the second part to vaccinate my students against the temptation to engage in factor analysis. Because of frequent malpractice in the use of this statistical tool, mass immunization is needed.

In a series of volumes, *Freedom in the World*, Raymond D. Gastil (1979–90) has ranked countries with the help of experts according to two basic dimensions: political rights and civil liberties. The rating is on a seven-point scale by univocal ranking. Published annually since 1979, this series has become an important source of documentation for comparative politics in general and for empirical quantitative research in particular.

After decades of progress in comparative politics we still face this dilemma: whether to have recourse to judgemental variables or to neglect some of the most important aspects of political life.

Obstacles to Sophisticated Statistical Analysis in Survey Research

In the literature on comparative survey research many theoretical and methodological issues are carefuly discussed. Here I shall raise only one. Given the errors which are theoretically admitted in random sampling, how much statistical treatment might be applied to survey data? It is necessary to remember an elementary rule in the theory of probabilities, a rule that students are supposed to know but that eminent scholars forget too often. In a sample of 1000 individuals the chances are 95 in 100 that the sampling error is not larger than 5 percentage points in the case of a dichotomous category (men versus women, for instance). Theoretically the error increases rapidly if the sample is divided into four or five categories (age groups). It increases even more in case of a triple cross-tabulation (age groups by gender across political parties). Nor should we neglect the errors generated by sampling procedures, weighting of data, unclear questions, insufficient training of interviewers and so on.

Given such a theoretical margin of error within the data, is it reasonable to treat survey results by sophisticated statistical methods? The gap between the softness of the data and the sophistication of the technique used to treat it denotes uncritical reasoning and forgetting the theory of probability.

Ronald Inglehart, in *The Silent Revolution* (1977), gives a good example of the limits to sophistication in the statistical treatment of survey data:

> A carefully designed and validated question about satisfaction with one's own life was asked twice in the same survey, with a time interval of about ten minutes. The correlation between responses was 61.6 In the context of survey data, this is a very high correlation: it reflects the fact that fully 92 percent of the respondents gave answers at the two time points that were in either identical or adjacent categories on a seven-point scale. Yet statistically speaking, the responses at Time 1 'explain' only 37 percent of the variance in responses at Time 2 – a mere 10 minutes later. If this were a question about diplomatic relations with mainland China, one might argue that the failure to explain something close to 100 percent of the variance was due to the fact that many of the informants were too poorly informed or uninterested to have any real opinion. But this was a very clear and simple question concerning a subject about which everyone knows and cares; the man in the street may not have any real preference about China policy but surely he is able to judge whether the shoe pinches him or not. (Inglehart, 1977, p. 26)

A fruitful method for analysing survey data was proposed long ago by Paul Lazarsfeld, particularly the refinement of the analysis by a chain of cross-tabulations. His methodology based on critical reasoning avoids the risks of overquantification. He has never practised factor analysis and rarely regression analysis.

The richness of studies based on survey research depends on the validity of the theoretical framework and the pertinence of the questions asked, and very little on the power of statistical techniques used for the treatment of the data (see, for example, Harding et al., 1986; Stoetzel, 1983; Turner, 1992; Inglehart, 1977, 1990; Barnes and Kaase, 1979; Dogan, 1988). None of these scholars uses sophisticated techniques of analysis. *Political Action* (Barnes and Kaase, 1979) has avoided unnecessary methodological complications. None of its nine authors has gone beyond mean scores, mean coefficients of dissimilarity, attitudes scales and a variety of typologies. Consequently, the book includes interesting tables and graphs. The same is true of Inglehart's *Culture Shift* (1990) and Stoetzel's *Les Valeurs du temps présent* (1983). The tree-analysis, which consists of a chain of dichotomies, is the only methodological pedantry that can be found in *Electoral Behavior*, edited by Richard Rose (1974), a very rich 'comparative handbook' full of empirical evidence, with tables and graphs on most of its 745 pages. The book edited by Charles Glock, *Survey Research in the Social Sciences* (1967), concentrates on reasoning and logic, and not on statistical techniques, for analysing the data.

Survey research has pushed further the new frontiers of comparative research. Important aspects, such as regime legitimacy, trust in rulers, religious feelings, national identities, perception of national symbols and many others, are analysed cross-nationally today by using survey research. Enormous progress has been achieved since the old *Civic Culture*. In 1969, in an inventory of comparative surveys, Rokkan et al. counted 982 cross-national surveys. In a bibliographical follow-up, published three years later, several hundreds titles have been added (Delatte and Almassy, 1972). The first European Values survey (1981) covered some 20 countries; the World Values survey (under the leadership of Ronald Inglehart 1990–3), about 40 countries.

Survey data and aggregate data should be combined wherever possible. Such a combination requires standardized indicators, not as yet pressed far enough and largely limited to the efforts of individual scholars. A good strategy for combining aggregate data and survey research has been proposed by Juan Linz (1969). Another solution has been proposed by S. Barnes and M. Kaase (1979, p. 18): 'By studying countries with relatively similar political structures we minimize the impact of systemic factors and amplify the importance of individual level factors.'

Feeding the Computer

After the discovery of the 'ecological fallacy' by W.S. Robinson in 1950, analysis of aggregate data was neglected, even by those who were not directly interested in the inference from ecological correlations to individual behaviour. But not for long. A few years later the analyses of aggregate data had been resuscitated in cross-national comparisons by United Nations statisticians. The accompanying spread of the computer facilitated the treatment of masses of data. At a certain moment comparative research was the privileged locus for analysing aggregate data.

There is no need to recall how the computer has increased enormously the research capabilities in all sciences. What must be emphasized is the temptation to feed the computer.

The first experiment in feeding the computer with as much statistical data as possible, without any selection, was by Brian J.L. Berry in 1972 for a study on American cities. This experiment was so unsatisfactory that it served as a lesson for many social scientists even outside the field of urban sociology.

Many examples of the unimaginative use of the computer could be given. In an article on 'Patterns of democratic development' the authors (it is unnecessary to indicate their names) attempted to examine the conditions under which democratic systems have flourished or failed through an analysis of longitudinal comparative data on 44 countries for the period 1800–1960. Their measure of democracy was an eight-point index based on the presence or absence of four basic characteristics of the political system. Data were collected for each decade. A mountain of data! The article was published in 1971. Since then, how many times has this contribution been cited in the literature on comparative politics? Clearly, the success of an article is not proportional to the amount of data computerized.

In an article on income distribution patterns in developing nations, covering more than 40 countries, the authors used the technique of tree-analysis, based on dichotomies, by reducing the diversity of the groupings. The tree-analysis, a powerful technique, over-simplifies causal relationships. It has been used in a satisfactory way only when the number of units is high, in electoral research for instance. The technique of tree-analysis is inappropriate for comparing entire countries, necessarily limited in number.

In an article published in the APSR some years ago, on macro-economic policy in 12 advanced democracies, the author treated an impressive amount of data by computer. One has to admire his methodological virtuosity, even if the result is a platitude: 'the general conclusion is that governments pursue macroeconomic policies broadly in accordance with the objective economic interests and subjective preferences of their class-defined core political constituencies'.

Well-known practitioners of quantitative comparative politics have strongly reacted against doping the computer, for instance Charles Taylor (1974):

Frequently everything was correlated against everything else and linear coefficients were taken quite seriously although nothing at all had been done to check on the true nature of the relationship. The power of the new computers and the availability of statistical programming packages encouraged quick, superficial data grindings that revealed little about data structure. More recently the pendulum has swung and we have heard a great deal about the movement from data analysis to model building, somehow as if the two were opposites. Political sophistication must be at least as important as methodological sophistication.

Since he wrote these lines the gap between technique and data has increased.

Giovanni Sartori, in this volume (ch. 1. n. 28), is also pitiless: 'many current failings of comparative politics are not of the method itself but result from shaky data. The more massive the information, and the larger the number of countries from which it is drawn, the less the person at the computer is in control of his evidence ... Printout giants are easily erected, but over a marsh.'

Factor Indigestion

Mea culpa: in a study of the relationship between social class, religious attitude and political behaviour based on aggregate data for 2477 French cantons, I used several analytic techniques including multiple regression. The results were satisfactory. At a certain moment I was advised by a respected statistician to adopt a more powerful technique of investigation, rarely applied because of the difficulties of constructing an orthogonalized plan: the convariance analysis which is a variety of factor analysis. From the strictly statistical point of view the article could be considered as valid. But for a social scientist it is useless. What I did in reality was to throw out of the window the statistical information that I had painfully collected (2477 units). This is a good example of what I call overquantification (Dogan, 1968). The lesson to be learned is that by using very sophisticated factor analysis I jeopardized my data; on the contrary, with simpler techniques I arrived at rewarding results (Dogan and Derivry, 1988). Since that time, I have became immune to factor analysis.

Theoretically, factor analysis replaces many variables by a few 'factors', each being correlated with a group of variables, highly correlated among themselves. In other words, a series of indicators is combined in a single factor, which reduces the number of explanatory variables (Janson, 1969). Factor analysis as a method was elaborated by social psychologists for their own needs. It played a crucial role in the advancement of this discipline. Today, it is used in various domains. In the natural sciences it is practised in preliminary research, as a lantern in an obscure gallery, in order to get a first picture of the causal relationships. In the social sciences some scholars adopted it with enthusiasm, but many found it finally deceptive, because in practice it is very difficult to interpret its results.

In his book *Social Statistics*, Hubert Blalock (1960) dedicates only 12 out of 450 pages to factor analysis. This great methodologist was not one of its apostles. What he wrote is confirmed three decades later: 'it is very possible to end up with a set of factors which have very little theoretical meaning. We then have merely replaced a large number of clear-cut operational indices by a smaller number of theoretically meaningless factors'. (p. 384).

In the literature on factor analysis one can find a wide spectrum of sophisticated techniques. Not all of them are valid for comparative research. Two seem promising: the so-called 'structural equation model' and so-called 'confirmatory factor analysis' designed by Karl Joreskog and adopted by Melvin L. Kohn and his colleagues in a recent study of the causal connection between social structure and personality in Poland and the United States (Kohn and Slomczinski, 1990). Confirmatory factor analysis may be extremely useful in psychometrics, and the structural equation model in econometrics, but in comparative politics – which have not yet become politicometrics – their utility remains to be demonstrated.

For each meaningful and valuable factor analysis one could find in comparative sociology and political science many more frustrating attempts. In fact, it is impossible to suggest here a ratio, because most of the studies that use the tool of factor analysis in an unimaginative way are never printed. They remain as mimeographs presented at academic meetings. Nevertheless, a few see the light. I shall give only one example; the reader will easily find others. In an article published in a prestigious journal of sociology many years ago on 'Dimensions of nations: size, wealth and politics', the author, after reviewing earlier studies on 'correlates of democracy' uses data for 82 countries and 236 variables producing nearly 20,000 cells. He incorporates many of the variables separately included in one or another of the earlier studies. From three previous factor analyses the study reintroduces nine of Schnore's 12 modernization and urbanization variables, 27 of Berry's 43 economic development variables, and 36 of Cattell's 72 variables. Product-moment correlations are computed between each pair of variables. 'The resultant 236 × 236 correlation matrix was factored by the method of principal components, which produced fifteen factors ....' After a careful reading one is entitled to ask if this article brings anything new, unknown from the previous studies, and if the slight improvement in a correlation coefficient justifies so much effort not only by the author but also by the reader.

I have already mentioned the factor analysis by Adelman and Taft-Morris (1971). The authors undoubtedly felt guilty, otherwise why would they end their statistical exercise with a 'poem for the skeptic'?

Graduate students in political science, sociology and economics are the most vulnerable victims of overquantifiers. We should not follow this pernicious advice: 'in these days of powerful computers and packages of statistical programs, it seems gratuitous to put students through the anxiety of confronting complex calculations when machines can perform the bulk of the work' (Bryman and Cramer, 1990, p. xiii). The reaction to such a philosophy can only be ironical: 'give up on the ideas, but equip the student with a computer package-based veneer of competence ... giving instructions on SPSS commands ... anything more than a quite telegraphic account of essential ideas is crowded out' (Economic and Social Research Council, *Data Archive Bulletin*, May 1992, 25).

What Cannot be Analysed in Statistical Terms

Overquantification is not a new fashion. Twenty years ago, Derek Phillips had already asked: 'why is it that sociologists concerned with explanation and prediction are unable to account for more than a small portion of the variance in their research?' (Phillips, 1971, p. 9). And he cites Hubert Blalock (1968, p. 157), who has offered several explanations, in particular the possibility of a wrong set of independent variables and of an inadequate measurement. In *Causal Inferences in Nonexperimental Research*, (1961) Blalock raises extremely important issues, but an essential question is missing: How often has the practising social scientist, and in particular the comparativist, enough good data in hand to analyse such causal inference? During the last quarter of a century few quantitative analyses in comparative political science and sociology have succeeded, despite growing statistical sophistication, to explain more than 15 per cent of the variance. This is a balance sheet, which indicates one of the limits of quantification. In many cases the alternative to the statistical method is what Neil Smelser (1976, p. 157) calls the 'systematic comparative illustration'. In fact, the binary analysis, which is the most frequent kind of comparative research, is in many cases a systematic comparative illustration.

No wonder that many comparativists are today sceptical about the potential of intensive and extensive statistical analysis. 'In quantitative cross-national studies, cases lose their identities as they are disaggregated into variables. Relations between variables are studied, not similarities and differences among whole cases' (Ragin, 1989, p. 60). 'Most of the features of small-N research are antistatistical' (ibid., p. 70). This is a plaintive leitmotiv in the literature: 'We have too few nation-states in our sample. Nor do we have much confidence in our ability to measure anything as complex as responsiveness on the level of the nation-state. We are by no means completely happy with our measurement of this phenomenon on the community level and would find such analysis on the national level much more difficult' (Verba, 1977, p. 185). So, when we have few countries, their features are 'antistatistical': when we have a very large number, including poor countries, we encounter the obstacle of inaccurate statistical data.

The appropriate dose of quantified data depends of the kind of question that you ask and the goals pursued by comparing. For instance, a reply to the question: Is the gap between poor and rich countries increasing? has to be based on solid statistical data, carefully analysed. By contrast, when Samuel Huntington asks: 'Will more countries become democratic?' the analytical reasoning becomes more important than the statistical evidence.

Excessive recourse to quantified data can be of little help in finding answers to some major questions. Why did China not collapse into rival feudalities, as did the Roman empire? The non-quantitative comparativist Fred Riggs believes that the existence of mandarins prevented such a collapse. This plausible explanation cannot be tested with statistics. But I would not go so far as Arthur Schlesinger Jr who proclaimed: 'Almost all important questions are important precisely because they are not susceptible to quantitative answers' (cited by Kousser, 1981). This is a gross exaggeration.

Some observable phenomena are not quantifiable. Take, for instance, political corruption. There cannot be statistics on a phenomenon which by its very nature is concealed. In an impressive book of 1000 pages on this topic, edited by A.J. Heidenheimer, M. Johnston and V.T. Le Vine (1990), there are no numbers; but some numerical evaluation would be useful.

According to certain comparative theories, India should not be democratic. It is not by using statistical methods that one would likely be able to explain this enormous deviant case. If we have ten cases and one is deviant, the correlation coefficient is seriously diminished.

Some interesting theories in comparative research cannot be tested statistically. The attempts to test the dependency theory with regression equations have not resulted – despite the great statistical expertise of the authors – in a great advance of the theory as it was formulated previously, without using powerful statistical techniques, by Frank Cardoso, Furtado, Falitto, Amin, O'Donnell and others. There could be, but there is not, a single regression equation in Deutsch's *Nationalism and Social Communication* (1953).

Nor should we forget Weberian comparisons using ideal types, which played a seminal role in the past and which is the opposite of the inductive statistical method. Because of the kind of questions that they have asked, none of the great classic comparativists, from Marx to Tocqueville, has used the statistical techniques available in their time, not even Durkheim. Today, most of the great comparativists are not adepts of the statistical method, from Almond, Apter and R. Aron to Wallerstein, Weiner and Wittfogel. What Barrington Moore (1966, pp. 519–20) wrote a quarter of century ago is still valid today:

> Although statistics can shed considerable light on this thesis and similar ones, there may also be a point at which quantitative evidence becomes inapplicable, where counting becomes the wrong procedure to use. In the analysis of qualitative changes from one type of social organization to another, let us say from feudalism to industrial capitalism, there may be an upper limit to the profitable use of statistical procedures .... The more definitions the investigator make in order to catch up with structural changes, the smaller and less useful and trustworthy become the statistical piles with which he works.

Final Remarks

Briefly stated, overquantification results from an imbalance between data and method. If the data are inaccurate, the statistical technique should not be too ambitions. If the data are reliable, a sophisticated methodological design is justified and recommended.

In comparative politics every year dozens of books and articles are published, and ten times more unpublishable texts are written. Among those that have seen the light, how many are cited during the 12 years following their publication? We may divide these publications into two categories of 50 titles each: those written in vernacular language and those characterized by overquantification, by an unnecessarily high dose of statistical analysis. From consulting the *Social Science Citation Index* for 1979–88 it appears that publications in the first category are cited 20 to 30 times more often than those in the second category. About one-third of the overquantified studies are never cited, or are cited only once or twice, in 12 years; only a few of the vernacular publications are also totally ignored. This count can easily be contested, because there are more books than articles in the first category, the reverse being the case with the second category. Nevertheless, most articles were published in prestigious journals.

Clearly, the majority of comparativists are not addicted to over-quantification. But how can we explain that, until recently, three or four of the best-known American professional journals in political science and sociology have often been vectors of overquantifiers, having frequently published articles that only a small minority of scholars were interested in or ready to cite? Few of the books and articles in comparative politics that have lasted decades after their publication have been based on sophisticated statistical techniques. They have the same short life-expectancy as the grand theories built on shifting sands. By advancing on the middle road, comparativists have a better chance of finding the truth. It appears that the scientific community harbours its own correctives for the ailment of over-quantification.

Note

Several colleagues have read earlier drafts of this paper and given me wise suggestions. I am grateful in particular to Seymour Martin Lipset, Dwaine Marvick, Samuel C. Patterson, Gilbert Rozman, Peter Merkl and Frederick Turner. None of them is responsible for the errors that this paper may still contain.

References

Adelman, Irma and Morris, Cynthia Taft 1971: *Society, Politics and Economic Development: a quantitative approach*. Baltimore, Md: Johns Hopkins Press.

Alker, Hayward R. 1965: *Mathematics and Politics*. New York: Macmillan.

Apter, David E. 1988: *Pour l'état, contre l'état*. Paris: Economica.

Banks, Arthur S. and Textor, Robert B. 1963: *A Cross-polity Survey*. Cambridge, Mass.: MIT Press.

Barnes, Samuel H. and Kaase, Max (eds) 1979: *Political Action Mass Participation in Five Western Democracies*. London: Sage.

Bartolini, Stefano 1990: 'Tempo e Ricerca Comparata', *Rivista Italiana de Scienza Politica*, xx: 530–71.

Beckerman, Wilfred 1966: *Comparaison internationale du revenu réel*, Paris: OECD.

Bernhard, Richard C. 1972: 'Mathematics, models and language in the social sciences'. In Uphoff and Ilchamn, 1972, pp. 497–506.

Blalock Hubert M. 1960: *Social Statistics*, New York: McGraw-Hill.

—— 1961: *Causal Inferences in Nonexperimental Research*. Chapel Hill, N.C.: University of North Carolina Press.

—— 1968: 'Theory building and causal inference'. In Hubert M. Blalock and Ann B. Blalock (eds), *Methodology in Social Research*, New York: McGraw-Hill, pp. 155–98.

Bollen, Kenneth A. 1979: 'Political democracy and the timing of development'. *American Sociological Review*, 44: 572–87.

—— 1980: 'Issues in the comparative measurement of political democracy'. *American Sociological Review*, 45: 370–90.

Bryman, A. and Cramer, D. 1990: *Quantitative Data Analysis for Social Scientists*. London: Routledge.

Censis 1976: *L'occupazione occulta*. Rome: Censis.

Charlesworth, James C. (ed.) 1963: *Mathematics and the Social Sciences: the utility and inutility of mathematics in the study of economics, political science and sociology*. Philadelphia, Pa: American Academy of Political and Social Sciences.

Cutright, Phillips 1963: 'National political development: measurement and analysis'. *American Sociological Review*, April: 253–64.

Dahl, Robert A. and Tufte, Edward R. 1973: *Size and Democracy*. Stanford, Cal.: Stanford University Press.

Delatte, J. and Alamsy, E. 1972: *Comparative Survey Analysis: a bibliographical follow-up*. Paris: International Social Science Council.

Deutsch, Karl W. 1953: *Nationalism and Social Communication*. Cambridge, Mass.: MIT Press.

—— 1960: 'Toward an inventory of basic trends and patterns in comparative and international politics'. *American Political Science Review*, 54(1): 34–57.

—— 1961: 'Social mobilization and political development'. *American Political Science Review*, 55(3): 493–514.

Documentation Française (La) 1980: 'Economie souterraine'. In *Problèmes politiques et sociaux*, Paris: La Documentation Française, October.

Dogan, Mattei (1968): 'Une analyse de covariance en sociologie électorale'. *Revue française de sociologie*, IX: 537–47.

—— 1988: *Comparing Pluralist Democracies: strains on legitimacy*. Boulder, Col.: Westview Press.

—— and Derivry, Daniel 1988: 'France in ten slices: an analysis of aggregate data'. *Electoral Studies*, 7(3): 251–67.

—— and Kasarda, John D. (eds) 1988: *A World of Giant Cities and Mega-cities*, 2 vols. London: Sage.

—— and Pelassy, Dominique 1990: *How to Compare Nations*, 2nd edn. Chatham, N.J.: Chatham House.

—— and Rokkan, Stein (eds) 1969: *Quantitative Ecological Analysis in the Social Sciences*. Cambridge, Mass.: MIT Press. Reprinted as *Social Ecology*, 1974.

Economic and Social Research Council (ESRC) 1992: *Data Archive Bulletin*, May.

Eulau, Heinz 1969: *Micro-Macro Political Analysis*. Chicago, Ill.: Aldine.

Flora, Peter 1983: *State, Economy and Society in Western Europe: a data handbook*. Frankfurt: Campus Verlag.

—— (ed.) 1987: *Growth to Limits: the Western European welfare states since World War II*, 5 vols. Berlin: De Gruyter.

—— and Heidenheimer, Arnold J. 1981: *The Development of Welfare State in Europe and America*. New Brunswick, N.J.: Transaction Books.

Freedman, David 1987: 'As others see us: a case study in path analysis'. *Journal of Educational Statistics*, XII: 101–28.

Gastil, Raymond D. 1979–90: *Freedom of the World, Political Rights and Civil Liberties*. Westport, Conn.: Greenwood Press, various volumes.

Gillespie, John V. and Nesvold, Betty A. (eds) 1971: *Macro-quantitative Analysis: conflict, development and democartization*. Beverly Hills, Cal.: Sage.

Glock, Charles Y. 1967: *Survey Research in the Social Sciences*. New York: Russell Sage Foundation.

Harding, S., Phillips, D. and Fogarty, M. 1986: *Contrasting Values in Western Europe*. London: Macmillan.

Heidenheimer, A.J., Johnston, M. and Le Vine, V.T. (eds) 1990: *Political Corruption*. New Bruswick, N.J.: Transaction Publishers.

Huff, Darrell 1973: *How to Lie with Statistics*. London: Pelican.

Huntington, Samuel P. 1968: *Political Order in Changing Societies*. New Haven, Conn.: Yale University Press.

—— 1984: 'Will more countries become democratic?' *Political Science Quarterly*, 99(2): 193–218.

Inglehart, Ronald 1977: *The Silent Revolution*. Princeton, N.J.: Princeton University Press.

—— 1990: *Culture Shift in Advanced Industrial Society*. Princeton, N.J.: Princeton University Press.

Jackman, Robert W. 1985: 'Cross-national statistical research and the study of comparative politics'. *American Journal of Political Science*, 29(1): 161–82.

Jain, Shail 1975: *The Size Distribution of Income: a computation of data*. Washington, D.C.: World Bank.

Janson, Carl-Gunnar 1969: 'Some problems of ecological factor analysis'. In Dogan and Rokkan, 1969.

Kamarck, Andrew M. 1976: *The Tropics and Economic Development: a provocative inquiry into the poverty of nations*. Baltimore, Md: Johns Hopkins University Press and World Bank.

King, Gary 1986: 'How not to lie with statistics: avoiding common mistakes in quantitative political science'. *American Journal of Political Science*, 30(3): 665–87.

Kohn, Melvin L. (ed.) 1989: *Cross-national Research in Sociology*. Newbury Park, Cal.: Sage.

Kohn, Melvin L. and Slomezynski, K.M. *Social Structure and Self-direction: a comparative analysis of the US and Poland*. Oxford: Basil Blackwell.

Kousser, J. Morgan 1981: 'Quantitative social-scientific history'. In M.G. Kammen (ed.), *The Past Before Us*, Washington, D.C.: American Historical Association.

Kurian, Georg Th. 1984: *The New Book of World Rankings*. New York: Facts on File.

Laponce, Jean A. 1987: *Languages and their Territories*. Toronto: University of Toronto Press.

Lazarsfeld, Paul and Barton, Allen 1951: 'Qualitative measurement in the social sciences classification, typologies and indices'. In D. Lerner and H.D. Lasswell (eds), *The Policy Sciences*, Stanford, Cal.: Stanford University Press, pp. 155–92.

Lazarsfeld, Paul F. and Rosenberg, Morris (eds) 1955: *The Language of Social Research*. New York: The Free Press.

Lerner, Daniel 1958: *The Passing of Traditional Society*. New York: Free Press.

Lijphart, Arend 1971: 'Comparative politics and the comparative method'. *American Political Science Review*, 65: 682–93.

Linz, Juan J. 1969: 'Ecological analysis and survey research'. In Dogan and Rokkan, 1969, pp. 91–131.

—— and Amando de Miguel 1966: 'Within-nation differences and comparisons: the eight spains'. In Merritt and Rokkan, 1966, 267–320.

Lipset, Seymour Martin 1959: 'Some social requisites of democracy: economic and political legitimacy'. *American Political Science Review*, 53: 69–105.

——, Seong, Kyoung-Ryung and Torres, John Charles 1993: 'A comparative analysis of the social requisites of democracy'. *International Social Science Journal*, 2: 153–75.

Marsh, Robert M. and Parish, William L. 1965: 'Modernization and communism: a re-test of Lipset's hypotheses'. *American Sociological Review*, 30: 934–42.

Merritt, Richard 1970: *Systematic Approaches to Comparative Politics*. Chicago, Ill.: Rand McNally.

—— and Rokkan, Stein (eds) 1966: *Comparing Nations: the use of quantitative data in cross-national research*. New Haven, Conn.: Yale University Press.

—— and Russett, Bruce M. 1981: *From National Development to Global Community: essays in honor of Karl Deutsch*. London: Allen & Unwin.

Moore, Barrington 1966: *Social Origins of Dictatorship and Democracy*. Boston, Mass.: Beacon Press.

Morris, David M. 1979: *Measuring the Condition of the World's Poor*. New York: Pergamon Press.

Naroll, Raoul 1972: 'A holonational bibliography'. *Comparative Political Studies*, 5(2): 211–30.

Needler, Martin 1968: *Political Development in Latin America: instability, violence and evolutionary change*. New York: Random House.

Neubauer, Deane E. 1967: 'Some conditions of democracy'. *American Political Science Review*, 61: 1004.

Nisihira, Sigeki 1975: 'L'erreur et la precision des sondages au Japon'. Paper presented to the 1975 congress of the World Association of Public Opinion Research.

Nowak, Stefan 1989: 'Comparative studies and social theory'. In Kohn, 1989, pp. 34–56.

O'Donnell, Guillermo A. 1979: *Modernization and Bureaucratic Authoritarianism: studies in South American politics*. Berkeley, Cal.: Institute of International Studies.

OECD 1992: *Purchasing Power Parities and Real Expenditures*. Paris: OECD.

Olsen, Marin E., 1968: 'Multivariate analysis on national political development'. *American Sociological Review*, 33: 699–712

Phillips, Derek L. 1971: *Knowledge from what? Theories and methods in social research*. Chicago, Ill.: Rand McNally.

Putnam, Robert 1967: 'Toward explaining military intervention in Latin American politics'. *World Politics*, 20(1).

Ragin, Charles 1981: 'Comparative sociology and the comparative method'. *International Journal of Comparative Sociology*, xxii: 1–2.

—— 1989: 'New directions in comparative research'. In Kohn, 1989, pp. 57–76.

—— (ed.) 1991: *Comparative methodology*. London: Sage.

Riggs, Fred W. 1981: 'The rise and fall of political development'. In J.L. Long (ed.), *The Handbook of Political Behaviour*, vol. 4, New York: Plenum Press, pp. 289–348.

Rokkan, Stein (ed.) 1968: *Comparative Research Across Cultures and Nations*. Paris: Mouton.

——, Viet, J., Verba, S. and Almasy, E. 1969: *Comparative Survey Analysis*. Paris: Mouton.

Rose, Richard (ed.) 1974: *Electoral Behavior: a comparative handbook*. London: Macmillan.

Rueschemeyer, Dietrich 1991: 'Different methods – contradictory results? Research on development and democracy'. In Charles C. Ragin (ed.).

Russett, Bruce et al. 1964: *World Handbook of Political and Social Indicators*. I. New Haven, Conn.: Yale University Press.

Sartori, Giovanni 1994: 'Comparing, miscomparing and the comparative method'. Chapter 1 in this volume.

Sauvy, Alfred 1984: *Le Travail noir et l'économie de demain*. Paris: Calman-Levy.

Scheuch, Erwin K. 1966: 'Cross-national comparisons using aggregate data: some substantive and methodological problems'. In Merritt and Rokkan, 1966, pp. 131–68.

Shaw, Timothy M. and Olajide Aluko (eds) 1985: *Africa Projected*. New York: St Martin's Press.

Siegelman, Lee and Naroll, Raoul 1974: 'Holonational bibliography'. *Comparative Political Studies*, 7(3): 357–82.

Simon, Herbert A. and Newell, Allen 1956: 'Models: their uses and limitations'. In Leonard White (ed.), *The State of the Social Sciences*, Chicago: Chicago University Press, pp. 66–83.

Smelser, Neil 1976: *Comparative Methods in the Social Sciences*. Englewood Cliffs, N.J.: Prentice Hall.

Smith, Arthur K. 1969: 'Socio-economic development and political democracy: a causal analysis'. *Midwest Journal of Political Science*, Feb. 95–125.

Smith, Brian H. and Turner, Frederick C. 1982: 'The quality of survey research in authoritarian regimes'. Paper presented at the World Congress of Political Science, Buenos Aires.

Stoetzel, Jean 1983: *Les Valeurs du temps présent: une enquête européenne*. Paris: PUF.

Sullivan, Michael J. 1991: *Measuring Global Values: the ranking of 162 countries*. New York: Greenwood Press.

Tanzi, Vito 1982: *The Underground Economy and the United States and Abroad*. Washington, D.C.: International Monetary Fund.

Taylor, Charles L. 1974: 'The uses of statistics in aggregate data analysis'. In James F. Herndon (ed.), *Mathematical Applications in Political Science*, vol. vii. Dallas, Tx.: Southern Methodist University Press.

——(ed.) 1980: *Indicator Systems for Political, Economic and Social Analysis*. Cambridge, Mass.: Oelgeschlager Publishers.

——(ed.) 1983: *Why Governments Grow*. London and Beverly Hills, Cal.: Sage.

——and Hudson, Michael C. 1972: *World Handbook of Political and Social Indicators*, ii. New Haven, Conn.: Yale University Press.

——and Jodice, David A. 1983: *World Handbook of Political and Social Indicators*, iii. New Haven, Conn.: Yale University Press.

Turner, Frederick C. 1992: *Social Mobility and Political Attitudes, Comparative Perspectives*. New Brunswick, N.J.: Transaction Publishers.

United Nations 1990: *Conference on the Least Developed Countries*, Paris. New York: United Nations.

United Nations Conference on Trade and Development (UNCTAD) 1985: *The Least Developed Countries*. New York: United Nations.

United Nations Development Programme 1990: *Human Development Report, 1990*. Oxford: Oxford University Press.

Uphoff, Norman T. and Ilchman, Warren (eds) 1972: *The Political Economy of Development*. Berkeley, Cal.: University of California Press.

Vanhanen, Tatu 1984: *The Emergence of Democracy: a comparative study of 1919 states, 1850–1979*. Helsinki: Finnish Society of Sciences and Letters.

——1989: 'The level of democratization related to socio-economic variables in 147 states, 1980–85'. *Scandinavian Political Studies*, 12(2): 95–127.

Verba, Sidney 1971: 'Cross-national survey research: the problem of credibility'. In Ivan Vallier (ed.), *Comparative Methods in Sociology*, Berkeley, Cal.: University of California Press, pp. 309–56.

——1977: 'The cross-national program in political and social change'. In A. Szalai and R. Petrella (eds), *Cross-national comparative research*, Oxford: Pergamon Press, pp. 169–99.

Wiarda, Howard J. 1985: 'Comparative politics, past and present'. In H.J. Wiarda, *New Directions in Comparative Politics*, Boulder, Col.; Westview Press, pp. 3–25.

Winham, Gilbert R. 1970: 'Political development and Lerner's theory: further test of a causal model'. *American Political Science Review*, 64: 810–18.

World Bank 1987: *Social Indicators of Development 1987*. Washington, D.C.: World Bank.

—— 1989a: *Social Indicators of Development*. Baltimore, Md.: Johns Hopkins University Press.

—— 1989b: *World Development Report 1989*. New York: Oxford University Press.

3

Conceptual Homogenization of a Heterogeneous Field

Presidentialism in Comparative Perspective

FRED W. RIGGS

The frequent collapse of presidentialist regimes in about 30 Third World countries that have attempted to establish constitutions based on the principle of 'separation of powers' suggests that this political formula is seriously flawed. By comparison, only some 13 of over 40 Third World regimes (31 per cent) established on parliamentary principles had experienced breakdowns by *coup d'état* or revolution up to 1985 (Riggs, 1993a)[1].

This empirical data substantiates Juan Linz's argument that parliamentarism 'is more conducive to stable democracy' than presidentialism (Linz, 1990, p. 53). While Linz admits that a presidentialist regime may be stable, as the American case shows, he does not try to explain this exception. Here I shall speculate about some of the practices found in the United States which seem to have helped perpetuate an inherently fragile scheme of government. These speculations need to be tested by systematic comparisons with the experience of the presidentialist regimes that have broken down. Pending such analysis, however, I shall offer some impressionistic evidence to support the hypotheses presented below.

The discussion which follows is divided into three parts. First, we need to clarify the institutional features found by definition in all presidentialist regimes; the second part identifies some critical problems inherent in any constitution based on 'presidentialist' principles; and the third part considers American practices or traditions − frequently 'undemocratic' in character − whose absence has apparently contributed to the collapse of presidentialism elsewhere.

I Presidentialism: What Is It?

Traditional institutional analysis antedated the Second World War and, unavoidably, focused attention on the well-established polities of North America and Europe. Because all the stable industrial democracies (except the US) adopted parliamentary forms of government and the other presidentialist systems were so unstable, however, the comparative analysis of presidentialism languished. Generalizations were based on a universe that included only one 'viable' presidentialist regime and a good many parliamentary systems. Perhaps unavoidably, in this context, comparativists often assumed that the unique properties of governance in the US could be attributed to environmental factors (that is, geography, history, culture, economy, social structure and so on) rather than to its institutional design.

After the Second World War comparative government experienced a radical re-evaluation of its fundamental premisses in the light of the entry into the world system of over 100 new Third World states. Many of them adopted constitutions that were quickly repudiated when military groups seized power in *coups d'état*, and it became apparent that formally instituted structures of government, typically based on Western models, did not or could not work as they were expected to. New approaches to comparative politics stressed functionalism or socio-economic determinism, and emphasized the crucial importance of external forces generated by the world capitalist system and international 'dependency.' Political anthropologists emphasized the continuing vitality of traditional cultures and the comparative study of institutions languished.

1 The institutional framework

In this context, formal institutions of governance were downplayed as having secondary, if not trivial, importance. The fact that virtually all presidentialist regimes except that of the United States experienced authoritarianism and military coups was attributed to cultural, environmental or ecological forces rather than to any inherent problems in this constitutional formula. Comparative presidentialism was neglected because it was considered useless to take 'unsuccessful' cases seriously: how could failures teach us anything about the workings of a political system?

Moreover, since there was only one 'successful' case, it could scarcely prove anything about the requisites for success in a presidentialist regime. It never occurred to anyone to think that the failures of presidentialism outside the US were due to deep structural problems with the institutional design rather than with ecological pressures caused by the world system, poverty, Hispanic culture, religion, geographic constraints, demographic forces and so on. Nor did anyone imagine that constitutional failures could be used to test hypotheses about why American presidentialism had survived, or to learn more about the risks involved in this kind of system.

A counterintuitive hypothesis might explain why presidentialism in the Third World has been so unsuccessful. The newer presidentialist regimes may have rejected, as undemocratic, some practices that, perhaps unintentionally, have helped American presidentialism to survive. If so, these regimes were unconsciously caught in a double bind: to be more democratic involved taking risks that could lead to dictatorship, whereas to perpetuate representative government meant accepting some patently undemocratic rules. Unfortunately, I believe, our ignorance of the regime-maintaining requisites of presidentialism blinds us to the negative impact of progressive reforms on the survival of this type of democracy.

In the US itself, debates about proposed 'reforms' fail to consider their likely impact on the viability of the constitutional system. An old example involves the use of 'primaries' to select candidates for election to public office, a nominally 'democratic' innovation that has weakened its political parties. The current debate about limiting the terms of legislators in order to enhance democratic values fails to consider how it might affect the capacity of Congress to maintain the precarious legislative/executive balance of power that is so crucial for the survival of presidentialism.

A recent critic of President George Bush's proposal for a constitutional amendment to limit Congressional terms to 12 years points out that it would increase the number of legislative 'lame ducks,' reduce the incentives for 'men [and women] of potential public excellence' to compete for elective office, increase the dependence of neophyte legislators on their professional staff and on bureaucrats and lobbyists, and diminish the scope of effective electoral choice open to voters. The same author, who directs political and social studies at the conservative Hudson Institute, argues that other solutions can be found to overcome the unfair advantages – mainly financial – that incumbents have when seeking re-election, without incurring the grave defects of the limited term option. I agree with all of these arguments, but they do not consider how the proposed change would affect the vitality and viability of presidentialism in America (Blitz, 1990).

Without rejecting any of the important findings of functional, ecological and world systems analysis, should we not view all institutions

make their regimes 'presidentialist'. The term *president* is often
used also for the head of state in single-party and even military
authoritarian regimes, but they are not therefore 'presidentialist'.

In presidentialist regimes the elected head of government always
serves concurrently as head of state. However, we must avoid defining
a presidentialist system as one in which the head of state (president)
is elected to office, a criterion that includes many non-presidentialist
systems. A regime is presidentialist only if the effective head of
government (President) is elected for a fixed term: the mode of election
may be direct or indirect. To be 'effective,' a head of government
cannot be dominated by a single ruling party or a military junta, and
the 'fixed-term' rule precludes discharge by a legislative no-confidence
vote.[2]

To repeat, by *presidentialism* I mean only those *representative governments in which the head of government is elected for a fixed term of office*;
that is, he or she cannot be discharged by a no-confidence vote of
Congress. Note that this definition is onomantic rather than semantic:
I am not reporting what the word *presidentialist* already means; rather,
I am explaining a fundamental political concept and proposing a term
to name it. Of course, *presidential* can be used to name this kind
of system, but since this word is also used for other regime types
– notably parliamentary systems with an elected head of state –
there is less risk of ambiguity if we use an unfamiliar word such
as presidentialist, for the specific concept intended here.[3]

Admittedly, this usage is not yet established. Many writers will
say *presidential* when they mean *presidentialist*. However, generalizations
about 'presidential' regimes are often invalid because they lump
together non-presidentialist with presidentialist polities. In this chapter
it is always necessary to know whether one is talking about the
specific properties of a presidentialist system – as defined here – or
using a loose concept that can also include parliamentary systems.
These are different institutional forms of democracy and they have
radically different properties which we need to understand.[4]

2.2 *Scales of variation.*

The distinction between presidentialism and parliamentarism should
be viewed as logical contraries, not contradictories. They are ideal
types at opposite ends of a scale: in other words, representative
government is not necessarily either presidentialist or parliamentary.
There are intermediate possibilities, 'semi-presidential' and 'semi-
parliamentary' in character.

Consider, for example, the French Fifth Republic, which Maurice
Duverger (1980), among many others, has characterized as *semi-*

presidential. Although the head of state (president) is indeed elected for a fixed term of office, the head of government (premier) must command a parliamentary majority. So long as the president's party has such a majority, the president may choose a premier of his own party, thereby permitting him to rule as the *de facto* head of government. Otherwise, the head of government (premier) may come from an opposition party in order to gain parliamentary support, as happened between 1986 and 1988 when President François Mitterand had to name an opposition leader, Jacques Chirac, as premier. At such times, the president is not a President. Juan Linz refers to the Fifth Republic as a 'hybrid' (1990, p. 52).

Scott Mainwaring (1989, p. 159) also identifies Chile (1891–1924) and Brazil (1961–3) as semi-presidentialist, even though their constitutional rules differed from those of the French Fifth Republic. Luis E. Gonzalez (1989) uses the terms *semi-* and *neo-parliamentary* to characterize the changing Uruguayan constitutions. The 1934 and 1942 charters, for example, had neo-parliamentary features in so far as the President had the authority to dissolve the legislature, and the legislature could censure the ministers, compelling the President to resign – but these powers were never tested (Gonzalez, 1989, pp. 3–4). The 1967 Uruguayan constitution retained the President's right to dissolve Congress and hold new elections after a minister had been censured, but he would not, then, be required to resign (Gillespie, 1989, pp. 12–13).

Giovanni Sartori (1989) proposes a four-type scale running from pure 'presidential' (that is, presidentialist) to pure parliamentary regimes.[5] This typology presupposes the maintenance of representative government. We need, however, to consider a second dimension of variation which runs from truly representative government to open authoritarianism or personal rule. Presidentialist forms may be retained even though their essential functions are lost.

Quasi-presidential refers to a degenerated presidentialist system. Sometimes, regimes that were originally presidentialist become modified in practice when the principle of separation of powers is breached even though it remains nominally in effect. This has usually occurred when Presidential powers were expanded at the expense of the legislature which became a pliant legitimizing body, ratifying without resistance the decisions of the President. Although such regimes are presidentialist *de jure*, *de facto* they are not. We might put *'President'* in quotation marks to signify a role that appears to follow presidentialist rules but, in fact, violates them.

It is often said that a weak legislature combined with 'Presidential' domination is endemic in Latin America – countries such as Argentina, Chile, Costa Rica and Uruguay provide the exceptions. Quasi-presidentialism may mask the dominant position of a hegemonic political party but it occurs more often, I believe, because an autocratic 'President' or a dominant family or clique gains control of the presidential office. Sometimes, also, unseen military 'bosses' determine key policies while the formal office-holders, including the 'President', become their 'puppets'. One may argue that most Latin American regimes are only 'quasi-presidential'.

Whereas quasi-presidentialism results when an authentic presidentialist regime disintegrates, *pseudo-presidentialism* arises when a presidentialist charter is promulgated as a façade to cover some form of authoritarianism. For example, a military dictator establishing personal rule (Jackson and Rosberg, 1982, p. 10) may adopt the title of 'president' and sponsor a charter that copies the presidentialist formula: its elected assembly is politically impotent and the outcome of its presidential elections is predetermined.

2.3 Constitutional transformations.

When a presidentialist regime experiences serious crises, one might assume (or hope?) that its political leaders would recognize the need for fundamental reforms and adopt constitutional amendments or new constitutions that move in the parliamentary direction. Instead, what usually happens is a regime breakdown which moves toward authoritarianism, whether formalistically through quasi-presidentialism or more overtly, after a *coup d'état*, into pseudo-presidentialism.

Authoritarianism, whether in the form of quasi- or pseudo-presidentialism, is no more stable than pure presidentialism. Ultimately, all forms of dictatorship (including single-party and military authoritarianism) may be overthrown and replaced by constitutional regimes and representative government. Whenever this happens, serious attention is usually given to the design of a new constitution that might overcome the liabilities of earlier schemes.

In such episodes of re-democratization, parliamentary or semi-parliamentary options are often seriously debated, as happened recently in Brazil, Argentina and Chile. However, it seems to be true that almost all ex-presidentialist regimes opt again for a new form of presidentialism. Under these circumstances, it is truly important to understand the survival problems inherent in the presidentialist formula. The practices which have enabled presidentialism to last in the United States might, perhaps, be institutionalized in other countries. However, I believe that most reformers would consider these practices (not presidentialism as such) so essentially undemocratic that they would reject them. When they recognize the costs involved in perpetuating presidentialism, they may be more willing to embrace options that move in the direction of parliamentarism. Until then, they are more likely, unwittingly, to approve presidentialism in a form that also involves quite democratic practices which, unfortunately, undermine the viability of the regime.

Presidentialism, *per se*, may be neither more nor less 'democratic' than parliamentarism, although the American 'founding fathers' explicitly prescribed a 'republican' formula that they thought would avoid the dangers of populist 'democracy'. However, even if one were to grant, provisionally, that presidentialism creates a more open and democratic regime than parliamentarism, one would have to balance this argument against the claim that, if presidentialism is likely to collapse into authoritarianism, then we ought to embrace a less democratic option that has better prospects of survival. I do not claim that presidentialism is less democratic than parliamentarism. I only argue that if presidentialism is to survive as a regime type, heavy costs must be born, and some of these costs involve accepting undesirable (undemocratic?) practices.

II   The Troubles of Presidentialism

In order to maintain the constitutionally prescribed separation of powers based on the election of a head of government for a fixed term of office, several fundamental and typical problems have to be solved in every presidentialist regime. Even though some of them may be solved in a given polity, failure to handle others can lead to deterioration or breakdown. Each major presidentialist problem is a kind of handicap: by itself it may not cause a breakdown but it becomes part of a cumulative and mutually reinforcing set of ruinous forces.

An executive/legislative relationship based on the fixed term of office set for the head of government constitutes the core problem: it generates other difficulties, however, each of which might precipitate a breakdown. Thus the separation vs. fusion of powers issue is not the only critical issue. In addition, each institutional feature of presidentialism – including the presidential role, the Congress, the political party and electoral system, and the bureaucracy, as they relate to each other – needs to be examined. Questions involving a powerful third branch, the judicial system, are also relevant, but space limitations prevent discussion of this complex subject here. Might it be true, for example, that even a strong Supreme Court could not rescue a presidentialist regime about to collapse, or that a weak judicial system would not undermine such a regime if it had found other ways to cope with its major intrinsic problems? Such doubts reinforce my decision to ignore this important question here, but some tentative thoughts on it can be found in Riggs (1988c, pp. 255, 269–72).

3 The presidential establishment

Although the presidentialist formula only requires, by definition, the election for a fixed term of office of the head of government, presidents also always serve as the head of state. In addition, the President is typically also the commander-in-chief and sometimes heads a leading party (or coalition of parties). These overlapping roles create vast expectations. The power vested in the office seems overwhelming, and regime stability appears to be assured. Since presidentialist regimes are vulnerable to collapse, however, this is an illusion. No doubt, so long as the regime persists, the fixed term of a President's office assures more continuity of leadership – despite possible cabinet reorganizations – than can be found in a multiparty parliamentary system vulnerable to frequent cabinet crises. In practice, nevertheless, Presidents are severely hampered in their leadership roles, and their inability to fulfil popular expectations often leads to crises and regime breakdowns. These limitations may be viewed from several perspectives.

3.1 Fusion of roles.

As head of government, every President has to make controversial policy decisions which unavoidably alienate substantial portions of the population. Even when a government's policies are widely supported, failures and injustices in their implementation are often blamed on the President. Yet Presidents, in their capacity as heads of state, are expected to symbolize and attract everyone's loyalty, providing a common focus of patriotism for all citizens. Clearly, the requirements of the first role often clash with those of the second.

In parliamentary regimes, where loyalty to the head of state ('king' or 'ceremonial president') can easily be dissociated from support for/opposition to the head of government (prime minister in cabinet), citizens can more easily sustain their patriotic loyalty to the state while opposing the policies of the government. When the two roles are linked, however, citizens easily confuse their dissatisfaction with government with disloyalty to the state. As a result, opposition to the current administration may produce discontent with the constitution and provide support for coups and revolutionary movements:

opposition to government easily becomes treason to the state; dissent becomes revolution. The absence of a separate head of state may also deprive the regime of an important moderating force to help conciliate opposing political movements or tendencies in times of emergency.

3.2 Fixed term of office.

The fixed term poses a double liability. In the case of effective Presidents it forces them out of office prematurely: one example may be that of Nobel prize-winning President Oscar Arias Sanchez of Costa Rica: his four-year term expired in 1990 and he could not be re-elected. The more usual cost, however, is that paid for an ineffectual President who, nevertheless, cannot be constitutionally discharged from office (except for criminal conduct as determined by impeachment). Ironically, one of the reasons for such ineffectiveness is precisely the fixed term: ambitious politicians, even in the President's own party, often feel that they can best advance their own careers by distancing themselves from the President, building an independent (oppositional) base for future political campaigns, and establishing themselves as opponents of the current regime.

This lame duck phenomenon occurs in the US near the end of every President's second term in office, but in many other countries we might even speak of a dead duck syndrome which afflicts new Presidents shortly after they assume office. In part this is due to constitutional barriers to any re-election of a President: in the American case, the possibility of at least one re-election (two or more until the enactment of Amendment 22 in 1951) enables a President to postpone the lame duck syndrome.

A lame duck President is not only gravely handicapped, but the growth of political opposition and popular discontent may well bolster the ambitions of a military cabal conspiring to seize power. A *coup d'état* is the functional equivalent, under presidentialism, of a removal effort that in parliamentary regimes can be achieved by a no-confidence vote. Since coups involve suspending the constitution, Congress is also dissolved, whether or not its resistance contributed to the failures of the Presidency.

3.3 Veto groups vs. opposition.

A President's role as head of government is also severely limited by the pervasiveness of veto groups such as the legislature, the courts and the bureaucracy, plus a fractionalized party system. Although these diverse bodies can block executive action, they cannot formulate the coherent alternatives that the political opposition can often produce in parliamentary regimes. Such an opposition may also compel government to modify policies in a consociational direction (Lijphart, 1989, p. 8), something which presidential veto groups normally fail to do. The possibility that an opposition can replace them means that cabinets must take their views seriously, whereas Presidents are tempted to view their opponents merely as hostile forces to be subdued.

Mainwaring (1989, p. 162) tells us that in the Latin American presidentialist democracies, Presidents have often been able to initiate policies but unable to win support for their implementation. Thus veto groups can block action but they are powerless to bring alternative (opposition) parties to power. Since all Presidents, despite growing opposition and political impotence, must cling to office until they meet their scheduled deadlines, a kind of self-induced nemesis drives them into the dead end of their lame duck terms.

3.4 The 'winner-take-all' syndrome.

In parliamentary systems, the election of a ceremonial president means relatively little, while the election of party members to Parliament means a great deal – especially to party supporters. Even small parties may 'win' to the degree that some of their candidates become Members of Parliament and may even join the government.

By contrast, in presidentialist systems the electoral stakes are much higher and more concentrated because so much hinges on the selection of a governing President – often, indeed, it is more of a personal than a partisan victory. Presidentialism, writes Juan Linz (1990, p. 56), 'is ineluctably problematic because it operates according to the rule of "winner-take-all" – an arrangement that tends to make democratic politics a zero-sum game, with all the potential for conflict such games portend'. There are many losers under presidentialism. Not only defeated parties but even members of a winning party – especially rival candidates for nomination – may feel that they have lost everything when a President is elected, leading to great discontent, alienation and the dead duck syndrome, as noted above.

To the degree that patronage prevails – and it is pervasive in all presidentialist regimes – a host of public officials may feel that their continuation in office depends on victory for the ruling party, and private interests supported by the government also have a large stake in its survival. Consequently, a Presidential victory is a triumph for supporters of the winning candidate and a great loss for opponents (Linz, 1990, p. 56). Understandably, their frustrations easily translate into popular resistance to the regime rather than loyal opposition to the government.

In pathological cases, the stakes seem so high that Presidents resort to unconstitutional means to maintain their power, including corruption, violence and sponsoring protégés (relatives and cronies) so as to perpetuate a 'family' dynasty, or even to compel constitutional changes that permit their own re-election. Corruption and violence at the polls often occur as a likely consequence of the high-stakes winner-take-all contest.

Such contentiousness may be amplified by the electoral rules. In Peru, for example, until 1979 a President could be elected by a one-third plurality, and Congress could name the President when no candidate won a third of the votes. In Peru's 1962 election, the leftist (APRA) party's leader, Haya de la Torre, 'beat Balaunde [of the centrist Accion Popular party] by less than one percentage point, 32.9% to 32.1%, with Odria third at 28%'. Since this threw the final choice to Congress, Haya sought first to make an alliance with Balaunde, who rejected him, calling instead for new elections (APRA had been charged with electoral irregularities). Haya then turned to his arch rival, Odria, of the right wing PPC. 'The specter of a government led by the presidential candidate who had finished third, in an ideologically disparate coalition between two parties that had been enemies for decades, may have been the last straw for the military. The coup came within two days' (McClintock, 1989, pp. 28–9). Thus the high-stakes winer-take-all game may even lead the losers to support the desperate expedient of a military coup.

3.5 A fragile political/administrative base.

The institutional foundations of a President's rule are inherently fragile. We may analyse this problem separately at the political (partisan) and the administrative (bureaucratic) levels, although in fact the two are closely interlocked.

At the political level, the contrast with parliamentary systems is instructive. The dependence of cabinets on parliamentary support means both that party discipline is necessary and that a government without parliamentary support must resign. The resulting fusion of powers often enables parliamentary governments to act decisively. By contrast, no such interdependence occurs under the presidentialist separation of powers where a persistent stalemate can block executive action.

Ideally, perhaps, a President's authority ought to rest on a party system which mobilizes voters to support candidates for election to public offices so that a winning party can ensure Congressional support for Presidential policies. In fact, however, this rarely occurs. Presidentialist party systems vary widely in their capacity to mobilize political support for a President. Some are highly disciplined and others extremely loose, two equally dysfunctional extremes. Disciplined parties, as found in Chile, have prevented the President from getting necessary Congressional support whenever he lacked a majority. Alternatively, as in Brazil, where party members freely vote their personal preferences, Presidents have responded by flagrantly over-riding or flouting the parties which had formally supported their candidacy (Mainwaring, 1990b, p. 21). Even in the United States, the majority party in Congress need not be the President's party, setting the stage for persistent conflict and deadlocks.

In multiparty systems, the President is likely to win only a plurality of popular votes, even though a technical majority may be formed in second-round run-off elections or Congressional voting. Such majorities are *ad hoc* coalitions that soon fall apart, denying the President genuine legislative support for his or her policies: according to Mainwaring (1990b, p. 25). 'The combination of presidentialism and a fractionalized multiparty system is especially unfavorable to democracy.' (See also Valenzuela, 1989, p. 33.)

Even when, in a two-party system, the President's party has a Congressional majority, the fact that the President cannot be dis-charged by a majority vote of no confidence may mean that members of the President's party have little to lose by not supporting a govern-ment bill they do not like. Moreover, party factionalism can also mean that many members of the ruling party consistently vote against the chief executive's policies and leadership. No doubt, when party discipline is strong, as it has been in Argentina, a Congressional majority will assure support for Presidential policies. Nevertheless, even though the separation of powers may serve its original purpose of preventing arbitrary government, it often fails to provide the political support Presidents require in order to govern effectively.

The inability of Presidents to implement policy is compounded at the administrative level, as illustrated pointedly by the precarious dynamics of 'cabinet' formation. A President needs the help of a highly qualified top echelon of department heads and bureaucrats who can administer public policies effectively and also secure Con-gressional and legal support for administration policies. However, Presidents jeopardize the separation of powers if they rely either on members of Congress or on career officials to head their departments and form a cabinet. Accordingly, they seek to enhance Congressional support by naming party activists from outside Congress, or they recruit personal followers (even relatives) from the private sector to fill these posts, and to staff the Presidential apparatus, by-passing both elected politicians and experienced public administrators. Consequently, a highly personal style, inter-departmental conflicts and lack of institutionalization at the top levels of Presidential administration typically hamper the processes of governance in presidentialist regimes.

4 The legislative–executive chasm

Consider the case of Ecuador, which has experienced frequent regime breakdowns, but has restored democratic procedures since 1979. Nevertheless, acute tensions between President and Congress persist, according to Catherine Conaghan (1989, p. 20), who tells us that shortly after the elections of 1984, 'Congressional activity came to a stand still after sessions were marred by tear-gas bombings, fisticuffs on the floor of the assembly, and walk-outs by legislators on both sides. Meanwhile, [President] Febres Cordero had decided to physically bar the new appointees [named by Congress to the Supreme Court] from using their offices and banned the publication of the appointments ....' In 1987 the President was kidnapped by Air Force paratroopers who released him only after he had agreed to confirm the amnesty granted by Congress to two leading opponents of the administration (pp. 23–4).

'From 1979 through 1988, Ecuador staggered through a succession of executive–legislative confrontations that created a near permanent crisis atmosphere in the polity' (Conaghan, 1989, p. 25). 'Even when Presidents enjoyed a pro-government majority in Congress, the majority could easily erode under the pressures of interest groups and electoral calculations. Congressional opposition was a standard feature in the interruption of Presidential terms with interest groups and the armed forces joining in the fray' (ibid., p. 8).

When a President is 'incapable of pursuing a coherent course of action because of congressional opposition ... in many cases, a coup appears to be the only means of getting rid of an incompetent or unpopular president' (Mainwaring, 1989, p. 165). A similar argument can be found in Linz (1990, p. 53). Stalemate is even more unavoidable when – as noted above – the President's party has only a minority in the Congress.

To overcome such impasses, Presidents frequently strive to dominate the assembly, a tendency that, in effect, vitiates the principle of separation of powers and leads to quasi-presidentialism and the erosion (or destruction) of presidentialist legitimacy. Embattled Presidents are often tempted to resort to desperate and even unconstitutional measures in order to bypass Congress and achieve their goals (Mainwaring, 1989, pp. 168–9). Sometimes, as in the

Philippines in 1972, the President suspends Congress and rules by martial law and executive orders.

More often, as in Brazil, according to Mainwaring (1990b, p. 15), all its democratic Presidents sought 'to bypass Congress by implementing policy through executive agencies and decree-laws ... the practice of creating new agencies and circumventing congress for major programs' has grave costs. 'When Quadros and Goulart were frustrated with Congress ... they appealed to popular mobilization – with disastrous results in both cases .... This strategy was catastrophic, as it further alienated major institutional actors, including the armed forces' (p. 16).

Military interventions are not often explicitly due to an overt impasse between the President and Congress, but rather are attributed to habitual executive abuse or misuse of power provoked by a long-festering history of such conflict. The absence of a coherent opposition that could replace the government – as noted above – often tempts a President to persist in unwise projects that undermine popular support. No cabinet office-holder or legislator is powerful enough to compel the President to make serious policy revisions. The frequent replacement of cabinet members not only reflects Presidential weakness but, reciprocally, generates sycophancy and intimidates those who might be able to correct a misguided President.

Since impeachment cannot replace the government by an opposition party, even fierce opponents may oppose a procedure that will merely replace the President with an even more objectionable vice president. Consequently, the fixed electoral cycle of presidentialism creates structural rigidities that are readily overcome in the alternative parliamentary model by the threat of a cabinet crisis and/or new elections whenever the current leadership is seriously discredited. Is it, therefore, surprising that in such an environment a cabal of officials, mainly military officers, should seize power and overthrow the presidentialist regime?

4.1 Congressional problematique.

Since the presidentialist formula requires that members of Congress as well as the President be elected for a fixed term of office, it is apparent that every effective Congress will have to cope with a vast and inherently unmanageable agenda. By contrast, in any Parliament, members usually need only to agree or disagree with government policies. Even members of a government party who disagree with its policies will usually support them in order to avoid the possibility of an election in which they might lose their seats.

In all contemporary polities the number of complex issues calling for attention is so vast and controversial that it is really impossible for any body of legislators to study and reach collective agreements on all of them. The danger, then, is that an overloaded Congress will fail to act or will find itself deadlocked in major controversies. If it is too compliant with Presidential policy demands it becomes a mere rubber stamp, or it may simply refuse to consider many of the issues that have been placed on its agenda. If, however, it habitually rejects government proposals, or offers alternatives that the President is sure to veto, it can bring the processes of governance to a halt.

Moreover, members of Congress face competing demands that must be terribly frustrating. They are pressured by clients seeking patronage appointments, by local constituencies seeking funds for 'pork barrel' projects, and they must mobilize support for re-election campaigns. Essentially, every Congress is placed in a kind of 'no-win' situation from which it vainly struggles to extricate itself. Ultimately, it must share with the President a heavy burden of criticism that, all too often, generates military intervention and the breakdown of the regime.

5   The Party system

Since a presidentialist regime is, by definition, a form of representative government, it needs to have an open party system: that is, it needs electoral competition between two or more effective parties. This is because the maintenance of genuine legislative power is impossible whenever one party regularly dominates the elected assembly. A one-party system (as in communist regimes) leads to complete party control of the elected assembly. Even a hegemonic party, in a polity which permits genuine opposition parties, nearly suffocates the Congress. Mexico provides a classic case: all the advantages resulting from electoral success belong repeatedly to the PRI, and the Congress becomes a pliant legitimizing instrument. The separation of powers required, by definition, in a presidentialist regime is, therefore, incompatible with hegemonic or one-party rule – what I shall refer to as a closed party system. By definition, although opposition parties may be permitted to run candidates in free elections, if they have no real chance of winning power then the party system is really 'closed.'

An open party system, by contrast, is one in which two or more parties have real possibilities of winning power. We cannot use *multiparty* for this concept because a *two-party* system is also 'open.' No doubt the distinction between *two* and *multiparty* systems is significant – as is the distinction between single and hegemonic party systems. However, I see them as sub-types of a more fundamental distinction, that is, between open and closed party systems. Moreover, among open party systems there is a more fundamental difference based on the dynamics of interparty competition which we need to consider here.

5.1 Dynamics of centrifugalism.

Among open party systems, the most fundamental distinction involves the degree to which power is centrifugalized (polarizing) or centri-petalized (centring). In the context of this distinction, we can better understand the two-party/multiparty contrast[6]. I believe that the survival of presidentialism is promoted by an open centripetal party system and undermined by one that is centrifugal or closed.

Centripetal forces arise when different parties compete mainly for centre votes; that is, the support of regular, mainstream voters who think of themselves as 'independents', willing to support candidates of any party or even to split their tickets, as current interests, policy issues or political personalities suggest. By contrast, centrifugal forces prevail when more extreme positions are taken by parties seeking to attract the support of non-voters. This typically involves proposing dramatic, populist, costly and controversial policies likely to win the support of apathetic or alienated citizens who normally cannot or will not vote. Unfortunately, most presidentialist regimes have developed centrifugal party systems, thereby creating self-destructive spirals based on circular causation.

5.2 Multiparty systems.

A voting system that rewards small parties offers strong incentives for marginal groups to become organized and present extremist platforms that can mobilize special interest groups of many kinds, be they street sleepers, religious sects, ethnic communities or social classes. Such pressures produce multiparty systems that undoubtedly create grave problems for parliamentary systems but they need not destroy them. No doubt each party represented in a coalition cabinet can exercise a veto power by threatening to withdraw, but it also needs the support of other coalition members to achieve any of its goals, often leading even extremists to support consociational accommodations.

By contrast, a centrifugal multiparty system undermines any presidentialist regime because its polarized parties lack pressure points *vis-à-vis* a fixed-term head of government. Although presidential candidates may temporarily seek the support of extremist parties, as when forming pre-election coalitions, the withdrawal of partisan support will have little influence on Presidents in office. Small parties lack bargaining power and Presidents have no built-in structures to counteract the polarizing tendencies of a centrifugal party system. Indeed, any President who seeks to meet the demands of extremists in Congress soon antagonizes the main-line parties and loses the support needed for policies of more general interest.

Multiparty systems usually lead to minority governments, in two senses. First, a *plurality government* is one in which a President has won office with a plurality vote but no absolute majority of the popular vote. Secondly, a *divided government* is one where the President continually faces an antagonistic majority in Congress. (Where the same party prevails in both branches we may speak of *party government*.) Minority government in both senses is almost unavoidable because of the centrifugal dynamics inherent in multiparty systems: plurality Presidents lack the popular mandate needed to lead effectively, and minority governments cannot gain Congressional support for their policies.

In most of Latin America, multiparty systems prevail. Among them, the most successful was probably Chile, 'the only case in the world of a multiparty presidential[ist] democracy that endured for 25 or more consecutive years' (Mainwaring, 1989, p. 168). In Chile, Congress was called upon to make the final choice of a President but, in this situation, a temporary coalition of highly disciplined parties, formed to support the winning candidate, usually soon fell apart (Valenzuela, 1989, p. 32). Thus, 'there was an inadequate fit between the country's highly polarized and competitive party system, which was incapable of generating majorities, and a presidential[ist] system of centralized authority .... As minority Presidents ... Chilean chief executives enjoyed weak legislative support or outright congressional opposition. And since they could not seek reelection, there was little incentive for parties, including the President's own, to support him beyond mid-term' (Valenzuela, 1988, pp. 33–4). The resulting sense of 'permanent crisis' culminated in 1974 in the Pinochet coup and dictatorship.

A different kind of multiparty presidentialism is found in Brazil where 'Presidents could not even count on the support of their own parties, much less that of the other parties that had helped elect them. Brazilian parties in the two democratic periods have been notoriously undisciplined and incapable of providing consistent block support for presidents' (Mainwaring, 1990b, p. 5). They have tried to cope with the deadlock of congressional opposition based on an extremely fragmented and fluid party system by developing an 'anti-party discourse' and have 'engaged in anti-party actions'. Often they were 'recruited from outside or above party channels'. They usually avoided strong links with any party in order to enhance their political appeal to a broad range of public opinion (Mainwaring, 1990b, pp. 9–10).

Whether the individual parties are disciplined or not is certainly important, but I believe that a more important consideration is the centrifugal dynamism of all multiparty systems. Although these dynamics may even invigorate parliamentary systems, they ultimately destroy presidentialist regimes, producing both plurality and divided governments.

5.3 Two-party systems.

It is widely thought that two-party systems are generated by presidentialism and conducive to their survival. Actually, multipartyism is more common in presidentialist regimes, and two-partyism by no means assures their survival. According to Mainwaring, 'Two party systems are the exception rather than the rule in Latin America, but among the regions's more enduring democracies, they are the rule rather than the exception' – including Colombia, Costa Rica, Uruguay and Venezuela (Mainwaring, 1990b, p. 25).

However, a two-party system is not necessarily a permanent feature of any presidentialist regime, and by no means assures its survival. Since the 1984 election, Uruguay may no longer be classed as a 'two-party system' and Venezuela has been a two-party system only for the last 20 years or so. In Asia, two-partyism prevailed in the Philippines from 1946 to 1972, after which President Ferdinand Marcos imposed martial law, suspended Congress and created his closed system dominated by the New Society Movement (KBL) (De Guzman and Reforma, 1988, pp. 87–95). Actually, it is very difficult to maintain a viable two-party system: it may evolve into a multiparty or hegemonic party system.

Ideally, a two-party system will enable Presidents to secure a majority vote and a popular mandate to rule, with the support of a party majority in Congress. This premiss is based on the familiar parliamentary model and fails to appreciate the basic fact that, because of the fixed term, presidentialist regimes lack the basic motor of parliamentarism which promotes party discipline. Even when the President's party has a Congressional majority, there is no way to guarantee support for the President's programme.

To understand the acknowledged linkage between two-partyism and presidentialism we must first recognize that a two-party system may be centrifugal or centripetal: overcoming executive/legislative conflicts is much easier with a centripetal two-party system than it is when that system is centrifugalized. To visualize the dynamics of a centrifugal two-party system, consider the situation in Uruguay, often mentioned as a leading example of successful two-party democracy. There, the Colorado party actually held power from 1865 to 1973 – except for a brief interim period (1958–62) of control by the opposition Blanco party – suggesting a *de facto* hegemonic party situation. A military group seized power in 1973; democracy was not restored until 1985.

Centrifugalization in this 'two-party system' was driven by party factionalization and high voter turnouts, leading to deep cleavages between the President and Congress (Gillespie, p. 1989, 15; Gonzalez, 1989, p. 14). The main explanation can be found in Uruguay's exceptional scheme of proportional representation which permits party factions to present separate lists. This system, known as the 'double simultaneous vote', has produced highly contentious intraparty factions (Gillespie, 1989, p. 15). Even though each list goes under the label of a major party, the candidates on each faction's list compete with each other, just as they would in a multiparty system, and they also provoke widespread electoral participation. Consequently, Presidents typically face strong resistance within their own party – in addition to that from the opposition party.

Thus, when Oscar Diego Gestido was elected in 1967, his faction controlled only a fraction of the Colorado deputies. The resulting standoff, complicated by some quasi-parliamentary features of the constitution, resulted in no 'real control over the Executive but a permanent hindrance of its functioning which ironically increases the tendency toward coups'. In 1973 a military group seized power and dissolved Congress, although Juan Maria Bordaberry was allowed to remain as nominal 'President' (Gillespie, 1989, pp. 15–17; Gonzalez, 1989, pp. 7–8).

A similar rule permits party factions to run separate electoral lists in Colombia and helps to explain the complexity of this country's highly factionalized and centrifugal 'two-party' system. 'Factionalization forced each President to create and recreate an effective governing coalition within Congress, making the National Front period resemble a multiparty system' (Hartlyn, 1989, p. 16). Although leading factions of the two main parties supported the government, other factions of each party went into opposition. Immobilism and deadlock resulted. (For further details, see Hartlyn, 1989, pp. 15–20.)

Since multiparty systems are necessarily centrifugal, only a two-party system is compatible, in the long run, with presidentialism. However, this is possible only if the system is centripetal, and as

Uruguay and Colombia demonstrate, two-party systems may be highly centrifugal. We shall clarify the problem, therefore, if we say that a centripetal open party system is needed. If, as I have argued, multi-party systems are necessarily centrifugal, this means that it must be a two-party system, but having only two parties is not sufficient.

5.4 Electoral Foundations.

When our focus is on the centripetal/centrifugal distinction among open party systems, we can easily see that the electoral system provides the most important explanation. In general, a wide variety of multimember-district proportional representation (PR) systems produce centrifugalized party configurations (normally, but not always, with more than two parties). The attempt to secure a popular majority for the President by means of a second-round run-off election cannot nullify the effects of PR in the first round. Moreover, when congressional elections coincide with the first round balloting for President, as may often be the case, it becomes most 'unlikely that a President will enjoy a clear-cut majority in Congress'. This proved to be the case in Ecuador where many parties have proliferated (Conaghan, 1989, pp. 12–13).

The rhetoric of two- and multiparty systems lulls us into our preoccupation with the number of parties in a polity and distracts attention from an equally necessary factor: the internal distribution of power in a party. I believe the survival of presidentialism is as much affected by party structure as it is by party system. Yet we cannot easily discuss this dimension because our vocabulary is inadequate. We tend to make a simplified dichotomy between 'disciplined' parties, such as we normally find in parliamentary systems, and the 'catch-all' parties found in the United States and, for example, in Brazil. We may also assume that PR leads to disciplined parties and single-member-district (SMD) voting to loose parties – generalizing from US/European comparisons.

The comparative study of presidentialist regimes will show us, however, that such notions conceal a far more complicated reality in which, assuredly, electoral systems play a role, in combination with regime type. We need to distinguish between at least three dimensions of power distribution found in all political parties: geographic, functional, and relational. We can use *centralized/localized* to talk about the geographic dimension; *concentrated/dispersed* for the functional dimension; and *integrated/isolated* to discuss relations between political parties and other social organizations based on religion, ethnicity, class, occupation and so on. Here I shall focus on the first two, leaving the third for later comment.

I shall use *centred* to characterize a political party where power is both centralized and concentrated; and *fluid* for a pattern in which power is both localized and dispersed. *Discipline* is properly used for the willingness of all legislators belonging to a given party to vote as instructed by their leaders. Clearly, the more centred a party, the greater the likelihood that its parliamentary members will be disciplined. By contrast, members of a fluid party are likely to be undisciplined, often refusing to follow their party's line. We need to retain this distinction between the internal power structure of a party and the voting behaviour of its members in an elected assembly.

A party in which power is both centralized and dispersed is *factionalized*, as illustrated by the Uruguayan and Colombian parties. This pattern is produced by an unusual form of PR (the 'double simultaneous vote') which produces a centrifugalized two-party system. Legislative voting will be disciplined (within the factions) and undisciplined (in an all-party sense). A neologism may be required to talk clearly about such cases: we might speak of *dia-discipline* in the case of factionalized parties.

Party power may be both localized and concentrated in the form of urban *machines*, such as Tammany Hall and many other political clubs typical of an earlier period in US history. Rather awkwardly, we might speak of such a party as *machined* or *machinist*, but I use these words here only to illustrate our need for better terms. Legislative voting in such parties might also be dia-disciplined, but with members following orders from local machine bosses rather than from national faction leaders.

More importantly, however, we need to see that normally PR in a presidentialist regime produces a multiparty system in which the power distribution in individual parties can vary between centred and fluid. Fluid parties are found in Brazil, producing a chaotic Congressional arena where Presidents have to bargain with many individualistic members in order to secure clientelistic support for their policies, often by means of patronage and local (pork-barrel) projects. 'The extremely loose nature of Brazilian parties has added to the problems caused by the permanent minority situation of Presidents' parties. Presidents could not even count on the support of their own parties, much less that of the other parties that had helped elect them' (Mainwaring, 1990b, p. 5).

Similarly, in Ecuador, 'politicians of every stripe appear to be afflicted with a significant amount of distaste and disdain for the party system in which they operate. ... Rather than using presidential resources to build up his own party, Febres Cordero [as other

Presidents had done] preferred to by-pass parties altogether and create a clientelist network' (Conaghan, 1989, p. 30). Thus, the efforts of Presidents and other politicians to undermine party solidarity often stimulates, by circular causation, the disruptive effects of fluid parties on legislative performance and the growing frustrations of the chief executive. Conaghan remarks: 'What is striking in Ecuadorean political culture and style is the extent to which it has been permeated by an anti-party mentality' (p. 29). Alternatively, as I propose, one might see the extreme fluidity (localization and dispersal) of such parties as a normal feature of presidentialist regimes that use PR electoral systems.

It is equally normal, however, for such systems to produce highly centred parties, and they are equally dysfunctional for the maintenance of presidentialist regimes. The best example can be found in Chile, where well-disciplined (ideological) parties often combine to produce a solid opposition front whenever a President cannot sustain the majority coalition in Congress which brought him to power (Valenzuela, 1989, pp. 32–3).

In parliamentary systems, of course, PR also leads to centred parties – the dynamics of parliamentarism simply renders a fluid party non-viable. Moreover, centred parties are functional for the maintenance of parliamentary accountability because they produce discipline. Reciprocally, the need for discipline has a feedback effect which encourages electoral rules that generate centred parties. In presidentialist systems, by contrast, PR can produce parties which are fluid, centred or factionalized: always in a centrifugalized party system and always dysfunctional for the maintenance of presidentialism. Moreover, neither president nor Congress seems to have any systemic means to counteract these party dynamisms.

Fortunately, between the polar extremes identified above some intermediate intraparty power distributions are also possible. Here our vocabulary is, again, quite inadequate. Provisionally, I shall use *'responsive'* to characterize an intraparty distribution of power that combines local autonomy with headquarters guidance, and permits intraparty groups to organize informally but not to become oppressively prominent. On the two basic power dimensions, responsiveness falls between centred and localized, and between concentrated and dispersed. In sub-section 9.2 I shall try to show that the survival of presidentialism in the United States hinges, among various factors, on the responsiveness of its political parties and the *semi-disciplined* voting patterns which this engenders. The causes are no doubt complex, but they surely include reliance on a single-member-district plurality system for the election of legislators, plus the freedom to abstain from voting and a variety of other factors that will be explained below, in sub-sections 11.2 and 11.3.

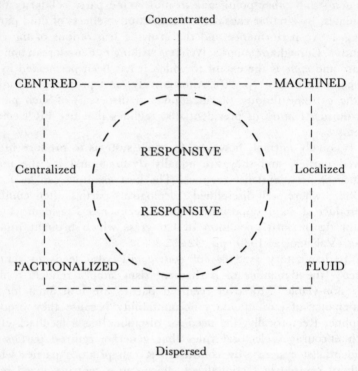

Figure 3.1: A typology of political parties by internal distribution of power

A *centred* party is centralized and concentrated; a *fluid* party is localized and dispersed; a *factionalized* party is centralized and dispersed; a *machined* party is localized and concentrated; a *responsive* party is intermediate on both dimensions.

6 Bureaucratic dilemmas

The urgent need of any chief executive to be surrounded by competent and loyal officials capable of managing and co-ordinating the administration of government directs attention to a major problem that is easily overlooked by analysts predisposed to focus on the 'political' aspects of governance at the expense of its 'administrative' dimensions. Yet failure to administer well has dire political consequences. Public confidence declines and discontents soar, producing the kinds of unrest that lead, so often, to revolutionary movements and coups.

Moreover, many activities that are nominally administrative in character actually have strong political implications – for example, appointments to public office and administrative reorganizations, including the establishment of new agencies, can vitally affect a President's power position and influence the disposition of members of Congress to support or oppose a President's policies. Perhaps, above all, bureaucratic power often expands to such a degree that public (especially military) officials become major actors in the political arena – sometimes even seizing power by a *coup d'état*. Because the political implications of bureaucratic dilemmas are so often misunderstood, we need to take a closer look at these problems as they occur in presidentialist regimes.

6.1 The power of modern bureaucracy.

The main instrument for administering any modern government is typically a bureaucracy whose members – military as well as civil – depend largely on their salaries to support themselves and their dependants. This feature of modern bureaucracy contrasts with the situation found in traditional bureaucracies where modest official stipends were usually supplemented by various kinds of legal but non-official income (Riggs, 1991, pp. 2–6).[7] The significance of this fact becomes apparent when we remind ourselves that officials, like all other people, have their own interests to defend. However, their control over public offices and resources gives them weapons of power (especially in the armed forces) not available to most citizens. Unless their incomes are secure and their conduct is well monitored, guided and supervised by constitutional organs and popular forces, bureaucrats are easily able to exploit public office for personal advantage, as by widespread corruption and sinecurism. When they feel really threatened, they can also, under military leadership, seize power by a *coup d'état*.[8]

6.2 The need for patronage.

The public interest in contemporary societies requires that many bureaucrats, especially those in leadership and technocratic positions, be experienced and highly qualified to perform difficult tasks. The necessary qualifications are best assured by the establishment of a 'merit' system designed to recruit well-trained persons whose continuing (tenured) experience in government service enables them to perform effectively.

In parliamentary democracies – and even under single-party domination and in traditional monarchies – the development of experienced cadres of public officials is usually possible, and ruling

elites or cabinets are able to rely for the most part on career bureaucrats to staff and implement their politically driven policies in ways
that are essentially technocratic and professional.

By contrast, in *presidentialist* regimes, the structurally precarious
position of Presidents, for reasons discussed above, would be seriously jeopardized were they to depend on career officials to staff the
highest bureaucratic offices, including cabinet positions. Moreover,
Presidents cannot recruit sitting members of Congress to serve as
cabinet members without endangering the autonomy and power of the
executive office, nor is it possible for non-elective cabinet members
to hold seats in the assembly without jeopardizing the balance of
power. In this necessarily precarious position, Presidents have no
option but to recruit a large number of leading officials, starting at
the cabinet level, from outside the government service: they can be
neither career officials nor elected politicians.

Consequently, heavy reliance on patronage appointments (clientelism, cronyism and spoils) is a prevalent and necessary feature of
all presidentialist systems. It entails fateful political and administrative
costs. The most apparent is a lack of experience, qualifications and
dependability: Presidents must, on very short notice, try to assemble
a team of personal supporters to manage the government and direct
a host of subordinates whose interests and obligations often conflict
with those of the President.

Members of Congress also have a compelling interest in patronage.
They typically seek posts for their supporters (clients) in order to
maintain the political support without which they could not be
elected. This gives them a powerful incentive and basis for bargaining with a beleaguered President: they can trade votes for favours. This
is no trivial matter because their own power base may be seriously
undermined if they cannot secure appointments for their protégés.
Consequently, the indispensable minimum of political appointees
needed to staff a presidentialist regime's top posts is vastly inflated
because both the President and the Congress need patronage to
maintain the system.

Presidents typically need patronage to gain legislative support
for their policies. Hartlyn reports that in Colombia a 'President
had massive appointive powers, whose significance was augmented
by the importance of spoils and patronage to the clientelist and
brokerage oriented parties and by the absence of any meaningful
civil service legislation. Presidents could appoint cabinet ministers
without congressional approval' (1989, p. 13). The effect of the
growing power of the President was 'to marginalize Congress
further from major decisions, reducing its functions to ones of

patronage, brokerage and management of limited pork barrel funds' (p. 21).

Mainwaring reports that, in Brazil, 'The only glue (and it is a powerful one at times) that holds the President's support together is patronage – and this helps explain the pervasive use of patronage politics' (1990b, p. 7). 'Both Vargas and Kubitschek pressed for reforms that would strengthen the merit system and protect state agencies from clientelistic pressures, but they were defeated by a Congress unwilling to relinquish patronage privileges' (p. 6).

Here we find a classic double bind: the President needs patronage to secure Congressional support and members of Congress cannot abandon clientelism without undermining their own political support base. Only a judicious use of patronage can sustain the separation of power needed for presidentialism to survive. Thus, although both President and Congress need a non-partisan *career* system in the bureaucracy in order to implement their policies effectively, neither can afford to embrace a merit system without undermining their own precarious power base and threatening the presidentialist balance of power.

6.3   The tenacity of retainers.

In every polity bureaucratic self-interest produces additional problems that involve officials in office. Most conspicuously, in presidentialist regimes this concerns the retention/rotation dilemma. In all non-presidentialist regimes, as noted above, almost all appointed officials are recruited and retained on a career basis. In presidentialist systems, by contrast, powerful forces lead to patronage appointments under a succession of elected officials, including both the President and members of Congress. What happens to these appointees when new elections bring new personalities and political parties into power? Will they be able to keep their jobs, or will they be discharged?

It is much easier to hire than to fire, and those in office fight to keep their jobs: no doubt they are more interested and powerful than are candidates seeking new posts. We need to recognize a large class of political appointees who are able to retain their positions – I refer to them as *retainers*. Although they remain in office, they are often down-graded and humiliated (siberianized) when new political appointees replace them in higher office. Only their dependence on salaries and their eagerness to protect their personal security and fringe benefits lead them to put up with many humiliations. Predictably, however, demoralized and underpaid officials do unsatisfactory work and lower the quality of public administration.

Moreover, because bureaucratic retainers work on a salary basis and depend on the government for their income and security, they will often (when their livelihood is threatened) support a coup. Its military leaders are not only enraged by the policy failures of a regime but they want to safeguard the interests of all public employees, not just themselves. In all bureaucratic revolts, military officers play the dominant role because they control the means of violence, but they need the support of civil servants in order to run the government successfully. This is why I use *'bureaucratic polity'* for the resultant dictatorships, rather than the superficial term, 'military authoritarianism'.

Merit-based careerism will surely help any regime to cope with the serious crises that might lead to a coup simply by improving the quality of public administration. However, it is extremely difficult to establish such a system, not only because of short-term Presidential and Congressional resistance, but also because retainers see it as a threat that must be fiercely resisted. In order to pave the way for careerists to replace retainers, rotation in office must first be accepted. A government must be able to discharge incumbents in order to create the vacancies that a new class of careerists can fill. Yet attempts by any presidentialist regime to enforce a rotation policy generate fierce resistance and usually compel governments to compromise with incumbents rather than risk the serious costs of mass lay-offs, including a possible *coup d'état*.

A costly alternative to rotationism was developed in Chile, where civil servants could retire 'with fifteen years service and a relatively good pension. Agency heads, however, would retire with what was known as *la perseguidora* – a pension that kept pace with the salary of the current occupant of the post retired from .... Agency heads were thus appointed as a culmination of their careers and could be persuaded to retire to allow a new President to make new appointments' (Valenzuela, 1984, p. 262). Another common bureaucratic practice in Chile deprived officials of significant functions while respecting their job security: 'The *huesera* (or common grave), a series of offices for individuals with no official responsibilities ... became a feature of many agencies' (ibid., p. 264). Moreover, 'new agencies ... that could carry forth new program initiatives of the new administration were brought into existence without having to abolish older ones. Even the conservative and austerity-minded Jorge Alessandri added 35,000 new employees to the public sector during his tenure in office' (ibid., p. 263). This practice enables a President to make patronage appointments without discharging incumbent officials.

Similarly, in Brazil Presidents often expanded the apparatus of government by creating new state agencies in order to enhance their power and overcome Congressional resistance (Mainwaring, 1989, p. 169). By such means, some of the short-term political benefits of rotationism have been achieved, but only at immense cost. Most importantly, by thwarting the establishment of merit-based career systems, they have perpetuated a deep flaw that helps us explain the collapse of most presidentialist regimes.

6.4 Structural poly-normativism.

A second fundamental problem for all presidentialist bureaucracies involves the need of bureaucrats to be responsive concurrently to the separate authority of the President, Congress and the courts. This results, as David Rosenbloom (1983) has pointed out, in three sets of criteria governing bureaucratic performance which frequently clash with each other, generating bureaucratic poly-normativism. Presidential authority can lead to emphasis on the managerial values of efficiency and effectiveness; Congressional demands may generate insistence on political responsibility and responsiveness; and judicial decisions often give priority to standards of legality and the protection of citizens' rights versus bureaucratic abuse of power. A fourth criterion, suggested by the discussion of patronage, involves partisan pressures. Indeed, it may be true that in all political systems partisanship can play an important role in public bureaucracies. This is especially true of presidentialist regimes, however, where it has disastrous consequences.

Even where a 'non-partisan' merit system has been established, as it was in the Philippines because of American influence, career officials are often openly partisan. Carino reports that 'a third of middle-level bureaucrats in a survey mentioned helping in an electoral campaign – against civil service rules. Another third acknowledged nurturing political ambitions.... Civil servants also sometimes played off the executive against Congress, claiming the ability to get appropriations despite the absence of the President's support' (1989, pp. 12, 14). In addition to the career officials, of course, in the Philippines, as in all presidentialist polities, there were always a good many overtly partisan Presidentially appointed 'agency heads and such aides as could be justified as "policy determining, highly technical or primarily confidential" ' (p. 10).

This was the 'normal' pattern of bureaucratic politics in the Philippines, always involving substantial Congressional intervention, before the advent in 1972 of the dictatorship of President Ferdinand Marcos. He sought to institutionalize an intermediate, highly politicized and well-paid layer of political appointees, the 'Career Executive Service', to become vehicles of his authoritarian regime and to help him perform functions of the dissolved Congress. Since the advent of President Corazon Aquino in 1986 and the attempt to re-establish a democratic presidentialist regime, there have been sweeping bureaucratic replacements, purges of many officials and tumultuous reorganization schemes. The partisanship involved in this highly traumatic and often unsuccessful effort to 'de-Marcosify' the bureaucracy are summarized by Carino (1989) and described in more detail in her monograph (1988).

In Chile a partisan type of merit system evolved. According to Valenzuela (1984, p. 271), 'The Chilean civil service was recruited and promoted through a Chilean version of the spoils system: party recommendations, and legislative support, in addition to formal credentials, were important in gaining entry and crucial in rising to higher office. The civil service was fragmented ... by strong partisan loyalties that prevented the development of institutional loyalties.'

In practice, therefore, public officials in presidentialist regimes are typically cross-pressured from four main sources: the President, Congress, courts, and political parties. Although comparable cross-pressures can no doubt be found in non-presidentialist regimes, they are less disruptive of administrative performance in them than they are in presidentialist systems where they augment the forces contributing to the collapse of these regimes mentioned above. Further details on this subject can be found in Riggs (1993b).

III Survival of Presidentialism

All the inherent difficulties resulting from the presidentialist design that have been enumerated above compel us to conclude that it would be amazing if any country could maintain such a regime for any length of time. The likelihood of catastrophe is simply too great. Any one of these major problems could lead to disaster, but normally, we may assume, adverse results are due to the cumulative and mutually reinforcing consequences of many unsolved problems. No one of them by itself can be blamed for the collapse of a presidentialist regime but cumulatively they generate insoluble difficulties that lead to catastrophe.

Moreover, disasters typically occur in stages. The economy may stagnate and civil strife break out, provoking foreign interventions, even though the formalities of presidentialism are maintained. Sometimes, a frustrated and angered President will then usurp power and bypass Congress, leading to quasi-presidentialism. Power may become concentrated in the hands of an authoritarian 'President' or, more often, in behind-the-scenes military, family or social elites and factions. Eventually, revolution, military or foreign intervention may occur, accompanied by complete suspension of the constitution.

It is, perhaps, comforting to note that military bureaucratic and autocratic regimes are themselves unstable. They provoke growing resistance and even external pressures which often lead to their collapse and, possibly, to the restoration of constitutional government. At such times it is important to understand the prospects and costs of presidentialism by contrast with its parliamentary alternatives. An explanation of the survival of presidentialism in the US by contrast with its fate elsewhere will, surely, contribute immensely to such an understanding.

7 A procedure

In the light of the problems identified in Part II, we need not be astonished at the fate of the 30 or so polities that adopted the American presidentialist scheme, by contrast with the greater ability of parliamentary regimes to survive. No doubt, some contextual variables help to account for the striking US exception: for example, are North Americans more 'practical', 'tolerant' or 'problem orientated' than the citizens of Latin America, as some analysts assert? Have geographic, economic, cultural, historical or social advantages of various kinds facilitated the perpetuation of presidentialism in America? Such claims are often made to explain the apparent viability of American presidentialism.

I feel helpless to evaluate these claims. Moreover, in so far as we may be interested in the possibility that other states – especially the new Republics in Eastern Europe – will want to emulate the American model, we need to consider the proposition that, if environmental conditions are the determining factors, they cannot be replicated in other countries; but if rules and practices that can be changed by political decisions are decisive, their adoption by others might enable them to establish or perpetuate presidentialist regimes.

To the degree that important political practices found in the United States are not found in other presidentialist regimes, their absence may have explanatory significance. The single American case cannot provide conclusive evidence to support any important causal explanations, but it can suggest hypotheses that may be tested by the comparative study of presidentialist regimes. If practices which seem to be associated with the survival of American presidentialism are missing in countries where presidentialism has failed, then this evidence provides empirical support for the hypotheses. We must not reject comparisons between the US and other presidentialist regimes because of the failures of the latter – rather, they provide the information we need in order to explain the relative success of the US.

I say 'relative success' because some observers now wonder whether or not American presidentialism can continue to survive in the face of growing world complexity and interdependency. For example, Philip Cerny has recently offered an English political scientist's opinion that 'The Madisonian formula of checks and balances – federalism and the separation of powers – provided a resilient and flexible means during the nineteenth centurys ....' By contrast, he argues, at the present time 'the capacity of the United States to play an effective role in an increasingly interpenetrated world has frequently been undermined in significant ways by the workings of the system. ... as other countries adapt more effectively than the United States to contemporary conditions, the American system of government both exacerbates crises and stalls solutions. Such counterproductive propensities threaten continually to turn an otherwise manageable hegemonic decline into a steep and slippery slope' (1989, pp. 47–8). 'The effects of Madisonian entropy are already reaching a critical point, seriously compromising the capacity of the United States to respond coherently to the challenges of the future' (ibid., p. 55). Although federalism may well be a liability in presidentialist regimes, it may also be an asset, in my opinion, for reasons explained in section 11.5 (see also note 19).

No doubt, foreign friends will increasingly become more aware than Americans of the serious limitations of presidentialism. Fortunately, however, there are a few American political scientists who are seriously studying the problems inherent in the American presidentialist system and proposing significant constitutional reforms. In 1963 Quentin Quade argued that 'American government is inadequate for the responsibilities confronting it' and that we need 'a fundamental alteration of our political institutions' (Quade, 1963, p. 73). A collection of documents offering diagnoses of the problem and proposed reforms is contained in Robinson (1985). This work reflects the efforts of the Committee on the Constitutional System – under the leadership of Nancy Landon Kassebaum, Lloyd N. Cutler and C. Douglas Dillon – to promote serious inquiry into the need for and possibility of some basic reforms in the American constitution (cf. also Hardin, 1974 and 1989; Robinson, 1985 and 1989; and Sundquist, 1986).

7.1   *The fruits of comparison.*

So far, unfortunately, these analyses pay scant attention to comparisons with other presidentialist regimes. Instead, they focus on parliamentary democracies and on the strategic considerations that might block or support proposed reforms. To view the American case in a broader perspective, consider the sad Argentinian experience. By the 1920s, according to an article in the *Wall Street Journal* cited with approval by N. Guillermo Molinelli (1988, pp. C6–7), Argentina was 'one of the world's richest countries, had a democratically elected government, an elaborate university system, a literacy rate close to 90%, one of the best credit ratings in the world, and its per capita output of goods and services in 1929 was four times higher than Japan's'.

Since then, starting with the first of six military coups in 1930, political instability has prevailed, and 'Argentinians have suffered an increasing economic downward trend, characterized by more and more inflation and less and less growth. Today, most Argentinians know that theirs is the only underdeveloping country of the world, "going back from the First World to the Third in a generation"' (ibid.). The explanation of this huge disaster, I believe, is primarily political (and institutional) rather than ecological. Carlos Waisman (1989, pp. 160–2) offers a somewhat different but relevant explanation. Argentina's fate can, assuredly, happen to any other country, including the US, that strives to govern itself by the antiquated and increasingly non-viable eighteenth-century presidentialist model: past successes provide no assurances for the future.

The Argentine case illustrates another point: although we often assume that economic conditions determine political systems – as when we compare 'industrialized democracies' and relegate comparisons among 'Third World' countries to a separate category – we may also want to consider the possibility that political institutions affect, though they do not determine, the nature and extent of economic growth or 'development'. Put differently, political systems may provoke economic decline, as the ex-communist countries have now discovered.

Finally, and ironically, democratizing reforms in some Latin American countries undermined the stability of presidentialist regimes that had previously seemed to work rather well. Many of the traditions which seem to explain the survival of American presidentialism appear to have 'undemocratic' implications. Not surprisingly, they have often been rejected elsewhere in favour of rules or practices that seemed to be more 'democratic'. In fact, some American traditions are currently under severe attack in the US precisely because of their undemocratic implications and, if my conjectures are correct, reforming them may undermine the continuing viability of the US system. In this connection, see the last paragraph of sub-section 2.3.

The analysis offered here includes points routinely made in constitutional studies by American political scientists. However, several differences should be pointed out. Most importantly, the usual premiss of these analyses is that the separation of powers not only safeguards democratic freedoms but it poses no serious problems for system survival. When constitutional issues have been debated in the US, according to James Sundquist, they have focused on such details as the length of presidential and congressional tenure, links between the cabinet and Congress, the direct election of senators, the amendment process, approval of treaties, the war power and (in a limited academic environment) questions of leadership and accountability growing out of the divided (executive/legislative) powers (Sundquist, 1986, 41–74). Sundquist also notes, 'no amendment that would contravene the separation of powers principle has ever been debated on the floor of either house of Congress, and few have even been proposed .... When structural amendments have been debated in the halls of Congress, proponents have been at pains to insist ... that their proposed changes would certainly not weaken, or would even reinforce, the constitutional structure of checks and balances' (pp. 40–1).

No doubt, some American political scientists have questioned the long-term viability and utility of presidentialism, but their ideas have not provoked much general interest or debate. For example, almost half a century ago Charles McIlwain (1947, p. 143) wrote that, 'For this dissipation of governmental power [that is, the separation of powers inherent in presidentialism] with its consequent irresponsibility I can find no good precedents in the constitutional history of the past. The system has worked disaster ever since it was adopted, and it is not the outcome of earlier political experience .... It is a figment of the imagination of eighteenth-century doctrinaires who found it in our earlier history only because they were ignorant of the true nature of that history'.

Had McIlwain's warnings been seriously heeded, we would long since have undertaken a serious popular debate on presidentialism and the high costs of preserving the archaic American constitutional system. Today, in the light of comparative analysis based on the experience of countries that have emulated the American model, it is even more urgent to engage in such a debate, not only for the sake of the US itself, but also for the future of other countries – notably the newly independent Republics of the USSR and Eastern Europe – that are today seriously considering the possibility of new constitutional frameworks for representative government and democracy.

In the discussion that follows, I shall try to identify some of the important practices – paraconstitutional in character (Riggs, 1988c) – which appear to play a significant role in enabling the American presidentialist system to survive. I do not argue that any one of them is a *necessary* condition for the persistence of presidentialism, and certainly no one is a *sufficient* condition. Taken as a whole, however, we need to ask ourselves how the presence, or absence, of these practices affects the survival of presidentialism. I shall now discuss each of the major problems identified in Part II (omitting the need for a powerful judicial system only because this question is too complex for the kind of brief treatment that might be possible here), starting with the role of a head of government (President) elected for a fixed term of office.

8 The American Presidency

No good solution has been found to overcome the essential limitations on the Presidency dictated by the separation of powers and its precondition, a fixed term of office. In presidentialist regimes the role of President has been called a 'winner-take-all' competition, leaving many powerful and frustrated losers whose bitterness in defeat undermines the viability of the new government (Linz, 1990, pp. 55–8). However, in the United States the stakes appear to be considerably lower than they are in other countries with the same rules for choosing the head of government – resulting in fewer embittered losers and hence less antagonism against the President.

8.1 Lower stakes.

A number of significant features of the American political system reduce the weight of the Presidential sweepstakes. Similar features are found in some but not most other presidentialist systems.

Because of federalism, real power in the United States is distributed by constitutional mandate among the 50 sovereign 'states'. Much of the decision-making power that affects the average citizen, the success or failure of most politicians and the fate of office-seekers is determined at the local level – not only in the sovereign states but also in cities, counties, towns and other jurisdictions having delegated authority. Although presidential power rises above that of all sub-national politicians, it is nevertheless shared with a host of elected officials. Because of the 'responsive' two-party system (see sub-section 11.6) the President cannot command the loyalty nor control the actions of innumerable locally powerful politicians – including members of his own party – with whom his/her power is shared.

By contrast, to a large degree power is much more centralized in most presidentialist systems, even when the system is formally 'federal'. Although Venezuela is a 'federal republic', the governors of its states are appointed by the President; in the Philippines power is highly centralized despite changing constitutional and legial provisions for local self-government. The Mexican federal constitution authorizes each member state to have its own constitution and elect its governor, but in practice only candidates of the President's party, the PRI, win these elections and power is highly centralized. Argentina has a federal constitution which authorizes the provinces to elect their own governors and legislatures, but in practice the central government exercises overwhelming power.

Brazil has long been a genuine federation, but since 1930, under the domination of President Getulio Vargas, central power has increasingly prevailed over state power. According to Abdo Baaklini (1992, p. 3), 'Vargas' reforms and programs transformed the federal government's role in the socio-economic realm. ... The role of state governments was irrevocably diminished. ... The decentralized federal system of government which Brazil enjoyed until 1930, gave way to a more centralized system. ... The governor's role as a counterbalance to the President during the old republic was undermined. From then on the presidency became the undisputed power center of the entire political system.'

The separation of powers in the Federal government also means that Presidential power is shared with Congress and an extremely powerful judicial system. In addition, there are many autonomous governmental bodies, such as the Federal Reserve Board, whose powers are not subject to Presidential control. Because of the vigorous independence of the private sector in the United States, including not only capitalist profit-making corporations but also a vibrant non-profit (third) sector, the range of Presidential decision-making is also significantly restricted. Except in times of grave national emergency, as during an economic depression or war, when central controls over the economy multiply, it may not make much difference who occupies the Oval Office. By contrast, in other presidentialist systems, despite the existence of capitalism and free market institutions, governmental powers are often more extensive than in the United States, especially where corporatism prevails.

Within the Federal bureaucracy, the overwhelming majority of offices are now filled on a non-partisan career basis. Because career advancement occurs primarily within specific programmes and government agencies are strongly orientated to legislative committees, Congressional influence over career officials is very strong by contrast with the relative weakness of Presidential control. This means that extremely powerful structures within the bureaucracy exercise considerable autonomy – in collaboration with private interest groups and legislative committees (the 'iron triangles') – again limiting the real power of the President. By contrast, in other presidentialist regimes, the number of people whose jobs hinge on the outcome of a Presidential election is terrifyingly great, magnifying the stakes of the game.

Finally, the moderate, compromising platforms offered in the context of a centripetal (non-ideological) two-party system (see subsection 11.1) means that the actual programmes of the government are never radically transformed, regardless of who wins the Presidential elections. By contrast, in most presidentialist regimes a new head of government is more likely to initiate far-reaching changes with important consequences for large sectors of the population.

In so far as a crisis atmosphere created by the winner-take-all character of Presidential elections prevails in most presidentialist systems, we can understand why it contributes so much to the instability of these regimes. By contrast, the relatively low stakes involved in the American Presidential sweepstakes contributes to the capacity of this system to survive.

8.2   Surrogates for the head of state.

No doubt, a dampened role as elected head of government permits American Presidents to serve better as head of state. Nevertheless, because Presidents must still take sides in many controversies, their actions as head of government are necessarily more salient than their ceremonial role as head of state. To compensate for the inherent weakness of the President as head of state, impersonal symbols play an exceptionally important role in America, contributing to a sense of national unity or patriotism that the President, in person, cannot sustain.

Americans pledge allegiance to the flag (consider the recent outrage about flag burning and calls for a constitutional amendment to ban such protests), sing the national anthem, visit patriotic monuments and the Statue of Liberty: above all, they honour the Constitution and take oaths to support it, even though they often know little about its real meaning. Thus the American 'Constitution' is reified, a glamourized myth, more or less loosely based on the written charter. Eric Black (1988, p. 173) tells us that 'the Constitution that binds us is the one we have in our heads. That mythic Constitution performs functions no 200-year-old parchment ever could. It functions as the bible of our national civic religion.'

Recently John Rohr has written: 'it is our Constitution – and perhaps our Constitution alone – that holds us together as a people' (1991, p. 293). Rohr's argument is reinforced by the fact that the French have never required public officials to swear loyalty to their Constitution nor to any person or institution during periods of parliamentary government – except that since the Fifth Republic was constituted In 1958, members of the *Conseil Constitutionnel*, the body charged with responsibility for maintaining the Constitution, are required to swear that they will be completely impartial 'with respect to the constitution'. By contrast, all American public officials must swear to 'support and defend the Constitution of the United States, against all enemies, foreign and domestic'.

The logic of this difference seems clear enough. In France, during the Third and Fourth Republics, parliamentary supremacy was clear – the Parliament served 'as surrogate of the supremacy of the people' and the 'Constitution' of the Third Republic was itself only a series of laws passed by Parliament. By contrast, in the US 'Neither Congress, nor the President, nor the judiciary is supreme because all three are creatures of the Constitution, which alone is supreme and which alone is a worthy object of a compulsory oath' (Rohr, 1991, p. 293).

American oath-takers pledge themselves to 'bear true faith and allegiance' to the Constitution, without any mental reservation or purpose of evasion'. Such an oath is a 24-hour commitment, not just to govern official behaviour but to inspire every waking moment. In effect, the civil liberties protected by the Constitution's Bill of Rights are suspended for American public officials, and all citizens are, in effect, socialized to regard the 'Constitution' as a sacred text immune from the kind of critical analysis – save for marginal amendments – that other public documents are vulnerable to.

The presidentialist formula everywhere provides no single institution that can *re-present* the people as their surrogate. All its branches are but creatures of a Constitution. Yet such a belief blocks serious consideration of fundamental changes. Advocates of fundamental reform are seen as endangering the basic framework of legitimacy that enables democratic and representative government to survive in the United States. When the President and Congress engage in bitter contest, as they do today, each blames the other, but who dares to risk the charge of blasphemy and treason by wondering out loud if the Constitution itself is to blame.

No doubt other presidentialist regimes also have some functionally equivalent symbols, though I cannot comment on their potency. However, I believe it would be rare to find a presidentialist Constitution that commands so much unquestioned patriotism as does the 200-year old American prototype. As the recent flurry of constitution-drafting in ex-presidentialist countries reveals, there is a widespread willingness to question and reassess pre-existing constitutions, even though in every case the new version has been some form of presidentialist charter. In most presidentialist regimes, I suspect, the Constitution is viewed as a product of expediency, a more or less useful set of rules for the conduct of government, but far from a sacred symbol of national identity.

8.3 *Presidential powers.*

Considerable variation exists among presidentialist regimes concerning the powers constitutionally assigned to the office, ranging from extensive authority, especially in emergencies, to carefully limited powers. May we assume that both extremes are dysfunctional, leading to imbalances in the executive/legislative relationships? The intermediate powers assigned to the American President are probably conducive to system survival, but this is not a question about which I feel able to say anything more concrete. Certainly, however, it deserves careful study.

It is also clear that historical and personal factors affect the vigour with which different Presidents exercise whatever powers they hold by constitutional fiat. Energetic leaders, during emergencies such as war or depression, exercise more power than weaker persons in ordinary times. A weak President during a great crisis may be faulted for the collapse of a regime, but because of the low stakes discussed above, even a relatively ineffective American President is not likely to cause a breakdown of the system. Variations in Presidential leadership style and capabilities naturally interest historians – especially those who focus on one country in a non-comparativist mode – and may help explain a particular constitutional débâcle. However, they have little bearing on the questions studied here.

One restriction, however, has important implications that need to be mentioned here: namely term limits that produce the lame duck phenomenon, a drastic reduction of Presidential powers during a final term in office. American Presidents were not truly vulnerable to this phenomenon until 1951, when the twenty-second Constitutional amendment (to limit American Presidents to two terms in office) was adopted. Even now, during the President's first term, the lame duck syndrome is avoided.

By contrast, in many if not most Latin American countries, Presidents are limited to one term. This restriction was often imposed as a democratic safeguard against serious abuses caused by incumbent presidents who used unconstitutional means to enable them to repeat their terms in office. However, such term limitations seriously hamper many presidents who find that, almost as soon as they have been sworn in, rival and defeated candidates begin to organize campaigns against them and to undermine their efforts to govern effectively. This is a good example of a democratic reform that undermines the viability of presidentialism.

9   The legislative–executive balance

All modern representative governments require the concurrent exercise of authority by a dynamic leader (or small group) and a restraining/ legitimizing representative body.[9] The relationship between the two countervailing centres of political legitimacy are never easy to manage, but the parliamentary principle works more smoothly than the presidentialist one. When a cabinet can be ousted at any time by a parliamentary no-confidence vote, the leadership can act vigorously so long as it retains a majority, and yet it can be held strictly accountable. By contrast, a fixed term of office for the head of government sets up a built-in opposition ('separation of powers') between President and Congress in every presidentialist regime. Presidents must often choose between abuse of their powers in order to accomplish much-needed policy objectives or a supine posture of doing only what Congress mandates.

The formula invented by the American founding fathers was designed to prevent the abuse of power by safeguarding the interests of minorities (especially propertied minorities). It has worked well to accomplish this goal, but it could not anticipate the growing need of modern governments to provide effective policy leadership and implementation over a wide range of extremely complex issues. Moreover, a formula that can, indeed, safeguard civil rights and human freedoms offers small comfort for democracy when it collapses in the face of problems it cannot solve, only to be replaced by dictatorships. Juan Linz, commenting on the dangers of imbalance in the legislative/executive relations of presidentialist regimes points out that presidentialism is based on 'dual democratic legitimacy: no democratic principle exists to resolve disputes between the executive and legislature about which of the two actually represents the will of the people' (1990, p. 63).

To illustrate this problem, consider the Argentine experience where, according to Guillermo Molinelli, executive/legislative relations have evolved in such a way as to enhance Presidential powers at the expense of Congress. One result has been the erosion of the authority of the regime and the 'probable role of this low level [of authority] in a general loss of political legitimacy as a concurring factor for *coups d'etat*' (1988, p. 22). This long-term trend has been reinforced by the norms promulgated by authoritarian rulers during Argentina's six periods of *de facto* (military) rule, between 1930 and 1983. Each time, when democratic government was restored, these decisions might have been revoked by the new President, 'but it seems unrealistic to expect such generous behaviour: power is power is power'. Although Congress would have good reason to revoke new norms which typically curtailed legislative authority, any such law would be 'subject to Presidential veto, which can only be overridden with ⅔ of the votes in each chamber' (p. 31).[10]

9.1 The party line.

A critical element affecting the legislative/executive relationship in presidentialist regimes involves the role of political parties. In the American case, exceptionally, a centripetal open party system prevails, and the distribution of power within each of the main parties is responsive (see sub-section 5d). No doubt, in America it has often happened that the President's party also held a majority in Congress. Between 1796 and 1945 the same party dominated both the Presidency and Congress three-quarters of the time, the ratio fell to less than half after 1945 and to less than one-third since 1968 (Robinson, 1989, p. 43). Thus the phenomenon of divided government has been increasing in the US while its opposite, party government, has declined. However, we must not exaggerate its importance. Having an undivided government by no means assures Presidents of Congressional support for their policies, though it surely helps. Our habit of comparing presidentialism with parliamentary systems leads us to assume that the solution involves party discipline and, somehow, finding a way to give Presidents a partisan majority in Congress.

In fact, however, American Presidents who lack a partisan majority in Congress – a continuing recent phenomenon – have, nevertheless, been able to secure legislative support for many of their main policies and, because of the veto power, they can abort laws that they seriously oppose. Consequently, despite continuous tension between President and Congress in the US, it has been possible to reach sufficient accord on fundamental issues for the two institutions to coexist. We need to learn why this has been possible – and how the main problems due to the separation of powers can be overcome.

The grave disadvantages for a President of fluid parties are well illustrated by the Brazilian situation where the extreme individualism or fluidity of Congressional voting puts every bill at risk and compels the President to bargain separately with every member in order to secure a winning package. 'Brazilian catch-all parties', writes Mainwaring (1989, p. 167), 'make the U.S. parties appear to be the paragon of well disciplined, cohesive parties'. By contrast, however, in a few countries, such as Chile and Venezuela, discipline in its centred parties is exceptionally strong. When the President lacks a Congressional majority, as was typically the case in Chile before 1974 when Major General Augusto Pinochet seized power, the President also experienced grave difficulties in maintaining Congressional support.

These examples suggest that the legislative/executive relationship may he impaired by excesses of partisan discipline or indiscipline. Both the domination exercised by party leaders over the votes of their members in centred parties, and the complete absence of such control found in fluid parties are equally dysfunctional for presidentialism, whereas party domination over the votes of legislators is both necessary for, and produced by, the dynamics of parliamentarism.

9.2 A predictable enigma.

In the American case, exceptionally, an intermediate degree of partisan responsiveness grounds Congressional support of Presidential policies, while always making the outcome of Congressional votes indeterminate. Enough party discipline exists to enable American Presidents normally to count on the support of a substantial number of members of their own party; they also know that a significant proportion of opposition party members will predictably oppose their initiatives. Consequently, they can focus their energies on efforts to sway enough opposition party members to secure a majority – and also, of course, to dissuade those members of the government party most likely to defect. No doubt 'responsiveness' is not a constant: at different times members of the US Congress have been more or less responsive to their party's leadership, but they have not ever gone to the extremes of party domination or extreme fluidity.

American Presidents who are sufficiently determined and adroit can often influence enough of the wavering party members to create a voting majority. Moreover, the President can usually count on the support of at least a third of the members of Congress, thereby permitting his/her veto of a measure to be sustained. Knowledge of an imminent veto can also influence waverers to compromise with the President so that at least some of their legislative goals will be accomplished. This means that preliminary negotiations, in which staff members and even the President personally take part, play a fundamental, though behind-the-scenes role in ameliorating clashes. These practices by no means assure legislative/executive congruence in the US but they do permit some agreements to be reached and help to prevent the bitter stalemates so often found in other presidentialist regimes. For American Presidents, Congress is a 'predictable enigma': the available options present soluble puzzles.

To explain the responsiveness of American political parties we need to understand the centripetalism of its two-party system, which appears to be truly exceptional among presidentialist regimes. Before discussing this phenomenon in section 11, however, a few thoughts may be inserted about the way the American Congress is organized.

10 An immense Congressional agenda

The separation of powers scheme can only be effective if Congress can make its own decisions on a vast agenda. This seems to be an impossible task, especially when compared with the modest burdens imposed on a Parliament which needs only to accept or reject its government's bills. Despite the growing attacks on Congress which we now hear, the American Congress handles its responsibilities exceptionally well – in large measure because of the effectiveness of its innumerable sub-committees – and this helps to explain its contribution to the viability of this presidentialist regime. I suspect, though I have no clear evidence, that the failures of other presidentialist regimes may be due in part to the inability of their Congresses to accept or process comparably large agendas. The American achievement, however, may be possible only because some important democratic values are sacrificed. We can evaluate them by examining the influence of senioritism, lobbyism, and bureaucratic functionism.

10.1 Senioritism.

According to the seniority rule, committees are usually chaired by members of the majority party who have been on that committee for the longest time. Moreover, in the absence of rules against re-election, incumbents are usually returned to office. These practices reinforce each other: members win the real rewards of office only after several terms, a consideration that motivates voters to return incumbents and incumbents to seek re-election, with the help of affluent contributors who tend, also, to support incumbents. I refer to both the seniority rule and the re-election of incumbents as *senioritism*.

Senioritism contributes to the power, prestige and subject-field expertise of long-term members of Congress. This enables them to build organizational networks and alliances while learning the complex rules and practices which govern legislative action. Seniority may also strengthen committee chairs because their leadership does not depend on popularity: where the members elect their chairs, they will presumably choose more congenial or less domineering personalities. Although seniority can, assuredly, produce ineffective and rigid leaders, it also favours capable and experienced persons, those most able to secure re-election and willing to provide strong leadership. Senioritism also enables legislators and committees to retain competent staffers whereas rapid turn-over of members, because of patronage, would reduce the professional expertise available to them.

In most presidentialist systems, by contrast, there is a widespread aversion to senioritism as being essentially undemocratic. Committee chairs are often filled on a non-seniority basis, incumbency in Congress is limited by rules against re-election, and restrictions are placed on the length of time that members may chair or remain on a single committee. Such rules, which vary greatly between countries, are usually supported because they enhance the representativeness of elected assemblies by favouring citizen 'amateurs', impede the growth of a professional class of 'elitist' politicians, and hamper the accumulation of power by old-timers and political insiders.

For evidence, consider the situation in Brazil where the rapid turnover of legislators and lack of senioritism greatly limits the effectiveness of the Congress (Baaklini 1989, pp. 17, 32). 'For ambitious politicians, serving in the legislature is a means to an end – executive positions – rather than an end in itself' (Mainwaring, 1990b, p. 23). Because executive branch positions – President, governors, mayors – offer much more power and prestige, ambitious politicians treat legislative seats as a short-term step in their careers, resulting in rapid rotation and a relatively low level of competence, both in policy areas and in knowing how to make a legislature work effectively.

The penalty for term limitations is that less experienced members of Congress will be more vulnerable, as 'lame ducks', to outside pressures, especially from special interest groups, local elites and, of course, public officials. Moreover, anti-senioritism rules mean that able and ambitious politicians are less likely to view legislative careers as an attractive vocation: at best they may think of it as a mere stepping stone to other more interesting political roles. In the contemporary American debate about this important issue, we hear much about the short-term advantages of tenure limitations for 'democracy', but the long-term implications of this important rule for the survival of presidentialism in America is never discussed.[11]

Instead, the frequent re-election of Congressional incumbents is deplored by American reformers who, quite rightly, regard it as a violation of democratic norms. However, from the point of view of system survival, the practice seems quite functional – it enables members to acquire relatively high levels of expertise, especially in the subject fields of the committees where they hold office for a long time, and their large bureaucratic and interest-group networks substantially enhance the power of Congress in relation to the President.

10.2 *Lobbyism.*

Lobbying includes the efforts of special interests to promote advantageous legislation in Congress – no doubt lobbying occurs in every democracy, parliamentary as well as presidentialist. In the US, lobbying is grounded in the institutionalization and legitimization of mutually advantageous long-term relationships between committee members in Congress and private organizations representing powerful constituencies. The agents of these constituencies enhance the informational, financial and political resources needed by their Congressional collaborators without thereby gaining the upper hand in this relationship. A term is needed for this broader framework, which I call *lobbyism*. Lobbyism benefits from senioritism and, reciprocally, senioritism is strengthened by lobbyism, but both need to be limited in appropriate ways. To control lobbyism presents issues as complex as those involved in the effort to restrict senioritism.

In some presidentialist regimes, lobbyism is strictly limited as an undemocratic practice that rewards the rich and better educated citizens at the expense of the masses. Unfortunately, anti-lobbyist policies, especially if combined with term limitation, have unintended consequences. In place of legally registered and controlled lobbyists, inexperienced legislators are easily influenced and manipulated by outside private interests which include rich and prestigious families, large landowners, merchants, industrialists and foreign corporations, working in a highly individualistic and invisible way. The bulk of the population lacks the resources needed to influence legislators, and anti-lobbyist rules hamper their efforts to become mobilized in mass-based public interest organizations. As with party discipline, presidentialism requires a balance between too much and too little power in the hands of lobbyists.

10.3 *Interest networks.*

The American pattern of recruitment and promotion for career officials normally places them throughout their professional lives in the service of a particular government programme. This pattern, which I call functionism, differs from the normal practice in parliamentary systems where officials often rotate between different departments (for more details see sub-section 12.3). As a result of the interactive linkages between bureaucratic functionism, senioritism and lobbyism there has emerged in the United States a complex set of interest networks ('iron triangles', 'subgovernments') which in large measure determine policy and its implementation in a host of specialized fields of public policy.

By yielding authority in these fields to its subcommittees, the American Congress is able to process a gigantic agenda, in close liaison with interested components of the federal bureaucracy and the constituencies most directly affected. Consequently, a vast 'infrastructure' of public business has become so self-governing and autonomous that it maintains itself without regard to political party and policy changes at the highest Presidential and Congressional levels.

When combined with the power of federalism, capitalism and a vast non-profit 'third sector', interest networks offer most Americans enough of a stake in the status quo so that they are not easily stirred to support widespread protest or revolutionary movements – including movements to make fundamental changes in the presidentialist constitution. In most presidentialist regimes, by contrast, political substructures such as the 'iron triangles' are weaker – not because of any specific opposition to them but because the fundamental practices which lead to them are discouraged as anti-democratic. Unfortunately, this means that vast populations have little reason to support the status quo.

10.4 Dispersal and decentralization of power.

However, the process of legislation by delegated authority, rooted in interest networks, carries heavy costs. It means that a few committee members (both in Congress and in state legislatures) allied with bureaucratic counterpart agencies and private constituency organizations can create mighty oligarchies. Public decision-making becomes so compartmentalized, as a result, that it replaces for the most part decisions by the whole Congress, to say nothing of 'all the people'. The resulting dispersal of power (not only within Congress but also in the bureaucracy) poses a tremendous challenge for Congressional and Presidential leadership: how to co-ordinate programmes that often contradict and clash with each other. Much of the business of governing proceeds independently of the President's preferences or the 'will of the people' as a whole.[12]

11 A centripetal open party system

In sub-section 5.1 I suggested that the prevalence of centrifugal party systems (whether two- or multiparty in structure) is dysfunctional for the survival of presidentialism. Although less common, a hegemonic (closed) party system, such as we find in Mexico, is equally dysfunctional. By contrast, perhaps alone among presidentialist regimes, the US has an centripetal open party system. We need to understand the practices or forces that have created and maintained this system, and how it has contributed to the development of responsive parties, as discussed above in sub-section 9.2. I shall first discuss party-system centripetalism and then the problematics of an open party system.

11.1 The maintenance of centripetalism.

The clearest evidence of centripetalism in the US can be found in the campaign strategies of its two major parties: each aims primarily to win the support of independent voters. To attract their votes, both parties adopt compromise platforms that are only marginally different from each other. This provokes the scorn of non-voters who believe they have little to gain from the victory of either party. A wide range of lower-class, ethnic and minority constituencies do not vote, thinking they have little to gain from either party. For many of the poor and less-educated, assuredly, the costs of voting outweigh the likely benefits. Most non-voters are bored by elections or view them with hostility as a no-win exercise, preferring to spend their spare time and effort on family, sports, religion or entertainments that promise immediate rewards.[13]

Each of the two US parties counts both on the abstention of non-voters and on the support of innumerable party regulars. It pays them, therefore, to target the independent voters: they do vote and, whatever ideology they embrace (whether 'conservative' or 'liberal'), it generates ambivalence towards both of the major parties. What is 'moderate' in the US is typically 'right of centre' in parliamentary systems. The point is that they are not party regulars and can, therefore, be swayed to vote either way or to split their votes.

The limitations of our vocabulary lead us to think of American political parties as 'loose' or unstructured. Clearly they are not *fluid* in the sense of having an extremely localized and dispersed power structure, nor are they centred (centralized and concentrated), as are most parties in parliamentary regimes. Instead, they are responsive (centralized/localized and concentrated/dispersed), and their members in Congress vote in a semi-disciplined way. This structure is often criticized by those who view centred and responsible parties as more 'modern' and preferable.[14] However, the responsiveness of American parties and politicians also permits American Presidents and Congress to make bargains, organize strong committees and find practical solutions to many of the crucial problems of presidentialism.

Two basic practices appear to be the main causes for the maintenance of centripetalism in the American party system: first, the SMD pluralist electoral system, and secondly, the right of citizens to abstain from voting. I shall discuss them next, reserving the problematics of an open party system for later treatment.

11.2 *SMD plurality voting.*

Concerning American electoral systems, Leon Weaver (1984, p. 195) reports that 'The numbers of PR and SPR [semi-proportional representation] systems constitute a very small proportion when compared with the total number of electoral systems in the United States, most of which are of the SMD variety (all national, virtually all state, and many local legislative seats), or in the AL [at-large] category, which are found mostly at the local level.'

Many critics condemn this situation, arguing that PR is a requisite for genuine democracy. J.F.H. Wright (1984, p. 127), for example, claims that 'The basic failure of any single-member-district system to provide for the representation of a large proportion of voters is sufficient to disqualify such systems for use in countries claiming to be democratic.' Similarly, George G. Hallett Jr (1984, p. 114) states, for the American case: 'Millions of voters across the country are regularly left with "representatives" whom they voted against because they were outvoted in the district where they resided. Though they are all sorts of people, they form together a major class of unrepresented citizens just as surely as if they had been denied "the free exercises of the franchise".'

Even if we accept this argument, viewing SMD majoritarianism as anti-democratic, we might also consider that it is a price which has to be paid for the survival of presidentialism. Interestingly, Arend Lijphart, who argues in favour of parliamentary-PR systems as the most democratic and effective kind of voting system, now says that 'the Latin American model of presidentialism combined with PR legislative elections remains a particularly unattractive option' (Lijphart 1991a, p. 77).[15] Charles Gillespie (1989, p. 2) remarks: 'very little thought has been given to the implications of Latin American democracies' peculiar combination of presidentialism with PR as the basis for legislative elections.' It is clear, nevertheless, that PR systems are widespread in Latin America, and they encourage the proliferation of centrifugal party systems.

By contrast, advocates of SMD plurality contend that it produces non-ideological and loose 'people's parties', appealing to a wide range of voter interests. Ferdinand Hermens (1984, p. 22) writes: 'Such parties do have different tendencies within them, but if these tendencies are organized (which, as a rule, they are not), their influence is limited and the entire line-up is characterized by fluidity and flexibility. The upshot is pragmatism and practicality in government.' As Hermens (1990, p. 6) has also pointed out, the essence of a two-party majoritarian system is not the absence of third parties or the possibility of winning by a mere plurality, but rather the likelihood that a single party will command a parliamentary (that is, Congressional) majority and will gain a majority mandate for the President. Consider that local, class, ethnic, racial, religious and linguistic interests which could easily, under PR rules, generate viable political parties, find in the American SMD context that their best hopes for political representation arise in the context of a major party since only one candidate can win in each district. To organize a 'third' (small) party is virtually to ensure defeat.

Whatever its costs for representative democracy, the rejection of PR strikes me as crucial to the survival of presidentialism in the US – and reliance on PR as fatal for its survival in Latin America. Moreover, I accept Hermens's argument that SMD majoritarianism is not totally undemocratic: each of the major parties recognizes that to enhance its electoral prospects it must offer hospitality, intraparty representation and participation in electoral tickets to any significant minority willing to support its candidates – especially when this minority commands a local majority. The impetus to win an electoral majority also leads both American parties to accept minority group planks that, they believe, would enhance their chances of winning. No doubt, groups joining a major party must also pay a price, sacrificing part of their special interests in the hope of winning some influence through the victory of a loosely structured but responsive political party.

SMD voting accounts for some basic differences between the responsive US political parties and the factionalized parties found in Uruguay: both are 'two-party systems', but they are very different. No doubt American parties are highly sectionalized and localized, lacking in discipline and sharply defined goals. They focus attention on candidates, their personalities and opinions, their weaknesses and strengths, at the expense of party or faction loyalties and ideological commitments. They produce 'tendencies' rather than 'factions'.[16]

They are also isolative – as I shall show. Those who prefer the centred and integrated parties produced in parliamentary PR regimes will easily find fault with the American parties. However, those committed to the perpetuation of American presidentialism may see that SMD plurality voting generates a type of party system that promotes its survival.

11.3 *The right to abstain.*

By itself the electoral system is not enough to assure the development of responsive parties in a centripetal party system. In addition, the right to abstain is necessary. When the American Constitution was adopted, state voting limitations were perpetuated. These typically required property qualifications that seriously restricted mass voting – and, of course, women could not vote and slaves were automatically excluded. Other kinds of restrictions can also impede the formation of new parties, thereby protecting the privileged position of the established parties. In the United States recently, such 'anti-democratic' restrictions have increased so much in states such as Florida, California, Oklahoma, Maryland, North Carolina and Massachusetts that it is almost impossible now for a third party to collect enough signatures, within the required time and cost limits, to put their candidates on the ballots (Harris, 1990, pp. 548–9). Over the years the right of all citizens to vote has been greatly expanded, but the duty to vote has never become institutionalized: indeed, the right not to vote, to abstain, has been viewed as a basic right. Quite unconsciously, this 'right' may contribute significantly to the survival of presidentialism in America.

Many writers condemn the low turnout in US elections as a very regrettable undemocratic phenomenon. Such an analysis is offered by Richard Pious (1986, pp. 139–40) who points to a 53.2 per cent turnout in the US in 1984 by contrast with between 72.6 and 91.4 per cent in the European democracies. Edward Greenberg (1980, p. 230) offers comparable data and points to a continuing decline in voter turnout in the US: for example, from 65 to 54 per cent in Presidential election years, and from 47 to 37 per cent in off-year congressional elections, between 1960 and 1978. A similar assessment can be found in Rodgers and Harrington (1985, pp. 129–34).

Unfortunately, none of these authors notes the connection between these data and their constitutional significance. Wherever PR systems prevail, the interests of those who would not otherwise vote can be espoused by political parties or factions that can attract their support. According to the prevalent myth of democracy, universal suffrage is not only a right of all citizens, but its exercise provides the basis for legitimizing representative government. Unfortunately, however, the high turnout levels PR systems produce are system-destroying for presidentialism because they generate strongly centrifugal political pressures that make it increasingly difficult for a president and a Congress to reach agreements on important policies.

In some presidentialist regimes concern for non-voters has led to compulsory voting. Politicians striving to capture the support of the new voters produced thereby have unintentionally centrifugalized party systems that might previously have been centripetal with SMD voting rules. In Argentina, for example, compulsory voting was mandated in 1912, trebling the voter turnout in the next (and succeeding) elections. As a result, the Radical and Peronist parties, at different times, came to power, permanently displacing the conservative parties which had hitherto monopolized power. Carlos Nino (1988, p. 19) reports that there was 'considerable political stability in Argentina prior to 1916 (from the enactment of the Constitution in 1853/60) and extreme unstability afterwards. Obviously, those displaced by the results of massive voting sought other ways of acceding to power.'

In Brazil, 'When popular participation was still quite limited, ideological consensus ... was reasonably strong, making it possible to form moderately stable, informal coalitions. Between 1945 and 1964 [the year of a coup] there was an explosion of popular participation in politics, with a significant impact on the parties. Politics ceased being an elite game and elite consensus eroded, and along with it so did the facility of forming these broad coalitions' (Mainwaring, 1990b, p. 12).

Chile's vigorous and ideological multiparty presidentialist system, rooted in PR, has generated high voter turnouts and centrifugal pressures. In its 1970 election, this turnout (83.7 per cent) gave Marxist candidate Salvador Allende a plurality of 36.3 per cent. The tragic denouement was the breakdown of 1973 and the Pinochet military dictatorship. Two opposing coalition parties, Popular Unity and the Democratic Confederation, were formed during Chile's 1973 congressional elections, but, as Arturo Valenzuela (1989, p. 31) notes, 'Rather than moderating the political spectrum, the two party configuration came to embody the ultimate in polarization [centrifugalization], a U-shaped curve with a total absence of any center force. ... under such circumstances the moderate forces within each coalition are pressured heavily by the extremes, reducing further any centripetal tendencies in the political system.' Apparently, even a two-party system with a large voter turnout and PR voting rules becomes centrifugalized.[17]

Non-voting in the US, by contrast, supports the viability of a centripetal party system. If the focus of a centripetal party system has to be on securing the support of independent voters, then it follows that centripetalism requires the right to abstain – compulsory voting assures centrifugalism in the party system regardless of whether it has two or more parties. PR always generates centrifugalized party systems, and SMD by itself does not assure a centripetal party system: it needs to be coupled with the right to abstain. Even an SMD-based two-party system will become centrifugalized when voting is made compulsory.

Low turnout, then, is neither a property of presidentialism nor of geographic exceptionalism (as comparisons of the US with European parliamentary polities alone suggest). Rather, either PR or compulsory voting will produce centrifugalized party systems and high levels of voter participation – as they typically have in Latin America. By contrast, party system centripetalism (as in the US deviant case) is associated with SMD voting, the right to abstain and widespread voter apathy or alienation. Of course, this pattern is reinforced by circular causation: the inability of elected politicians to deliver on their campaign promises because of the inherent problems in presidentialism fortifies the tendency of many citizens to abstain from voting.

11.4   A terrible paradox.

These considerations generate a terrible paradox: the more 'undemocratic' a presidentialist system (with low turnout), the more viable it will be. The more 'democratic' a presidentialist regime (with high turnout), the more likely it is to be overthrown and replaced by authoritarianism. The only way to achieve high turnout levels and safeguard democracy is to abandon the presidentialist 'fixed term' formula and move towards executive accountability to the legislature, that is, towards parliamentarism. A few pro-democracy rule changes unaccompanied by constitutional reform in the United States – notably the introduction of PR in multimember districts, compulsory voting and the elimination of barriers that prevent third parties from placing candidates on the ballot – would soon centrifugalize the party system and prevent any President securing a popular majority. This would throw the final choice of the President into the hands of Congress where a temporary coalition (Chilean style) would select the chief executive but deny him/her continuing support, thereby ensuring devastating stalemates between the President and Congress and enhancing the likelihood that a military group would seize power.

Unfortunately, even an SMD electoral system and the right to abstain cannot by themselves guarantee the maintenance of an open party system in a presidentialist regime. A comparison between multiparty and two-party systems indicates that the former are quite stable, even surviving periods of suppression under military dictatorships, but the latter are fragile and vulnerable to erosion. In particular, a two-party system easily slides into a hegemonic closed-party system, although continuation of SMD election rules will keep it from becoming a centrifugal multiparty system. To explain the persistence of an open two-party system, therefore, we need to introduce some additional factors among which the most important involve federalism and capitalism.

11.5 The role of federalism.

Even if we assume that SMD pluralities and a low voting turnout assure centripetalism in an open party system, we cannot assume that, somehow, one party will not become overwhelmingly successful at the expense of the other, engendering a type of hegemonic party situation. It is quite conceivable that, in every district, the same party will win and will be able by various means to prevent the opposition party from gaining power. Since each party acts in its own interests rather than that of the whole system of which it is a part, we cannot assume that idealism will lead a dominant party to help its rivals succeed.

Such a scenario can be found in some American states where a single dominant party has long held power at the expense of an impotent opposition party, such as in the long-standing Democratic domination of Georgia, Mississippi, Alabama – and Hawaii – and in the Republican control of New Hampshire and Vermont.[18] Because these state governments exist within the framework of the American federal system, their hegemonic parties cannot monopolize power but must share it with national and local authorities, often of a different party.

In a sovereign centralized state, however, the inability of an opposition party to win elections could well become a self-reinforcing vicious circle. The defeated party would have difficulty raising money or finding volunteers interested in jobs that are unlikely to materialize. Affluent contributors will support incumbents in preference to their opponents. Leaders of the opposition party naturally become discouraged and some, succumbing to the 'bandwagon effect', defect to the ruling party. Others, in frustration, abandon politics or try to form more-dynamic 'third' parties, covering a wide ideological spectrum, thereby dooming themselves to defeat so long as the SMD rule prevails. Only a unified opposition party can hope to defeat an entrenched hegemonic party under these rules.

One reason why, despite these inherent dynamisms, centripetal two-partyism persists in the US involves the framework of American federalism. Consider the fact that because the governors of each state, its legislators, mayors and city councils all stand for election, there are many opportunities for a defeated national party to win local victories on the strength of local issues and personalities. This is only possible because of the 'responsive' though not utterly localized structure of American parties.

In the two major American parties, local organizations nominate candidates and control their campaigns, including those for members of Congress. So long as each of these parties can dominate local politics in a substantial number of states, the members of Congress will represent both parties, and the majority in Congress will be independent of the ruling party in the White House, even when it has the same name. Moreover, inasmuch as having party competition in a legislature sustains that body's power position, members of both parties in Congress may perhaps unite in support of measures that help them maintain the strength of the legislature and consequently their own power and prestige, simply by safeguarding the openness of the party system (Riggs, 1973).

If the President's party apparatus could control a permanent majority in Congress, the effectiveness of that body would collapse, as it has in other countries with hegemonic or single-party regimes. Although divided government unavoidably hampers the ability of a presidentialist regime to make and implement policy effectively, it also contributes to the maintenance of an open party system. Such a contribution may well be a necessity if democratic presidentialist government is to survive.

Remember that the national party is only a coalition of local parties designed to conduct presidential campaigns and has no authority over the conduct of the local parties. Because local party organizations in a centripetalized party system cannot have strong ideological commitments but would love to place their own candidate in the White House, they will form a coalition with kindred party organizations in other states for the sole purpose of sponsoring a presidential candidate. The continuing local power of party organizations affiliated with a defeated national party surely helps to explain the survival of an open party system in the US.

To say that federalism supports the maintenance of an open centripetal party system in the US clearly is not to imply that federalism will always have this effect. Indeed, a centrifugalized multiparty system may well be weakened by federalism. If its parties are centred – as in Chile, for example – they would view federalism as a threat. To maintain centralized control in each party, a unitary state is functional.

In a multiparty system with fluid parties, we may expect federalism to aggravate the localization and dispersal of power so as to undermine the capacity of Congress to perform in any coherent way. In the Brazilian case, an unusual electoral system which combines PR with open lists that permit voters to choose among rivals in the same party (a kind of quasi-primary system) augments the weight of locally sponsored political appointments in the state bureaucracy. The combination of these factors undermines all sense of party solidarity by favouring individualistic local clientelism (Mainwaring, 1990a, pp. 26, 28–9).[19] By holding its primaries before an election, the American national party organization, although weakened, can still generate a moderate sense of responsiveness, and not all of its local party organizations are victims of the primary system.

The Uruguayan system could be viewed as a refutation because there a two-party system has survived despite a centralized system of government. However, the unique form of PR used in Uruguay supports the formation of powerful intraparty factions which, in effect, operate much like the centred parties in a multiparty system.

My conclusion, therefore, is that only federalism enhances the prospects for survival of an open party system, provided SMD plurality voting and the freedom to abstain from voting combine to make it a centripetal system. Such a system, I now think, may be a *sine qua non* for the long-term survival of a presidentialist regime.

11.6 The business of capitalism.

By itself, however, even the momentum of federalism might not be strong enough to perpetuate an open party system in the US. Additional reinforcement may be attributed to the requirements of campaign financing in the context of a dominant capitalist economic system. Wealthy and powerful individuals, corporations and associations recognize the advantages they enjoy as a result of the open party system. By direct contributions and through 'Political Action Committees' they support individual candidates and campaign committees in both parties, enabling them to conduct costly primary and electoral campaigns.[20]

During the heyday of the spoils system, volunteers hoping for political appointments powered the American party system. Since expansion of the career system (see section 12), however, and the development of modern media campaigning, plus the burdens of extensive pre-electoral primaries, the costs of political campaigning have radically escalated. The result, of course, has been a vast expansion of the importance of corporations and wealthy contributors in the political process. The direct primary was introduced in order to bring the people into the process of candidate selection and to bypass the inner-circle nominating process formerly dominated by local party bosses at national conventions.

Its critics claim that primaries have actually weakened democracy in America. For example, Edward Greenberg (1980, p. 222) writes, 'With the coming of the direct primary, prospective candidates could bypass the party organization, thus weakening it as an important entry to politics. It soon became apparent that the people best able to conduct direct primary campaigns were those with ready access to money ... and to a favorable press, persons who were rarely a threat to dominant groups.' Rodgers and Harrington (1985, pp. 325–8) also show how primaries have gravely weakened the political parties. Primaries have also enhanced the salience of the President's personal preferences and political appointees, bringing them daily into the living rooms of most Americans. These effects have increased the influence of wealthy contributors who support political party activities. Not only do they enhance the electoral prospects of pro-capitalist candidates, but winners are reluctant to betray those who finance them by supporting social programmes that appear to curtail the scope of a free market system.

Here, however, we have to raise a different question: how does this system affect the viability of American presidentialism and, more specifically, does it safeguard the survival of an open party system? To answer this question, do we not need to re-think the relations between bourgeois capitalism and the American system of government? They have usually been assessed in the context of theories which hold that property holders have contrived (plotted?) to design and maintain a regime that protects their interests.[21] Little attention has been given to a different hypothesis, namely that the maintenance of an open party system depends on capitalist support for candidates both parties.

The survival of capitalism is, we may assume, a basic goal in all capitalist systems. Because of its own 'contradiction', to use a Marxist term, it is vulnerable to self-destructive tendencies currently manifested in the US savings and loan crisis, junk bonds and insider trading, bankruptcies produced by monopolistic competition among giant firms, and so on. To overcome such risks, capitalism requires regulation by a state that is not just its pawn. The point is that this is not an 'either/or' situation – either socialism or rampant capitalism. There are many degrees of regulation and control over free market institutions, and some of them are, indeed, prerequisites for the survival of capitalism.

However, a state dominated by a hegemonic party can easily be seen as a threat to capitalism. Once securely in control of the state apparatus, the leaders of a dominant party are free to impose oppressive regulations which undermine private property and the market system. At least, property holders may reasonably fear such domination and feel helplessly threatened whenever an open party system is crushed.

Without further discussion of this admittedly controversial hypothesis, we may use it to ground a corollary, namely that shrewd capitalists will use their resources to perpetuate an open party regime within which they may feel their prospects for enhancing their more specific interests are also enhanced. To accomplish this goal, they will want to see both parties succeed, and the collapse of either party will be viewed as a threat. They understand that their interests lie with the system rather than with either political party. By supporting candidates in both parties whose views support capitalism, even though tinged with enough commitment to social justice to ameliorate the most flagrant causes of unrest, contributors help to maintain the system. So long as the party system remains centripetal, politicians know that they need not commit themselves to policies that will mobilize a mass electorate. Plenty of issues remain to attract the attention of independent habitual voters and to swing the election to one side or the other. I have to admit that this argument is speculative, but it seems reasonable enough to deserve study.

Moreover, it can be tested by the comparative study of party systems in other presidentialist countries. These dynamics do not apply in parliamentary systems, however. In them, mass-based popular parties have a good chance of winning power because of the PR electoral system and the dynamics of cabinet government. The commitment of their members also greatly reduces the dependence of parliamentary parties on generous financial support. Consequently, it is much easier for social democratic or labour parties to gain power, and they can regulate capitalism quite strictly while ensuring its survival.

In most presidentialist regimes, however, capitalist interests are much weaker than they are in the United States, and they are also vulnerable to external pressures. They may not understand how an open centripetal party system would help them, nor how it could be created. Moreover, if PR electoral systems and compulsory voting have already been established, they may feel helpless to promote the general interest and compelled to concentrate on their own short-term personal problems. In the context of an established multiparty system, they will tend to sponsor a party committed to their specific interests, as will their various class and ethnic opponents. The option of supporting coalitional catch-all parties, such as those produced by a centripetal two-party system, is simply not available to them.

To conclude, it seems to me that capitalism – in conjunction with federalism – helps to perpetuate an open party system in the US, even though it could not create such a system. This effect occurs only because the party system is centripetal, a fact that may be attributed to the prevalence of SMD plurality voting and the right to abstain. Finally, it is the responsiveness (not the discipline) of party members that enables Presidents to bargain with and reach accomodations with Congress, even when confronted with an opposition party majority. Such accommodations are no doubt easier to reach when the President's party has a majority in Congress – but the lack of party discipline means that even then such agreements are not guaranteed. This is fortunate for the survival of American presidentialism because it sustains the independent power of Congress and probably also helps perpetuate the openness of the party system.

12   American bureaucracy

A ubiquitous patronage system and poly-normativism are inescapable consequences of the separation of powers, as explained in section 6. They hamper public administration and promote corruption in such a way as to undermine support for any regime, providing a basis for all kinds of popular complaints, military coups and protest or revolutionary movements. Although we habitually take public administration for granted as a non-political function of government, clearly the effective administration of public policies is a *sine qua non* for the success of any political regime; bad administration can lead to the overthrow of representative government, especially when bureaucrats themselves feel threatened by the status quo and, under the leadership of military officers, take measures to discharge elected officials and appropriate their functions. The reasons why the risk of such a catastrophe are significantly greater under presidentialism than they are in other types of constitutional system are also discussed in section 6.

12.1   A unique experience.

To explain the deviant American case – why it alone has never experienced the type of breakdown that other presidentialist regimes have suffered – we need to pay attention to the structure and role of bureaucracy in the United States. The topic is so important and complex that it deserves separate treatment and I have, therefore, written another paper that explores the subject in some detail (Riggs, 1991c). An earlier discussion of related problems can be found in Riggs (1988a). Here I shall only summarize the argument.

Two decisive reforms ameliorated the effects of patronage and poly-normativism and limited their negative impact in the US – though, of course, they never eliminated them. These involved the establishment of large-scale non-partisan merit-based career services rooted in the principle functionism. The reforms which led to this development have deep historic roots that need be understood: they involved the development of a spoils system based on the principle of rotation in office – I shall explain below.

However, other factors also need to be taken into account. Admittedly, the relative efficacy of the political superstructure (President, Congress, courts and party system) meant that the temptation for public officials (especially military officers) to seize power was probably never as great in the US as in many other presidentialist regimes. Some commentators argue that the indoctrination of American military officers to accept civilian rule may be the most important variable. I accept this argument as part of the explanation. Historically it can perhaps be attributed to the small size and intermittent existence of the armed forces during the early days of the Republic, and the relative importance of state militias in contrast to the small and weak Federal forces. By the time national forces had become permanently institutionalized, their political subordination had become well established and culturally reinforced. Even so, as Dwight Eisenhower warned, the 'military–industrial complex' has become an extremely powerful actor in American politics and, despite lip-service to civilian rule, I suspect that in a time of major political crisis it would be as able and willing to seize power as any other military establishment.

Another important factor is the federalist configuration of the American government: more officials serve in state and local government than in the federal government. Consequently, no unified 'national' bureaucracy has ever existed and the kind of co-ordinated action among dissidents that is possible in unitary polities would not be possible in the US. Moreover, in so far as the 'winner-take-all' game applies also to US presidentialism, its effects are greatly ameliorated by the distribution of patronage powers among a great many jurisdictions: the President controls only a small part of the total pie to be divided among the winners of political power.

It must also be considered that a powerful capitalist market system and innumerable private associations in the US offer many job opportunities that for most people are highly prized and often more attractive than public office. By contrast, in most presidentialist systems the demand for government jobs is disproportionately large because of the relative weakness of the private sector. This point affects all Third World countries, regardless of the degree to which they have market economies. It may well be one of the environmental variables that most powerfully affects the survival of American presidentialism. Indeed, it may now also be true that the President's need to appoint officials who are not only loyal but also well qualified has changed the dynamics of political patronage. Although the supply of applicants is undiminished, those who are most wanted are often reluctant to serve. Accordingly the stakes in the Presidential winner-take-all game are reduced.

Because of its strong capitalist (free enterprise) influence (see subsection 11.6) the US offers fewer social benefit – health, social security, welfare – than other democracies (mainly parliamentary) that have universalized such services. This relatively 'undemocratic' feature of the US system greatly reduces the number of government positions. Moreover, the tendency to 'privatize' many operations that elsewhere would be handled by government agencies curtails the number of officials in the state bureaucracy. By contrast, most presidentialist regimes employ a larger percentage of the population as bureaucrats, thereby increasing the opportunities for patronage (and for the resulting corruption and mismanagement of these functions).

Perhaps above all, the successful introduction of non-partisan merit-based careerism has radically reduced the pressure for making a large number of patronage appointments. Americans now take this development for granted, but comparative analysis shows how truly exceptional it is for presidentialist systems. How can we explain this exception?

12.2   Non-partisan merit-based careerism

Different kinds of careerism are well established in most presidentialist regimes, but they they are typically partisan and based on favouritism. Indeed, this was the way the American public service started: according to Leonard White (1948, pp. 514, 180), 'The Federalists took for granted permanence of tenure and were sensitive to the claims of officeholders except where they proved untrustworthy'. By the end of the 1790s, 'the rule of continuing tenure had become established'.

Despite the important political changes which occurred at the century's end when Jeffersonian Republicans succeeded the Federalists, public administration remained under the control of 'gentlemen', to whom, Thomas Jefferson wrote, he 'would wish to give office, because they would add respect and strength to the administration' (White, 1951, p. 550). In fact, without any contracts or examinations, a conservative upper class of retainers (see sub-section 6.3) dominated the public administration for 40 years from 1789 to 1829.

The rotation system in America was established during the Jacksonian period when, as White (1954, pp. 4–5) explains, President Andrew Jackson (1829–37) 'did not introduce the spoils system', but he did 'introduce rotation into the federal system'. Although we normally associate the Jacksonian era with the rise of the 'spoils' system, the introduction of rotation was historically more critical. It opened the doors of public office to ordinary people (not just 'gentlemen') and it also enabled succeeding Presidents to discharge many (though not all) officials in large numbers. Thereby, it not only created vacancies to he filled by patronage but it also dampened the natural growth which occurred in other patronage-based retainer bureaucracies. In such bureaucracies, as top officials retain their salaries although they have been downgraded and replaced (siberianized), the costs of government rise and the quality of public administration declines.

The rotation principle made government more 'popular' in the sense that, by opening the doors of public office to those of humble background, it made bureaucracy more 'representative'. At the same time, public administration became more formal as increasingly rules and regulations replaced the idiosyncratic habits and traditions that had been established by the long-term gentlemen retainers of the first 40 years (Crenson, 1975, pp. 131–9).

If we assume that the tendency of public officials to cling tenaciously to their posts and their perquisites is even stronger than the zest with which applicants seek new appointments, we may understand how persistently the retainer tradition has maintained itself in most other presidentialist regimes. In a comparative perspective, the Jacksonian achievement was truly remarkable and paved the way for a new type of merit-based non-partisan careerism that was to emerge 50 years later.

Had the patronage-based retainer bureaucracy established by the founders been permitted to continue, it would assuredly have become an incubus on the body politic, encouraging corruption and oppression while encumbering the public administration. A good example can be found in Brazil where, according to Scott Mainwaring (1990a,

p. 20), 'The political class has been acutely aware of the over-shadowing of the legislature by the bureaucracy and has responded by expanding their influence within the bureaucracy ... [with] deleterious consequences upon the efficacy of the state apparatus.'

In the American case, by contrast, Jacksonian rotationism and spoils generated a new set of problems and opportunities that paved the way for the successful movement to establish the merit-based career services. First, the spoils system, by itself, created so much abuse of office and incompetence in administration that it spawned a growingly powerful middle-class reform movement which ultimately succeeded in launching a new kind of non-partisan and merit-based careerism (for details, see Van Riper, 1958, pp. 60–95; and Hoogen-boom, 1961).

Although the spoils system generated powerful incentives for reform, it also created opportunities that have been little noticed. Any well-entrenched class of retainers in public office is sufficiently experienced to administer better than inexperienced spoilsmen. At the same time, they clearly have good reason to resist the introduction of a merit-based system that might bring better-qualified newcomers into office and, eventually, undermine their own security. By contrast, a host of American ex-spoilsmen, having some experience in public office, may join forces with reformers in the expectation that they could qualify themselves for re-employment on a permanent career basis. After the merit system was introduced, many patronage appointees were actually 'blanketed' into the career services: facing discharge because of continuing rotationism, they may have supported the extension of the career-based reforms.

Finally, it must be emphasized that the new careerists were em-phatically non-partisan. It was clearly in their interest, in order to avoid being rotated out of office when a new party came to power, to emphasize their own non-partisanship. The myth of a dichotomy between 'politics' and 'administration' served as a powerful argument to support the reforms and thereby helped to preserve the American constitution. At the time, *politics* clearly meant *partisanship*. As 'politics' came to be used for a much broader concept that includes non-partisan policy-oriented and organizational competition (in the Lasswellian sense), it informed a growing disjunction in the study of government which separated the academic disciplines of Political Science and Public Administration, with adverse consequences for both.

The success of the reform movement was also affected by the subsequent emergence of 'lobbyism' as a powerful force in American politics (see sub-section 10b). In many countries, parliamentary as well as presidentialist, political parties have closely associated themselves with religious and social movements – thus one party may bring together conservative Catholic farmers, another radical Protestant workers, and a third liberal anti-clerical intellectuals. Many professional, class, religious and policy-orientated movements become identified with a single *integrative* political party, one whose 'ideology' includes a variety of explicit policy commitments.

By contrast, the *isolative* American political parties reduced their linkages with a wide range of interest groups and embraced bland, essentially non-ideological party platforms. The rhetoric of bureaucratic politics has been shaped by this difference: transient appointees are orientated to party politics and hence are 'partisan', whereas careerists are associated with policy politics and interest group lobbies on a 'non-partisan' basis. In countries where integrative parties prevail, such a dichotomy is scarcely viable: bureaucrats necessarily link party loyalties with interest-group policies. However, the American solution required not only a disjunction between political appointees and careerists, but also a separation of career-ladders on a programmatic or policy-orientated basis, which may be discussed under the heading of *functionism*.

12.3 The significance of functionism.

The success of the merit system in the US may well hinge on its adoption of the principle of functionism, whereby candidates are admitted to a programme-orientated[22] career service (based on functionally specific examinations) that produces a host of functionaries (rather than mandarins). An important obstacle to the formal adoption of a career system in America involved resistance to the British model of the Administrative Class which produces a powerful 'mandarinate' of generalists who rotate between different government departments. Paul Van Riper (1958, pp. 100–1) explains that the American functionist adaptation was due to the rejection of youthful recruitment (by permitting entrance at all levels) and academic criteria (in favour of practical tests). He also tells us that the Congressional debate thoroughly explored 'the likely effects of the proposed legislation upon the constitutional position of the President and Congress, upon the party system', but it appears that the main issue involved the constitutionality of Congressional action to restrict the President's power of appointment, in view of his unrestricted removal powers (p. 97). More practically, Congress insisted on a quota system that would ensure recruitment of personnel from all the states, a safeguard against its loss of patronage but also a barrier to the rise of an elitist bureaucracy recruited from the most prestigious universities – the American counterparts to Oxbridge.

Perhaps unconsciously – though I have no positive evidence – members of Congress might have sensed that careerists, rooted in functionism, would be more responsive to legislative committees and more dependable as political allies than an elite core of bureaucratic generalists (mandarins) shaped according to the typical parliamentary mode (Riggs, 1988a, pp. 363–5, 376 n. 40). In fact, this adaptation of the British model has surely fostered the survival of American presidentialism. Had the British system (itself derived from the Chinese Confucian prototype via the Indian Civil Service) prevailed, an elite class of career generalists would have become so powerful that it could have unbalanced the separation of powers principle, first by undermining the power position of the Presidency, and ultimately by subordinating the Congress itself. As it turned out, career functionaries became closely attached to Congressional committees and their programmatic goals. Through evolving interest networks, career bureaucrats became ambivalently interdependent with members of Congress and thereby augmented the power of the legislative branch (see sub-section 10.3).

Some reformers apparently hoped eventually to replace all patronage appointees by merit-based careerists. Their efforts were reinforced by the teachings of the newly emergent academic field or discipline of Public Administration which, borrowing from business management theory, tended to see the President as a kind of chief executive officer (CEO) of a gigantic corporation in which norms of efficiency and effectiveness prevail over political and legal norms. Had their efforts succeeded, however, the independence of the Presidency would surely have given way to the growing power of an 'Imperial Congress'. Some alarmists think this has already happened, as Charles Kesler (1988, p. 23) explains: 'the principal beneficiary of the growth of the executive bureaucracy has been Congress, not the president'.

Confirming the image of American bureaucrats continuously caught in a cross-fire between the three branches of government that David Rosenbloom (1983) has given us, John Rohr (1986, p. 89) writes 'American Public Administration ... is necessarily and appropriately caught in the perennial cross fire involving a Congress, a president, and courts – all fiercely independent of one another.' However, in Rohr's view, career officers should 'become active participants rather than feckless pawns in the constitutional struggle for control of the Public Administration'. By deciding for themselves which 'branch to favor and for how long', they could preserve 'a certain autonomy within the framework of the Constitution and would thereby capture the professionalism that was at the heart of the reforms [Woodrow] Wilson and [Frank J.] Goodnow had in mind' (ibid.). In short, 'The Public Administration' has a responsibility to help 'Run the Constitution' and thereby preserve the balance of power between its constitutional branches which undergirds the American presidentialist regime.

If careerists alone were employed in the Federal Government, however, I suspect they would dangerously unbalance the separation of powers. To maintain the balance it is necessary to retain the President's patronage powers, although it was not until the Presidencies of Woodrow Wilson and Franklin D. Roosevelt that those powers became well entrenched in the continuously expanding apparatus of the White House and the Office of the President. These powers have proved increasingly effective both in helping the President to influence the outcome of Congressional votes and also, one hopes, to co-ordinate the mutually competitive, not to say antagonistic, branches of the functionist career bureaucracy. Although the balance between (non-partisan) careerists and (partisan) transients in the Federal bureaucracy remains at best conflicted and hazy, it has to be coped with as one of the costs of survival of a presidentialist regime (Durant, 1990).

The manifest purpose of the merit system reform was administrative rather than political: it provided a growing body of experienced officials whose institutional memory and personal competence enabled them to implement public policies with some consistency and efficiency, despite changes in the Presidency. However, these improved administrative capabilities had important political consequences which strengthened both the Congress and the Presidency. Through the creation of stable interest networks ('iron triangles' or 'subgovernments'), the state bureaucracy directly enhanced Congressional power.

Moreover, since authorized public policies could, as a result, be implemented with minimal intervention from the White House, the President's work-load was greatly reduced (Riggs, 1988a, pp. 363–5), and Presidents could also become more selective in choosing their patronage appointees, singling out those who could really help them to achieve their major political goals (Newland, 1987). Simultaneously, they could claim credit for the continuous implemention of a vast array of public programmes that were uninterruptedly administered by experienced career officials whose work required no direct intervention by the President. Concurrently, better public administration reduces popular discontent and also helps the regime survive.

Paradoxically, the American Presidency, as a result of these changes, has become both more institutionalized and more personalistic. The stability of interest networks involving career officials, members of Congress and professional lobbyists has institutionalized governance in the US to such an extent that it proceeds 'autonomously', regardless of who occupies the White House. However, the growing importance of television and the primaries and the resultant loosening of party organization throws a spotlight on the personalities of the President and key political appointees, giving each administration an idiosyncratic flavour that sets it apart from its predecessors and challenges American political historians and journalists to focus public attention on every eccentricity in the kaleidoscopic White House scene. Confusingly, it occurs to me that this public theatre, by distracting attention from more basic problems, may also contribute to the survival of this complicated and precarious political system.

I cannot prove that the absence of non-partisan, merit-based functionist bureaucracies or the ubiquity of patronage (cronyism, spoils, clientelism) in other presidentialist regimes has contributed to their collapse, but I believe it is an important possibility that deserves careful study. Put differently, I think the presence of non-partisan, merit-based and functionist careerists in the American government has contributed significantly to its survival in the twentieth century at a time when the challenges facing all contemporary governments have escalated.

IV   The Outlook for Presidentialism

A comprehensive explanation of the survival of presidentialism in the US should, admittedly, include an assessment of the environmental conditions that have favoured it. These might include the Common Law system, inherited from Britain, which may have helped the courts exercise their powers of judicial review and maintain the system of federalism. The Puritan tradition in church organization may have paved the way for widespread acceptance of collegial decision-making through elected assemblies. The historical sequences that permitted the thorough institutionalization of representative institutions prior to the development of a modern administrative state were surely important. The availability of jobs in the private sector facilitated the establishment of the rotation principle in the public bureaucracy, and the existence of a vast frontier that could easily be seized from its indigenous inhabitants provided opportunities that alleviated socio-political pressures.

Many other environmental conditions could be mentioned: their significance for comparative analysis would require that we evaluate the effects of their presence or absence in other presidentialist systems of government. I cannot do that here. Moreover, in so far as there may be some interest in discovering the conditions that might enable other presidentialist regimes to survive after their recovery from bouts of authoritarian dictatorship, it is surely relevant to focus on practices rooted in constitutional prescriptions and laws that can be adopted by political choice – after all, environmental conditions based on culture, geography, history and socio-economic circumstances are more difficult to manipulate and defy transfer from one country to another.

13 Comparing presidentialist regimes

The structural dynamics of presidentialism as a whole system of government, moreover, seems to have received little attention. Only by comparing the operations and fate of different presidentialist regimes – including those that broke down as well as those that persisted for varying lengths of time – can we gain an understanding of the inherent problems of this system and how they might be solved. This chapter highlights some of the dangers inherent in the presidentialist design, and points to some of the practices which have helped the system survive in the United States, including federalism, SMD plurality voting, the right to abstain, senioritism, lobbyism, rotationism, functionist careerism and capitalism.

The strength of these practices (traditions) should not be taken for granted. Many them have been attacked by reformers as 'un-democratic'. Because we have not studied presidentialism com-paratively we were unable to see how some proposed reforms (such as proportional representation) could undermine the viability of representative government in the US.

In this context, widespread support for the fundamental reforms required to overcome the essential constraints of the presidentialist formula will not arise until the country has experienced deeper crises than any so far encountered. Moreover, the Constitutional myth based on the separation of powers principle is itself so necessary as a supplement (if not replacement) for the compromised role of the President as head of state that we cannot seriously challenge it without undermining the viability of the regime and gaining a sinister reputation for ourselves.

The Committee on the Constitutional System (see section 7) has struggled heroically to mobilize interest in fundamental reform and has no doubt provoked some academic interest (see Hardin, 1974 and 1989; Sundquist, 1986; Robinson, 1985 and 1989). Unfortunately, however, the comparisons made by Committee members usually involve only parliamentary systems: the index to Robinson (1989), for example, lists about 15 parliamentary democracies with which some comparisons are made, but the only presidentialist polities mentioned are Nicaragua and El Salvador, where the text only takes up US foreign policy issues. Until specific comparisons are made with other presidentialist regimes, we cannot really understand the deeper problems inherent in the presidentialist design. Such an understanding, moreover, will enable us to attract the interest of a large constituency composed of many kinds of frustrated reformers who will discover that, until the regime itself is transformed, they will continue to be frustrated, for reasons they cannot understand.

It is surely important and feasible for us now to engage in a serious analysis of the political/administrative implications of presidentialism, and to re-evaluate the American experience in a comparative framework that takes into account the ordeals suffered by other countries following the American model. Such an analysis will help us to understand the plight of other presidentialist regimes, why presidentialism has survived in the US, and what other countries must do if they want their presidentialist constitutions to succeed. We shall also, I hope, become very wary about recommending presidentialist constitutions to any of the new republics that are now emerging from long periods of single-party domination.

14   Para-constitutional practices

Elsewhere (Riggs, 1988c) I have characterized the fundamental traditions, rules and practices that seem to help maintain the American presidentialist system, despite its great inherent problems, as *para-constitutional*. These include rules that favour the re-election of members of Congress, reward seniority in committee assignments and delegate great power to their sub-committees, and recognize lobbies that represent affluent and well-organized constituencies while permitting them to subsidize the re-election of incumbents. They must tolerate the frequent rotation in office of political appointees who have to work in antagonistic co-operation with career officials, and they embrace the formation of stable interest networks, including the notorious 'iron triangles'. They must put up with an electoral system based on federalism, special interest funding, the right to abstain and SMD plurality voting.

No doubt, even compliance with all these para-constitutional practices may not ensure the survival of a presidentialist regime –

especially if environmental conditions are not also auspicious. Of course, the lack of any one or more of these practices may not, by itself, precipitate the collapse of a presidentialist regime: it is their cumulative effect that is important. However, I believe that each of them does contribute significantly to the survival of such a regime and its absence acts like a handicap that, cumulatively, jeopardizes its continued existence.

I do not have systematic data on all presidentialist regimes, but my impression is that most of them abhor many of these practices and, in fact, have adopted more 'democratic' rules which, tragically, have the paradoxical effect of undermining any presidentialist regime and leading to military, personalist or hegemonic-party authoritarianism. Any constitution-makers who are unwilling to pay the price needed to enhance the prospects for survival of presidentialist governance ought to consider seriously the alternative designs that are based on executive accountability to an elected assembly. Whenever the head of government can be succeeded in a crisis by a responsible political opposition rather than by a military junta or a personal dictator, the prospects for the survival of representative government will, I believe, be enhanced and the viability of various democratic practices and public policies will also be increased.

Notes

1. Between 1946 and 1984 Bolivia had experienced 12 coups, Argentina 8, Ecuador 7, Brazil, Venezuela and South Vietnam 6, El Salvador, Guatemala and Peru 5, Panama 4, Dominican Republic 3, Colombia and South Korea 2, Chile, Cuba, Honduras, Nicaragua and Uruguay 1. The Philipines fell under presidential authoritarianism in 1972. Although Costa Rica and Mexico did not experience coups during this period, Mexico, after a stormy political history, came under the domination of a hegemonic party, the PRI; and Costa Rica experienced uprisings in 1917 and 1948, but since promulgation of the Constitution of 1949 has had the most stable presidentialist regime, after the United States. All but forgotten are the abortive Chinese (1913) and Philippine (1898, Malolos) republics and the unfortunate Liberian case.

   Most of the surviving parliamentary regimes are mini-states, but they also include gargantuan India, plus Jamaica, Mauritius, Papua New Guinea, Sri Lanka, Trinidad and Tobago. Fiji had not experienced a coup before 1984, but succumbed to one in 1987. These data are unavoidably rough because complex historical events defy simple codings.

2. By contrast, Giovanni Sartori suggests that a polity should be defined as presidential only if (a) the head of state is popularly elected; (b) during his pre-established tenure cannot be displaced or removed by a

parliamentary vote; and (c) is both head of government and head of state (Sartori, 1993, p. 1). The first criterion conflates presidentialist with parliamentary systems, many of which have elected heads of state (presidents), and Presidents may also be elected indirectly (see note 4). My single criterion covers the essential points in all three of Sartori's stipulations while excluding those that are not necessary.

3. Additional distinctions are made here: I shall refer to the elected assembly in any presidentialist system as a *Congress* and in a parliamentary system as a *Parliament*, while using *legislature* as a generic term for both. Since *presidential* often refers to the office of a president as well as a system of governance, I shall use either *Presidential* (capitalized) or *President's* to characterize properties of the office in presidentialist systems only.

4. The approach used here distinguishes between the defining, accidental and redundant characteristics of a concept. A *defining* (essential) characteristic is one that is always found in members of a defined class. When only some members of that class have a characteristic it is called *accidental* (accompanying), and if non-members also have it, it is *redundant* (superfluous).

   These distinctions are often ignored in definitions of *presidential* systems. For example, since some presidents may be re-elected but others may not, this is an *accidental* property. Similarly, the head of government is normally just one person, but a small group (board or commission) may also exercise presidential functions, as happened in Uruguay from 1917 to 1933 and 1951–67. Consequently, to specify that the president is one person is to identify an accidental rather than a defining characteristic of presidentialism – though most presidents, assuredly, are individuals. All Presidents, as heads of government, serve concurrently as heads of state. However, since presidents are also elected in such parliamentary regimes as Austria, Finland, France, Germany, Iceland, India and Ireland, it is *redundant* to define Presidents as elected heads of state.

   Although presidents are usually elected by a *direct* popular vote, this is not true by definition. The American Constitution provides for the *indirect* election of Presidents by an Electoral College – a rule which is still formally observed. The final choice may actually be made in Congress, as it has been in Bolivia and Chile and even in the US where the Constitution gives the House of Representatives the authority to choose the President when no candidate secures a majority in the Electoral College. Exceptionally, this happened in 1801 when the House chose Jefferson over Burr to break an Electoral College tie, and in 1824 when it selected Adams, although Jackson had a plurality. Since most Presidents are, indeed, popularly elected, this is an important *accidental*, but not a defining, feature. Moreover, since presidents are also directly elected in some non-presidentialist (parliamentary) regimes, such as Austria, Iceland, Ireland, Finland, the direct election of the President is also a *redundant* characteristic in any definition of presidentialism.

5. Sartori's scale recognizes semi-presidential and semi-parliamentary forms of government which intervene between the pure presidentialist (*primus solus*) and the pure parliamentary (*primus inter pares*) models. His preference is clearly for the two 'semi-' types: semi-presidential illustrated by France and Finland, and semi-parliamentary illustrated by Great Britain and West Germany (Satori, 1989, p. 6). I shall not discuss the parliamentary alternatives in this paper, but we could usefully examine the experiences of several Latin American countries which have experimented with semi-presidentialist features. Some proposed fundamental reforms of the American constitution also go in the direction of semi-presidentialism rather than full parliamentarism.

6. The dangers of 'polarized pluralism' have been lucidly explained by Sartori (1976, pp. 131–45). However, his treatment focuses on parliamentary multiparty systems (except for Chile) and he draws a basic line between 'moderate' and 'polarized' pluralism, using five or six parties as the dividing line. My analysis supplements his by emphasizing the parliamentary/presidentialist context and by arguing that even a two-party system can be highly polarized (centrifugal) by PR-based factionalism, as in Uruguay and Colombia.

7. Because much if not most of the income of traditional officials was secured from extra-governmental sources, hureaucrats lacked the incentives found in modern polities for seizing power and we find no examples of a real *coup d'etat* in these societies, with the possible exception of the Mamlukes in Egypt (Riggs, 1991, pp. 7–8).

8. The historical reasons for this phenomenon are elaborated in Riggs (1991 and 1993a). Most importantly, the new states have inherited well entrenched modern bureaucracies whereas the institutions of representative government required to control them were established, usually, only as independence approached. Not surprisingly, when and if these new-born institutions failed to handle serious problems, especially those involving public finance, threatened officials were willing to support a coup that promised to stabilize their own incomes.

9. No elected assembly can, by itself, govern effectively: it always falls into disarray and deep cleavages. According to Douglas Verney (1959, p. 57), 'Convention government, the domination of a political system by the Assembly, has generally been unsuccessful.' Until the development of both the presidentialist and parliamentary models in the nineteenth century, political theorists tended to think that the only option for governing a society involved a choice between the rule of one (as in monarchy) or the rule of an assembly (as in classical Greek democracy). Monarchic absolutism remains as a political fossil in a dozen or so countries (mainly in the oil-rich Arabian peninsula) but convention government has been severely discredited ever since the disaster of the French Convention of 1792–5.

10. What determines the capacity of a legislature to sustain its power position in the face of Presidential pressures is a complex and important

problem that I shall not address here. However, in an earlier essay I offered some reflections on the need for party competition as a basis for legislative power, pointing out that legislatures in countries with a single-party or hegemonic party system are reduced to political power-lessness (Riggs, 1973).

11. A strong political campaign is now under way in the United States to restrict senioritism by setting limits to the time legislators may remain in office. This campaign appears to be partly motivated by the hope of Republicans that, thereby, they might regain 'parity in Congress and in most of the legislatures of America' (Cannon, 1990). California has recently adopted, by referendum, a rule that limits members of its state Assembly to six years in office. Since some 96 per cent of its members who sought re-election during the last decade were returned to office, this will force a mass turnover by 1996. Meanwhile, many state legislators, 'concerned about their political and economic futures [will] seek other offices or leave government altogether' (Cannon, 1990). By contrast, the state of Washington, in November 1991, rejected a proposition that would also have set term limits – mainly because of a desire to retain their own long-term member of Congress, Speaker Tom Foley.

12. This situation has generated an interesting academic debate: the class-ical preference of American political theory for democratic values rooted in liberal notions of the importance of *majority rule* has been largely replaced by theories rooted in *pluralism*, the idea that it is in the general interest to permit many special interests to compete freely for their share of the public patrimony, the sum of these claims adding up, supposedly, to the general interest. As Trudi Miller has noted, the prevalence of a *pluralist* orientation among American intellectuals wel-comes special-interest politics as desirable. She calls for a revival of eighteenth century *liberal* theory in a modernized form. Such a theory, rooted in the notions of individualism, rationality and *majoritarianism*, is attributed, among others, to James Madison who wrote in *The Federalist*, no.10, 'If a faction consists of less than a majority, relief is supplied by the republican principle, which enables the majority to defeat its sinister views by regular vote' (Miller, 1989, p. 80).

13. Juan Linz (1990, p. 57) argues that 'In countries [e.g., the US] where the preponderance of voters is centrist ... and expects both rightist and leftist candidates to differ only within a larger, moderate consensus, the divisiveness latent in presidential[ist] competition is not a serious problem. With an overwhelmingly moderate electorate, anyone who makes alliances or takes positions that seem to incline him to the extremes is unlikely to win ....' By contrast, my analysis of the American party system attributes its ability to sustain a centripetal dynamic to the reluctance or inability of most poor and uneducated citizens to vote, rather than to any consensus that can be ascribed to moderate 'independent' voters. Indeed, I believe that there are as many potential voters with extremist views in the US as in any other country. The big

difference is that they see no reason to vote. Perhaps charismatic candidates, such as Jesse Jackson on the left or David Duke on the right, could mobilize many apathetic non-voters, but only at the cost of centrifugalizing the party system, encouraging candidates to espouse extreme positions that would appeal to white racist non-voters as well as impoverished and disaffected ethnic minorities – a good example can be found in the defeat of David Duke for governor of Louisiana in November 1991, where an unprecedentedly large turnout of black voters was generated in reaction to Duke's racist history.

14. Linz (1990, p. 53), for example, writes about 'the diffuse character of American political parties – which, ironically, exasperates many American political scientists and leads them to call for responsible, ideologically disciplined parties ....' He notes, however, that the American case is exceptional by contrast with the 'development of modern political parties' elsewhere.

    From a different perspective, Edward Greenberg (1980, pp. 229–34) attacks the American party system as too loose, uncommitted, and elitist and argues that, although 'Elections play an important function in the overall maintenance of the American system, and of the capitalist order at its base, ... [they] do so even though – indeed precisely because – they perform largely ceremonial and symbolic functions' (p. 229). Greenberg fails to see that the kind of parliamentary (ideological) party which he prefers as more inherently democratic would centrifugalize the party system and jeopardize the survival of presidentialism in America.

15. By contrast, PR is clearly compatible with parliamentarism where small minorities can actually participate in coalition governments. PR may even be compatible with two-party parliamentary systems, but this combination is unusual. Maurice Duverger (1984, p. 37), while advocating PR systems in general, has pointed out that 'it can happen that PR does not prevent the formation of a two-party system, as in Austria and the German Federal Republic. But these cases are exceptions and depend on special circumstances'.

    In view of the rejoinders to Lijphart (1991a) by Lardeyret (1991) and Quade (1991), I am not persuaded that PR necessarily improves the performance of parliamentary regimes but, on the basis of Lijphart's response (1991b), I agree it might be better than plurality systems. My argument here is simply that, by promoting centrifugalism, PR undermines the viability of presidentialism.

16. *Faction* is often used loosely, especially when describing local party organization in the US (Henry, 1984, pp. 83–85). In fact, however, local intraparty groups rarely combine to form coherent national 'factions'. A lucid explanation of the difference between *factions* (well-organized intraparty groups) and *tendencies* (loosely patterned attitudes) is contained in Sartori (1976, pp. 75–82). He classes both as *fractions*. A good example of an American party 'tendency' would be the 'Boll

Weevils' in the Democratic Party who helped President Ronald Reagan gain Congressional support for some of his key programmes. A counterpart Republican group, the 'Gypsy Moths', frequently defected from their party's position. How Reagan and his followers managed to secure the support of the Boll Weevils and prevent defection by the Gypsy Moths is explained in colourful detail by Hedrick Smith (1988, pp. 471–7). Although one may well deplore this amorphous pattern of 'tendencies' in American political parties and its affinity for elitist 'back-room' wheeling and dealing, it seems to be conducive to the survival of presidentialism in America.

17. Under presidentialism, it is almost impossible for a centrist governing coalition to form when a centrifugalized party system prevails. A possible exception might have been Chile, but even in this case, as Valenzuela (1989, p. 14) explains, 'centrist movements only minimally represented a viable centrist tendency and were in fact primarily reflections of the erosion of the two extreme poles . . . . The instability of centrist movements . . . contributed to the difficulties in building common public policies because centrist consensus at the decision making level was so fragile. The erosion of centrist consensus accelerated dramatically during the Allende years and contributed to the crisis culminating in regime breakdown.'

Linz (1990, p. 57) also recognizes this problem when he writes: 'One of the possible consequences of two-candidate races in multiparty systems is that broad coalitions are likely to be formed (whether in run-offs or in preelection maneuvering) in which extremist parties gain undue influence.' Consequently, 'a Presidential election can fragment and polarize the electorate'. He sees the American system as exceptional because, there, 'the preponderance of voters is centrist, agrees on the exclusion of extremists, and expects both rightist and leftist candidates to differ only within a larger, moderate consensus' thereby overcoming 'the divisiveness latent in presidential competetion'.

However, Linz ignores the possibility that the American exception is not so much due to a 'centrist consensus' as it is to the *centripetalism* of a party system based on SMD voting and the right to abstain which, together, enhance the weight of a relatively small number of independent voters while dampening participation by peripheralized people. The point is that we may better understand the attitudes of American voters and non-voters if we view them, structurally, as a *consequence* of the centripetalized party system. My guess is that any presidentialist polity would generate popular responses similar to the American if it were to develop a centripetalized rather than a centrifugalized party system. However, to do that, it would have to sacrifice important democratic values, for example by relying on SMD plurality electoral systems and accepting the right of citizens to abstain from voting. Under these conditions, no doubt, the behaviour of voters might create the illusion of a centrist consensus as the *cause* of political moderation, rather than the *consequence* of electoral rules and widespread non-voting.

18. For a summary of one-party domination in the states and the shifts that have occurred, together with analysis of the reasons for these changes and their significance, see Henry (1984, pp. 98–106).

19. Mainwaring (1990a, pp. 23–4) argues that the 'combination of presidentialism and a multiparty system is further complicated by the strong federalist bases of Brazilian politics'. I would argue, instead, that Brazil's fluid multiparty system is primarily caused by its open-list PR electoral system, which is simply reinforced by its federalism. Mainwaring also points out that the extreme fluidity of party identification in Brazil leads 'clientelistic politicians to join the party in power, regardless of what it is' (p. 24). There is a similar tendency in the US, before elections, but party responsiveness dampens the tendency and, once elected, legislators will be strongly sanctioned by their local supporters if they try to jump to the other party.

20. Elsewhere, I have argued that presidentialist regimes have to be conservative in order to survive whereas parliamentary regimes may well move much further in the direction of social democracy and the regulation of capitalist enterprises (Riggs, 1990, pp. 230–2). However, in that context I failed to appreciate the importance of an open centripetal party system as the linkage mechanism which both enables *capitalism* to dominate the regime while compelling the regime to protect and regulate *capitalism* in order to assure its own survival.

21. A pioneer exposition of the class basis of the American Constitution was offered in Beard (1913). The founding fathers counted on the indirect election of both the President and the Senate, plus the prevalence of property qualifications in the state laws governing elections to the House of Representatives to assure support for the minority interests of property-holders (augmented by the obstacles to be overcome by decision-makers subjected to the severe constraints of an institutional design based on the separation of powers). Subsequent constitutional changes have eliminated these electoral safeguards, rendering all three of these basic institutions subject to popular elections (despite the anachronistic survival of the Electoral College).

    Contemporary radical explanations of the American government rely, more explicitly, on the Marxist view that bourgeois *capitalism* is an autonomously powerful socio-economic actor capable of imposing its preferences on a government subject to its domination. Greenberg, for example, writes that '. . . the building blocks of a general understanding of the political economy appear in that body of work known as Marxist social theory.' In that context, Greenberg (1980, pp. 13–14) sees 'Government . . . as the institutional expression of the needs and interests of those who own property, and not as a popular tool for the redress of grievances,' and views 'what we might call *normal politics* (elections, representation, petition, and the like) only from within the more general framework of *capitalism* as a whole'.

    By contrast with the position I am offering here, Greenberg views *capitalism* in a unilinear perspective as accountable for the performance of both government and the party system, while dismissing the relation of the party system to government as unimportant or purely symbolic. By ignoring the properties both of parliamentary government and of other presidentialist regimes, his interpretation is essentially non-comparative (parochial).

More conventional authors often ignore the linkages between presidentialism and the capitalist system. Comparisons with other presidentialist (and parliamentary) regimes, however, should enable us to formulate a more adequate understanding of the interdependence of *capitalism* and presidentialism in a context of circular causation, via the party system. Here my focus is more specifically on the linkages between capitalism and the maintenance of an open party system.

22. American specialists on Public Administration normally use the term *program-oriented* in contrast with *career-oriented*, a juxtaposition that emphasizes positions rather than rank as a focal concept. This distinction also separates the American from the British practice, but here I need to emphasize a different dichotomy: the specialist (departmentalist or functional) by contrast with the generalist (class) criterion. Functionaries are career specialists, by contrast with transient generalists (the political appointees) – they constitute the two main divisions of the American bureaucracy. In the British, as in most parliamentary systems, elitist mandarins are career generalists by contrast with lower level functionaries (career specialists).

References

Aberbach, Joel D., Robert D. Putnam, and Bert A. Rockman 1981: *Bureaucrats and Politicians in Western Democracies*. Cambridge, Mass.: Harvard University Press.

Baaklini, Abdo 1989: 'Presidentialism and Brazilian Politics'. Unpublished paper.

—— 1992:*Brazilian Legislature and Political System*. New York: Greenwood Press.

Beard, Charles 1913: *An Economic Interpretation of the Constitution*. New York: Macmillan.

Black, Eric 1988: *Our Constitution: the Myth that binds us*. Boulder, Co: Westview Press.

Blitz, Mark 1990: 'Term limits a poor solution'. *Honolulu Advertiser*, 18 Dec., A14.

Broder, David 1990: Column. *Honolulu Advertiser*. 14 March, A8.

Cannon, Lou 1990: 'Term limits: GOP's big hope'. *Honolulu Advertiser*, 15 Dec., A8.

Carino, Ledivina 1988: *Bureaucracy for a Democracy: the struggle of the Philippine political leadership and the civil service in the post-Marcos period*, Occasional Paper no. 88–1. Manila: University of the Philippines, College of Public Administration.

—— 1989: 'A dominated bureaucracy: an analysis of the formulation of, and reactions to, state policies on the Philippine civil service'. Unpublished paper.

Cerny, Philip G. 1989: 'Political entropy and American decline'. *Millenium: Journal of International Studies*, 18(1): 47–63.

Conaghan, Catherine M. 1989: 'Loose parties, floating politicians, and institutional stress: presidentialism in Ecuador, 1979–88'. Paper for Georgetown University Symposium.

Crenson, Matthew A. 1975: *The Federal Machine: beginnings of bureaucracy in Jacksonian America*. Baltimore, Md: Johns Hopkins University Press.

De Guzman, Raul P. and Mila A. Reforma (eds) 1988: *Government and politics of the Philippines*. Singapore: Oxford University Press.

Dogan, Mattei (ed.) 1975: *The Mandarins of Western Europe*. New York: John Wiley.

Durant, Robert F. 1990: 'Beyond fear or favor: appointee-careerist relations in the post-Reagan era'. *Public Administration Review*, 50(3): 319–31.

Duverger, Maurice 1980. 'A new political system model: semipresidential government'. *European Journal of Political Research*, 8: 165–87.

—— 1984: 'Which is the best electoral system?' In Lijphart and Grofman, 1984, pp. 31–9.

Federalist Papers 1961: Alexander Hamilton, James Madison, and John Jay. New York: New American Library.

Gillespie, Charles Guy 1989: 'Presidential-parliamentary relations and the problems of democratic stability: the case of Uruguay'. Paper for Georgetown University Symposium.

Gonzalez, Luis E. 1989: 'Presidentialism, party systems and democratic stability: the Uruguayan case'. Paper for Georgetown University Symposium.

Greenberg, Edward S. 1980: *The American Political System: a radical approach*, 2nd edn. Cambridge, Mass.: Winthrop Publishers.

Hallett, George H. Jr 1984: 'Proportional representation with the single transferable vote: a basic requirement for legislative elections'. In Lijphart and Grofman, 1984, pp. 113–25.

Hardin, Charles 1974: *Presidential Power and Accountability*. Chicago, Ill.: University of Chicago Press.

—— 1989: *Constitutional Reform in the United States*. Ames, Iowa: Iowa State University Press.

Harris, James W. 1990: 'Third parties out'. *The Nation*, 12 Nov., 548–9.

Hartlyn, Jonathan 1989: 'Presidentialism and Colombian Politics'. Paper for Georgetown University Symposium.

Heclo, Hugh 1987: 'The in-and-outer system: a critical assessment'. In C. Calvin Mackenzie (ed.), *The In-and-Outers: Presidential Appointees and Transient Government in Washington*, Baltimore, Md: Johns Hopkins University Press.

Henry, Nicholas 1984: *Governing at the Grassroots: state and local politics*. Englewood Cliffs, N.J.: Prentice-Hall.

Hermens, Ferdinand A. 1984: 'Representation and proportional representation'. In Lijphart and Grofman, 1984, pp. 15–30.
—— 1989: 'Making democracy safe for the world'. Unpublished paper.
—— 1990: 'From tyranny to democracy'. *Freedom at Issue*, 114, 6–9.
Hoogenboom, Ari 1961: *Outlawing the Spoils: a history of the civil service reform movement, 1865–1883*. Urbana, III.: University of Illinois Press.
Jackson, Robert H. and Carl G. Rosberg 1982: *Personal Rule in Black Africa: prince, autocrat, prophet, tyrant*. Berkeley, Cal.: University of California Press.
Kesler, Charles 1988: 'Separation of powers and the administrative state'. In Gordon S. Jones and John A. Marini (eds), *The Imperial Congress*, New York: Pharos Books (Heritage Foundation).
Lardeyret, Guy 1991: 'The Problem with PR'. *Journal of Democracy*, 2(3): 36–41.
Lasswell, Harold D. and Abraham Kaplan 1950: *Power and Society: a framework for political inquiry*. New Haven, Conn.: Yale University Press.
Lijphart, Arend 1989: 'Presidentialism and majoritarian democracy: theoretical observations'. Paper for Georgetown University Symposium.
—— 1991a: 'Constitutional choices for new democracies'. *Journal of Democracy*, 2(1): 72–84.
—— 1991b: 'Double-checking the evidence'. *Journal of Democracy*, 2(3): 42–8.
—— and Bernard Grofman, 1984: *Choosing an Electoral System*. New York: Praeger.
Linz, Juan 1990: 'The perils of Presidentialism'. *Journal of Democracy*, 1(1): 51–69.
Mainwaring, Scott 1989: 'Presidentialism in Latin America: a review essay', *Latin American Research Review*, 25(1): 157–79.
—— 1990a: 'Brazilian party underdevelopment in comparative perspective', Working Paper no. 134. Notre Dame, Ind.: University of Notre Dame, Kellog Institute. (Revised version of a paper presented at the International Political Science Association congress, 1988.)
—— 1990b: 'Dilemmas of multiparty presidential democracy: the case of Brazil'. Paper prepared for the World Congress of Sociology.
McClintock, Cynthia 1989: 'Presidential or parliamentary democracy: does it make a difference? The Peruvian case'. Paper for Georgetown University Symposium.
McIlwain, Charles Howard 1947: *Constitutionalism: Ancient and Modern*. Ithaca, N.Y.: Cornell University Press.
Mezey, Michael L. 1989: 'Congress within the United States presidential system'. Paper presented at the APSA Annual Meeting, Atlanta, Ga.
Miller, Trudi C. 1989: 'The operation of democratic institutions'. *Public Administration Review*, 49(6): 511–21.
Molinelli, N. Gullermo 1988: 'President-Congress relations in Argentina: 1860s–1980s'. Paper presented at the IPSA World Congress, Washington, D.C.
—— 1989: Personal letter with extended comments on Riggs (1988c) sent to the author on 11 Sept.

Newland, Chester A. 1987: 'Public executives: imperium, sacerdotium, collegium?' *Public Administration Review*, 47(1): 45–56.

Nino, Carlos Santiago 1988: 'Transition to democracy, corporatism and constitutional reform in Latin America'. Unpublished paper.

Pfiffner, James P. 1987: 'Political appointees and career executives'. *Public Administration Review*, 47(1): 57–65.

Pious, Richard M. 1986: *American Politics and Government*. New York: McGraw-Hill.

Quade, Quentin 1963: 'Presidential leadership: paralyzed or irresponsible'. *Parliamentary Affairs*, 17(1): 65–76.2

—— 1991: 'PR and democratic statecraft'. *Journal of Democracy*, 2(3): 30–5.

Riggs, Fred W. 1965: 'The political context of administrative reform: relearning an old lesson'. *Public Administration Review*, 25(1): 70–9.

—— 1973: 'Legislative structures: some thoughts on elected national assemblies'. In Allan Kornberg (ed.), *Legislatures in Comparative Perspective*, New York: McKay.

—— 1985: 'Bureaucratic power and administrative change'. *Administrative Change* (Jaipur, India), 11(2) (1984): 105–58.

—— 1988a: 'Bureaucratic politics in the US: benchmarks for comparison'. *Governance*, 1(4): 343–79.

—— 1988b: 'The interdependence of politics and administration'. *Philippine Journal of Public Administration*, 31(4) (1987): 418–38.

—— 1988c: 'Survival of presidentialism in America: para-constitutional practices'. *International Political Science Review*, 9(4): 247–78.

—— 1989: 'The political ecology of American public administration: a neo-Hamiltonian approach'. *International Journal of Public Administration*, 12(3): 355–84.

—— 1990: 'A neo-institutional typology of Third World polities'. In Anton Bebler and James Seroka (eds), *Contemporary Political Systems: classification and typologies*, Boulder, Col.: Lynne Rienner.

—— 1991a: 'Bureaucratic links between administration and polities'. In Ali Farazmand (ed.), *Handbook of Comparative and Development Public Administration and Policy*, in press New York: Marcel Dekker, pp. 587–609.

—— 1993a: 'Fragility of the Third World regimes'. *International Social Science Journal*, 136: 199–243.

—— 1993b: 'Bureaucracy and the constitution'. *Public Administration Review*, forthcoming.

Robinson, Donald L. (ed.) 1985: *Reforming American Government: The bicentennial papers of the Committee on the Constitutional System*. Boulder, Col. and London: Westview Press.

—— 1989: *Government for the Third American Century*. Boulder, Col.: Westview.

Rodgers, Harrell R. and Michael Harrington 1985: *Unfinished democracy: the American political system*, 2nd edn. Glenview, Ill.: Scott, Foresman.

Rohr, John A. 1986: *To Run a Constitution*. Lawrence, Kan.: University Press of Kansas.

—— 1991: 'Ethical issues in French public administration'. *Public Administration Review*, 51(4): 283-97.

Rosenbloom, David 1983: 'Public administrative theory and the separation of powers'. *Public Administration Review*, 43(3): 219-27.

Rourke, Francis E. 1984: *Bureaucracy, Politics, and Public Policy*, 3rd edn. Boston, Mass.: Little, Brown.

Sartori, Giovanni 1976: *Parties and Party Systems*, vol. i. Cambridge: Cambridge University Press.

—— 1993: 'Democracy: presidential or parliamentary'. In Juan Linz and Arturo Valenzuela (eds), *Stable Democracy in the Third World*, Baltimore, Md: Johns Hopkins University Press.

Severn, Bill 1969: *John Marshall: the man who made the court supreme*. New York: David McKay.

Smith, Hedrick 1988: *The Power Game: how Washington works*. New York: Random House.

Suleiman, Ezra N. 1989: 'French presidentialism and political stability'. Paper for Georgetown University Symposium.

Sundquist, James L. 1986: *Constitutional Reform and Effective Government*. Washington, D.C.: Brookings Institution.

Valenzuela, Arturo 1984: 'Parties, politics, and the state in Chile: the higher civil service'. In Ezra N. Suleiman (ed.), *Bureaucrats and Policy Making*, New York: Holmes & Meier.

—— 1988: 'Chile: origins, consolidation and breakdown of a democratic regime'. In Larry Diamond, Juan Linz and Seymour Martin Lipset (eds), *Democracy in Developing Countries: Latin America*, vol. 4, Boulder, Col.: Lynne Rienner. [References based on pre-publication draft].

—— 1989: 'Party politics and the failure of presidentialism in Chile'. Paper for Georgetown University Symposium.

Van Riper, Paul A. 1958: *History of the United States Civil Service*. Evanston, Ill.: Row, Peterson.

Verney, Douglas V. 1958: *The Analysis of Political Systems*. Glencoe, Ill.: Free Press.

Waisman, Carlos H. 1989: 'Counterrevolution and structural change: the case of Argentina'. *International Political Science Review*, 10(2): 159-74.

Weaver, Leon 1984: 'Semi-proportional and proportional representation systems in the United States'. In Lijphart and Grofman, 1984, pp. 191-206.

White, Leonard D. 1948: *The Federalists*. New York: Free Press.

—— 1951: *The Jeffersonians*. New York: Macmillan.

—— 1954: *The Jacksonians: a study in administrative history, 1829-1861*. New York: Macmillan.

Winger, Richard (ed.) *Ballot Access News*. San Francisco, Cal.: Coalition for Free and Open Elections.

Wright, J.F.H. 1984: 'An Electoral basis for responsible government: the Australian experience'. In Lijphart and Grofman, 1984, pp. 127-34.

4

Binary Comparisons

American Exceptionalism — Japanese Uniqueness

Seymour Martin Lipset

Japan and the United States are two of the foremost examples of industrial success in the contemporary world, and they took very different paths to reach that position.[1] Efforts to account for America's past success have emphasized that it had fewer encrusted pre-industrial traditions to overcome, in particular, that it had never been a feudal or hierarchically state church dominated society. All of Europe and, of course, Japan were once feudal, organized in terms of monarchy, aristocracy and fixed hierarchy, with a value system embedded in religious institutions which both emphasized the virtues inherent in agrarian society and deprecated commercial activities. Japan's feudal period, however, did not end until the latter half of the nineteenth century.

Analysts of the social prerequisites for industrialization have suggested that such conditions existed optimally in America. An efficient market economy is seemingly best served by an emphasis on individualism, on achievement, on meritocratic competition, by a value system which regards the individual as the equivalent of a commodity within the market. Ideally, under capitalism, people seek to maximize their own positions and deal with others without being concerned with inherited or ascribed qualities. Academic economic historians are not the only ones who believe that America has had the optimum conditions for development.[2] Nineteenth- and early twentieth-century Marxists, analysing the expansion of capitalism, also pointed to the United States as the purest of bourgeois societies, the least feudal one, and therefore the most successful.[3] In the 1920s, Antonio Gramsci, the justly celebrated Italian Communist theoretician, noted that his country had to Americanize socially as well as economically in order to develop the advanced capitalist industrial structure that, in his judgement, was a prerequisite for socialism.[4]

This chapter, part of a larger effort to explicate the nature of American exceptionalism, is based on an assumption recently enunciated by Kazuo Ogura: 'To define the "other" is to know one's nation.'[5] A person who knows only one country basically knows no country well. Comparing the United States or Japan with other nations is the best way to learn about each. In a previous work I dealt with Canada, and argued that 'it is precisely because the two North American democracies have so much in common that they permit students of each to gain insights into the factors that cause variations'.[6] Here, I shift to looking at the two outliers, the two developed nations which are most different from each other. They clearly have distinct organizing principles. And their values, institutions and behaviours fit into sharply different functional wholes. These variations, of course, have been written about in a myriad of comparative scholarly, business and journalistic works.[7] Given my limited contact with Japan (five visits covering a total of six months over 30 years), I cannot add to them observationally. This chapter, however, seeks to elaborate and test the validity of the qualitative analyses by a comprehensive examination of the comparative data on opinions, values and behaviour, collected by public opinion agencies.[8] As will be evident, there are astonishingly large differences between them.

Exceptionalism and Uniqueness

The United States is exceptional in starting from a revolutionary event.[9] It has defined its *raison d'être* ideologically. As historian Richard Hofstadter has noted, 'It has been our fate as a nation not to have ideologies, but to be one.'[10] The American Creed can be subsumed in five terms: liberty, egalitarianism, individualism, populism (the rule of the people) and *laissez-faire*. As Alexis de Tocqueville noted, egalitarianism in its American meaning has emphasized equality of opportunity and of respect, not of result or condition.[11] These values reflect the absence of feudal structures and monarchies and aristocracies. As a new society, the country lacked the emphasis on social hierarchy and deference characteristic of post-feudal cultures. These aspects, as Tocqueville and Max Weber stressed, were reinforced by the country's religious commitment to the 'nonconformist', largely congregationally organized, Protestant sects which emphasized voluntarism with respect to the state, and a personal or individual relationship to God, one not mediated by hierarchically organized churches which have predominated in Europe, Canada and Latin America. The United States was 'born modern'.[12] In Japan and much of Europe, on the other hand, the historic national values are derivative from monarchical and mercantilist pasts, feudal class and hierarchial religious structures and traditions, which have favoured an emphasis on hereditary status and family origins. These nations identify with their history, not with an ideology.

The focus of the American value system, of the American Creed, has been on the individual. Individuals have been expected to demand and protect their rights on a personal basis. The exceptional emphasis on law in the United States, derivative from the Constitution and the Bill of Rights, has stressed individual rights against those of the state and other powers and persons. America began and continues as the most anti-statist nation.

Japan, on the other hand, as many commentators have noted, is the world's exemplar of a group-orientated society and 'non-socialist' state-influenced economy. As Naohiro Amaya has stated:

> Japan's history is much different from that of the United States. Japan did not establish the atomistic individual as the basic unit of society and rarely had individuals who 'spun off' from society and lived by themselves. Today, as in the old days, the basic unit of Japanese society is not 'atomistic' individuals, but 'molecule-like' groups. These groups consist of 'villages' and 'families'. One may consider 'families' as monomers and 'villages' as polymers. Individuals live as an organic element of their groups within this group structure.
>
> The fundamental ethic which supports a group has been 'harmony'. Such American values as individual freedom, equality, equal opportunity, and an open-door policy can be considered 'foreign proteins' introduced into the traditional body of Japanese society.[13]

The interpretation which identifies post-feudal structures and values as antithetical to the development of modern industrial society is in many ways challenged by the history of Japan, which boasts the most successful economy of the postwar era. Rising from a terrible military defeat and the almost total destruction of its economy, Japan experienced a level of sustained economic growth which enabled it to become, in per capita terms, one of the wealthiest countries in the world and also to compete successfully with the United States. But this postwar 'miracle' continues a successful development pattern which began in the latter part of the nineteenth century long after Northern Europe and North America began their industrial revolutions. Self-starting industrialization and modernization took place almost entirely in a few European countries and the English-speaking overseas settler societies. Japan is the earliest non-Western country to become wealthy and industrially developed. Its record, compared to that of the United States or, to some degree, of Western Europe, seems to contradict much of what economic historians and comparative social scientists generally had thought they learned from the American experience. The question which now interests the West is: what is it about Japan that enabled this to happen? The Japanese themselves are-fascinated with discussions of Japanese uniqueness, *Nihonron*, their counterpart to American exceptionalism.[14] The 're-iterated refrain underlying the literature on Japanese identity is that of uniqueness'.[15] One literature survey estimates that over 2000 works dealing with Japanese uniqueness have been published since the Second World War.[16]

Revolution from Above

Japan has modernized economically while retaining many aspects of its pre-industrial feudal culture. Until the mid-nineteenth century, the social structure under the Tokugawa Shogunate was still feudal; its culture still resembled that of Renaissance Europe. Japan was an extremely hierarchical society which placed a tremendous emphasis on obligation to those higher up as well as to those down below. Inferiors were expected to show deference and give loyalty while superiors were obliged to protect and support them.

By the mid-nineteenth century, Japan had avoided a prolonged breakdown of feudalism, but the Japanese aristocratic elite decided that the country had to industrialize if it was to escape being conquered by the imperialist West. Determined to avoid dependence on or takeover by Western powers, this elite sought to remake the country economically along Western lines. To do so, they recognized the need to consciously remould the social structure so as to create the conditions for economic development, a dauntingly gargantuan task.[17] If individualism, egalitarianism and liberalism (a weak state) are highly conducive to economic development, Japan has been more disadvantaged than most nations. Comparatively, it is still status conscious (the vernacular language and social relations are particularly hierarchical), politically centralized and, above all, by Western standards, collectivity orientated and particularistic (group centred).

Few Westerners, other than scholars, are knowledgeable about the reorganization of Japan. The record of the country's mid-nineteenth-century barons, that brilliant group of oligarchs who took over the country determined to modernize it, makes that of any group of communist rulers seem like indifferent bumblers. The changes which occurred in Japan from the 1860s on were among the most remarkable societal transformations that have ever occurred. The barons planned a sociological transformation using Emperor Meiji to legitimate it.[18]

The Meiji planners were faced with the need to reorganize the status system. In a feudal agrarian society, banking and other commercial activities were held in low repute. This had been true in Europe where merchants, even when wealthy, were looked down upon by the feudal rulers. They were necessary, but they were not considered equals by the aristocracy. The Meiji elite realized that Japan had to encourage commerce and industry, the pursuit of profits. The populace, and the elite as well, had to regard business pursuits as important and worthy occupations. The solution was to foster the merger of aristocratic and business statuses by encouraging the lowest aristocratic stratum, the *samurai*, to become businessmen. This was possible since the *samurai* had been functionless even before the end of feudalism.[19]

The Meiji transformation highlights the widely discrepant roles of the state in developed societies. The ideological heritage of Japan, derivative from a post-feudal alliance of throne and altar, engenders a positive sense of the role of government, the same as a somewhat similar background has produced in much of Europe. Industrialism in Japan, as in Imperial Germany, was planned for by the government, indicating that Japan has been less unique in this respect than many now believe.[20] Thorstein Veblen, writing in 1915, noted these developments in terms which resemble recent writings:

> It is in this unique combination of a high-wrought spirit of feudalistic fealty and chivalric honor with the material efficiency given by the modern technology that the strength of the Japanese nation lies. In this respect ... the position of the Japanese government is *not unique* except in the eminent degree of its successful operation. The several governments of Europe are also ... endeavoring similarly to exploit the modern state of the industrial arts by recourse to the servile patriotism of the common man.[21]

The 'evolution of Japan', as Emile Durkheim stressed, corresponded in many ways to European 'social evolution. We have passed through almost the same phases.'[22] Norman Jacobs, Carmi Schooler and Ken'ichi Tominaga emphasize that feudalism and consequent statist centralization facilitated industrialization in Japan and Europe.[23] The never-feudal, classically liberal (*laissez-faire*) United States developed with much less government involvement in the economy than almost all other presently industrialized countries, making it truly exceptional.

The Ministry of International Trade and Industry (MITI) has continued the tradition of guidance set by the Meiji economic planners.[24] MITI's contemporary 'approach is anticipatory, preventive, and aimed at positively structuring the market in ways that improve the likelihood that industry-specific goals will be achieved'. The Ministry views the operations of a 'pure' market economy as flawed, in part because *laissez-faire* ideology entails the pursuit of narrow interests, and thus a lack of attention to 'collective interests ... and ... national goals'.[25] Conversely, the classically liberal, *laissez-faire*, anti-statist ideology is the political tradition of the United States.[26] The American polity stands out in resisting state leadership in the economic arena.[27] In contrast to the Japanese experience, the government 'tends to deal primarily with failures after they have occurred. ... [It] suggests a preference for leaving the market alone unless there is tangible evidence of a breakdown. ... Whereas Americans are content to let the chips fall where they may, the Japanese prefer to remove as much of the element of uncertainty from the market processes' as possible.[28] In an exaggerated sense, the Japanese economy may be described as a form of market socialism, or, as Shin-ichi Nakazawa, a popular social critic, comments: 'It's as if Japan has a kind of Communistic capitalism, or state socialism without the socialism.'[29] Chalmers Johnson describes the system as a 'different kind of capitalism', one which operates in 'ways that neither Adam Smith nor Marx would recognize or understand', one which is fundamentally different from the American.[30]

Although this chapter deals almost exclusively with comparisons between the United States and Japan, it should be noted that most European countries fall in between, so they are more like Japan than is the United States, but more like America than is Japan. As Ronald Dore notes in concluding a book comparing Britain and Japan: 'In the dimension ... which I have called "individualism-collectivism", "individualism-groupism", the United States and Japan stand at opposite ends, with Britain somewhere in the middle.'[31]

The culturist group or consensus model of Japanese society and the individualist and conflict model of American society, which are followed by much of the literature and are employed in this chapter, have been criticized by some scholars. They suggest that others, including the structuralist, stratification, social exchange (focusing on the emphasis on reciprocity and gifts) models, provide alternative ways to conceptualize the two nations. But these are not mutually exclusive approaches.[32] Nations develop new institutions, patterns of acting, which fit into their organizing principles. Receptivity to particular modes of behaviour is a function of the larger value system. Quality circles invented in the United States, premised on group co-operation, took hold in Japan, not in America. Clearly, while it is possible to organize the analysis of any society along a variety of lines, it is necessary for comparative societal analysis to focus on organizing principles or values which encourage insight into sources of variation with other systems.

Societies are characterized by both ends of analytical polarities. A society is not either group-orientated or individualistic, or ascriptive or egalitarian, or consensual or not.[33] All societies are marked by stratification, conflict and consensus. There is considerable individualism in Japan as well as particularism (group orientation) in the United States. Such concepts must be treated in a comparative context, as measured by relative rankings; that is, as more or less. Viewed in such a fashion, Japan, as noted above, appears to be the most group-orientated culture among developed societies; the United States is the most individualistic. Harumi Befu has suggested as an alternative model for Japan a social exchange one. He notes correctly that the Japanese stress the need to repay all obligations, indebtedness to others who may have helped out or given favours of any kind; while Americans feel less impelled to act in such ways, especially when to do so may create the impression of cronyism, of special favours in return for 'bribes'.[34]

Duty and Obligation

A fundamental difference between Japan and the United States lies in the fact that the Japanese governing elite made a conscious effort to merge the traditional with the modern. The Japanese have continued to uphold values and institutions which, from the perspective of Western market economics analysis, make little sense. They maintain a society in which deference and hierarchy are important, in which there is a 'continuing ethos of patrimonial relations [derivative] from Japan's feudal past'.[35] In theory, the person does not exist as an individual, but only as a member of certain larger groups: family, school, community, company, nation.[36] A 1990 Japanese government study of American and Japanese high school students concludes that, unlike the situation in the United States,

child rearing in Japan, the educational system, the style of education play against individualism. Rote learning is favoured over a creative approach to study. In addition, the Japanese do not want to STAND OUT as individuals. The proverb about the nail sticking up which must be pounded down implies that the individual who behaves in an individualistic way, is significantly different from the group will be punished and not rewarded.[37]

The continuity in the American emphasis on individuality and the Japanese on conformity to the group may be seen in the cross-national variation in polls taken in 1989 which asked respondents to react to the statement: 'It is boring to live like other people.' Over two-thirds, 69 per cent, of the Americans agreed that conforming is tedious, compared to 25 per cent of the Japanese.[38]

The Japanese, whenever possible, seek to avoid individual responsibility. Notions of duty and obligation constantly come through in conversations with Japanese.[39] They have an obligation to each other and to the institutions of which they are a part. Individuals are indebted to their parents, teachers, employer, state. They must repay all favours, even casual ones. Gifts are exchanged frequently as a way of maintaining social relationships, of meeting and developing obligations.

Psychologist Janet Spence, in explaining how 'the Japanese character differs profoundly from the American one', notes that contrasting socialization processes result in sharp variations in ego, with individualism here leading 'to a sense of self with a sharp boundary that stops at one's skin and clearly demarks self from non-self'. For the Japanese, the *me* becomes merged with the we, and the reactions of others to one's behaviors gain priority over one's own evaluations'. These differences are related to the varying values and institutions of the two nations.

> These contrasting senses of self in the two societies are produced by and lead to differing emphases on rights versus obligations, on autonomy versus personal sacrifice, and on the priority of the individual versus that of the group – differences that have broad ramifications for the structure of political, economic, and social institutions.[40]

According to psychological studies, the development of these distinct cultural identities begins in infancy. After noting 'sharply different styles of caretaking' in the two societies, William Caudill and Carmi Schooler comment: '[I]t would appear that in America the mother views her baby, at least potentially, as a separate and autonomous being who should learn to do and think for himself. ... In Japan, in contrast to America, the mother views her baby much more as an extension of herself, and psychologically the boundaries between them are blurred.'[41] A report on comparative surveys of children aged seven to eleven indicates that when questioned 'whether their mothers treated them "more like a grown-up or a baby", 65 per cent of the American children answered "more like a grown-up", compared to only 10 per cent of the Japanese children'.[42] A similar cross-national view of the parent–child relationship is found in the answers samples of fathers gave in 1986 to the question: 'Do you try to treat your child like an adult as much as possible?' An over-whelming majority of American fathers, 79 per cent, replied 'Yes', compared to less than half, 43 per cent, of Japanese.[43] The same survey inquired of children aged 10 to 15 years: 'When you and your father disagree, does he listen to your opinion?' In tandem with the responses of the fathers, the majority of American offspring, 72.5 per cent, said, 'Yes, he does', compared to 45 per cent of the Japanese.[44] And when asked: 'What does your father usually do when you do something bad?' twice the proportion, 37 per cent, of the Americans chose the response, 'He doesn't get upset but tries to talk to me', contrasted to 18 per cent of the Japanese young people.[45] The latter were more likely than Americans aged 10 to 15 years to continue the pattern when dealing with younger siblings. Only 36 per cent of the Japanese, against 56 per cent of the Americans, said they would allow 'a younger child [who] wanted to watch some other [TV] program' to do so even when the older one would like to see another one.[46]

The strength of Japanese group allegiance is strangely and starkly illustrated by the Japanese prisoners of war who offered to engage in espionage against their homeland during the Second World War. 'The prisoners became excellent spies. Once they had changed ingroup, having been taken prisoner against the explicit instructions of their superiors, they no longer defined the self as Japanese'.[47] This behaviour, when compared to the intense sense of duty and com-mitment of kamikaze fighter pilots, seems to indicate that motivat-ing ideology is of secondary importance to the basic fact of group cohesion.

Ironically, the Japanese emphasis on obligation and loyalty to membership groups appears to result in a lower level of civic con-sciousness, a lesser willingness to help individuals or institutions to whom no obligation exists, than in the more individualistic America.[48] I have been told by Japanese that they are not supposed to assist strangers unless they are in very serious difficulty, since the person assisted will then have a new obligation which s/he does not want. Such reports are congruent with opinion poll findings. Youth surveys (ages 18–24) have been conducted in different countries by the Japanese Youth Development Office of the Department of Public Affairs. In 1977, 1983 and 1988 the Office asked: 'Suppose you meet a man lost and trying to find his way. What would you do?' Over half, from 51 to 60 per cent, of the Americans chose the answer 'Ask him if he needs help', while less than a third, 32 to 26 per cent, of the Japanese gave the same response.[49] Similar cross-national differences were reported in the study of 10–15 year-olds in 1986. They were asked: 'If you saw a person with more luggage or packages than he or she could comfortably handle, would you offer to help him or her even if you didn't know him or her?' Over three-fifths, 63 per cent, of the American young people said they would, while only a quarter, 26 per cent, of the Japanese would do the same.[50]

American parents are much more likely than Japanese ones to report that they try to teach their children to help those in need and to follow civic rules. A 1981 comparative survey conducted for the Prime Minister's Office in Japan, based on interviews with parents of children under 15 years old, reports that over two-thirds, 70 per cent, of Americans were instructed to 'care for the elderly and the handi-capped', compared to one-third, 33.5 per cent, of the Japanese. The corresponding figures for 'not to litter in parks and on roads' were 66 per cent for Americans and 33 for Japanese; for 'to wait one's turn in line', the percentages were 44 for Americans and 19 for Japanese.[51]

Change and Stability

A detailed review of the literature on Japanese uniqueness, inherently comparative like that on American exceptionalism, suggests major differences in structures, cultural styles and values, variations which 'are more or less identical with differences between industrial and preindustrial (feudal) civilization in the West'.[52] Japanese social scientists have been monitoring their values and 'national character' through survey research since the 1950s. Their findings indicate 'that no change in basic values has occurred in Japan. This evidence challenges the evolutionary view which posits the Western pattern as the end point, the culmination of societal development. Alternative patterns of family and human relations appear to be enduring rather than transitional.'[53] The studies stress that the 'central Confucian and Samurai values such as seniority, loyalty or priority of the group are still dominant'[54] Tatsuko Suzuki concludes from reviewing the Japanese experience that in spite of 'institutional changes ... in the areas of economics and politics ... the systems of belief in Japan owe their relative stability to the stability in the structure both of family relations and of supplementary, informal social relations'.[55] These findings seemingly reiterate Veblen's, reached in 1915, that it is 'only in respect of its material ways and means, its technological equipment and information, that the "New Japan" differs from the old'.[56]

Various reports on Japanese values indicate, however, that while many attitudes and values appear stable, a number have changed considerably between the 1950s and the 1980s. Some of these changes seem to involve an acceptance of Western values. For example, the proportion of Japanese who would 'adopt a child to continue the family line' (traditional behaviour for those without children) declined steadily over eight National Character surveys taken between 1953 and 1988, from 73 to 28 per cent. Those who say the prime minister should visit the Imperial Shrine annually moved down from 50 per cent in 1953 to 16 in 1988.[57] Asked repeatedly what sex they would choose to be if born again, the percentage of women who would prefer to be men fell off in linear fashion from 64 in 1958 to 34 in 1988. The proportion of men, however, who opt for a masculine rebirth has been constant at 90 per cent from 1958 on. In three American polls taken between 1946 and 1977, the same and unchanging percentage, also around 90, of American males preferred to be born in the same sex. American women, however, have consistently shown a much greater desire to retain their gender than Japanese, with the percentage wanting to be of the opposite one going down from 26 in 1946 to 17 in 1958 and 9 in 1977.[58]

Conversely, respondents to the National Character surveys, as well as to the youth studies, have become more traditional and less Western in their answers to many other questions. The varying patterns have been brought out in a review of the National Character studies by Scott Flanagan, in which he summarized the patterns of change for seven items, grouped by him into four value dimensions, about which respondents were asked in the six surveys taken between 1963 and 1988.[59] These are presented in table 4.1 below, in which the scores are the percentage differences between traditional and modern responses.

As is evident in the table, two items, 1 and 3, reveal changes in the direction of modernity, while four others, 4 to 7, show shifts toward more traditional beliefs. The one which seemed to produce the largest move toward modernity, 2, is a very dubious indicator in my judgement, since Flanagan classified the response, 'study earnestly and make a name for yourself' as traditional and 'work hard and get

Table 4.1: Patterns of change over 25 years across value dimensions

Year	Deference I-1	I-3	Conformity I-4	I-5	Personalism I-6	I-7	Survival I-2
			Traditional–modern scores				
1963	24	0	−8	12	−72	4	28
1968	26	−8	−8	10	−76	16	34
1973	38(b-34)	8	−10	6	−72	16	54
1978	28(c)	0	−20	−16	−80	2	50
1983	30(c)	−10	−26	−14	−82	−2	58
1988	34(c)	8	−20	−14	−80	−4	62
			Time change scores				
	10	8	−12	−26	−6	−8	34

NOTES   Item content is as follows: I-1 Leader vs. people; I-2 Enjoy oneself vs. self-denial, I-3 Individual vs. nation; I-4 Social obligation vs. individual freedom; I-5 Personal choice vs. follow custom; I-6 Specific vs. diffuse relations with boss; I-7 Merit vs. connections in hiring. (See below for full content and coding of items). There is a discontinuity in the time series on Item-1 owing to a shift in item format from a middle category to a forced dichotomy in the 1973b version of the question, which appears to depress the relative proportions of modern responses compared to the traditional format that was asked in that year. The dichotomized format was continued in the c version of the question beginning in 1978 but further word changes make it incomparable with the b version. Thus, the analysis of the I-1 type of change was carried only through 1973. The time change scores reported in this table ignore these changes and use the 1988 rather than the 1973 data in the computations. Traditional–modern scores were computed at each point by subtracting the percentages of responses classified as traditional from the percentages of those classified as modern, so that positive scores indicate predominantly modern responses.

Item content and coding
The item response categories are designated with a T if they were classified as traditional responses, M if they were considered modern responses, and U for unclassifiable if they could not be classified as traditional or modern.

Item-1   Some people say that if we get good political leaders, the best way to improve the country is for the people to leave everything to them, rather than for the people to discuss things among themselves. Do you agree with this?

    T – Agree
    M – Disagree
    U – Depends; other

Item-2   There are all sorts of attitudes toward life. Of those listed here, which one would you say comes closest to your feeling?

    T – Study earnestly and make a name for yourself.
    T – Resist all evils in the world and live a pure and just life.
    T – Never think of yourself; give everything in service of society.
    M – Don't think about money or fame; just live a life that suits your own tastes.
    M – Live each day as it comes, cheerfully and without worrying.
    U – Work hard and get rich.

Item-3 Which one of the following opinions do you agree with?

T – If Japan as a whole improves, then and only then can individuals be made happy.

M – If individuals are made happy, then and only then will Japan as a whole improve.

U – Improving Japan and making individuals happy are the same thing.

Item-4 If you were asked to choose two out of this list that are important, which two would you pick?

T – Being dutiful to one's parents.

T – Repaying social obligations.

M – Respecting individual rights.

M – Respecting freedom.

Item-5 If you think a thing is right, do you think you should go ahead and do it even if it is contrary to custom, or do you think you are less apt to make a mistake if you follow a custom?

T – Follow custom.

M – Go ahead.

U – Depends.

Item-6 Suppose you are working in a firm. There are two types of department chiefs. Which of these two would you prefer to work under?

T – A man who sometimes demands extra work in spite of rules against it but looks after you personally in matters not connected with the work.

M – A man who always sticks to the work rules and never demands any unreasonable work but never does anything for you personally in matters not connected with the work.

Item-7 Suppose you were the president of a company. The company decides to employ one person and then carries out an employment examination. The supervisor in charge reports to you, saying, 'Mr X (the son of parents who had been our benefactors) got the second highest grade. But I believe either he or the candidate who got the highest grade would be satisfactory. What shall we do?'

T – Hire the son of your benefactor

M – Hire the one with the highest grade.

SOURCE: Scott C. Flanagan, 'Value cleavages, contextual influences, and the vote'. In Scott C. Flanagan et al. (eds), *The Japanese Voter*, New Haven, Conn.: Yale University Press, 1991, pp. 97–9.

rich' as unclassifiable. I would have put these in the modern category, while the two choices which he considers modern appear to me as unclassifiable. I have, therefore, left item 2 out of the discussion, since I think it is irrelevant.

Ignoring item 2 leaves us with four shifts toward traditionalism and two moves in the modernity direction. All movements except item 5, which deals with following custom even when it is wrong, are relatively small. Flanagan's results indicate that the few early postwar shifts toward modernity began 'to halt or reverse in the 1970s, as a result of several factors'.

The 1973 Arab oil boycott sent shock waves through the Japanese
economy; the oil crisis diverted attention from the environmental,
quality-of-life, and participation issues that had come to the forefront
in the 1960s and refocused national attention on economic issues,
leading to a resurgence in conservatism. This period also coincided
with a renewed interest in Nihonjinron (essays on what it means to
be Japanese) as the Japanese began to reassess the enduring aspects
of their culture in light of the previous three decades of massive
importation of goods, ideas, and practices from the West. Toward the
end of the 1970s this renewed interest in the enduring traditions
of Japanese culture was reinforced by a growing nationalism and cultural
self-satisfaction with Japan's new international standing and dramatic
economic success.[60]

If we look at the specific content of items 4 to 7, as well as results
from other studies, we find further evidence for the continued strength
of traditional values. Thus, an increasing lack of confidence in
science, certainly a modern institution, appears to characterize the
Japanese, while Americans retain it. The belief that there is a loss
in 'the richness of human feelings as a result of the development
of science' increased from 30 per cent in 1953 to 47 in the National
Character studies of 1988. These results are supported by the findings
of 1980–1 World Values study, which asked: 'In the long run, do
you think that scientific advances we are making will help or harm
mankind?' It found the majority of Japanese critical or fearful of
science, while most Americans reacted positively. The latter were
distributed 56 per cent help to 22 harm, while only 22 per cent of
the former replied help to 59 harm.[61] Similar cross-national results
with comparable magnitudes of difference in response rates were
obtained to a number of questions seeking evaluation of the benefits
or damages derivative from the development of science and technology in surveys conducted in 1991 by the Japanese Science and
Technology Agency. For example, five-sixths of Americans, 85
per cent, compared to 54 per cent of Japanese, agreed that 'Scientific
development makes my daily life healthier, more safe and com-
fortable'. The Agency also reported much higher interest in 'news
and topics on science and technologies' in the United States in 1990
than in Japan in 1991.[62] Interest by Japanese young people in
science and technology is declining. It fell from 67 to 41 per cent
between 1977 and 1991. Studies of the occupational aspirations
of Japanese high-school students found that in spite of the fact
that 'the employment rate for science and engineering [university]
graduates is very high ... High school students are steering away
from the science and engineering disciplines'.[63]

Other responses in the National Character research also suggest a revival of traditionalism. Thus when asked to choose the 'two most important values', those answering 'respect individual rights' fell off from 49 per cent in 1958 to 36 in 1988. Those listing 'filial piety', being dutiful to one's parents, increased from 60 per cent to 71 over the same period, while 'respect freedom' declined slightly from 46 per cent in 1963 to 42 in 1983. And 'on the rather delicate question of whether or not the Japanese feel they are superior to the Westerners ... those who believe they are superior increased from 20% in 1953 to a massive 47% in 1968 ... [and to an even higher 55 percent in 1983]. The pattern observed here indicates the renewed self-confidence of the Japanese ....'[64]

Perhaps the best example of the strength of traditional practices, even when they appear dysfunctional for an economically developed society, is the nation's refusal to adopt the system of street names and consecutive numbers on buildings that exists in the West. Japanese streets are not named or numbered in the same systematic way, and house numbers refer to the order of construction in a given district. Strangers are expected to find their way through use of local maps or directions from a nearby landmark, such as a railway station. The Japanese had an opportunity to change after the Second World War when the American occupation forces assigned alphabetical or numerical names to streets. But this system, apparently so much more functional for commerce in a big city like Tokyo, was largely discarded as soon as the occupation ended.

Seemingly, in spite of the tremendous strides Japan has made toward technological modernization, higher self-esteem is leading toward a regained 'confidence in tradition', to a 'return to traditional values'.[65] These developments in turn should enhance the differences between Japan and the United States and other Western countries. The variations which have been suggested in the literature between the Japanese and American belief systems are summed up in table 4.2, a modified version of one presented by Peter Dale.

Many Japanese tend to agree with the stereotype that they are a less universalistic and more particularistic society than America. Thus, when asked by the Nippon Research organization in 1990 whether Japanese are more 'intolerant of other races', 40 per cent said they were, while only 13 per cent thought Americans were more intolerant than Japanese. A plurality of Japanese (35.5 per cent) replied their countrymen are more disposed to 'put priority on [matters concerning] one's own country' (nationalistically self-centred), compared to 22.5 per cent who believe the Americans are more nationally orientated. More Japanese, 33 per cent, see themselves as 'selfish',

Table 4.2: Differences between America and Japan

America	Japan
A. Society (*Gesellschaft*)	A. Community (*Gemeinschaft*)
B. Individualism	B. Groupism contextualism
C. Horizontality	C. Verticality
D. Egalitarianism	D. Hierarchy
E. Contract	E. 'Kintract'
F. 'Private'	F. 'Public'
G. 'Guilt'	G. 'Shame'
H. Urban-cosmopolitan	H. Rural-exclusive
I. Rights	I. Duties
J. Independence (inner-directed)	J. Dependence (other-directed)
K. Universality	K. Particularity-uniqueness
L. Heterogeneity	L. Homogeneity
M. Absolutism	M. Relativism
N. Rupture	N. Harmony, continuity
O. Artifice	O. Nature
P. Abstraction	P. Phenomenalism, concreteness
Q. Donative/active	Q. Receptive/reactive
R. Open	R. Closed

SOURCE: Adapted and modified from Peter N. Dale, *The Myth of Japanese Uniqueness*. New York: St Martin's Press, 1986, pp. 44, 51.

while only 12 per cent identify Americans this way. In each case, Americans answering the same questions for the NBC News/*Wall Street Journal* poll are more likely to give the converse response: to think themselves more tolerant of other races than the Japanese (by 46 to 40 per cent), less nationalistic (by 64 to 24 per cent) and less selfish (by 44 to 33 per cent).

Conflict and Consensus

The United States is a much more discordant society than Japan and, to a lesser extent, much of Western Europe. The combination of capitalist and Protestant sectarian values, to be found only in America, encourages conflict and moralism. As the purest example of a bourgeois nation, America follows the competitive norms of the marketplace in union-management and other relationships. Actors seek to win as much as they can and will ride roughshod over opponents if possible. As noted, American unions have been reluctant to co-operate with executives on management problems or to take responsibility for corporate welfare. They are described in the comparative labour literature as 'adversarial', as distinct from the behaviour of unions in post-feudal more social democratic corporatist nations.[66] They have pressed to secure as much from management as their strength permits. (In recent years, of course, their loss of membership, from one-third of the employed labour force in the mid-1950s to less than one-sixth in the early 1990s, has hampered their ability to gain concessions.) Unionists among the Japanese belong to company-wide labour organizations which show concern for the company's needs, not nationwide ones which include all in the same trade or industry, as in America. American unions historically have not been concerned about the welfare of specific companies. Japanese workers have been much less prone to strike than American unionists, although the emphasis on hierarchy has fostered Marxist and socialist beliefs among them, as it has among Europeans.[67] A '*de facto* incomes policy has grown organically out of a routinized set of norms, procedures, and institutions developed over years of interaction between labour and management'. The co-operative and 'self-regulating nature of labor-management relations has spared the Japanese government from being engulfed by the consuming task of binding up economic and social wounds following outbursts of labor unrest'.[68]

Related to the emphasis on obligation (exchange relations) is the ideal of a consensual society. 'The ideal solution of a conflict ... [is] not a total victory for one side and a humiliating defeat for the other, but an accommodation by which winner and loser could co-exist without too much loss of face.'[69] Labour relations reflect the more general patterns. 'Japanese dispute processing structures tend to minimize adversarialness. ... They parallel Japanese social structure in the sense that they tend to treat people as connected rather than separated, and to encourage solutions that minimize conflict and reduce the probability that relations between disputants will be permanently severed by the dispute.'[70] When conflict occurs, persons and groups linked by institutional relationships seek agreement. Majorities do not simply outvote minorities in parliament. Those who can win the vote (pretend to) allow their opponents to influence the final outcome. Japanese politicians, as one once told me, deliberately introduce sections of legislation which they do not want so they can yield them in the final negotiations with the minority opposition. In American election contests, the minority is voted down. The electoral system invariably produces a recognizable winner and loser even when the difference in votes between them is small. The Japanese method, on the other hand, encourages minority representation by a number of parties via the election of members of parliament representing disparate groups in the same multi-member constituency. But the myth of consensus, the rituals of agreement, remains dominant.[71]

In America, Protestant sectarian moralism helps to produce adversarialness, since political and social controversies are more likely to be perceived as non-negotiable moral issues than as conflicts of material interests which can be compromised. The United States always goes to war against Satan, and as a result demands unconditional surrender from the enemy.[72] Japanese religious traditions reinforce the need for consensus and compromise. They are synchronistic rather than sectarian. Many Japanese are Buddhists and Shintoists, praying at the temples of the former and the shrines of the latter. America, however, has been the most 'religiously fecund nation in the world', as the sects have divided. Unlike America, 'Japan never possessed a dogmatic religion which makes a sharp distinction between right and wrong. ... None of ... [Japan's] religions had a stern, omnipotent God. ... In a situation where no one fought for God or against Satan, it was easy to reach an accommodation once the fighting was over.'[73]

The varying consequences of a society which stresses obligation to groups as a major virtue and one which emphasizes individual success and rights are also reflected in the sharply different rates of crime. In America, the emphasis is on winning, 'by fair means if possible, and by foul means if necessary'.[74] The Japanese crime rate is much lower than the American on a per capita basis. As a result, while Americans worry about walking the streets of their cities, 'Japan is one of the few major nations – perhaps the only one – where one can walk the streets of its large cities late at night and feel in no danger.'[75] The serious crime rate in the United States is over four times the total crime rate of Japan. Only 1.1 per 100,000 of the Japanese population were victims of murder in 1989, compared with 8.7 Americans; for rape the relative rates were 1.3 and 38.1. The 1989 data were even more striking for robbery: 1.3 cases per 100,000 population in Japan, contrasted with 233.0 in the United States, while for larceny they were 1203 and 5077. As with other measures, European rates fall in between, closer to the Japanese than to the American.[76] As Hamilton and Sanders note: 'Japan and the United States occupy the opposite poles in the distribution of violent and property crimes among the major capitalist countries.'[77]

The trans-Pacific rates are not converging. Between 1960 and 1987 they increased in the United States for homicide (from 5.1) and larceny (from 1726), while in Japan they fell for murder (from 3.0) and remained constant for larceny.[78] As of 1986, 42 Japanese out of every 100,000 were in prison, as compared with 158 Americans.[79] Japan has a much smaller police force, about 60 per cent the size of America's in per capita terms, and many fewer lawyers.

There is frequent and much-exaggerated reference to the enormous difference between the number of lawyers in the two countries, 13,000 in Japan and around 800,000 in the United States. The second figure is correct: America has one-third of the world's practising attorneys; but the first refers only to *bengoshi* who, however, are the licensed litigators (barristers) handling 'only a small part of Japan's lawyering'. In fact, the country has about '125,000 suppliers of legal services', including all sorts of specialized persons dealing with particular aspects of law, and 'in-house corporate legal staffs filled with law graduates who never bothered to pass the bar exam'.[80] Adjusting for these results shows a difference of three to one, 312 lawyers per 100,000 for the United States and 102 for Japan.[81] There are many fewer tort cases in Japan; as a result, the 'tort tax' on business and the professions is much lower there. It is estimated that 'liability-loss payments in America totalled $117 billion in 1987, about 2.5% of the GNP. Japan's cost was eight times less, about 0.3%.'[82]

The vast differences have been explained by variations in structures, rules and culture, though the first two are in large part an outgrowth of the third. As a post-revolutionary new society, the United States has lacked the traditional mechanisms of social control and respect for authority that mark cultures 'based on traditional obligations which were, or had been, to some extent mutual'.[83] The American emphasis on individualism is therefore associated with the universalistic cash nexus and legally enforceable contractual agreements, a pattern which in comparative terms has continued to the present. Agreements among business firms are spelled out in much less detail in Japan than in America. Contracts are not written in anticipation of possible future litigation. It is assumed that if conditions change so as to benefit one party against the other, the two will modify the agreement, including adjustments in price. The Japanese 'prefer mediation. Even when suits are brought before a court, the judges prefer to use conciliation in order to avoid humiliating the loser.'[84] Legal informality, rather than litigiousness characterizes the Japanese approach to law.[85] On the other hand, the United States has, in Weberian terms, a legal-rational culture in which highly contractual, rather than traditional, mechanisms are emphasized, resulting in a very much higher rate of litigation. Tocqueville noted the contractual and litigious character of Americans in the 1830s; and writing in the 1990s, John Haley notes: 'In no other industrial society is legal regulation as extensive or coercive as in the United States or as confined and as weak as in Japan.' [86]

Japan has relied much more than the United States on informal mechanisms of social control, that is, on the sense of shame or loss of face, not only for individuals but for their families and other groups with which they are closely identified, including business. An Australian criminologist John Braithwaite explains the unique low rate of crime in Japan as a product of the 'cultural traditions of shaming wrongdoers, including an effective coupling of shame and punishment'.[87] Anthropologist George DeVos concludes 'that most social evidence points toward the greater continuing influence of informal social control and social cohesion within the Japanese groups than is found within their western counterparts'.[88] A 1983 survey of the opinions of national samples of 10–15 year olds, which inquired as to their having engaged in various socially disapproved activities, found only 28 per cent of the Japanese children admitting to such behaviour in contrast to 80 per cent of the Americans.

Behavioural as well as attitudinal data show that Japanese have been much less prone to violate traditional norms with respect to marital continuity than Americans, even though the proportions voicing discontent with the relationship are similar. Opinion poll data from the 1980s show Japanese much more opposed than Americans to divorce. The cross-sections of mothers of teenagers were asked whether they believed 'that a man and a wife, even if they want a divorce, should consider their children's future and remain married'. The question yielded overwhelming majority responses in both countries, but in opposite directions. Almost three-quarters of those in Japan said they should stay married, while three-fifths, 61 per cent, in the United States replied that they should get divorced.[89] The divorce rate, as of 1988, was much lower in Japan: 1.25 per 1000, than in the United States: 4.80 per 1000.[90]

Comparative surveys indicate that the Japanese are much more consciously committed to following the rules or customs than to innovating, while Americans take the opposite tack. In 1978, cross-sections interviewed for the Japanese National Character studies in both countries were asked to respond to the following question:

If you think a thing is right, do you think you should go ahead and do it even if it is contrary to usual custom, or do you think you are less apt to make a mistake if you follow custom?
  1. Go ahead even if contrary
  2. Depends
  3. Follow custom.

Fully three-quarters, 76 per cent, of the Americans replied 'go ahead' even if you have to violate traditional custom, as compared to less than one-third, 30 per cent, of the Japanese. Even when the issue does not involve illegitimate or socially disapproved activities, Japanese prefer to adhere to the rules, while Americans will innovate.[91]

Americans are much more likely than Japanese to say they will do anything necessary to get ahead individually. A majority of the former, 52 per cent, agreed in 1989 that 'I will do whatever I can in order to succeed', compared to only 14 per cent of the latter. Comparable differences were reported for the responses to the statement: 'I want to be successful no matter how much pain might be involved in doing so.' Over three-fifths, 63 per cent, of the Americans and 36.5 per cent of the Japanese agreed.[92]

Work and the Economy

Although a highly urbanized industrial nation, Japan retains many of the informal practices, norms and clientelistic relations of manorial societies.[93] Companies, particularly large ones, are obligated to their employees, for example to keep them employed and to establish pension funds, and are quite paternalistic: from arranging marriages to school placement for the offspring of employees. The 'corporation is a social unit in which everyone has a role and a stake'.[94] Ideally, boards of directors are not supposed to emphasize the maximization of profits. 'Many senior Japanese managers ... feel at least as obligated to the workers as to the owners of the corporation.'[95] Job supervisors even arrange marriages.

Employees are expected to be loyal to their companies; as indicated in table 4.3 the survey evidence confirms the generalization that employees in Japan are much less prone to change jobs than employees in America.[96]

These cross-national variations have also remained among the three samples of youth, with no change occurring between 1977 and 1988. Close to three-quarters, 72 per cent, of the Japanese said they were still in their first job, a reply given by only one quarter, 24 per cent, of the Americans. Almost a third of the latter reported having held four or more positions; only 1 per cent of the Japanese did the same.[97]

Some challenge the notion that prolonged employment and low separation rates in Japan have cultural components by the contention 'that life-time employment is only a large-firm phenomenon'. In

Table 4.3: Estimates of the number of jobs held by males over a lifetime, Japan and the United States

| | All Jobs | | | |
| | OECD | | Hashimoto–Raisian | |
Age group	Japan 1977	United States 1981	Japan 1977	United States 1978
16–19	0.54	1.07	0.72	2.00
20–24	1.19	2.54	2.06	4.40
25–29	1.54	3.69	2.71	6.15
30–34	1.75	4.57	3.11	7.40
35–39	1.92	5.35	3.46	8.30
40–44	2.05	5.98	4.21	10.25
45–49	2.15	6.45	4.91	10.95
50–54	2.26	6.90	–	11.15
55–64	2.62	7.50	–	11.16

SOURCES: *OECD Employment Outlook*, September 1984, 63; M. Hashimoto and J. Raisian, 'Employment tenure and earning profiles in Japan and the United States'. *American Economic Review*, 75 (September 1985), 724, as reprinted in Masahiko Aoki, *Information, Incentives and Bargaining in the Japanese Economy*, Cambridge: Cambridge University Press, 1988, p. 61.

fact, however, research by Masanori Hashimoto and John Raisian and also by Robert Cole indicate that although 'job tenure is longer in large Japanese firms, it is quite long even in the tiny and small firms', much longer in all size groups than in American ones.[98]

Japanese clearly exhibit much stronger ties to their employers than Americans do. Cross-national interviews with samples of male workers in 1960 and 1976 found that the proportions who said that they think of their company as 'the central concern in my life and of greater importance than my personal life', or as 'a part of my life at least equal in importance to my personal life' were very much greater in Japan than in the United States in both years and increased in absolute terms in the former. The combined percentages for the two company commitment responses, in surveys taken 16 years apart, were 65 rising to 73 for Japanese workers, compared to 29 declining to 21 for the Americans. The Americans were much more likely to choose other categories defining their relations to their employers in instrumental terms, that is, less important than their personal lives. It seems that the Japanese changed toward favouring a deeper involvement with their company, while the Americans became even less enamoured of such a stance over the decade and a half between the two surveys.[99]

Varying emphases toward particularism in economic life are
evident in the responses to 1978 surveys in both countries, which
indicated that Japanese were much more likely than Americans to
prefer a work supervisor who 'looks after you personally in matters
not connected with work' by 87 to 50 per cent. The alternative
formulation favouring someone who 'never does anything for you
personally in matters not connected with work' was endorsed by
10 per cent of the Japanese and 47 per cent of the Americans.'[100]
The difference in particularistic expectations about the role of
supervisors is brought out most strongly in the responses by samples
of male workers in 1960 and 1976 to the question: 'When a worker
wishes to marry, I think his (her) supervisor should [pick from four
alternatives].' Close to three quarters, 71–74 per cent, of the
Americans chose the category, 'not to be involved in such a personal
matter', as contrasted to 7 going down to 5 per cent of the Japanese.
The dominant answer of the latter, 66 per cent rising to 80, was
'offer personal advice to the worker if requested', an answer given
by 20 per cent descending to 15 of the Americans.[101] Similar cross-
national differences are reported by the World Youth Surveys when
they inquired in 1972, 1983 and 1988: 'Suppose you work under
a superior, do you think it is a good idea to have social contact with
him after hours?' The percentage replying, 'No' changed slightly
from 25.5 to 28 among the Japanese, a response given by a much
larger segment of Americans: 42 to 46 per cent.[102] Japanese workers
are, in fact, much more likely to socialize 'outside of work' with their
supervisors and managers, as well as with co-workers.[103]

The continued Japanese preference for particularistic relations is
also exhibited in the reactions to a question posed in 1973 and 1978
asking them to choose between working for a firm which 'paid good
wages, but where they did nothing like organizing outings and
sports days for the employees' recreation' and a 'firm with a family-
like atmosphere which organized outings and sports days, even if
the wages were a little bit less'. The Japanese respondents to both
surveys overwhelmingly chose the particularistic alternative, even
if it involved less pay, by 74 per cent in 1973 and 78 in 1978.[104]

Japanese seemingly work harder for, and are more loyal to, their
employers than Americans.[105] A review of the relevant behavioural
evidence appears to document this generalization thoroughly:

> Japanese workers put in more time on the job per week than American
> workers (43 vs. 37 hours) ... unexcused absenteeism is generally so
> low as to seem nonexistent; strike activity is lower in Japan than in
> the U.S. ... and unions cooperate with management in achieving
> corporate goals and in carrying out company programs ....[106]

Studies of leisure and family involvements, both attitudinal and behavioural, agree that Japanese devote less time than Americans to leisure pursuits and are more disposed to emphasize work over leisure or home life generally. Thus Lincoln and Kalleberg found 'only 35 percent of our Japanese sample (vs. 70 percent of the Americans) rate family life as more important than work responsibilities'.[107] The Japanese (49 per cent) were also more likely than Americans (28 per cent) to agree with the statement: 'Employees shouldn't take time off when things are busy, even though they have a right to take time off.'[108] A 1980 survey by NHK (the public broadcasting system) found that more than a quarter, 27 per cent, of Americans gave the highest priority to leisure activities, while 18 per cent of Japanese did. The World Youth Study reported that when asked in 1977, 1983 and 1988, 'Which do you find more worthwhile, work or something else?', two-thirds, 67–71 per cent, in the United States replied 'something other than work', as compared to around half, 49–57 per cent, of those in Japan.[109]

Behaviour corresponds to opinions. A survey-based comparison by the Leisure Development Center of Japan in 1989 of work and leisure in seven developed nations notes that the Japanese work the most and have the least time off. Two out of three Japanese employees work more than 45 hours a week. In every other country surveyed, the majority of workers spend less than 45 hours per week at their jobs. 'The American figure [for more] is 42.5 percent. As for weekend holidays, the most common pattern in Japan is one day off, and less than 20 percent of workers have two-day weekends every week. On the other hand ... 68 percent of Americans are assured two-day weekends every week.'[110] Not surprisingly, 'leisure participation is comparatively low in Japan. Japan was last in 23 – or more than half – of the [42 leisure activity] categories.'[111]

Although Japanese groups and firms are intensely competitive, individuals within them are not expected to be – nor do they want to be – in overt competition with colleagues in seeking to get ahead. Promotion and salary increases within Japanese firms tend to be a function of seniority much more than in American ones, including among white-collar employees and executives, although judgements of ability do play an important role.[112] Seniority is even more important and strictly respected within the civil service, where political appointees do not intervene in personnel matters.[113] Chie Nakane points out: 'In the West, merit is given considerable importance, while in Japan the balance goes the other way. In other words, in Japan in contrast to other societies, the provisions for the recognition of merit are somewhat weaker, and the social order is institutionalized largely by means of seniority.'[114] When national cross-sections of employed young adults (18 to 24 years of age) were asked in 1977, 1983 and 1988 for their preferred basis for promotions and pay increases, an average of 80 per cent of the Americans favoured giving more weight to performance than to seniority, compared to 36 per cent of the Japanese. Preference for seniority basically stayed constant from 1977 to 1988 at 46 to 44 per cent among the Japanese and 16 to 15 per cent for the American youth.[115]

The two World Values studies conducted in 1981–2 and 1990–1 also found that Americans are much more likely than Japanese to believe in merit pay; more of the latter are inclined to pay the same to all in a given type of work. Thus in the first survey, when asked whether a secretary who 'is quicker, more efficient and more reliable at her job' should be paid more than one of the same age who does less, over three-quarters of the Americans, 79 per cent, said the more useful one should be paid more, compared to 54 per cent of the Japanese.[116] The second survey asked respondents whether 'there should be greater incentives for individual effort', or should 'incomes be made more equal'. As in the response to the earlier question, the Americans favour greater emphasis on 'incentives' by 68 per cent compared to 47 for the Japanese.[117]

Surprisingly, however, much, though not all, of the comparative survey results dealing with work-related attitudes appear contradictory. On a subjective verbal level, different surveys have found Japanese are less work-orientated, less satisfied with their jobs and less positive in feelings about their companies than Americans.[118] James Lincoln and Arne Kalleberg, who have reported these inconsistencies between behavioural and survey findings, note, correctly I believe, that there are 'cultural biases operating to generate overly positive assessments of work life on the part of American employees and understatements by the Japanese'.[119]

The cultural biases are in part an 'apparent manifestation of Japanese collectivism and Western individualism ... [as in] the tendency for Japanese respondents to give average or non-committal answers, while Anglo-American respondents are somewhat more prone to take strong, even extreme stands on issues'.[120] Ronald Dore suggests that variations in 'average personality' also affect cross-national attitudes, such as 'a difference on a dimension which has cheerfulness and good-humored complacency at one pole and a worried earnestness and anxious questing for self-improvement on the other'. He believes this affects varying propensities to express job satisfaction.[121] Answers to questions about job satisfaction, working hard or ratings of employers are also relative; they are affected by conceptions of what hard work means, by expectations about a job or organization, by perceptions about fellow workers or supervisors. It has been argued that 'precisely because the Japanese subscribe to a strong work ethic ... that they are less likely to feel that their expectations have been met'.[122]

I can suggest other cultural dispositions which may affect differences in verbal responses. Japanese are not disposed to boast, to express positive judgements about themselves, a trait which extends to groups of which they are part, such as pride in country, on which they rank close to the bottom in international comparisons. Americans, conversely, are almost uninhibited in such terms. They lead the world in positive expressions about America.[123] Americans also show up as among the most optimistic people in Gallup Polls conducted in 30 countries, while the Japanese are among the least optimistic. The polls, taken annually near the end of each year from 1976 to 1987 and again in 1990, posed the following question: 'So far as you are concerned, do you think [next year] will be better or worse than [last year]?'[124] Even in December 1990 after the recession began, the United States was still in the lead, because 48 per cent of Americans, compared to only 23 per cent of the Japanese, who had not yet entered a recession, replied that next year would be better.

Individualism may also press Americans to give positive responses about satisfaction with job and company, while embeddedness in strong group allegiances reduces the propensity of the Japanese to answer in comparable terms. Since Americans believe in personal choice of jobs, schools and mates, a response that one does not like his/her situation raises the question: what is wrong with the individual? Why does he/she not quit? Japanese, in contrast, do not have the option to break from a group relationship. If he/she says that he/she does not like his/her spouse or company, there is no implication that there is something wrong with the respondent. Hence, Japanese will be much more outspoken than Americans about voicing negative feelings. Individualism constrains speech, group allegiances liberate.

Group-orientated commitments are weak in the United States where the religious tradition, linked to its Puritan origins, emphasizes individualism and personal rights. Bourgeois norms enjoin the same behaviour. Americans do not feel obligations, other than familial, if these conflict with the requirements of efficiency or income. They expect people to do their best for themselves, not for others.

Status Patterns

The dominant stratification orientations of the two societies are also quite different. America stresses equality: equality of opportunity, equality of respect, but not of income. As previously noted, Tocqueville suggested that Americans believe that individuals should give and receive respect because they are human beings. Everyone recognizes that inequality exists, but it is impolite to emphasize it in social relations. Tocqueville and others have even argued that personal service is un-American; though there are exceptions, Americans generally do not like to be servants or to use them.

In Japan, as the industrialized society most recently derivative from feudalism, hierarchy remains important in defining social relations. However, as will be noted in a subsequent section, there is much greater stress on reducing income inequality. Reischauer has written that no other people place a greater emphasis on status differentiation in social relationships than the Japanese.[125] Living in a relatively collectivist society, Japanese 'show much more status consciousness and accept [social] inequality to a greater extent than individualists', such as Americans.[126] Each person and institution has a place in the prestige order. The comparative surveys of youth aged 18–24 conducted in 1977, 1983 and 1988 found, in response to questions concerning the factors valued about a college education, that the Japanese were much more likely than their trans-Pacific counterparts to say 'having gone to a top ranking college' is to be valued by an average margin of 25 to 16 per cent, while Americans put much more emphasis than Japanese on 'school performance and school record' by 39 to 10 per cent. The proportion of Japanese who mentioned performance fell from 11 to 7 per cent over a decade, while it increased among Americans from 36 to 43 per cent.[127] The results of a detailed study of the relationship of college status and occupational attainment in Japan and the United States on a mass level challenges the thesis that educational credentialism is greater in Japan than in the United States. However, 'when we focus on the process of elite formation, a different picture emerges. *The linkage between the summit of educational stratification and top of the corporate managerial [and civil service] hierarchy appears to be much stronger in Japan than in the United States'.*[128]

Hierarchy is particularly evident in the Japanese use of words, many of which are laden with social status connotations. Japanese employ different terms in conversations with superiors, equals and inferiors. In this way, their language is one in which status determines how people talk to each other. When two people meet, they must be able to place one another in order to determine how to interact, although for a brief meeting persons who are unacquainted may use status-neutral terms. A friend of mine, an anthropologist at Stanford, tells of an experience during a stay in Japan as a visiting professor. He invited two Japanese colleagues, who did not know one another, to dinner. They devoted considerable time trying to place each other hierarchically. Not only would this determine the language they used to each other, but even who would walk through the door to the dining-room first. My friend could not get them to move to go in to dinner. At last, acting like a hungry, uncouth American, he literally shoved them into the dining room. To those who may think this story is unrepresentative, I submit the observation by Chie Nakane: 'In everyday affairs man who is not aware of relative ranking is not able to speak or even to sit or eat. When speaking, he is always expected to be ready with differentiated, delicate degrees of honorific expressions appropriate to the rank order between himself and the person he is addressing. The English language is inadequate to supply appropriate equivalents in such contexts.'[129]

Although both countries are political democracies, the Japanese are more respectful to political leaders, to persons in positions of authority, and are less likely to favour protest activities. Americans, on the other hand, tend to be more anti-elitist and suspicious of those in power. George DeVos notes that in Japan '[a]uthority figures – political, administrative, and familial – are for the most part, granted a degree of respect rare in the United States'.[130] These generalizations are borne out by comparative survey research which indicate that Japanese are more likely than Americans to agree that 'if we get outstanding political leaders, the best way to improve the country is for people to leave everything to them, rather than for the people to discuss things among themselves'. Both, however, express a low level of 'confidence' in their current crop of politicians. Japanese respect for authority is also evident in the finding that a much greater percentage of them than of Americans feel that parents should support teachers by refusing to repeat to their child a story 'that his teacher had done something to get himself in trouble', even if the rumour is true.[131]

The Japanese are also less disposed to give verbal support to extraparliamentary activism, although the behaviour of students during the 1960s contradicted such statements. The youth surveys conducted in 1972, 1977, 1983 and 1988 found that the Japanese were the least likely among persons aged 18 to 24 in six countries (France, Sweden, the United Kingdom, the United States and

West Germany) to say that if they 'are not satisfied with the society', they would 'engage in active actions as far as they are legal' to change things (21 per cent in 1988, down from 37 in 1972) while the Americans were the most disposed among the six to favour activism (55 per cent, falling from 62). The modal response (39 to 41 per cent) for the Japanese was: 'I will use my voting rights but nothing more.'[132] Here is further evidence of the different attitudes of Americans and Japanese (as well as Europeans) to conformity.

Gender Relations

Gender presents a major anomaly in any effort to evaluate the extent to which the United States and Japan continue to vary along the modern–traditional axis and of the ability of Japan to maintain its historic values and behaviour.

Structural changes in the economy have forced the Japanese to choose between admitting large numbers of foreign workers, thereby upsetting their traditional aversion to accepting outsiders, or to allow a sizeable increase in employed married female labour, thereby undermining the norms defining the relations between the sexes. The Japanese have chosen to do the latter, although they remain behind the United States and almost all other industrialized nations in participation by women in the employed labour force.[133]

Japan remains, however, 'a persistent outlier among industrial societies, demonstrating a greater male–female wage differential and more pronounced sex segregation across a range of indicators, including employment status and occupation'.[134] The United States differs from Japan on all of these variables.[135]

The almost 40 per cent decline in the marriage rate in Japan over the past two decades and the increase in the average age of newly-weds have been greater than in any other society, while fertility rates there are among the lowest anywhere. They have fallen from 5.3 in Japan and 3.3 in the United States in 1921 to 3.2 in both countries in 1951 then down to 1.6 and 1.9 respectively in 1988.[136] Marriage rates have changed little in America in recent years, hovering around 15 per 1000 population aged 15 to 64 between 1960 and 1986, while dropping from 14.5 to 8.6 in Japan in the same period.[137] The age of marriage in Japan was the highest in the world in 1985.[138] Not surprisingly, the changes in behaviour have been paralleled by shifts in attitude. The proportion of Japanese females agreeing with the statement: 'Women had better marry because women's happiness lies in marriage', declined from 40 per cent in 1972 to 14 per cent in 1990.[139]

Despite these changes, gender relations remain much more traditionally hierarchical, more asymmetrical in Japan than in Western nations, particularly the United States.[140] The traditional male-dominated family is much more characteristic of the former. Comparative survey data gathered by NHK in 1980 indicate that three-fifths of the Japanese think males 'have higher analytical ability' than women; most Americans, 72 per cent, believe that 'by nature there are no differences between men and women'. The same NHK study reports that 80 per cent of Japanese men and 74 per cent of the women say the 'husband should have the final deciding voice' in the family, compared to 40 per cent of American men and 34 per cent of women. When asked how the household chores should be divided when the husband and wife both work, 90 per cent of the Americans said 'equally between the spouses', a position taken by only slightly over half of the Japanese, including 54 per cent of the women.[141] That these cross-national variations in opinions correspond to behavioural differences is evident in table 4.4 below. In Japan, between 1965 and 1990, an unchanging nine-tenths or more of the time spent on household chores is by women, compared to 79 per cent declining to 64 per cent in the United States.

Table 4.4: Percentage distribution between women and men of average time spent per week in housework and child care: Japan, 1965–90, and the United States, 1965–86

Country	Year	Percent share of:		
		Women	Men	Total
Japan	1965	92	8	100
	1970	92	8	100
	1975	91	9	100
	1980	91	9	100
	1985	92	8	100
	1990	90	10	100
United States	1965	79	21	100
	1975	75	25	100
	1986	64	36	100

SOURCE: Noriko O. Tsuya, 'Work and family life in Japan: changes and continuities'. Unpublished paper, Tokyo: Department of Sociology, Nihon University, 1992, table 4.

Given these cross-national differences, it is not surprising that the Prime Minister's Office multinational study of parents of children, which inquired in 1981 whether women should have jobs after marriage or 'after childbirth', found that a majority of Americans, 52.5 per cent, replied, 'Yes, at any time', in contrast to 30 per cent of the Japanese.[142] The Japanese-conducted international youth surveys reported cross-national differences running in the same direction when they asked respondents to react to the more general statement: 'Men should go out to work while women stay home and take care of the house.' In each year (1977, 1983 and 1988), the large majority of Americans disagreed by 71, 81 and 81 per cent, compared to minorities, albeit increasing ones, of Japanese who felt the same way: 35 and 44 per cent.[143] The Prime Minister's Office also reported that American spouses are much more likely to socialize together than Japanese. The percentages for 'eating out' are 48 American, 17 Japanese; for 'films and theaters', 40 and 7 per cent; for 'social parties' 37 and 5 per cent; and for 'travel', 33 and 5 per cent.[144]

Polls conducted in 1990 by the Roper Organization and the Dentsu Institute for the Virginia Slims Company in both nations supply more-recent evidence of continued Japanese traditionalism in gender relations.[145] Working females were asked whether 'the men you work with really look on you as an equal or not?' American women replied by 59 to 29 per cent that they are viewed as equals. The Japanese response pattern was diametrically opposite with 55 per cent of the women saying they are not looked upon as equals and only 31 per cent thinking they are. Asked whether women's opportunities are the same as those of men in various job-related areas, American females are much more likely than Japanese to perceive equality for salaries − 65 to 24 per cent; for responsibility − 74 to 37 per cent; for promotion − 60 to 18 per cent; and for becoming an executive − 49 to 15 per cent. These attitudinal differences correspond to variations in national behavioural patterns. As of 1990, two-fifths, 40 per cent, of administrative and managerial positions in the United States were filled by women, up from 27.5 per cent in 1981, compared to only 7.9 per cent in Japan, up from 5.3 per cent in 1981.[146] Clearly, women are gaining more rapidly in America than across the Pacific in 4 the attainment of executive positions.

A 1991 survey of mothers of junior high school students in Japan and America found again that women in the former are much more traditional than their trans-Pacific peers with respect to gender roles of adults and their treatment of and expectations for their offspring. Thus, over half, 53 per cent, of the Japanese mothers agree that 'Husbands should work outside and wives should take care of the family', in contrast to 39 per cent of the Americans. Similarly, over three-fifths, 61 per cent, of the latter reject the statement: 'Men are supposed to play a central role and women are supposed to support them', a point of view held by less than half, 44 per cent, of the Japanese mothers.

Japanese mothers are more disposed than Americans to vary their treatment of siblings according to gender. Just over half the former, in contrast to 38 per cent of the latter, say 'boys and girls should be raised differently'. More specifically, when asked: 'What education level do you want your child to achieve?', Americans do not differentiate their expectations for sons and daughters; 83 per cent want both to graduate from university. Japanese mothers, on the other hand, vary anticipations according to the sex of their children. Sixty-seven per cent want their sons to go to university, while only 35 per cent wish the same for daughters.[147]

Cross-national attitudinal and behavioural differences are linked closely. Of the 38 per cent of Japanese males who continue their education beyond high school, fully 95 per cent attend four-year universities; among the one-third of females who are in post-high-school studies, 'nearly two-thirds ... go on to junior colleges and the rest enroll in four-year universities'.[148] The situation is reversed in the United States, where a larger proportion of college-age women (64 per cent) than of men (55 per cent) are enrolled in tertiary institutions, more or less proportionally distributed by gender in different types of higher education.[149]

The distinctive gender-linked attitudes and behaviours in Japan and America appear to be supported by friendship patterns. Both younger (18–24) and older (65 plus) Japanese are much more likely than comparably aged Americans to say that all their close friends are of their sex. Among the youth, the ratio of Japanese to Americans to report this is 51 to 10 per cent; among the aged, it is 57 to 32 per cent. The drop-off between the generations in traditional behaviour is clearly much greater in the United States. Over four-fifths of American youth reported having friends of both genders in 1977, 1983 and 1988; less than half of the Japanese did so, although the percentage was increasing from 32 per cent in 1977 to 49 per cent in 1988.[150]

Family Relationships

The family has been an area of considerable change as societies have moved from predominantly rural and small-town environments to industrial and metropolitan ones. There has been a shift everywhere from single-household multgenerational stem families to nuclear ones, fertility rates have declined greatly, and the role of parents in arranging marriages has been replaced by an emphasis on love. The United States has been in the forefront of such developments; Japan has been a laggard among industrialized nations, although it too has moved considerably.[151]

Familial relations seemingly reflect the continuity of traditional elements in Japan. In spite of the strains of adjusting to the rapid social change encompassed in the pace of industrialization and urbanization in postwar Japan, the family is more secure there than in the United States. As Nathan Glazer emphasizes: 'The Japanese family is undoubtedly changing; but for a developed country it still maintains a remarkable stability, which underlies the stability of the value patterns.'[152] Divorce rates, as noted earlier, are much lower in Japan. Aged parents are more likely to live with or near their offspring and to receive deference and assistance from them. A 1980 international study of 'human values' found 89 per cent of a national cross-section of Japanese in favour of adult children living with their parents and older parents residing with a married son or daughter, a position taken by only 25 per cent of a comparable sample of Americans. Surveys of the elderly, 65 and older, taken in 1981, 1986 and 1991 found that the majority of the Japanese in each year (59, 58 and 54 per cent) said they wished always to 'live together' with their children and grandchildren, compared to very few Americans (6.5, 2.7 and 3.4 per cent).[153] Cross-sections of mothers of teenagers in the two societies, when interviewed in 1983, also varied in their responses to a question concerning their desired relationship with their children in old age. The overwhelming majority of Americans, 87 per cent, said they would like to dwell apart from their offspring; 56 per cent of the Japanese preferred to be with them. These attitudes correspond to behaviour. In the 1980s three-fifths of Japanese 65 years of age or older were living with relatives, compared to one-seventh of similarly aged Americans. The 1981, 1986 and 1991 studies of people aged 65 and over found that in the United States, about four-fifths of the 'elderly were either living alone or were living alone as couples. In Japan, about 50 per cent of the elderly interviewed were living with children.' Even more strikingly, the data showed that 'roughly 35 percent of the Japanese are living in three [adult] generation households against [almost] no Americans'.[154] Conversely, during the 1980s 30.4 per cent of Americans 65 years of age or older were living by themselves, as contrasted to 8.6 per cent of elderly Japanese. Comparative research finds that 'except in Japan, the one-person household has shown the most rapid growth of all household types since 1960'.[155]

These findings reinforce the conclusion reached in 1992 by Junko Matsubara, that Japanese society basically 'recognizes families as basic social units and disregards individualists who desire to live alone'. An unmarried freelance writer in her mid-forties, Matsubara was told by landlord that she was unqualified to rent an apartment by herself.[156] Grown children among the Japanese are more disposed to remain with their parents in the (physically small) family households than Americans, who generally live in much larger dwelling units. Surveys of 18–24-year-old Japanese youth report that from 79 per cent in 1977 to 83 per cent in 1988 were residing with parents, compared with 59 per cent to 62 per cent of the same age group of Americans.[157]

The Perpetuation of Tradition

The argument has frequently been made that to develop economically, less developed countries (LDCs) must become modern, individualistic and meritocratic. In other words, they must come to resemble America. As noted above, even Marxists, writing in a period when the United States was perceived as the great capitalist success (not yet the great capitalist villain), saw America as the equivalent of modernity.

The Japanese elites were able to employ the country's traditions in ways which made industrialization possible. They could use religion because pre-Meiji beliefs contained elements that encouraged rationally orientated work and economic behaviour. Robert Bellah concludes that Japanese economic development was causally linked to its Buddhist and Confucian heritages.[158] Shinto, one of the country's two major faiths, is older than most Western religions and helped to legitimate the Meiji transformation. Travelling around Japan one can see business people enter Shinto shrines and clap to get the attention of the local god, the god of a river, of aviation, of a district. They are practising a form of the same animist or shamanist religion that existed in the pagan Western past and persists today in tribal societies.[159]

Religion everywhere tends to institutionalize values and practices from previous eras. As Weber emphasized, traditionalism in the form of religion helped to modernize America and facilitated the development of a competitive capitalist society. The same Protestant sects which fostered individualism and rational market behaviour also sustained many values and beliefs derivative from the pre-industrial history of Western societies. Tocqueville noted a century and a half ago that Americans formed the most devout population in the West. They still do. Business executives and members of Congress attend prayer breakfasts. When Americans are asked whether they believe in the Devil, close to half say yes; in most other Christian countries, the percentage is around 5–10 percent. Most Americans believe in Hell and the afterlife, most Europeans do not. Americans accept far more fundamentalist biblical teachings than do Europeans.[160]

The Japanese, of course, not being Christians, cannot be expected to accept biblical teachings, but in any case they are much less religious than Americans. The three youth surveys report that, over an 11-year period, more than 90 per cent of Americans said they believe religion should be important in their life (41–47 per cent 'very'; 45–46 'somewhat'), contrasted to around two-fifths of Japanese (6–10 percent 'very'; 31–35 'somewhat').[161] The 1990 World Values study found 79 per cent of Americans and only 17 per cent of Japanese reporting religion as an important value. It is interesting to note that similar differences showed up when the responses of a national cross-section of Japanese were compared with those of a sample of Japanese Americans in Hawaii, both taken at the beginning of the 1970s. For example, only 31 per cent of the Japanese said they had a personal religious faith compared to 71 per cent of the Hawaiian Japanese.[162]

The lesser religiosity of the Japanese may explain the findings in the Roper–Virginia Slims polls that Japanese are more permissive or liberal with respect to sexuality-related issues. Thus, they are 10 per cent less likely than Americans to believe that 'pre-marital sexual intercourse is immoral', and 14 per cent more disposed to agree that 'legal abortions should be available to women who choose to have them'.

Various observers of American values have indicated that there has been little change over time in the key characteristics which have defined American culture when viewed comparatively, for example, with Europe or Canada. As noted, this judgement is premised on the assumption that the United States was 'born modern', that values like universalism, egalitarianism, individualism and an emphasis on meritocracy were present from the beginning of the republic.[163] However, the European post-feudal societies, with their earlier stress on hierarchy, particularism and ascription (hereditary status), while remaining different from America, changed greatly to meet the functional requirements of industrial society. But Japan, as we have seen, has modernized economically while retaining many traditional ways which were discarded in most of post-feudal Europe.

The United States, however, like Japan, contradicts the assumption that the emergence of a developed urban economy necessarily undermines tradition. As noted, most Americans still adhere to pre-modern religious beliefs. In some ways, therefore, America is a more traditional society than Western Europe, or even Japan. Public opinion studies conducted since the Second World War in the United States attest to the strength of ancient sacred traditions, which are much stronger than in almost all other Christian countries. One of the foremost sociologists of American religion, Andrew Greeley, has documented the basic continuity of practice and belief. He concludes that those who believe in 'the ever-increasing power of secularization' or in 'a "surge" of religious fundamentalism' are both wrong. 'When George Gallup ... asked the first question about whether you "happened" to attend church or synagogue last week in the early 1940s, the proportion that had "happened" to attend church was 40 percent. It's still 40 percent almost a half-century later'. Summing up the findings of survey research – 'twenty-five years for most items, almost fifty for some' – he concludes:

> Most of the lines one would draw on a graph of American religious behavior through the years are straight lines: more than 95 per cent believe in God; 77 per cent believe in the divinity of Jesus; 72 per cent believe in life after death with certainty, while another 20 per cent are unsure; 70 per cent believe in hell, 67 per cent in angels, 50 per cent in the devil; 34 per cent belong to a church-related organization; a third have had some kind of intense religious experience; half pray at least once a day and a quarter pray more than once a day; a third have a great deal of confidence in religious leadership; more than half think of themselves as very religious. Defection rates have not increased since 1960 and intermarriage rates have not changed significantly across Protestant and Catholic lines in the same period.
>
> Only three indicators show a decline – church attendance, financial contributions, and belief in the literal interpretation of the scripture. All three declines are limited to Catholics. ... [I]t is a decline accounted for by a change to a position which is quite properly orthodox for Catholics – acceptance of the general message of the scripture as inspired without believing the literal interpretation of each word.[164]

The supposedly greater commitment of Japanese than Americans to traditional ways of life, such as living in small towns, also did not appear when samples in both countries were asked in the late 1970s by Gallup International about preferences for community of residence. The Americans turned out to be more wedded to older models. Close to three-fifths (56 per cent) of those interviewed in the United States stated they would like to live in rural areas or in a small town of up to 10,000 persons, as compared to only a quarter (27 per cent) of the Japanese. Although the latter are closer in time (generations) to residence in small communities, with many now living in highly congested urban conditions, 36 per cent said they would prefer to live in a large city, while only 13 per cent of the Americans expressed the same choice.

Antagonism to big cities in America has been linked for many decades to an image of these communities as centres of moral corruption, sin and irreligion, an image held by fundamentalists and evangelical Protestants. As Earl Raab and I documented, such views have given rise to anti-modernist and anti-urban movements from the Anti-Masonic Party of the 1820s and 1830s through the Know-Nothing-American Party movement of the 1850s, the Ku Klux Klan of 1920s, and the right-wing religious-linked groups, of whom the most publicized has been the Moral Majority of the 1970s and 1980s.[165]

On a completely secular level, the refusal by Americans to give up the ancient systems of pounds and ounces, miles and inches and the Fahrenheit temperature scale in favour of metric measurements, while Canadians went along with the proposal of the two governments that the North American nations join most of the world in using more logical and economically more functional methods, is another illustration of an American attachment to tradition. By the criterion of measurement, America (and Britain) are more traditional than Japan. But the latter, as noted earlier, insists on retaining an equally dysfunctional approach to street names and numbers.

Another major pattern in the United States which involves the perpetuation, even the extension, of traditional behaviour is race and ethnicity. Until recently, most scholars of this topic agreed that ethnicity reflected the conditions of traditional society, in which people lived in small communities isolated from one another, and mass communications and transportation were limited or non-existent. They expected that industrialization, urbanization and the spread of education would reduce ethnic consciousness, that universalism would replace particularism. Sociologists in Western countries assumed that modernization would mean the end of ethnic tension and consciousness. Assimilation of minorities into a larger integrated whole was viewed as the inevitable future. Nathan Glazer and Daniel P. Moynihan note that it was generally believed that divisions of culture, religion, language, [and race] ... would inevitably lose their weight and sharpness in modern and modernizing societies, that there would be increasing emphasis on achievement rather than ascription, that common systems of education and communication would level differences, that nationally uniform economic and political systems would have the same effect. Under these circumstances the 'primordial' (or in any case antecedent) difference between groups would be expected to become of lesser significance.[166]

But, as we know, this has not happened in the United States, or in a number of other European countries. The image of the universalistic 'melting pot' into which all American groups would blend has been de-emphasized in favour of an ethnically pluralist society that legally and otherwise accepts the rights of national origin groups, such as Blacks, Asian Americans, Hispanics, Jews and so on. Affirmative action policies are a part of this phenomenon, whereby the modernist and market economy emphasis on universalism has declined, while particularism has become more important.[167] Japan remains highly particularistic and race conscious, a point to be elaborated below.

Modernity and Conservatism

The assumption that Japan is an exception to the theory that economic development necessitates a shift from tradition to modernity, because it retains major-aspects of the value systems associated with feudalism, is clearly invalid. Every industrial country is a combination of tradition and modernity. As Weber, Reischauer and Bellah have suggested, development in the Western sense is an outgrowth of certain traditions which fostered rational economic behaviour, elements present more strongly in Northern Europe, North America, Japan and Confucian East Asia than in other parts of the world. The new is introduced as an outgrowth of the right combination of the old. And the strains of social change, of adjusting to new forms of behaviour, of rejecting the old, can only be moderated if societies are able to link the new with the old, if they maintain considerable elements from previous stages of development. Not all cultures have equally usable cultural elements.

Tatsuko Suzuki draws conclusions from examining the responses to five Japanese National Character surveys conducted over a quarter of a century which apply to some degree to the United States and other developed countries:

First, the processes of social change did not bring about a total dis-appearance of a 'traditional' outlook, to be replaced by a 'modern' outlook. Despite all the changes in the postwar era, the systems of values in Japan have continued to provide culturally legitimate and meaningful outlets for different ideas.

Second, large-scale institutional changes may occur without drastic shifts in the systems of attitudes. In fact, in view of the Japanese experience, we are inclined to argue that it is precisely the relative stability in the systems of beliefs which allows institutional changes to take place, for example in the areas of economics and politics, without major social dislocations.[168]

The Japanese differ from Americans and some Western Europeans in having done much more to plan their economic development. One of the reasons they were able to do this was that they were latecomers on the industrial scene and, as noted earlier, were pushed into modernizing by the desire to prevent being colonized. The Meiji elite sought to maintain what was truly Japanese, to restore the status of the Emperor, and at the same time to become an industrial power. The United States was fortunate in having the right com-bination of traditional values to make use of its economic resources. It is important to note that the great Japanese postwar reforms (for example, land reform, democratization, demilitarization, the elimina-tion of the peerage) were legitimated by the same mechanism as in the Meiji Restoration, the Emperor's approval. Those most upset by the changes were the most bound to the Emperor. General MacArthur played out the classic role of a controlling Shogun stand-ing behind the Emperor, but by doing so he helped preserve many of the older traditions. More than a quarter of a century earlier Winston Churchill had urged a similar role for the German Kaiser, arguing that by retaining him the Allies would avoid the alienation of the right wing and the military from the new German democracy.

From a perspective of the diverse indicators of 'traditionalism' discussed here, Japan and America appear more traditional than most West European and Australasian cultures, while being as or more modern or developed technologically. If the ability to maintain traditionalism is linked to or identified with conservatism, then both are also conservative cultures.

Conservatism tends to be a political term, and from a political perspective both are conservative societies. America is exceptional in its lack of an important labour or socialist party. And while Japan does have a major socialist party, as well as a moderately strong communist one, unlike those of industrial Europe and Australasia it has never been the ruling party, except for a brief period in an early stage of the occupation. In 1985 the socialists explicitly gave up adherence to Marxism and the doctrine of class struggle, a change typical of many of the world's left parties.[169] Class solidarity, as reflected in trade union strength as of 1990, is also weaker in both countries than elsewhere, albeit with a much smaller percentage of the non-agricultural labour force organized in the United States (16 per cent) than in Japan (25 per cent).[170] Membership is declining in both. In recent years, commentators have been wont to emphasize the fact that 90 per cent of Japanese identify themselves as 'middle class', rather than 'upper' or 'lower', as evidence that their country has become classless. The interpretation is wrong. Americans and Europeans distribute themselves similarly when responding to this question. All these answers mean is that few people will choose to say they are sufficiently privileged to be in the upper class or that they belong to the invidiously labelled lower class. When faced with further choices which include 'working class' or 'lower middle class', 40 to 50 per cent choose these options in America and Europe.

The meaning of conservatism is quite different in the two societies. In America, it involves support of *laissez-faire*, anti-statist doctrines, which correspond to bourgeois-linked classical liberalism. In Jefferson's words, 'that government governs best which governs least'. In Japan, as in post-feudal Europe, conservatives have been associated with the defence of the alliance between state and religion (that is, between throne and altar), the maintenance of elitist values and the use of the state for national purposes. Aristocratic monarchical conservatives have favoured a strong state. From Meiji onwards, this meant a state bureaucracy and politicians who consciously planned the use of national resources to enhance economic growth and, in prewar times, military power. The business community, in so far as it took an independent stance, was more liberal, more supportive of laissez-faire, and less militaristic than the aristocracy, but it was weak politically.

In Europe, aristocratic agrarian-based conservatism, which favoured a strong state, fostered the *noblesse oblige* communitarian values of the nobility, disliked the competitive, materialistic values and behaviour of the capitalists, and introduced the welfare state into Germany and Britain. The socialists, when they emerged, also favoured a powerful state and extensive welfare programmes, as well as democratization of the polity. In Japan, the conservative post-feudal impulse led, as we have seen, to state guidance of the economy but, unlike Europe, the emphasis on *noblesse oblige* and communitarianism has been expressed more within the confines of private institutions – in the obligations of firms to their employees (lifetime employment, company-provided annuity payments), what Ronald Dore calls 'welfare corporatism' – than in state institutions.[171] Hence, direct state payments for welfare have been weaker in Japan than anywhere else in the developed world.

America and Japan have made important moves in the extension of the welfare state, but they remain at the bottom of the international list of OECD nations with respect to levels of taxation generally and spending for welfare purposes particularly. In 1980 Japan was last among these countries, with 7.5 per cent of its GDP spent on social benefits, while the United States was third last with 9.6 per cent.[172] However, when presented in 1990 by the World Values study with a choice between the classical liberal or Tory– socialist positions in the form of a ten-point scale running from 'Individuals should take more responsibility for providing for themselves' to 'The state should take more responsibility to ensure that everyone is provided for', 53 per cent of the Japanese placed themselves on the Tory-statist side of the scale while only 26 per cent chose individual responsibility. Conversely, fully four-fifths of the Americans, inheritors of an anti-statist individualistic value system, favoured individualism, less than a fifth, 17 per cent, answered that the state should be responsible. Although, as noted, both countries have private insurance rather than state coverage for health care, their employee benefit systems differ greatly, reflecting these differences in national values. As Tomoni Kodama of the Japanese Ministry of Health notes:

> The U.S. structure of employee benefits seems to be based on diversity and individualism. Companies have a real choice in selecting and planning their employee benefit system. ...
> ... [T]he structure of Japanese employee benefits is equity and uniformity for everyone. The Japanese priority has been to assure equal access to benefits for everyone. ... [I]n order to provide equal access to all employees, health insurance is strictly regulated across the board by Japanese government. In other words, employees of a small company on the verge of bankruptcy are provided basically the same coverage as employees of a well-known big company such as Honda or Toyota. ... The same type of equity and uniformity is more or less a common feature among other Japanese employee benefits such as pension plans and health care.
> As a result ... it is not the companies but the central government that has consistently taken the key role in planning and implementing the employee benefit system.[173]

Japan, throughout its postwar decades of economic growth and prosperity, has had a conservative government; one, however, whose business-related Liberal Democratic administration has responded quite differently to the recession of the early 1990s than has the American Republican one. The former would improve the economy by Keynesian pump-priming policies, including 'more public investments to boost the economy ... public works and housing. ... [A]n additional ¥1.12 trillion will be allocated to public funds for investment in stocks. This is separated from the ¥10.7 trillion stimulus ... [most of which] will be spent on public works and housing. ... Economic Planning Agency officials [announced] ... "the package will fill the gap between demand and supply in the economy ...".'[174] The Bush administration, and even the Clinton campaign, reject comparable policies for the United States as too leftist. The Japanese government remains centralized; its bureaucracy and politicians continue, as under Meiji, to influence strongly general economic policies. The American rejects proposals for a state-co-ordinated 'industrial policy', although the Clinton Democrats use the term in suggesting a version much more moderate than the Japanese one. The dominant business sector adheres to a *noblesse oblige* sense of obligation to employees in Japan, one almost totally lacking in America. Feudal or post-feudal values penetrate Japanese life and economy in ways which are largely absent from the American.

Japan, as noted, also has a relatively strong Marxist socialist party, a much weaker and more moderate (social democratic) Democratic socialist party, and a fairly radical Communist party. Their combined vote has ranged up and down between 36 per cent in 1958 and 32 in 1990; such tendencies have almost no electoral support in the United States. The disparity between America and the rest of the industrialized world has given rise to an extensive literature seeking to explain 'Why No Socialism in the United States?'[175] Many analysts, following Louis Hartz, have suggested that the group orientated, corporatist, *noblesse oblige*, statist norms dominant in monarchically rooted Tory conservatism have legitimized support for social democratic statist policies.[176] Further evidence that the variations in political orientation and social policies between Japan and America are linked to basic differences in orientation toward individualism and equality may be found in the first 1981–2 World Values survey, which asked respondents to choose between two statements:

Q – Here are two opinions about conditions existing in our country. Which one do you happen to agree with?
A – There is too much emphasis upon the principle of equality. People should be given the opportunity to choose their own economic and social life according to their individual abilities.

B – Too much liberalism has been producing increasingly wide differences in people's economic and social life. People should live more equally.

Table 4.5: Attitudes to individualism and equality (%)

| | Japan | | America | |
	Individualism	Equality	Individualism	Equality
Total	25	71	56	32
Social class				
High	47	53	62	33
Upper middle	38	59	61	26
Middle	25	72	58	31
Lower middle	22	75	49	43
Low	13	80	56	20

SOURCE: Adapted from Elizabeth H. Hastings and Philip K. Hastings (eds), *Index to International Public Opinion, 1980–1981*. Westport, Conn.: Greenwood Press, 1982, p. 519; 'Survey in thirteen countries of human values'. Leisure Development Center, Tokyo, 1–5 October 1980.

As indicated earlier and reiterated by the data reported in table 4.5, the Japanese have been very much more disposed to favour equality than individual competition. Although support for meritocracy increases with social class, a majority of the 'high' class opt for equality. Conversely, most Americans, including a majority of the 'low' stratum, prefer a competitive race for position.

The second World Values Study did not include the individualism–equality question, but it repeated one that requested respondents to choose between statements emphasizing freedom or equality. As might be expected, in both years Americans were more likely to opt for freedom over equality.[177] The question posed was:

Q – Which of these statements comes closest to your own opinion?
    A – I find that both freedom and equality are important. But if I were to make up my mind for one or the other, I would consider personal freedom more important, that is, everyone can live in freedom and develop without hindrance.
    B – Certainly both freedom and equality are important. But if I were to make up my mind for one of the two, I would consider equality more important, that is, that nobody is underprivileged and that social class differences are not so strong.

Table 4.6:   Attitudes to freedom and equality (%)

	Japan		America	
	1980–1	1990–1	1980–1	1990–1
Agree with freedom	37	39	72	66
Agree with equality	32	32	20	22

SOURCE: News release by CARA (Center for Applied Research in the Apostolate), 1981; and International Study of Values Interim Report. Tokyo: Dentsu Institute for Human Studies, 1991, p. 20.

The data in table 4.6 point out the greater emphasis on individual freedom in American culture than in Japanese. Seemingly there was little change in Japan over the decade of the 1980s, while the very high commitment in the United States for the freedom choice went down slightly, though it remained the opinion of the large majority.

Conclusion

The two nations follow different organizing principles. National traditions continue to inform the cultures, economies and politics of both countries in very dissimilar ways. One, the United States, follows the individualistic essence of bourgeois liberalism and evangelical sectarian Christianity; the other, Japan, reflects the group orientated norms of the post-feudal aristocratic Meiji era. The former still stresses equal respect across stratification lines; the latter still emphasizes hierarchy in interpersonal relations. The first continues to suspect the state; the second places heavy reliance on its directing role. They are both among the world's most successful societies as measured by levels of productivity and political stability. Clearly, nations which have reached the same point of technological development and economic success can still be very different culturally, can continue to be anomalies, outliers, among the developed countries, exceptional or unique compared to most others.

But as noted earlier, while America has been exceptional, Japanese patterns resemble those in Europe, particularly Northern Europe. Japanese and European corporations have shown a propensity to co-operate with each other and with the government. Americans are low with respect to both orientations.[178] Efforts to introduce quality circles and worker involvement in industrial production have succeeded in Japan, Sweden and other Northern European countries. They have failed in the United States.[179]

There is an increasing body of literature which concludes that
Japan will do better than the United States in the future, consideration of industrial policy apart, because its group-orientated culture is better suited to the economic structure of a post-industrial
society. The argument is that engineering innovations, the key to
economic growth, are more successfully fostered by *groups* while
scientific discoveries, yet-to-be-applied basic research, are more likely
to occur in societies which stress individual initiative. The latter
lead to Nobel prizes, but the contention is that they are less likely
to have a direct impact in the post-industrial marketplace. This
hypothesis is far from the only one presented to account for Japanese
economic success. Others stress the impact of group solidarity values
on the willingness of Japanese – including corporate business executives, stockholders and employees – to earn less than comparably
placed Americans or Europeans, while the gap between those who
run companies and ordinary workers is also much smaller in Japan.[180]
Sony Corporation Chairman Akio Morita has 'described in detail
the corporate management style of Japan – thin profit margins,
low dividends to stockholders, overwork [by and low pay to] ...
employees, seizing market share above all'.[181]
The comparative evidence indicates that:

[T]he employees of the Japanese company share more equally in the
cash benefits available from the company than is the case in other
countries [particularly the United States]. ... Surveys of executive
attitudes indicate that Japanese executive pay levels are set with a
conscious awareness of the need to stay within reasonable ranges with
regard to other levels of compensation. ... Organizational pressures
work to limit executive pay at least as much as do self-sacrificing
impulses by the executives themselves.[182]

Survey data bear out the generalization that Japanese executives
place the goal of increasing market share, one which benefits workers,
ahead of profits and short-term gains for stockholders. A 1980 cross-
national poll of 291 Japanese and 227 American top corporate executives found the Americans giving first and second place to return
on investment and increasing the value of company shares, while
the Japanese put enlarging market share first, and placed enhancing
the worth of shares at the bottom, ninth.[183]
The answers to various other questions posed in this survey re-
iterated the differences presented in the qualitative and case-study
literature. The Japanese reported close relationships with 'distri-
butors, customers, suppliers, and subcontractors', and 'somewhat

cooperative relationships with competitors', while the Americans noted 'remote relationships' and 'rivalry'. The Americans followed a pattern of 'head-on competition stressing cost efficiency', while the Japanese emphasized 'coexistence with competitors stressing "niche" and differentiation'. The Japanese sought 'information-oriented leadership' and generalists; the American preference was for 'task-oriented leadership' and specialists. The American executives were inclined 'toward innovation and risk-taking', the Japanese towards 'interpersonal skills'. The survey responses indicate that American managers were disposed to handle 'conflict resolution by confrontation ... [and] decision-making [by] stressing individual initiative', while the Japanese engaged in 'group-oriented consensual decision-aking'.[184]

The Japanese postwar success, when contrasted to the much slower growth rate and the loss or decline in markets in major industries by American business, has led various analysts to argue that the United States should adopt comparable policies to those followed across the Pacific. Assuming that various specific Japanese ways are responsible for higher productivity, the fact remains that these have developed in a very different context. 'The literature on Japanese development is generally pessimistic regarding the transfer of Japanese organization. It suggests that Japanese organizations derive from cultural factors such as homogeneity, familism, and group loyalty.'[185] Yet a comprehensive study of Japanese 'transplants' in the automobile industry in America indicates both that they have done well economically and that they 'have been successful in implanting the Japanese system of work organization in the U.S. environment. The basic form of Japanese work organization has been transferred with little if any modifications.'[186] These do not involve major practices such as lifetime employment or the emphasis on seniority, but include a very much lower number of job classifications, more job rotation, greater emphasis on worker initiative and quality circles. It appears that a Japanese management can secure acceptance of practices which fail when sponsored by Americans. (Quality circles, as noted earlier, were originally an American idea which, ironically, was not accepted in its native land.)

The Japanese are bound together by a common history, by an enduring desire to remain distinct from foreign culture. From the start of the seventeenth century to the mid-nineteenth, they maintained barriers against contact with other societies and economies. They had to be forced by Commodore Perry and the American navy to recognize the greater power of the West and to open the door to outside influences.

But even though open to intellectual, commercial and physical contact with the rest of the world, they have insisted on preserving their separateness. As a nation, Japan emphasizes ancestral purity. As James Fallows notes: 'Rather than talking about race ... the Japanese talk about "purity". Their society is different from others in being pure.' The system is closed, unlike the United States, where 'in theory anyone can become an American. A place in Japanese society is given only to those who are born Japanese.'[187] Legal immigration is close to impossible. The more than half a million Koreans, left over from the period when Korea was ruled by Japan, do not have citizenship, even though most of them were born in Japan. For a long time the Japanese government refused to accept a quota of Vietnamese boat people on the grounds that the Japanese people would not treat them well. It finally reluctantly agreed to take in 10,000. The traditional concern for 'purity' has not declined. If anything, the 'discrimination against the Korean, Chinese and other minority people who permanently reside in Japan' has been increasing rather than decreasing since the 1970s.[188] The protectionist zeal of the country, the barriers to the import of foreign goods, is a related form of behaviour.

The United States, on the other hand, is, as noted earlier, united around an ideology, the American Creed, which is anti-statist, individualistic and populist. It has welcomed foreigners to enter and join up. It is an immigrant, multicultural, multiracial society. Those who accept the Creed are Americans, those who reject it or transgress it, even though American-born, are 'un-American'. From a comparative, particularly Japanese, perspective, the United States has been an open society, open to imports as well as people. The past decade witnessed more newcomers to the United States than at any previous time; and the immigrants now are overwhelmingly from the Third World, not from Europe.

The American emphasis on individualism and competition has resulted in a 'star' system in all areas of American life, with enormous rewards to those on top: business executives, scholars, professionals, entertainers, athletes. The income spread from the top to the bottom is much higher in the United States than elsewhere in the developed world, particularly Japan. This is true in spite of the fact that formal hierarchical distinctions and family background are of greater importance in Japan and, to a lesser extent, in other post-feudal nations as well. In Japan, the emphasis is on the group winning, on the individual, whether athlete, executive or worker, subordinating his/her concerns to those of the larger unit. Such behaviour occurs even at the summit of politics. Prime Ministers tend to be prosaic figures who hold office for two to four years. They have little authority over their cabinet or party colleagues.[189] This pattern stands in sharp contrast to the American system, where elections focus on the individual rather than the party, and emphasize the role of the President, even though he must rely on influence, not authority, when dealing with Congress.

My stress here on the continued distinctions between the two economically most powerful Pacific Rim societies is not intended to deny that both have been changing culturally. As they moved from being primarily agrarian societies to industrial giants, with the bulk of their populations living in cities, they changed greatly in norms and behaviour. Their family systems are now nuclear; their birth rates are low; they are more meritocratic than in their nineteenth-century formats. Both have become more post-industrial or post-materialistic, to use Daniel Bell's and Ronald Inglehart's terms (they do not mean the same). Reflecting worldwide changes in the developed nations, their young people are more permissive with respect to traditional morality, particularly with regard to sexual relations and the position of women. They are more concerned about protecting the environment, they are more interested in the 'quality' of life. But their organizing principles remain different. They vary from each other in much the same way as a century ago. The value and behavioural differences reported here are much greater than have been found in any other comparison of industrialized nations. Each maintains much of its unique or exceptional character. To reiterate an analogy I first used in discussing Canada and the United States, 'The two are like trains that have moved thousands of miles along parallel railway tracks. They are far from where they started, but they are still separated.'[190]

Japan, as much of the quantitative survey and behavioural data presented here indicate, has challenged the assumption that technological development leads to convergence with the cultural models that emerged in Western industrialized societies. It appears now to be rejecting aspects which it seemed to accept during the postwar decades. Some attribute the reversals to the country's changed international and economic status. As a defeated, economically 'backward' society, many Japanese consciously took America as a model to be emulated. Now that Japan thinks of itself as 'number one', it can return to its own traditions.

The dean of the four-decade-old Japanese National Character studies, Chikio Hayashi, emphasizes the way in which Japan's changed position over a century of development has affected popular response to its culture:

Intent on the assimilation of Western culture and ways of thought, people naturally tended to neglect and even denigrate traditional customs and practices.

Now, however, the Japanese lead the world in many areas of technology, and they are rapidly losing their infatuation with imported culture. ... For this reason the new breed will be motivated to reassess the Japanese heritage and turn its attention to what makes the Japanese Japanese.[191]

Frank Upham, an American student of comparative law, makes a similar point in noting that

two decades of increasing Japanese social and economic success *vis-à-vis* the West have led many [domestic] observers to reverse the normative evaluation, so that sociolegal characteristics formerly seen as embarrassingly premodern are now celebrated as models for the overly individualistic and litigious West. The 'modern' legal system exemplified by the rule-centred model ... has ceased to be the ideal and assumed destination of a Japanese social and legal evolution. Instead, commentators envision a legal system that preserves the social interconnectiveness which they perceive as Japan's unique cultural foundation and which is immune to the corrupting influence of the same individualistic rights consciousness that previous observers had considered a prerequisite to a modern democracy.[192]

American individualism won the major international competitions in the twentieth century. Will it continue to be number one in the twenty-first? The American economy is still the more productive of the two, while 'per capita consumption in Japan was only 63 percent of the US level', as of 1988.[193] Still, the Japanese have clearly moved ahead of and are more efficient than the United States in industrial organization in major areas, such as automobile and electronics production. Some contend that their systems, which are leaner in the scope of management, more egalitarian in economic reward and place more emphasis on worker participation in quality control, are more 'modern' than the American, that the United States should modernize, learn from a more efficient system, much as the Japanese did for a century. In the coming years, will the world be more interested in American exceptionalism or Japanese uniqueness?

Notes

This paper was presented to a conference of the Research Committee on Comparative Sociology of the International Sociological Association at Kurashiki, Japan, on 5 July 1992. I am obligated to the Japan Society for a two-month fellowship awarded in 1984 to 'non-Japanologists', which led to my first work on the subject, and to the International House of Japan which hosted and supported me beyond all expectations in 1984 and 1992. Various Japanese, particularly Tatsuo Arima, Takako Kobori and Joji Watanuki, assisted me greatly by locating and/or translating materials. The scholars of the Institute of Statistical Mathematics of Tokyo were also particularly helpful. I am particularly grateful to Jennifer Bagette, Jeff Hayes and Janet Shaw for helping to find research reports. A number of American Japanologists gave important intellectual assistance, including Robert Cole of Berkeley, Daniel Okimoto of Stanford and Henry Rosovsky of Harvard. The John C. Olin Foundation helped to fund the project. The Hoover Institution of Stanford University enabled me to write up the research findings. Finally, I must acknowledge a deep intellectual debt to my friend of over three decades, Michio Nagai, now President of International House, who first introduced me to the basic differences between his country and mine.

1. On reasons for comparing these countries, see V. Lee Hamilton and Joseph Sanders, *Everyday Justice: responsibility and the individual in Japan and the United States*. New Haven, Conn.: Yale University Press, 1992, pp. 1–3. On the serious difficulties faced by foreigners who seek to understand Japan, see Joseph M. Kitagawa *On Understanding Japanese Religion*. Princeton, N.J.: Princeton University Press, 1987, pp. 294–6.

2. Max Weber, *The Protestant Ethic and the Spirit of Capitalism*. New York: Scribner, 1935, pp. 55–6; Max Weber, 'The Protestant sects and the spirit of capitalism'. In Hans Garth and C. Wright Mills (trans.), *Essays in Sociology*, New York: Oxford University Press, 1946, pp. 309, 313.

3. Friedrich Engels, *Socialism, Utopian and Scientific*. New York: International Publishers, 1935, p. 25. See also Seymour Martin Lipset, 'Why no socialism in the United States?' In Seweryn Bialer and Sara Sluzar (eds), *Sources of Contemporary Radicalism*, vol. i, Boulder, Col.: Westview Press, 1977, pp. 32–8.

4. Antonio Gramsci, *Selections from the Prison Notebooks*. New York: International Publishers, 1971, pp. 21–2, 272, 318.

5. Quoted in Raymond Lokker, 'Sake cup philosophy'. *Mainichi Daily News*, 2 July 1992, 2.

6. Seymour Martin Lipset, *Continental Divide: the values and institutions of the United States and Canada* New York: Routledge, 1990, p. xvii.

7. For good examples of the first, see Ezra Vogel, *Japan as Number One*. Cambridge: Harvard University Press, 1979; Ronald Dore, *Taking Japan Seriously: a Confucian perspective on leading economic issues*. Stanford, Cal.: Stanford University Press, 1987; of the second, Clyde V. Prestowitz Jr, *Trading Places: how we are giving our future to Japan and how to reclaim it*. New York: Basic Books, 1989; and of the third, James Fallows, *More Like Us: making America great again*. Boston, Mass.: Houghton Mifflin, 1989, esp. pp. 28–47. See also Hugh Patrick and Henry Rosovsky (eds), *Asia's New Giant: how the Japanese economy works*. Washington, D.C.:

Brookings Institution, 1976, particularly the article by Nathan Glazer, 'Social and cultural factors in Japanese economic growth', pp. 813–96.

8. For an earlier and briefer comparable effort, see ibid., pp. 853–61.

9. The phrase is Tocqueville's. For a review of the concept and the American evidence, see Seymour Martin Lipset, 'American exceptionalism reaffirmed'. In Byron E. Shafer (ed.), *Is America Different?: a new look at American exceptionalism*, Oxford: Clarendon Press, 1991, pp. 1–45.

10. Quoted in Michael Kazin, 'The right's unsung prophet'. *The Nation*, 248 (20 February 1989), 242.

11. Alexis de Tocqueville, *Democracy in America*, vol. I. New York: Alfred A. Knopf, 1948, p. 51.

12. Lipset, *Continental Divide*, pp. 74–9.

13. Quoted in Frank K. Upham, *Law and Social Change in Postwar Japan*. Cambridge, Mass.: Harvard University Press, 1987, pp. 205–6.

14. See James Fallows, 'The Japanese are different from you and me'. *Atlantic Monthly*, 258 (September 1986), 38–9; Chalmers Johnson, 'The people who invented the mechanical nightingale'. *Daedalus*, 119 (Summer 1990), 73.

15. Peter N. Dale, *The Myth of Japanese Uniqueness*. New York: St Martin's Press, 1986, p. 25. For an analysis of the background of *Nihonron*, see Harumi Befu, 'Civilization and culture: Japan in search of identity'. *Senri Ethnological Studies*, 16 (1984), 66–74.

16. Tamotsu, Aoki *Nihon-Bunka-ron no Henyo* (Evolutionary Japanology). Tokyo: Chuo-Koron Sha, 1990, p. 24.

17. Yohio, Sakata 'The beginning of modernization in Japan'. In Ardath W. Burks (ed.), *The Modernizers*. Boulder, Col.: Westview Press, 1985, pp. 69–83. See also Marius B. Jansen (ed.), *Changing Japanese Attitudes Toward Modernization*. Princeton, N.J.: Princeton University Press, 1965; William W. Lockwood (ed.), *The State and Economic Enterprise in Japan*. Princeton, N.J.: Princeton University Press, 1965; Ronald P. Dore (ed.), *Aspects of Social Change in Modern Japan*. Princeton, N.J.; Princeton University Press, 1967; Robert E. Ward (ed.), *Political Development In Modern Japan*. Princeton, N.J.: Princeton University Press, 1968; Donald Shively (ed.), *Tradition and Modernization in Japanese Culture*. Princeton, N.J.: Princeton University Press, 1971; James W. Morley (ed.), *Dilemmas of Growth in Prewar Japan*. Princeton, N.J.: Princeton University Press, 1971; Bernard S. Silberman and H.D. Harootunian (eds), *Japan in Crisis: essays on Taishō Democracy*. Princeton, N.J.: Princeton University Press, 1974; W.G. Beasley, *The Meiji Restoration*. Stanford, Cal.: Stanford University Press, 1971.

18. See Edwin O. Reischauer, *The Japanese*. Cambridge, Mass.: Belknap Press, 1977, pp. 78–87; Robert J. Smith, *Japanese Society: tradition, self and the social order*. Cambridge: Cambridge University Press, 1983, pp. 9–36.

19. George A. DeVos, *Socialization for Achievement*. Berkeley, Cal.: University of California Press, 1973, pp. 173–4.

20. David S. Landes, 'Japan and Europe: contrasts in industrialization'. In Lockwood (ed.), *The State and Economic Enterprise*, pp. 100–5, 119–43. See also: on Japan, Henry Rosovsky, *Capital Formation in Japan, 1868–1940*. Glencoe, Ill.: Free Press, 1961; on Germany, Thorstein Veblen, *Imperial Germany and the Industrial Revolution*. New York: Viking Press, 1939. For reference to Japan, see Thorstein Veblen, *Essays in Our Changing Older*. New York: Viking Press, 1934, pp. 248–66.

21. Ibid., p. 251 (my emphasis).

22. As quoted in Carmi Schooler, 'The individual in Japanese history: parallels to and divergences from the European experience'. *Sociological Forum*, 5:4 (1990), 569.

23. Norman Jacobs, *The Origins of Modern Capitalism in Eastern Asia*. Hong Kong: Hong Kong University Press, 1958; Schooler, 'The Individual in Japanese history'; Ken'ichi Tominaga, 'Max Weber on Chinese and Japanese social structure'. In Melvin L. Kohn (ed.), *Cross-national Research on Sociology*, Newbury Park, Cal.: Sage Publications, 1989, pp. 125–46.

24. Chalmers Johnson, *MITI and the Japanese Miracle: the growth of industrial policy, 1925–1975*. Stanford, Cal.: Stanford University Press, 1982, esp. pp. 198–304; Prestowitz, *Trading Places*, pp. 100–50.

25. Daniel I. Okimoto, *Between MITI and the Market*. Stanford, Cal.: Stanford University Press. 1989, pp. 11–12.

26. Louis Hartz, *The Liberal Tradition in America*. New York: Harcourt Brace, 1955.

27. Lester Thurow, *Head to Head: coming economic battles among Japan, Europe, and America*. New York: Morrow, 1992.

28. Okimoto, *Between MITI*, pp. 11–12.

29. Quoted in Steven R. Weisman, 'An American in Tokyo'. *New York Times Magazine*, 26 July 1992, 27.

30. Chalmers Johnson, 'The Japanese economy: a different kind of capitalism'. In S.N. Eisenstadt and Eyal Ben-Ari (eds), *Japanese Models of Conflict Resolution*, London: Kegan Paul International, 1990, p. 44.

31. Dore, *Taking Japan Seriously*, p. 245.

32. Harumi Befu, 'Four Models of Japanese society and their relevance to conflict'. In Eisenstadt and Ben-Ari (eds), *Japanese Models*, pp. 213–38; Robert M. Marsh and Hiroshi Manneri, *Organizational Change in Japanese Factories*. Greenwich, Conn.: JAI Press, 1988, pp. 8, 284–5.

33. Seymour Martin Lipset, *The First New Nation: the United States in historical and comparative perspective*, enlarged edn. New York: W.W. Norton, 1979, pp. 209–13.

34. Harumi Befu, 'The Group Model of Japanese Society and an Alternative'. *Rice University Studies*, 66:1, pp. 178–80.

35. Johnson. 'The People', p. 78. For a detailed exposition of the importance of hierarchy and seniority in Japan, see Chie Nakane, *Japanese Society*. Berkeley, Cal.: University of California Press, 1972.

36. Tadashi Fukutake, *The Japanese Social Structure*. Tokyo: University of

Tokyo Press, 1989, pp. 44–56; Reischauer, *The Japanese*, pp. 127–37; Daniel Pipes, 'Japan invents the future', *Society*, 2 (March/April 1992), 61.

37. Japan Youth Institute, 'A comparison of Japanese and American high school students' perceptions about what their lives would be like when they will be thirty years old'. Tokyo: Japan Youth Research Institute, 1990, p. 91.

38. *Nanakakoku Hikaku: Kokusai Leisure Chosa '89* (International Leisure Survey '89: Comparative Survey of Seven Countries). Tokyo: Yoka Kaihatsu Center (Leisure Development Centre), 1989, p. 47.

39. Smith, *Japanese Society*, pp. 45–7.

40. Janet T. Spence, 'Achievement American style. The rewards and costs of individualism'. *American Psychologist*, 40 (December 1985), 1287–8 (emphasis in original).

41. William A. Caudill and Carmi Schooler, 'Childrearing and personality formation'. In Daniel I. Okimoto and Thomas P. Rohlen (eds), *Inside the Japanese System*. Stanford, Cal.: Stanford University Press, 1988, pp. 16–17.

42. William A. Caudill and Carmi Schooler, 'Children and their mothers'. In ibid., p. 19.

43. *Japanese Children and their Fathers: a comparison with the United States and West Germany*. Tokyo: Youth Affairs Administration, Management and Coordination Agency, Prime Minister's Office, 1988, p. 31.

44. Ibid.

45. Ibid., p. 33.

46. Ibid., p. 38.

47. Harry C. Triandis, 'Cross-cultural studies of individualism and collectivism'. In John J. Berman (ed.), *Cross-cultural Perspectives*, Lincoln, Neb.: University of Nebraska Press, 1990, p. 81.

48. See Takeo Doi, *The Anatomy of Dependence*. Tokyo: Kodansha International, 1973, pp. 40–4; Mitsuyuki Masatsugu, *The Modern Samurai Society*. New York: AMACOM Book Division, 1982, pp. 88–9.

49. *A Summary Report of the World Youth Survey 1989*. Tokyo: Youth Affairs Administration Management and Coordination Agency, Prime Minister's Office, 1989, p. 74. The results from the Youth Survey nd some others reported here are also given in Elizabeth Hann Hastings and Philip K. Hastings (eds), *Index to International Public Opinion, 1988–89*. New York: Greenwood Press, 1990; and Sigeki Nihira and Christine Condominas, *L'Opinion japonais: société–travail–famille à travers*. Tokyo: Sudestasie, 1991.

50. *Japanese Children*, p. 38.

51. Prime Minister's Office, *International Comparison on Youth and Family*. Tokyo: Foreign Press Center, June 1982, p. 3.

52. Dale, *The Myth*, p. 44.

53. Çiğdem Kağitçibasi, 'Family and socialization in cross-cultural perspective: a model of change'. In Berman (ed.), *Cross Cultural Perspectives*,

p. 161. See C. Hayashi and T. Suzuki, 'Changes in belief systems, quality of life issues and social conditions in post-war Japan'. *Annals of the Institute of Statistical Mathematics*, 36 (1984), 135–61.

54. Trommsdorf, 'Some comparative aspects of socialization in Japan and Germany'. In I.R. Lagunes and Y.H. Poortinga (eds), *From a Different Perspective: studies of behavior across culture*, Lisse: Swets & Zeitlinger, 1985, p. 232.

55. Tatsuko Suzuki, 'Ways of life and social milieus in Japan and the United States: a comparative study'. *Behaviormetrika*, no. 15 (1984), 100.

56. Veblen, *Essays in Our Changing Order*, p. 251.

57. Kinji Mizuno et al., *A Study of the Japanese National Character*, vol. 5. Tokyo: Idemitsu Shoten, 1992, pp. 523, 525, 529; Yasumasa Kuroda, Alice K. Kuroda, Chikio Hayashi, and Tatsuzo Suzuki, 'The end of westernization and the beginning of new modernization in Japan: attitudinal dynamics of the Japanese, 1953–1983'. In Chikio Hayashi and Tatsuko Suzuki (eds), *Beyond Japanese Social Values: trends and cross-national perspectives*, Tokyo: Institute of Statistical Mathematics. 1990, p. 253.

58. *Fortune* and Gallup Poll results from the files of the Roper Data Library.

59. Two other surveys were conducted by the Institute of Statistical Mathematics in 1953 and 1958, but they did not include all these items.

60. Scott C. Flanagan, 'Value cleavages, contextual influences, and the vote'. In Scott C. Flanagan et al. (eds), *The Japanese Voter*, New Haven, Conn.: Yale University Press, 1991, p. 101.

61. From analysis by the Roper Data Center.

62. Hajime Nagahama, 'International comparisons of the public understanding of science and technology based on opinion surveys'. Unpublished paper, Tokyo: National Institute of Science and Technology Policy, Science and Technology Agency, 1992, pp. 16–17.

63. Shin'ichi Kobayashi, *Savages in a Civilized Society: young people's drift away from science and society*. Tokyo: National Institute of Science and Technology Policy, Science and Technology Agency, 1991, pp. 4–5.

64. Mizuno et al., *A Study*, pp. 528, 530; Kuroda et al., 'The end of westernization', pp. 257–9. The 1983 data on Japanese feelings of superiority are from Chikio Hayashi, 'Statistical study on Japanese national character'. *Journal of the Japanese Statistical Society*, Special Issue (1987), 77.

65. Kuroda et al., 'The end of westernization', pp. 258–9.

66. G.J. Bamber and R.D. Lansbury, *International and Comparative Labor Relations*. London: Allen & Unwin, 1987.

67. Reischauer, *The Japanese*, p. 186; Fukutake, *The Japanese*, p. 113.

68. Okimoto, *Between MITI*, pp. 121–2. See also *Labour–Management Relations in Japan 1992*. Tokyo: Japan Institute of Labour, 1992, pp. 13, 21, 27.

69. Ben-Ami Shillony, 'Victors without vanquished: a Japanese model of conflict resolution'. In Eisenstadt and Ben-Ari (eds), *Japanese Models*, p. 127.

70. Hamilton and Sanders, *Everyday Justice*, p. 37.
71. Karel van Wolferen, *The Enigma of Japanese Power: people and politics in a stateless nation.* New York: Alfred A. Knopf, 1989, pp. 337–9, 409–10.
72. Lipset, *Continental Divide*, pp. 78–9.
73. Shillony, 'Victors without vanquished', p. 127.
74. Robert K. Merton, *Social Theory and Social Structure.* Glencoe, Ill.: The Free Press, 1957, p. 169.
75. Walter L. Ames, *Police and Community in Japan.* Berkeley, Cal.: University of California Press, 1981, p. 1.
76. *Japan 1992. An international comparison.* Tokyo: Keizei Kohu Center, 1992, p. 93.
77. Hamilton and Sanders, *Everyday Justice*, pp. 158–9.
78. Ibid.
79. Data taken from ibid., p. 194.
80. 'The legal profession', Survey, *The Economist*, 18 July 1992, 12. See also Hamilton and Sanders, *Everyday Justice*, p. 23.
81. 'The legal profession', p. 4.
82. Ibid., p. 13.
83. Russell Ward, *The Australian Legend.* New York: Oxford University Press, 1959, p. 27.
84. Shillony, 'Victors without vanquished', p. 135.
85. Upham, *Law and Social Change*, pp. 166–227.
86. John Owen Haley, *Authority Without Power: law and the Japanese paradox.* New York: Oxford University Press, 1991, p. 14.
87. John Braithwaite, *Crime, Shame and Reintegration.* Cambridge: Cambridge University Press, 1989, p. 61; see also pp. 61–5.
88. George DeVos, 'Dimensions of the self in Japanese culture'. In Anthony V. Marsella, George DeVos and Francis L.K. Hsu (eds), *Culture and Self: Asian and western perspectives*, New York: Tavistock Publications, 1985, pp. 145–46.
89. *Chugakusei no Hahaoya – Amerika no hahaoya to no hikaku* (Mothers of Junior High School Students – a comparison with American mothers). Tokyo: Somucho Seishonen Taisaku Honbu, Youth Affairs Administration Management and Coordination Agency, 1991.
90. *1989 Demographic Yearbook.* New York: United Nations, 1989, pp. 513–14.
91. Suzuki, 'Ways of life', p. 89.
92. *Nanakakoku Hikaku*, p. 48.
93. On clientelistic relations, see S.N. Eisenstadt and L. Roniger, *Patrons, Clients and Friends.* Cambridge: Cambridge University Press, 1984, esp. pp. 145–50, 174–8.
94. Charles A. Anderson, 'Corporate directors in Japan'. *Harvard Business Review*, 62 (May/June 1984), 30.
95. Ibid.; Prestowitz, *Trading Places*, pp. 289–317.
96. Tadao Kagano, Ikujiro Nonaka, Kiyonori Sakakibara and Arihiro Okumura, *Strategic vs. Evolutionary Management: U.S.–Japan comparison*

208   S. M. Lipset: American and Japanese Exceptionalisms

of strategy and organization. Amsterdam: North-Holland, 1985, pp. 55–90;
Labour-Management Relations, pp. 31–2; Masahiko Aoki, Information,
Incentives and Bargains in the Japanese Economy. Cambridge: Cambridge
University Press, 1988, pp. 61–4.

97. The World Youth Survey, p. 60.
98. Masanori Hashimoto and John Raisian, 'Employment tenure and earn-
     ings profiles in Japan and the United States'. American Economic Re-
     view, 75 (September 1985), 726–7; Robert Cole, Work, Mobility and
     Participation. Berkeley, Cal.: University of California Press, 1979,
     pp. 87–90.
99. Shin-chi Takazawa and Arthur M. Whitehill, Work Ways: Japan and
     America. Tokyo: Japan Institute of Labour, 1983, pp. 58–61.
100. Suzuki, 'Ways of life', pp. 88–9; Vogel, Japan as Number One, p. 152.
101. Takezawa and Whitehill, Work Ways, pp. 118–20.
102. The World Youth Survey, 1989, p. 62.
103. James R. Lincoln and Ame L. Kalleberg, Culture, Control and Commit-
     ment. A study of work organization and work attitudes in the United States and
     Japan. Cambridge: Cambridge University Press, 1990, p. 88.
104. Hayashi, 'Statistical study on Japanese national character', 174–5.
105. See Takeshi Inagami, 'The Japanese will to work'. In Okimoto and
     Rohlen (eds), Inside the Japanese System, pp. 32–6.
106. Lincoln and Kalleberg, Culture, Control, p. 56.
107. Ibid., p. 63.
108. Ibid., p. 68.
109. The World Youth Survey, 1989.
110. Leisure and Recreational Activities in Japan. Tokyo: Leisure Development
     Center, 1991, pp. 19–20; see also Labour–Management Relations, p. 38.
111. Leisure and Recreational Activities, pp. 20–2.
112. Ronald Dore, British Factory – Japanese Factory: the origins of national
     diversity in industrial relations. Berkeley, Cal.: University of California
     Press, 1973, pp. 67–70. See also Labour–Management Relations, p. 33.
113. Kazuo Yawata, 'Le recruitments et la carrière des hauts fonctionnaires
     japonais'. Era Promotions Revue de l'Association des Anciens Elèves de l'Ecole
     Nationale d'Administration, no. 113.
114. Chie Nakane, 'Hierarchy in Japanese society'. In Okimoto and Rohlen
     (eds), Inside the Japanese System, pp. 10–11.
115. The World Youth Survey 1989, p. 62.
116. From an analysis of the original data by the Roper Data Library.
117. The data from this study are reported in International Study of Values
     Interim Report. Tokyo: Dentsu Institute for Human Studies, 1991. The
     1991 study was directed by Ronald Inglehart.
118. Lincoln and Kalleberg, Culture, Control, pp. 57–61.
119. Ibid., p. 61.
120. Ibid., p. 50; Dore, British Factory – Japanese Factory, p. 232.
121. Ibid, p. 218.
122. Lincoln and Kalleberg, Culture, Control, p. 61; Robert E. Cole, Japanese

Blue Collar: the changing tradition. Berkeley, Cal.: University of California Press, 1971, p. 238.

123. Richard Rose, 'National pride in a cross-national perspective'. *International Social Science Journal*, 37:1 (1985), 86, 93–5; Russell V. Dalton, *Citizen Politics in Western Democracies*. Chatham, N.J.: Chatham House Publishers, 1988, p. 257; 'American Values'. *The Economist*, 11 September 1992, p. 20.

124. Alex C. Michalos, 'Optimism in thirty countries over a decade'. *Social Indicators Research*, 20 (1988), 178–9. The data for 1990 are from a Gallup Poll release. The Poll did not ask the question from 1986 to 1989 or in 1991.

125. Reischauer, *The Japanese*, pp. 162–5.

126. Triandis, 'Cross-cultural Studies', p. 103.

127. *The World Youth Survey, 1989*, p. 58.

128. Hiroshi Ishida, *Educational Credentialism, Class and the Labor Market: a comparative study of social mobility in Japan and the United States*. Ph.D. Dissertation, Harvard University, 1986, p. 176 (emphasis in original). For a discussion of the emphasis on ranking schools and universities, as well as companies, see Befu, 'Four models of japanese society', pp. 220–2.

129. Nakane, 'Hierarchy', p. 11.

130. George DeVos. 'Confucian hierarchy versus class consciousness in Japan'. Berkeley, Cal.: Department of Anthropology, University of California, unpublished paper, 1990.

131. Suzuki, 'Ways of Life', 88–9.

132. *1987 New Social Indicators*. Tokyo: Social Policy Bureau Economic Planning Agency, 1987, p. 91; *The World Youth Survey, 1989*, p. 86.

133. Patricia A. Roos, *Gender and Work: a comparative analysis of industrial societies*. Albany, N.Y.: State University of New York Press, 1985, pp. 15–16, 131; Constance Sorrentino, 'The changing family in international perspective'. *Monthly Labor Review*, 113 (March 1990), 53.

134. Mary C. Brinton, 'The social-institutional bases of gender stratification: Japan as an illustrative case'. *American Journal of Sociology*, 94 (September 1988) 308.

135. Roos, *Gender and Work*, pp. 146–7.

136. Sorrentino, 'The changing family', 42. 'The total fertility rate is defined as the average number of children that would be born per woman if all women lived to the end of their childbearing years, and at each year of age they experienced the birth rates occurring in the specified year.'

137. Ibid., 44; Robert V. Smith, 'Work and family in contemporary Japan, background information'. Data distributed for a talk at the Woodrow Wilson Center for International Scholars, 17 September 1992.

138. Ibid.

139. Ibid.

140. Reischauer, *The Japanese*, pp. 204–12.

141. For similar findings from 1988 data, see Tatsuko Suzuki, 'Cultural link analysis: its application to social attitudes – a study among five nations'. *Bulletin of the International Statistical Institute*, Proceedings of the 47th Session, Paris, 1989, 368.
142. Prime Minister's Office, 'International comparison', p. 5.
143. *The World Youth Survey, 1989*, p. 86.
144. Prime Minister's Office, 'International comparison', p. 8.
145. See the Dentsu Institute's *Virginia Slims Report, 1990: a comparative study of opinion polls on women's issues between Japan and the United State.* Tokyo: Dentsu Institute for Human Studies, 1990.
146. *Yearbook of Labour Statistics.* Geneva: International Labour Office, 1991, pp. 108, 409, 418.
147. *Chugakusei no Hahaoya*, pp. 1, 14–15, 34.
148. Mary C. Brinton, 'Gender stratification in contemporary urban Japan'. *American Sociological Review*, 54 (August 1989), 554.
149. *Japan Statistical Yearbook, 1989.* Tokyo: Statistics Bureau, Management and Coordination Agency, 1989, p. 782.
150. *The World Youth Survey, 1989*, p. 64.
151. Fumie Kumagai, 'Modernization and the family in Japan'. *Journal of Family History*, 11:4 (1986), 371–82.
152. Glazer, 'Social and cultural factors', p. 861.
153. Management and Coordination Agency, *The Summary of International Comparative Surveys of the Life and Opinions of the Elderly.* Tokyo: Foreign Press Center, Japan, 1986, p. 5; and *Rojin-no Seikatso to Ishiki* (The Lifestyle and Attitudes of the Elderly). Tokyo: Somucho Chokan Kanbo Rujin Taisaku Shitsu, Elderly Affairs Administration, A Management and Coordination Agency, 1991.
154. 'Presentation' by Chikako Usui and 'Comment' by George DeVos, in *Japanese/American National Character Conference.* Tokyo: Institute of Statistical Mathematics, and Stanford Hoover Institution, 1991, pp. 79–80. For same data, see Management and Coordination Agency, *The Summary*, p. 4; and for 1991, see *Rojin-no Seikatsu*.
155. Sorrentino, 'The changing family', 52.
156. Junko Matsubara writing in *Chuo koron* (June or July 1992), as reported in 'Japanese society ignores singles' rights', *Mainichi Daily News*, 5 July 1992, 2.
157. *The World Youth Survey, 1989*, p. 48.
158. Robert Bellah, *Beyond Belief: essays on religion in a post-traditional world.* New York: Harper & Row, 1970, pp. 116–18; see also Bellah, *Tokugawa Religion: the values of pre-industrial Japan.* Glencoe, Ill.: Free Press, 1957.
159. Masatsugu, *The Modern Samurai Society*, p. 18.
160. 'Religion in America'. *Gallup Report*, no. 236 (May 1985), 29, 38, 47–8.
161. *The World Youth Survey, 1989*, p. 74.
162. Tatsuko Suzuki et al., 'A study of Japanese-Americans in Honolulu, Hawaii'. *Annals of the Institute of Statistical Mathematics*, Supplement 7 (1972), 29.

163. Lipset, *The First New Nation*, pp. 99–139.
164. Andrew M. Greeley, 'American exceptionalism: the religious phenomenon'. In Shafer (ed.), *Is America Different?*, pp. 98–100.
165. See Seymour Martin Lipset and Earl Raab, *The Politics of Unreason: right-wing extremism in America, 1790–1977*, 2nd edn. Chicago: University of Chicago Press, 1978.
166. Nathan Glazer and Daniel P. Moynihan, *Ethnicity: theory and experience*. Cambridge, Mass.: Harvard University Press, 1975, pp. 6–7.
167. Seymour Martin Lipset, 'Two Americas, two value systems: blacks and whites'. *The Tocqueville Review*, 13(1) (1992), 137–77.
168. Suzuki, 'Ways of life', 100.
169. Seymour Martin Lipset, 'No third way: a comparative perspective on the left'. In Daniel Chirot (ed.), *The Crisis of Leninism and the Decline of the Left: the revolutions of 1989*. Seattle, Wash.: University of Seattle Press, 1991, p. 195.
170. *Japan 1992*, p. 72; *Labour–Management Relations*, p. 10.
171. Dale, *The Myth*, pp. 105–7; Dore, *British Factory*, pp. 202–3, 219–20, 370; Michael Shalev, 'Class conflict, corporatism and comparison: a Japanese enigma'. In Eisenstadt and Ben-Ami (eds), *Japanese Models*, pp. 73–7.
172. Vincent A. Mahler and Claudio J. Katz, 'Social benefits in advanced capitalist countries'. *Comparative Politics*, 21 (October 1988), 40. Data taken from International Labour Office, *The Cost of Social Security: eleventh international inquiry, 1978–1980*. Geneva: ILO, 1985. See also Fukutake, *The Japanese*, pp. 99–201.
173. Tomoni Kodama, 'Observations on the differences and similarities in the Japanese and US benefit systems'. *Employee Benefits Notes*, 13 (August 1992), 1.
174. Naoyuh Isomo, 'Stimulus size exceeds expectations'. *Nihon Weekly*, 5 September 1992, 4; T.R. Reid, 'Economic Recovery plan'. *Washington Post*, 31 August 1992, A1, A13.
175. For a review of the literature, see Lipset, 'Why no socialism in the United States?', pp. 31–149.
176. Hartz, *The Liberal Tradition in America*; Gad Horowitz, *Canadian Labour in Politics*. Toronto: University of Toronto Press, 1968; Henry Phelps Brown, *The Origins of Union Power*. Oxford: Clarendon Press, 1983.
177. The analysis of the 1990–1 survey directed by Ronald Inglehart is not yet complete. I have not seem much of the data.
178. T.J. Pempel and Keiichi Tsunekawa, 'Corporatism without labor? The Japanese anomaly'. In Philippe Schmitter and Gerhard Lehmbruch (eds), *Trend Toward Corporatist Intermediation*, Beverly Hills, Cal.: Sage Publications, 1979, pp. 231–70; Leonard Lynn and Timothy McKeown, *Organizing Business Trade Associations in America and Japan*. Washington, D.C.: American Enterprise Institute for Public Policy Research, 1988.
179. For an analysis of these experiences, see Robert E. Cole, *Strategies*

212 S. M. Lipset: American and Japanese Exceptionalisms

for Learning Small-group Activities in American, Japanese, and Swedish Industry. Berkeley, Cal.: University of California Press, 1989.

180. Vogel, *Japan as Number One*, p. 141.
181. Mike Millard, 'After the bashing'. *Japan Times Weekly*, 4 July 1992, 3.
182. James C. Abegglen and George Stalk Jr, *Kaisha: the Japanese corporation. The new competitors in world business*. New York: Basic Books, 1985, pp. 194–5.
183. Kagono et al., *Strategic vs. Evolutionary Management*, p. 38.
184. Ibid., pp. 48–9. The survey results are presented in 12 tables on pp. 26–46. The cross-national variations on well over 100 items are considerable.
185. Richard Florida and Martin Kenney, 'Transplanted organizations: the transfer of Japanese industrial organization to the US'. *American Sociological Review*, 56 (June 1991), 382. Karel Cool and Cynthia Legnick-Hall, 'Second thoughts on the transferability of the Japanese management style'. *Organization Studies*, 6 (1985), 1–22.
186. Florida and Kenney, 'Transplanted organization', 391.
187. Fallows, 'The Japanese are different', 37–8.
188. Johnson, 'The People', pp. 82–3.
189. Ibid., p. 82.
190. Lipset, *Continental Divide*, p. 212.
191. Chikio Hayashi, 'The national character in transition'. *Japan Echo*, 25 (Special Issue, 1988), 11.
192. Upham, *Law and Social Change*, pp. 206–7.
193. Johnson, 'The people', p. 82.

5

The Deviant Case in Comparative Analysis

High Stateness in a Muslim Society: The Case of Turkey

ALI KAZANCIGIL

An 'Interpretative/Deviant' Case

Lijphart (1971) and Eckstein (1975) elaborated taxonomies of case studies, which include a species which the former calls 'interpretative' and the latter 'disciplined-configurative' (following the terminology of Verba, 1967). Both authors describe such case studies as the application of theoretical propositions to particular cases. However, while Lijphart asserts that 'their value in terms of theory-building is nil' (1971, p. 692), Eckstein is less categorical in this respect, maintaining that they may 'point up a need for new theory in neglected areas. Thus, the application of theories to cases can have feedback effects on theorizing ...' (1975, p. 99).

This chapter which presents a comparative-interpretative analysis of certain features of the Turkish case, is closer to Eckstein's stance. Here, interpretative approaches should be understood as 'attempts to account for significant historical outcomes or sets of comparable outcomes or processes by piecing together in a manner sensitive to historical chronology and offering limited historical generalizations which are sensitive to context' (Ragin, 1987, p. 35). Furthermore, the present study is undertaken not only because of the intrinsic value of the specific case of Turkey, even if the latter displays a number of quite specific features (as single case analyses very often do), but also to pursue the complementary goal of being causal-analytic, that is offering 'limited generalizations concerning the causes of theoretically defined categories of phenomena ... common to a set of cases' (ibid.). Such phenomena can be, for example, processes of democratic transition, the emergence of the modern state, or changes in the party system from clientelistic to class patterns. Their analyses can be variable-orientated and quantitative, or historical and qualitative. More concretely, while this chapter interprets the historical path of the Turkish political system, it also attempts cautiously a formulation of some limited general propositions, which may have relevance to other cases as well. The causality is understood as probabilistic and not deterministic, the former being much better suited for macro-historical analyses such as this (Lieberson, 1991).

To the extent that the case-orientated analysis developed here has a theoretical relevance, it falls under another type in Lijphart's taxonomy: the 'deviant case', defined as bifurcating from established generalizations and aiming at uncovering the features which cause the deviation. Such case studies

> are implicitly comparative analyses. They focus on a particular case which is singled out for analysis from a relatively large number of cases and which is analyzed within the theoretical and empirical context of this set of cases. The deviant case may be likened to the 'experimental group' with the remainder of the cases constituting the 'control group'. Just as the analytical power of the comparative method increases the closer it approximates the statistical and experimental methods, so the analytical power of the case study method increases the more it approximates the comparative method in the form of deviant case analysis. (Lijphart, 1971, pp. 692–3)

Thus, the approach attempted below is a hybrid of the 'interpretative' and 'deviant' types. The application of such a hybrid type is not so obvious, since the joint pursuit of historical-interpretative and theoretical-comparative goals raises one of the most difficult methodological problems of historical sociology, a field in which interpretative approaches have generally yielded better results than comparative-causal analyses (Badie, 1992; ISSJ, 1992).

The Turkish social and political systems have been subjected to comparative analyses, from different theoretical perspectives. In the 1960 a wide-ranging comparative study brought together the Japanese and Turkish cases, analysing diverse dimensions of these societies from the perspective of political modernization. The comparison between these enormously different countries was inspired by the fact that they were early starters in modernization, having engaged in this effort in the nineteenth century, and its aim was to understand the reasons for which Japan was a more successful modernizer than Turkey (Ward and Rustow, 1964). Another theoretical approach was to compare Turkey with certain Latin American and Southern European countries, within the framework of the bureaucratic-authoritarian paradigm (O'Donnell, 1978). A third framework in which the Turkish case was compared with a whole set of cases was the theories of democratic transition (Özbudun, 1990; Sunar and Sayari, 1986).

In the study of the Turkish case presented here, the analysis will concern the conceptually defined phenomenon of stateness. The goal is to explore the reasons for which this phenomenon proves to be 'deviant' in the Turkish case, when compared to similar phenomena that can be observed in the set of cases considered, that is Muslim societies. The analysis aims at showing that the deviance from this set of cases consists in high stateness, together with the related processes of secularization and democratization. Let us note that, should such features be subjected to a comparative analysis within a different set of cases, the outcome might vary: for example, when the presence and impact of a strong state are studied comparatively between Turkey and certain selected Western European countries (Heper, 1992a), the element of deviance is greatly reduced. Hence, the analysis belongs in this configuration to the 'hypothesis generating' or 'theory confirming/infirming' type (Lijphart, 1971, p. 692).

A clarification regarding the category of Muslim societies is in order: the choice, for comparative purposes, of such a set of cases, conceptualized from a cultural perspective, is by no means due to a culturalist stance. Culturalism consists in holding the cultural variable to govern all the others and to be the major explanatory variable in the study of socio-political change. The category of Muslim societies, as it is used here, does not imply this kind of cultural determinism, which is based on the reification of culture, as well as on stereotypes, which prevails in certain currents of orientalist studies, as shown by critiques such as Saïd (1978) and Hudson (1980). Muslim societies are referred to empirically, that is, as entities in which the vast majority of the population is of Islamic faith, which controls the political system, without ascribing to this factor the capacity to explain all the characteristics of such societies. The latter, taken holistically, display too great a heterogeneity – just consider the differences between Turkey, Malaysia and Saudi Arabia – for the category of Muslim societies to constitute a useful analytical concept for comparisons. In comparative politics, as well as in historical sociology, the culture (or religion) is conceptualized, following Max Weber, not as a factor capable of apprehending the totality of social relations, but as a marker of whatever is historically specific in such relations, and as 'only one side of the causal chain' (Giddens, 1991, p. xvii;

Weber, 1991, p. 27). Culture is thus seen as one variable among many and as a body of symbols, codes and discourses relating to the meaning of action, rather than as the major source of change. In the approach adopted here, the analysis combines such various factors as historical structures, social praxis, state and culture. The state, rather than religion, is considered as an independent variable in the deviance under study, Islam being an intervening variable that provides a meaning to political and social processes and outcomes.

The Origins of Turkish High Stateness

Historical sociology has amply documented the considerable variations displayed by the state, even amongst countries that are geographically and culturally close to each other, such as the Western European nations, not to speak of the variations between the latter and the developing countries (Badie and Birnbaum, 1983; Evans et. al., 1985). It introduced the important conceptual distinction, between a political centre and a state. Badie and Birnbaum (1983, p. 65) maintain that 'state building is only one form of political centralization among others, and the methods followed in building states vary widely from one society to the next'. They provide evidence that there are political systems with both a centre and a state (France), a state but no centre (Italy), a centre but a weak state (Great Britain and the United States), or a weak state and no centre (Switzerland) (pp. 103–5). In their definition, 'the true state (as distinguished from what is merely the centre of a centralized political system) is one that has achieved a certain level of differentiation, autonomy, universality and institutionalization' (p. 60). Charles Tilly (1975, p. 35) has suggested a similar conceptualization of the stateness, to be measured according to the degree to which the government apparatuses are differentiated, centralized, autonomous and formally co-ordinated with each other. Out of such definitions a taxonomy takes shape, in which states are categorized from strong state or high stateness to weak state or low stateness. On such a scale, France appears closest to an ideal type of high stateness: the state attempting to run society through a powerful bureaucracy (others, such as Germany or Spain, belong in various degrees to this type); while Great Britain (and also the United States and Switzerland) is closest to the ideal type of low stateness, where civil society is capable of governing itself, thus making a strong state with a governing bureaucracy to a large extent irrelevant.

In such a taxonomy, the Muslim state belongs at the weaker end of the scale, Islamic polities displaying low stateness. A 'true' state is not part of the Islamic political tradition (Badie, 1986). In Gellner's formula, Muslim political systems are characterized by 'a weak state and a strong culture' (1981, p. 55).

The Turkish state, however, does not fall under this general rule, in terms of such criteria as the level of differentiation, autonomy, institutionalization and degree of control exercized over the social system through a powerful bureaucracy. Despite emerging and developing within an Islamic cultural context, the strong Turkish state appears to be closer to the French, or in certain respects to the German, state (Heper, 1992a) than to weaker, fragmented Muslim political centres facing strong primary and ethnic groups. The pattern found in Muslim formations is low stateness, often characterized by a patrimonial/personal rule, without the capacity to integrate a segmented social base. The causal factor in trying to explain the ability of the Turkish political system to evolve into a high degree of stateness appears be the emergence of a polity enjoying a non religious legitimation. The autonomization of the political sphere from the religious started around the eleventh century due to particular historical circumstances. Subsequently, the Turks were able to develop the institutional and bureaucratic formulas to consolidate, stabilize and perpetuate this feature for several centuries in the Ottoman Empire and later in modern Turkey.

The monism of Islam – the fusion of the spiritual and the temporal – is not unique amongst Abrahamic religions. Judaism is monistic as well (Dieckhoff, 1989), and Eastern Christianity – the Orthodox Church in the Byzantine and Russian Empires – also displayed comparable features known as Caesaro-Papism. However, it is the strongest and most far-reaching, due more to historical circumstances than to the religious doctrines themselves. Under the condition of the Diaspora, Jewish communities did not have the possibility of putting into practice the theocracy – a term invented by the Jewish historian Flavius Joseph (*c.*38–100 AD) to describe the Jewish 'political regime'. In contrast, the Muslims engaged in an imperial adventure as early as the seventh century, only decades after the death of the Prophet, creating the Omayyad and the Abbasid Empires. According to a very plausible hypothesis, this imperial adventure strongly consolidated in Islam the fusion of the spiritual and the temporal spheres, since the religious chief of the *Umma*, the Caliph, became the political and military leader of the Empire as well (Badie 1986: 43). The Islamic political systems would be marked by a pattern that resulted from the mutual reinforcement of the doctrinal monism of the Koran and the *Sunna* (the tradition) and the appropriation of the 'two swords' by the Caliph-Emperor. The Koranic laws (the *Shari'a*) claim to govern, beyond the spiritual life, the entire gamut of social, economic and political relations, following rules that were divinely revealed. Being beyond human reach, such rules could not be challenged. This had a profound impact on the actual modes of Islamic government: sovereignty belonged only to God, whose authority could not be delegated. Thus the Prince wielded power out of sheer necessity. Hence the political authority had very weak legitimacy, was precarious and often resorted to violence. Such a situation was to be a source of governmental instability and institutional weakness throughout history.

The Turkish case was to be an exception in the Muslim world, as regards the issue of the 'two swords'. After their Islamization in Central Asia, the Turks appeared prominently on the Middle Eastern scene in the tenth century in the Abbasid imperial context. Gradually, they came to control first the military, then the political power and by the middle of the eleventh century they created the Seljuk Empire, while the religious power remained in the hands of the Abbasid Caliphs. Hence the 'two swords' were dissociated, if not *de jure* at least *de facto*. Bearers of Asian political traditions, antedating their Islamization, and also borrowing from the Iranian, Abbasid and Byzantine statecraft, they later created the Ottoman Empire (1299–1922), the sovereigns of which laid no claims to the caliphate until the sixteenth century. After their conquest of Egypt, Syria and the Hedjaz (the Holy Places) in the sixteenth century, the Ottomans, as the unchallenged masters of the Sunnite Islam world, transferred the caliphate from Cairo to Istanbul. The Sultan was now also to be the Caliph, in order to acquire the legitimacy and prestige of the spiritual leader of the Muslims, as part of the power strategy of a world empire in which religion was put at the service of secular policies. As part of such policies, they organized a religious hierarchy of salaried clerics – the *ulemâ*, or scholars of Islamic law – which became part of the central bureaucracy and thus an apparatus in the service of the state. The *ulemâ* were in charge of judicial as well as educational functions. Monism continued at the doctrinal level, but the overlapping of the two spheres took on a shape reminiscent of Caesaro-Papism, since the Ottoman Sultan wielded religious power, somewhat as the Russian tzars dominated the Orthodox Church. The Ottoman political order was thus institutionalized according to modalities distinct from other Islamic political systems, on the basis of the relative autonomy of the political sphere, which had its own legitimation distinct from the religious sphere.

This was to be the major factor in enabling the Turks to build a state that was strong and long-lived by any standards, not only those of Muslim society (Gellner, 1981, p. 73).

The Turkish high stateness was achieved over a long period. During the first two centuries of the Empire (fourteenth and fifteenth), Ottoman-Turkish rule was patrimonial-personal, like other Islamic polities. Gradually, the central state institutions emerged and the Ottoman *Herrschaft* became less patrimonial, increasingly acquiring imperial features (Eisenstadt, 1981, pp. 132–3), with a sophisticated bureaucratic apparatus and a corpus of secular laws and regulations. In contrast, in other Islamic countries the political centre, which traditionally suffered from the debilitating effects of a weakly legitimized temporal authority, could not establish a stable rule and differentiate itself from a segmented society. The latter was regularly disrupted by cyclical competition between tribal groups and city dwellers, the dynamics of which was analysed by the fourteenth-century Arab sociologist, Ibn Khaldun.

The Ottoman Turks' way out of this 'Ibn-Khaldunian fatality' (Gellner, 1981, p. 76) was to elaborate a complex and powerful bureaucratic polity. The Ottoman bureaucracy proved to be the only successful and long-lasting one, while in the earlier Muslim polities, the attempts to create central bureaucracies consisting of Turkish slaves (the Mamluk system), in order to save the Empires, did not prevent their decline and demise. Not so in the Ottoman Empire, where this bureaucratic polity was elaborated early and became a powerful instrument of its expansion and stability; elsewhere it had been a late formula against decomposition. The Ottoman central bureaucracy was an example of institutional engineering within an autonomous and well-legitimized political space. The palatial bureaucracy that ran the state was differentiated, specialized and functioned according to a merit system. It was made up of an elite isolated from tribal or kinship ties, recruited individually through various procedures, the typically Ottoman one being the *devshirme* system which required the non-Muslim families in certain regions of the Empire to supply male offspring as recruits. They were socialized and educated in palace schools for administrative and military functions. These military (*Janissaries*), as well as civilian bureaucrats, called *Kapikulu* (slaves of the Porte), were completely subservient to the Sultan and did not constitute an estate, enjoying hereditary rights. Thus came into being a very complex and specialized central as well as provincial bureaucracy, forming the core of a state that was autonomous, even isolated, from the social base. Not only did the state tightly control the social base to an extent unknown in other Muslim formations, but it also reshaped it, through the *Millet* system, from the fifteenth century onwards. This system was another deviant feature, compared with the traditional Muslim polity. The *Millets* – Armenians, Greeks, Jews and Muslims, the latter made up of Turks, Arabs, Kurds and Albanians – were religious/ethnic communities that enjoyed the formal recognition by the central state, with which they could deal directly, while enjoying administrative and judicial autonomy in matters internal to the community.

The central bureaucracy eliminated the independent economic or social forces which challenged its power. In the latter part of the fifteenth century, Mehmet II, the conqueror of Byzance, eliminated the powerful landowning Turkish aristocracy by confiscating the land they owned. The land, the great majority of which belonged to the state, was administered by state-appointed officials without hereditary rights, who collected tax from the peasants and provided services to the state, mainly of a military nature. This system, called the *timar*, was the basic supportive formula of the state. Intermediary structures, such as the guilds and cities, were also denied autonomous power.

The high stateness generated a specific philosophy and a state tradition. The philosophy of the state was the 'Cycle of Equity' (different from Ibn Khaldun's destabilizing cycle between towns and the countryside, which characterized other Muslim systems): wealth can only be amassed under law and order; only the state can provide law and order; the state needs money to operate; the state can tax the available wealth to sustain itself (Gellner, 1981, p. 75). The state-orientated tradition (Heper, 1985) had its origins partly in the pre-Islamic Turkish governmental principle of *yasa*, which the ruler had to apply, basing his government on reason instead of on his personal desires. This led to the emergence of a strong, secular state tradition as well as a large secular legislation, next to the *Shari'a*, which was much wider in scope than in other Islamic systems (Veinstein, 1989). This legislation was formed by *Kânun* (law), codified in compendia called *Kânunname*, and was drawn from the Turkish *yasa* as well as from Islamic, Byzantine and Slav sources. All this contributed to the consolidation of a strong secular state tradition at the very core of the Ottoman-Turkish historical formation.

During the seventeenth and eighteenth centuries, however, the strong state went through a long period of decline under the joint impact of external and internal dynamics and low stateness prevailed. The Ottoman World Empire (Lapidus, 1988) was transformed gradually from the early seventeenth century into a peripheral formation, incorporated into the European World-Economy (Wallerstein,

1974). The *timar* system, which provided the socio-economic basis
of the state, became disorganized and was replaced by a tax-farming
system (*iltizam*), thus leading to the disruption of the countryside at
the same time as the social organization of the cities was breaking
down. The state entered a severe fiscal crisis, and the principle of
well-trained elite officials insulated from their ethnic or kinship ties
was abandoned. As a consequence, the central bureaucracy decayed
and lost its capacity to rule the country and the social base. By
the end of the eighteenth century the central authority was able
to control only a small portion of the provinces, which came under
the growing power of country notables, or potentates, called the
âyan. The most powerful amongst them – the *derebey* – had their
private armies. At this juncture, an age-old question concerning the
ways and means of saving the decaying state, which had been pre-
occupying Ottoman political thinkers since the end of the sixteenth
century, became acute. Contrasting responses were offered by two
different groups of elites: the religious officials – *ulemâ* – who came
to play an important political role in the eighteenth century, saw
the solution in a return to a strict application of the *Shari'a*, which
would stop the decay and enable the Empire to recover its former
glory. To the secular bureaucracy, the cause of the weakening
of the state was of a mundane nature and thus the solution had
to be this-worldly. The secular approach prevailed and lasted.
This outcome was an indication that, despite two centuries of a
weakened centre and a low stateness situation, the state tradition,
founded on an autonomous political sphere with its own legitimacy
had, at least partly, survived. Through a process of political and
administrative reforms, led by the central bureaucracy, throughout the nineteenth and the first part of the twentieth centuries, the
state institutions were gradually strengthened and high stateness was
recovered.

The Rise of a Strong Modern State

In the nineteenth century the Ottoman-Turkish state developed
more efficient means of administration, justice and education, and
increased its control over society. In pre-modern times this control
of a strong polity over the socio-economic base was exercised through
the mode of appropriation of land and was a major factor in explaining the non-availability of autonomous social forces. In this
respect, the Ottoman historical formation was very different from
the Western ones. Occidental feudalism uniquely combined personal

fealty of the vassal and the fiefs; in the Ottoman case, the Turkish cavalry (*timariots*) only held prebends, which were incorporated in the state, and as such were different from the fiefs (Weber, 1978, pp. 1070–85). Both the land and the offices were prebends and not fiefs, the latter in Weber's definition involving the specific fealty of vassals. In the West, relations between the lord and the vassal were based on contractual obligations of fealty and loyalty shaped by a code of honour which was binding on both parties. The Ottoman ruler had no such contractual obligations and his sovereignty was not limited by the contractual rights of the land-grant beneficiary. So, to Weber, the distinctive feature between Western feudalism and Eastern Empire is the type of sovereignty: shared by the lord and his vassals in the West, undivided and centrally concentrated in the hands of the ruler in the East. Conversely, Weber attributed much less importance to the hereditary character of the fief and the non-hereditary nature of the *timar*. The prebendal character of Ottoman land tenure, in which the sovereignty of the Sultan could not be 'detotalized' (Anderson, 1974), or shared, conditioned the institutionalization of the political system. When the central authority became very weak, because the prebends were part of the state structure their holders could not challenge the central bureaucracy from the periphery.

The social function of the producers – peasants, traders and artisans – was to engender a surplus for the political centre to appropriate, according to tributary relationships. The prevailing politico-economic rationality was incompatible with mercantilism, private economic accumulation or social mobility through market mechanisms. The only avenue of social ascent was through state service, and even there the advantages were non-hereditary prebends. This did not allow for the acquisition of political, administrative or judicial titles and functions which might, at the periphery, have led to legitimate and autonomous local powers in relation to the centre (Mardin, 1973; Heper, 1980). Basically, the *âyan* did not derive their power from a feudal-like control over land and agricultural labour, but from their being the local replicas of the political centre.

The mode of disintegration remained prebendal. In a system where the allocation of status and power was mediated not by market forces but by politico-administrative mechanisms, the *âyan* could not challenge the central authority from without. They shared the culture, value system and behaviour of the central bureaucracy. Thus, in the first decades of the nineteenth century, when the Ottoman central bureaucracy began to recover its capacity to control the social periphery thanks to administrative reforms, the power of the *âyan* was easily destroyed. The 1808 *Sened-i ittifak* (Document of Agreement), which the weak central authority was forced to sign with the powerful *âyan*, granting them certain privileges, was by no means the Ottoman Magna Carta. For the rest of the century, the *âyan* remained wealthy, but their power was abolished, some of them being forced to settle outside the areas they dominated and others brought to Istanbul to be incorporated into the central bureaucracy. The power of the political centre remained unrivalled and even at the end of the eighteenth century, when the state institutions became extremely weak, those holding prebends at the periphery (*âyan*), despite their representing strong communitarian resistances against the centre, were unable to mount a serious challenge to the Sultan and force him to share power. Disintegrative trends did not result in the *Ständestaat* (the states or orders of absolutist Europe), in the development of the market and of capitalism, the rise of a bourgeoisie, the constitution of civil society and the emergence of a dynamic 'from below'.

The subsequent changes – the reform of the Empire in the nineteenth century, the setting up of the Republic, the modernization of society and the beginnings of a democratic transition in the twentieth century – were all 'top down', through the initiatives of the state elites. All these characteristics explain why the civil society could not easily emerge as an entity distinct from the political centre, based on market relationships and economic rationality (by contrast with state-mediated relationships and administrative rationality) to form an organically cohesive network of voluntary associations, independent groups and individuals. In the Ottoman Empire the monopolization of power by a bloated centre, with both patrimonial and imperial dimensions, and the close administrative control of the economy and its agents, prevented these becoming a social force based on the market, since this was incompatible with civil society and pluralism, which had to wait until the second half of the twentieth century to start emerging.

The reforms undertaken by the state elites were first designed to strengthen the state and its administration, historically the centrepieces of Turkish social formation. These reforms were gradually extended to the establishment of a secularized judicial and educational system and improvements in the legal status of non-Muslim minorities. One important feature of the *Tanzimat* period (1839–76) was the gradual displacement of the power of the Palace towards the modernized bureaucracy, which Europeans were to call 'the Sublime Porte' (Davison, 1963). Thus, the Sultan had to share the power he traditionally exercised in the name of Islamic law with a Westernized state apparatus which, unlike the patrimonial bureaucracy of the Palace, from 1839 enjoyed legal guarantees granted by the *Tanzimat*. The conservatives, who desired a return to the 'golden age' of the Empire, vigorously opposed these developments, proposing instead the restoration of a Sultan who would not share power, in order to reinstate the reign of the Law of God (Abu-Manneh, 1990). By the second half of the century, the Ottoman polity had recovered high stateness, through a more efficient secular administration, as well as strong state-orientated norms. The spread of secular secondary and higher level schools led to the emergence of new generations of more numerous and socially more diversified modernizing elites, who were socialized to such a state tradition and norms. The *Tanzimat* elites considered that they were the servants of the state (Heper, 1992a), unlike the patrimonial bureaucrats of the Classical Age, who were the 'slaves' of the Sultan. They came to believe that they alone could modernize the country and defend its interests. This was to be the ethos of successive generations of state elites, the Young Ottomans in the 1860s and 1870s, the Young Turks in power from 1908 to 1918, and the Kemalists from the 1920s onwards.

The nineteenth-century state elites were almost exclusively concerned with the welfare of the state and much less with that of society, all the more so because the latter was devoid of organized social forces which could influence or interfere with the state bureaucracy. Until the end of the century, concern with economic matters was the exception amongst the state elites. 'The rather crude mercantilism of the statesmen of the *Tanzimat* was in any case hopelessly irrelevant, both to the bustling nineteenth century and to the fatalistic Turkish population' (Lewis, 1961, p. 451). They were not successful in solving the old financial crisis of the state by promoting economic activities. Although they can be credited with remarkable achievements, such as the instauration of the first constitutional monarchy (1876–8), the Young Ottoman elites were mainly seeking a limited introduction of Western-type modernity in administration, justice and education, while leaving untouched the Islamic communitarian lifestyle and interpersonal relations that characterized the Turkish and other Muslim ethnic groups. They believed that certain parts of the social formation could be exposed to Western modernity while others were kept immune from it, and that this kind of partial approach would suffice to save the state. In contrast, the post-*Tanzimat* modernizers, and particularly the Young Turks who came to power in 1908, developed a more radical view, considering that the mild reformism of the earlier period could not take the country further. They viewed the Western and the Ottoman civilizations as totally incompatible. The one they idealized from a distance had to win over the stagnant and backward one in which they were living. The Young Turks' most significant efforts concerned the socio-economic sphere. They were keenly aware of the absolute necessity to promote a national economy (Ahmad, 1980). The Young Turk experience, which ended in 1918 with the defeat of the Ottoman Empire in the First World War, was followed by the coming to power of the Kemalist elites, led by Mustafa Kemal, who pushed further the radical reforms to create a modern state.

Kemalists had had a Western education and held radical views, but they also shared the basic Ottoman-Turkish tradition of the state bureaucracy's dominance over society. These military and civil bureaucrats considered themselves pillars of the state and the unique holders of legitimate authority (Kazancigil, 1981). The transformations they achieved within two decades constituted a 'revolution from above', without mass mobilization. Whenever they needed the masses, particularly during the war of independence (1919–22), the latter participated as soldiers or commoners, never as revolutionary actors (Trimberger, 1978, p. 17). Victory in this war was won thanks to a national resistance movement based on the alliance between the state elites and the societal elites, that is, the emerging Turkish business class in major cities and small merchants, landowners and local notables in the Anatolian provinces. This alliance, concluded under the leadership of Mustafa Kemal, was also to provide the main social pillar of the emerging modern state. Like the Young Turks, the Kemalists had a sharp awareness about the creation of a national economy. The Turkish business class, which the Young Turks started to promote, found new opportunities to develop in the 1920s. The world economic crisis led the Turkish government to implement etatist economic policies, as of 1931. The state took the lead in industrialization and the public sector grew rapidly. The achievements of the state-led industrialization policy – in the 1930s only the Soviet Union and Japan did better than Turkey – resulted in considerable capital accumulation.

The Kemalist elites embarked on a very ambitious political, social and cultural modernization programme. It started with the proclamation of the Republic in 1923 and continued with the abolition of the Caliphate, the separation of religion and state, as well as the complete secularization of the educational and legal systems. It aimed at transforming all the cultural and symbolic aspects associated with the Islamic way of life: religious institutions, equal status and a public role for women, the language, the Latin alphabet, the calendar and the headgear. All these moves displayed, despite their great diversity, a remarkable coherence of purpose, aiming at the creation of a new national and cultural identity for the Turkish citizen and the liberation of the individual through the passage from a stagnant communitarian way of life to a contractual society, operating on the basis of instrumental rationality. The Kemalist elites' goal was the passage from *Gemeinschaft* to *Gesellschaft*. Such an ambitious social Utopia, imposed from above by a strong state, could not easily penetrate an old Islamic society with strong religious and communitarian traditions. This authoritarian reformism could have ended in complete failure, as did Iranian modernization under the Shah. It did not fail, even though the complete societal transformation the Kemalists wanted has taken longer than they expected. Four factors explain their success: first, the top-down modernization was in conformity with the old Turkish political tradition of state control over society and religion. There was no other autonomously organized social group with strong enough legitimacy to challenge the state elites. Secondly, the reform and modernization movement went uninterrupted for more than a century, so it reached relatively larger strata of society. Thirdly, Kemalist policies were successful in promoting the national economy, capitalist accumulation and bourgeoisie. Finally, the Kemalists were able to institutionalize adequately the new state and the political regime. High stateness enabled the Kemalist modernizing Utopia to take root in Turkish society and not be swept away like so many modernization attempts in other Islamic countries.

Two Outcomes Sustained by High Stateness: Democratization and Secularization

In the second half of the twentieth century, high stateness – the central historical feature of the Turkish polity – was to be a major factor sustaining the emergence of secularism and, somewhat paradoxically, political democracy. While a positive correlation between a strongly legitimized and institutionalized state and secularization is plausible, it appears more debatable as far as democracy is concerned. Indeed, older and stronger democracies correlate with low stateness, for example in the USA or the UK, whereas high-stateness countries, such as France or Germany, had greater difficulties in becoming democratic societies (Badie and Birnbaum, 1983). In the Ottoman-Turkish historical formation, the latter view appears to be even more obvious. Strong and autonomous as it was, the French state had to take account of and respond to the demands of the aristocracy and, later, the bourgeoisie, as Karl Marx showed in his analysis of the social classes and the state in France (1959). The same held for the relations of the Prussian-German state with the *Junkers* as well as with the middle classes. Unlike these two countries, the *Ständestaat* and a civil society did not exist in Ottoman history. The state was extremely autonomous from the social base; the state elites acted according to an ideology and professional norms which advocated responsibility *vis-à-vis* the state interests that they themselves defined, but did not involve the notion of responsiveness to the societal periphery. So, logically, the Turkish high stateness should not correlate positively with the emergence of a civil society and democratization. Yet the contemporary Turkey appears to be on its way towards a democratic society and, like many other major, *longue durée* phenomena in the Ottoman-Turkish polity, such an outcome is due to action from above taken by the state elites (as well as to the impact of external dynamics; Kazancigil, 1981 and 1986). This apparent paradox ceases to exist when the Turkish case is compared with other Muslim societies instead of with Western ones. Muslim societies, except Turkey, display low stateness accompanied by a conspicuous absence of an organized civil society, democracy and secularism. In these societies, several factors, to which reference was made earlier, prevented the political systems functioning effectively. A strong bureaucratic polity and high stateness that the Turks developed provided stability (Heper, 1992b) and enabled them to overcome the debilitating features of Muslim polities. Even if high stateness made more difficult the emergence of a secular, democratic civil society, the latter could not exist without the former, given the Islamic context.

Democratization

Quite typically, the origins of representative institutions are due not to some social pressure from below but to the initiative of Young Ottoman state elites, who persuaded Sultan Abdulhamit II to proclaim a Constitution in 1876 and to organize in the same year legislative elections (by restricted and indirect suffrage). The Ottoman Parliament was inaugurated in March 1877 and closed in February 1878 by the Sultan, who suspended the Constitution. The latter was to be restored in 1908 by the Young Turk Revolution, which inaugurated the second period of constitutional monarchy. Two competitive elections occurred in 1908 and 1912. Even though it was interrupted in 1913 by a *coup d'état*, this period constituted the first experience of parliamentarianism and of organized political parties with fairly wide social bases (Ahmad, 1969). During the war of national liberation (1919–22) against the Allied occupation of Anatolia, resulting from the Ottoman Empire's defeat in the First World War, the nationalists established the Turkish Grand National Assembly in Ankara to exercise legislative and executive powers under the leadership of Mustafa Kemal. In 1921 this Assembly adopted a Constitution the pillar of which was the principle of popular sovereignty. Following the victory of the Turkish nationalists in 1922, Mustafa Kemal created the People's Party, later the Republican People's Party (RPP), which ruled the country until 1950. Two attempts to found an opposition party, in 1924 and in 1930, failed. These years of single-party rule, from the foundation of the Republic in 1923 until 1946, witnessed the consolidation of the republican order through the radical reforms already mentioned. Mustafa Kemal exercised an authoritarian leadership until his death in 1938. However, unlike Nazism in Germany, Fascism in Italy and other authoritarian regimes in Central Europe and the Balkans, the declared objective of Kemalism was to progress towards a democratic polity. Mustafa Kemal succeeded in routinizing his largely charismatic power, strengthening the political institutions and establishing the regular holding of elections. Under Kemalism participation and mobilization were low, but the political institutionalization was high (Özbudun, 1990, p. 197).

The democratic transition began with the holding of pluralistic legislative elections in 1946. The founding act of the democratic regime was the alternation of power, thanks to the victory of the opposition in the elections of 1950, after 27 years of single-party rule. Gradual transition to democracy was facilitated by the absence of an official single-party ideology. Several factors contributed to the transition: some were external, such as pressures in favour of liberalization in economy and politics, originating from the United States; but internal factors, such as pressure from certain social groups (especially business circles and large-scale agriculturalists) to share political power, hitherto held almost exclusively by state elites, probably played a more important role. Confronted with such demands, the state elites preferred to opt for democracy, which the Kemalist regime had always proclaimed to be its long-term objective. Such an option seemed to them the best way to preserve the Republic's achievements. They naturally hoped to keep control of the state and a monopoly on republican legitimacy. The Turkish transition occurred in the context of *reformà* and *pactada*, not of *rupturà* (O'Donnell and Schmitter, 1986), with weak mobilization and participation, by agreement between certain elite groups. The leaders of the party in power and those of the opposition agreed on a new electoral law before the decisive parliamentary elections of 1950. Such a development was not alien to Ottoman-Turkish statecraft. However, in the nineteenth century such alliances had been restricted to the different bureaucratic factions of the Ottoman State. During the republican-Kemalist period, up to 1945, this alliance was controlled and directed by the state elites. The democratic transition resulted in some sharing of power between the state elites and political, economic and social ones, that is between the centre and the periphery. The latter polarity, rather than left–right tensions or those between the bourgeoisie and the subordinate classes, was to be the principal axis of the Turkish political system in the initial phases of transition until the 1960s, after which class relations dominated the polity. The 1950 elections were definitely a turning point, to the extent that the strong state, represented by a powerful central bureaucracy, had to become slowly but increasingly responsive to social forces. Such an outcome, although certainly not intentional, was none the less the result of state policies which fostered the social forces that would later challenge the state. Furthermore, the availability of high stateness provided, in the subsequent three decades of political turmoil, the necessary stability for the processes of democratic transition to be successful, despite several setbacks.

Those three decades between 1950 and 1980 were to witness the alternation of pluralistic politics and three military *coups d'état* with the authoritarian interludes of 1960–1, 1971–3 and 1980–3 (Kazancigil, 1991a). In the 1960s and 1970s the state elites, led by the military bureaucracy, competed with political elites representing the urban business class, Anatolian land-owners and the peasantry. Most of the competitive elections held between 1950 and 1980 were won and the country mostly governed by conservative parties (Democratic Party: 1950–60; Justice Party: 1965–80; with the exception of Republican People's Party-led governments: 1961–5, 1974–5 and 1978–9) representing these social groups, while the military questioned their legitimacy, accusing them of violations of Kemalist secularist republican principles. Thus the state elites interrupted the parliamentary system thrice, and tried to reorganize it so as to secure its functioning according to its own norms, before handing back power to politicians. By the 1970s the social basis of politics had been transformed and the party system had undergone a realignment. In the towns and the most-developed western regions, voters adopted more autonomous and instrumentalized criteria while in the less-developed regions clientistic relationships still predominated.

As the country industrialized and the market economy extended, political clientism tended to decline, even if it is still largely practised. On the whole the party system gradually lost the characteristics which it retains in other Muslim countries (Badie, 1989).

After the bitter experiences of the late 1970s, marked by bad political management and terrorism, and the very repressive military regime of 1980–3 Turkey appears to have established in the 1990s a democratic regime with a base sufficiently solid to last.

One important element of this democratic base is the existence of a dynamic, market-economy-based, autonomous civil society, by no means a foregone conclusion in a Muslim society. Again, somewhat paradoxically, this occurrence was possible, at least initially, thanks to policies implemented by the strong central state. The social transformation which led to this outcome started in the first two decades of the twentieth century. As already noted above, the Young Turks state elites had fully grasped the necessity to extend such transformations beyond the administrative, judicial and educational spheres. In 1917 one of the regime's thinkers, Yusuf Akçura, warned that 'if the Turks fail to produce amongst themselves a bourgeois class ... the chances of survival of a Turkish society composed only of peasants and officials will be very slim' (Berkes, 1964; p. 426). Later, the statist economic policies pursued by the Kemalist regime in the 1930s and 1940s allowed Turkey to enjoy considerable economic accumulation, but also helped the emergence of a class of financiers, merchants and entrepreneurs even though the state continued, as it still does, to play a very important role in the economy. This bourgeoisie as well as the dynamics of the market economy, are part of the structural elements indispensable to the consolidation and continued existence of democracy (provided they are balanced by other social and political factors). This fact was captured by Barrington Moore in his well-known formula: 'no bourgeois, no democracy' (1967, p. 428). Originally nurtured by the state bureaucracy and by 'top-down' action of a clientelistic type, the bourgeoisie gradually took hold so that, from 1945, it could defy the power monopoly held by the state elites. In subsequent decades the social groups supported by the market and economic activities gradually strengthened. The bourgeoisie increased its power. State elites, especially the military, remain very potent but since the 1970s, they no longer hold the monopoly of power. The Turkish social formation thus experienced, with ups and downs, that fundamental transformation which was at the root of Western political modernity, that is, the capacity of the bourgeoisie to project its economic power on to the political system. As the administrative rationality inherited from the Ottomans gave way to economic rationality, civil society became consolidated, it penetrated the state and shared power with the state elites. Republican and Kemalist modernity, imposed by authority from above, was gradually displaced by a modernity flowing from social and political forces and greater participation (Kazancigil, 1991b).

Nevertheless, the transformation of the relationships between state and civil society, favourable as it is to the emergence of a pluralistic and democratic order, does not *ipso facto* lead to polyarchy and citizens enjoying all the civic and political freedoms. The existence of an autonomous civil society, a bourgeoisie and a market economy are necessary but not sufficient conditions for democracy. For political democracy and citizenship in the West were won by very long struggles of the dominated classes against the bourgeoisie, against exploitation and the inequalities inherent in capitalism. When the Kemalist Republic undertook the transition from *Gemeinschaft* to *Gesellschaft* and encouraged the emergence of individuals free of communal restraints and active members of a contractual society dominated by instrumental rationality, it could not, or perhaps did not want to, recognize that the relationships between the market and democracy are at once close and contradictory: that the capitalist economy engenders inequality while citizenship is based on equality before the law (Polanyi, 1944; Dahl, 1985; Turner, 1986). The lessons of Western democracies, established after long struggles by the workers against the bourgeoisie to obtain and consolidate their rights and political freedoms, are relevant to contemporary Turkey (Giddens, 1981 and 1985; Marshall, 1973).

Such issues have been on the political agenda of Turkey since the 1970s. Voluntary associations grew tremendously in the 1960s and 1970s (Yücekök, 1971). Trade unions also became stronger. All these developments were severely restricted in 1980 but, with the restoration of a democratic regime, such restrictions are being lifted in the 1990s and a more open and free civil society is growing again. A lively democratic debate relayed by a pluralist press bears on political and economic questions, on environmental, cultural, religious, gender and human rights issues, as well as on the local administrative and cultural autonomy to be given to the important Kurdish minority (some 20 per cent of the population).

Secularization

The historical pattern of the Ottoman polity, involving control exercised over the religious sphere by a strong state enjoying its own legitimacy, displayed features that were favourable to the subsequent development of secularism. The nineteenth century reforms greatly enhanced secularist dimensions in the administrative, educational and judicial institutions. The Young Turks started to extend secularism to larger social groups. The failure of the pan-lslamist reform experience of Abdulhamit II (1876–1909), who, as the Sultan-Caliph, tried to mobilize and rally around his person the Muslim populations of the Empire by using Islamic symbols, reinforced the pro-Western orientation of the Young Turk state elites. They interpreted the Sultan's unsuccessful efforts as a further evidence of the impossibility of organizing modernization around Islamic values and way of life. The Kemalists went further in that direction in the 1920s and 1930s. Socialized to the ideas of Enlightenment, positivism and progress, they were committed to drive religion out of the public arena and relegate it to the sphere of individual conscience. The Kemalist reforms aimed at achieving a society and a cultural context structured by reason and science instead of by religious faith. This secularist orientation, which concerned the status of women and the family and even interfered with Islamic religious practices, such as the attempt to impose the use of the Turkish-language version of the Koran and public prayers in the Turkish language (which was quickly abandoned), culminated in the introduction of the principle of the separation of the state and Islam in the Constitution of 1937. Until the 1950s all this was adhered to by only a small portion of the population made up of Westernized elite groups. Because it was forcefully imposed by the state, the great majority of the population considered it a violation of the liberty to practice their Islamic faith. Kemalist secularism was a mixture of French Jacobinist laicism and the Ottoman tradition of keeping religion under the control of a strong state. These two elements were in fact contradictory, since French laicism is based on a strict separation between Church and state, rather than the supervision of the former by the latter.

The advent of a pluralist democracy in the 1950s created considerable strains for the state-imposed Kemalist laicism. Religious freedom became an electoral issue. Viewed by the Kemalist circles, and particularly the army, as a deadly threat against the most fundamental principle of the Republican order, the resurgence of political Islam was one of the motives invoked to justify the military *coups d'état* of 1960, 1971 and 1980. Democratic debate and pluralism allowed Islamic movements to participate in politics and Islamist parties appeared on the political scene in the 1970s. Their electoral score oscillated between 11.8 per cent in 1973 and 13 per cent in 1991, through 8.6 per cent in 1977 and 7.2 per cent in 1987.

They also participated in three coalition governments from 1973 to 1980. Besides the political formations, there are the *tarikat* (religious brotherhoods), cultural associations, a press generously financed by the 'Islamic international' (basically Saudi Arabia with at times Iran and Libya) and a remarkable intellectual elite. Thus, Islam benefited from Turkey's move from an authoritarian modernity imposed by the state to a modernity supported by a more autonomous, open and pluralistic civil society. Yet, the very characteristics which have allowed it to prosper inhibits Islamism from imposing its dogmatic and monolithic vision on society as a whole. While taking advantage of the opportunities for action offered by the democratic order, the Turkish Islamists, like their counterparts in Egypt and Algeria, consider democracy to be illegitimate. On the other hand, the secular powers in the country are sometimes tempted to control them by authoritarian methods which, of course, are incompatible with democracy. That is why the Islamist challenge is a crucial test for democracy in a Muslim society: either the Islamists are integrated with the political matrix and citizenship, which they will have to accept as legitimate, or the secular state will control (but for how long?) Islamic movements by authoritarian means, to the detriment of democracy.

The tensions between democratic and Islamist legitimacies in Turkish civil society recall those which arose in Protestant countries in the seventeenth century during the Puritan revolution. Just as zealous Puritans were unable to impose their absolutist faith on Protestant societies, so the zealous Islamists cannot overcome the secular forces which predominate in Turkish society. Kemalist secularism of the Jacobin variety, imposed by the state and thus in contradiction with democracy, is in the process of transmuting into a secularism of the Protestant type, with a free Islam but confined to the private sphere and individual conscience, facilitating the consolidation of a democratic order. This would require that the state withdraw the control it exercises over institutional Islam through the Directorate of Religious Affairs under the Prime Minister. Such a hypothesis is open to at least two objections. In the first place, given the pervasiveness of the state, is not Turkish secularism closer to the French model than to the Protestant one? Yet this parallel holds only for the state, not for religion; for in the French case there is the Catholic Church, a centralized institution holding its dialogue with the state, while in the Turkish case there is the nebula of Islam with no unified representation with which the state might negotiate. In the second place, although Protestantism – more precisely Lutheranism – like Islam, did not at its outset distinguish between the spiritual and the temporal (Hermet, 1986; Walzer, 1965), it none the less grew, particularly in its Calvinist variety, very much as part of the tradition of the dissociation of the two swords. Turkey obviously did not share any such history. Yet beyond the traditional autonomy of the political from the religious sphere, as we have emphasized already, over a long period the Republic separated religion from the political sphere by force, while a secular civil society and a market economy emerged. When, thanks to democratization, Islam reappeared on the scene, it was within the context of a society wherein individualism and pluralism were sufficiently rooted to accept the absolutist faith of the Islamists. In this respect, the relationship between social and political change, on the one hand, and theological and doctrinal issues, on the other, is far from being indifferent. Pursuing the parallel between Protestantism and Islam, the question is: what are the chances that those Islamic sects, 'revivalist' movements, the *tarikat*, which are more open to modernity, will prevail over the more conservative ones, as did Calvinism, which from the seventeenth and eighteenth centuries on, contributed to the rise of economic, social and political modernity, in contrast to Lutheranism which held a very absolutist and anti-democratic conception of the state and society (Troeltsch, 1912 and 1981; Weber, 1991)? In other words, does the Turkish experience of democratization and secularization offer a societal context from which a 'Calvinist' neo-Islam could emerge? This theological issue is significant because of its relation to the historical-sociological issue about the extent to which changing Muslim political traditions and institutions, as well as social conditions and class structures, can lead to the emergence of democratic polities (Esposito and Piscatori, 1991). The Turkish case is the only one to provide an affirmative answer to this question. The record of other Muslim societies' democratic transition or more limited parliamentary experiments and timid efforts towards secularization, spreading in some cases over decades, in Algeria, Egypt, Indonesia, Iran, Jordan, Morocco, Kuwait, Pakistan, Senegal, Sudan and Tunisia, has not been very encouraging.

So far, Turkish democracy has been able to keep Islamism under control. If the democratic regime shows its capacity to maintain economic growth while reducing social inequalities, political Islam will remain an extremist phenomenon, at most winning municipal elections in the least favoured areas. If the opposite happens, Islamism may become more dangerous, though not to the point of conquering the country. A constitutionally secular state, the market economy, an industrial and financial entrepreneurial class and a civil society made up of increasingly individualistic citizens make this threat incomparably less likely in Turkey than it is in other Muslim countries. The existence of high stateness over the *longue durée* has been a major factor in this respect.

Conclusion

Four central features of the Turkish state and society come out of the above case-orientated study as 'deviant', when compared to other Muslim polities. Amongst these features, two are independent explanatory factors: an autonomously legitimized political sphere, relatively dissociated from the religious sphere, and high stateness, with a strong centralized, bureaucratic polity. The other two – democracy and secularism – appear as dependent factors. The deviance is reduced when comparison is made with certain European states. Interestingly enough, the Turkish case of high stateness appears in many respects closer to European rather than to Muslim polities.

References

Abu-Manneh, B. 1990: 'The Sultan and the bureaucracy: the anti-Tanzimat concepts of Grand Vizier Mahmud Nedim Pasa'. *International Journal of Middle East Studies*, 22(3): 257–74.

Ahmad, F. 1969: *The Young Turks: the Committee of Union and Progress in Turkish politics, 1908–1914*. Oxford: Clarendon Press.

——1980: 'Vanguard of a nascent bourgeoisie: the social and economic policy of the Young Turks, 1908–1918'. In O. Okyar and H. Inalcik (eds), *Social and Economic History of Turkey (1071–1920)*, Ankara: Meteksan.

Anderson, P. 1974: *Lineages of the Absolutist State*. London, New Left. Books.

Badie, B. 1986: *Les deux Etats. Pouvoir et société en Occident et en terre d'Islam*. Paris: Fayard.

——1989: 'L'analyse des partis politiques en monde musulman: la crise des paradigmes universels'. In *Idéologies, partis politiques et groupes sociaux. Etudes réunies par Yves Mény pour Georges Lavau*, Paris: Presses de la Fondation nationale des sciences politiques, pp. 271–87.

——1992: 'Comparative analysis and historical sociology'. *International Social Science Journal*, no. 133: 319–27.

——and Birnbaum, P. 1983: *The Sociology of the State*. Chicago, Ill.: University of Chicago Press.

Berkes, N. 1964: *The Development of Secularism in Turkey*. Montreal: McGill University Press.

Dahl, R.A. 1985: *A Preface to Economic Democracy.* Cambridge: Polity Press.

Davison, R. 1963: *Reform in the Ottoman Empire, 1856–1876.* Princeton, N.J.: Princeton University Press.

Dieckhoff, A. 1989: 'Sionisme et Judaïsme: la difficile et fragile autonomie du politique'. *Revue française de science politique,* 39(6): 816–27.

Eckstein, H. 1975: 'Case study and theory in political science'. In F.I. Greenstein and N.W. Polsby (eds), *Handbook of Political Science,* Reading, Mass.: Addison-Wesley, vol. 7, pp. 79–137.

Eisenstadt, S.N. 1981: 'The Kemalist revolution in comparative perspective'. In A. Kazancigil and E. Özbudun (eds), *Atatürk: Founder of a Modern State,* London: C. Hurst, pp. 127–42.

Esposito, J.L. and Piscatori, J.P. 1991: 'Democratization and Islam'. *Middle East Journal,* 45(3): 427–40.

Evans, P.B., Rueschemeyer, D. and Skocpolt, T. (eds). 1985: *Bringing the State Back In.* Cambridge: Cambridge University Press.

Gellner, E. 1981: *Muslim Society.* Cambridge: Cambridge University Press.

Giddens, A. 1981: *A Contemporary Critique of Historical Materialism,* vol. 1: *Power, Property and the State.* London: Macmillan.

—— 1985: *A Contemporary Critique of Historical Materialism,* vol. 2: *The Nation State and Violence.* Cambridge: Cambridge University Press.

—— 1991: 'Introduction'. In M. Weber, *The Protestant Ethic and the Spirit of Capitalism,* London: Harper Collins Academic, pp. vii–xxvi.

Heper, M. 1980: 'Center and periphery in the Ottoman Empire with special reference to the nineteenth century'. *International Political Science Review,* no. 1, 81–105.

—— 1985: *The State Tradition in Turkey.* North Humberside: Eothen Press.

—— 1992a: 'Strong state as a problem for the consolidation of democracy: Turkey and Germany compared'. *Comparative Political Studies,* 25(2): 169–94.

—— 1992b: 'The strong state and democracy: the Turkish case in comparative historical perspective'. In S.N. Eisenstadt (ed.), *Democracy and Modernity,* Leiden: E.J. Brill, pp. 142-63.

Hermet, G. 1986: *Sociologie de la construction démocratique.* Paris: Economica.

Hudson, M.C. 1980: 'Islam and political development'. In J.L. Esposito (ed.), *Islam and Development: religion and sociopolitical change.* Syracuse, N.Y.: Syracuse University Press, pp. 1–24.

International Social Science Journal (ISSJ) 1992: 'Historical sociology', no. 133, August.

Kazancigil, A. 1981: 'The Ottoman-Turkish State and Kemalism'. In A. Kazancigil and E. Özbudun (eds), *Atatürk: Founder of a Modern State,* London: Hurst: 37–56.

—— 1986: 'Paradigms of modern state formation in the periphery'. In A. Kazancigil (ed.), *The State in Global Perspective,* Aldershot: Gower, 119–42.

—— 1991a: 'Democracy in Muslim lands: Turkey in comparative perspective'. *International Social Science Journal,* no. 128, 343–60.

—— 1991b: 'De la modernité octroyée par l'Etat à la modernité engendrée par la société'. In S. Vaner (ed.), *Modernisation autoritaire en Turquie et en Iran*, Paris: L'Harmattan, pp. 19–31.

Lapidus, I. 1988: *A History of Islamic Societies*. Cambridge: Cambridge University Press.

Lewis, B. 1961: *The Emergence of Modern Turkey*. London: Oxford University Press.

Lieberson, S. 1991: 'Small n's and big conclusions: an examination of the reasoning in comparative studies based on a small number of cases'. *Social Forces*, no. 70, 307–20.

Lijphart, A. 1971: 'Comparative politics and the comparative method'. *American Political Science Review*, 65(3): 682–93.

Mardin, S. 1973: 'Center-periphery relations: a key to Turkish politics?'. *Daedalus*, no. 102, 169–90.

Marshall, T.H. 1973: *Class, Citizenship and Social Development*. Westport, Conn.: Greenwood Press.

Marx, K. 1959: 'Eighteenth Brumaire of Louis Bonaparte'. In L. Fever (ed.), *Marx and Engels: basic writings on politics and philosophy*, New York: Doubleday.

Moore, B. Jr 1967: *Social Origins of Dictatorship and Democracy: lord and peasant in the making of the modern world*. Harmondsworth, Middx: Penquin Books.

O'Donnell, G. 1978: 'Reflections on the patterns of change in the bureau-cratic-authoritarian state'. *Latin American Research Review*, 13(1).

—— and Schmitter, Ph. C. 1986: *Transitions from Authoritarian Rule: tentative conclusions about uncertain democracies*. Baltimore, Md: Johns Hopkins University Press.

Özbudun, E. 1990: 'Turkey: crisis, interruptions, and requilibrations'. In L. Diamond, J.L. Linz and M.L. Seymour (eds), *Democracy in Developing Countries*, vol. 3: *Asia*. Boulder, Col.: Lynne Rienner, pp. 187–229.

Polanyi, K. 1944: *The Great Transformation: the political and economic origins of our time*. New York: Reinhardt.

Ragin, Ch. C. 1987: *The Comparative Method: moving beyond qualitative and quantitative strategies*. Berkeley and Los Angeles, Cal.: University of California Press.

Saïd, E.W. 1978: *Orientalism*. New York: Panther.

Shaw, S.J. and Shaw, E.K. 1977: *History of the Ottoman Empire and Modern Turkey*, vol. 2: *The Rise of Modern Turkey 1808–1975*. Cambridge: Cambridge University Press.

Sunar, I. and Sayari, S. 1986: 'Democracy in Turkey: problems and prospects'. In G. O'Donnell, Ph. Schmitter and L. Whitehead (eds), *Transition from Authoritarian Rule: Southern Europe*. Baltimore, Md: Johns Hopkins University Press, pp. 165–86.

Tilly, Ch. (ed.) 1975: *The Formation of National States in Western Europe*. Princeton, N.J.: Princeton University Press.

Trimberger, E.K. 1978: *Revolution from Above: Military Bureaucrats and De-*

velopment in Japan, Turkey, Egypt and Peru. New Brunswick, N.J.: Transaction Books.

Troeltsch, E. 1912: *Protestantism and Progress*. London: Williams & Norgate.

—— 1981: *The Social Teaching of the Christian Churches*, 2 vols. Chicago, Ill.: University of Chicago Press.

Turner, B.S. 1986: *Citizenship and Capitalism: the debate over reformism*. London: Allen & Unwin.

Veinstein, G. 1989: 'L'Empire dans sa grandeur'. In R. Mantran (ed.), *Histoire de l'Empire ottoman*. Paris: Fayard, pp. 156–226.

Verba, S. 1967: 'Some dilemmas in comparative research'. *World Politics*, 20(1): 111–27.

Wallerstein, I. 1974: *The Modern World-System: capitalist agriculture and the origins of the European world-economy in the sixteenth century*. New York: Academic Press.

Walzer, M. 1965: *The Revolution of the Saints: a study in the origins of radical politics*. Cambridge, Mass.: Harvard University Press.

Ward, R.E. and Rustow, D.A. 1964: *Political Modernization in Japan and Turkey*. Princeton, N.J.: Princeton University Press.

Weber, M. 1978: *Economy and Society*, vol. 2, ed. G. Roth and C. Wittich. Berkeley, Cal.: University of California Press.

—— 1991: *The Protestant Ethic and the Spirit of Capitalism*. London: Harper Collins Academic.

Yücekök, A.M. 1971: *Türkiye 'de Örgütlenmis Dinin Sosyo-Ekonomik Tabani 1946–1968* (The Socio-economic Basis of Organized Religion in Turkey). Ankara: A.Ü Siyasal Bilgiler Fakültesi.

6

Comparing Similar Countries

Problems of Conceptualization and Comparability in Latin America

JOHN D. MARTZ

Comparativists often find themselves confounded by the compulsive drive toward generalization about widely disparate political systems. The need to integrate insights and expertise from several disciplines-further challenges scholars' collective analytical capabilities. In recent decades, moreover, divisions between students of the Third World and those who concentrate on the Western industrialized states have also complicated efforts toward broad theorizing. All this has been reflected in the work of those who have specialized on the study of Latin America. The task of seeking broad theoretical themes by which to conceptualize the politics of the region has often foundered on the shoals of the pronounced diversity between and among more than two dozen nations.

The flow of current events has also compounded the problems facing the student of Latin America. Thus, the idealistic enthusiasm which accompanied the apparent upsurge of modernizing democracies in the early and mid-1960s nourished extensive theorizing about political development. The concomitant rise of armed rebellion and the radicalizing inspiration of the Cuban Revolution helped to nourish neo-Marxist elaborations of what became known as the dependency school of thought. The clash of political systems and competitive conceptual models led to ever more serious intellectual questioning by the scholars of the day. The challenge was renewed and rendered even more complex by the arrival of the authoritarian impulse of the 1970s.

As putatively democratic regimes fell right and left, there was heightened impetus to the formulation of corporatist ideas. A related

consequence was the bureaucratic-authoritarian paradigm which
was shaped by a host of scholars. The later wave of democratic
transitions which emerged in the 1980s helped to provoke yet another
renewal of theorizing at the macro level. Whatever one's individual
proclivities, the fact remains that such systemic changes demanded
concerted attention. For comparativists, the previous emphasis on
bureaucratic-authoritarianism inevitably gave way to efforts at explaining the emerging democratic transitions. Beyond this, yet another
intellectual current subsequently began to flow: the renaissance of
culturalist analyses which characterize much of our contemporary
effort to produce better and more systematic conceptualization.

Two broad characteristics have generally marked efforts to understand social change: regime stability and political behaviour. First,
they have tended to mount strong attacks on previous theorizing,
out of which new ideas then germinate. In addition, exclusivistic
claims to new insights scarcely obscure the fact that a cumulative
process has been operative. Theorizing which comes under fire from
new intellectual perspectives, then, can at the same time make its
own distinctive contribution to subsequent theorizing. This is no
less true for Latin America area specialists than it is for comparativist
generalists. Whatever a particular theoretical view, there is the
omnipresent necessity of defending it against charges that the cultural distinctions among countries and regions dilute the desired
degree of analytic comparability.

Political Science and Latin American Studies:
From Modernization Forward

There are long-standing tensions and contradictions between the
discipline and political studies of the region. More than three decades
ago the subfield of comparative politics was donning new and modern
clothing. Dedicated to the explanation of politics through new conceptual frameworks and theoretical perspectives, as well as gripped
methodologically by a compulsion to use newly evolving quantitative
techniques, the subfield was soon outstripping qualitatively more
specialized studies of Latin American politics. Through the 1960s
the relationship between comparativists and area specialists was
uneasy. In Merle Kling's seminal assessment of the field, the tone
was decidedly negative:

> Political research on Latin America resembles the area which is the
> object of its study. It retains underdeveloped and traditional features;

it is under both internal and external pressures to modernize. ...
Political scientists specializing in Latin America have not reached,
to borrow Rostow's familiar metaphor, the take-off stage. ... They
often have been content to play the role of consumers rather creators
of the newer conceptual products of modern political science. (Kling,
1964: 168)

Rosendo Gomez affirmed this view in no uncertain terms: 'It is
difficult to find any considerable assistance in the works of Latin
American scholars. In political science, there are very few studies
that would be significant by North American standards' (Gomez,
1967: pp. 37–8). Appearing the same year was a multidisciplinary
assessment by Kalman H. Silvert of Latin American studies. He
denied the allegation that the quality was uniformly low across the
disciplinary spectrum; at the same time, he was less than sanguine
towards political science, 'one of the most maligned of the disciplines'
(Silvert, 1967, p. 98). The disciplinary relevance of Latin American
political studies remained an empirical question, one which I
addressed in a 1971 essay subtitled 'A discipline in search of a
region' (Martz, 1971). While arguing that comparativists with
Latin American specialization were unduly apologetic, I also characterized the collective state of ongoing research as being in a state
of adolescence, with many pitfalls in the offing. At the same time,
practitioners were more than ever eager to place themselves within
the context of contemporary comparative political studies:

The record would seem to suggest that Latin American political studies
have more often than not been unimaginative in concept and pe-
destrian in approach. A certain healthy eclecticism has been diluted
by a Pavlovian tendency to respond to passing fads within the discipline. Political scientists committed to Latin American studies have
in recent years rushed to follow the comparativist pack. They have
been distinctly trend-followers rather than trend-setters. (Martz,
1971, 71)

The 1960s' thrust of modernization literature, then, was mirrored
in the work by students of the region. However, although Latin
Americanists produced a number of monographs which were framed
by that theoretical perspective, the broader conceptual contributions
were scarcely profound. Indeed, 'no matter how outstanding, this
work did not enter the mainstream of theorizing in comparative
politics, nor did Latin Americanists trained in the United States
provide new theoretical innovations for the field' (Valenzuela, 1988,

p. 68). The winds of fresher theorizing began to blow with the emergence of the dependency literature, the best of which was generated largely by Latin American scholars rather than their colleagues north of the Rio Bravo. Among the more influential contributors were Fernando Henrique Cardoso, Osvaldo Sunkel, Celso Furtado, and André Gunder Frank. With some exceptions on the part of Africanists, however, the concepts of dependency were notable in being applied almost exclusively by comparativists whose major focus was Latin America. Consequently, dependency came to be associated much more with the work of Latin Americanists than with the comparative politics field at large.

The so-called *dependencia* literature also extended beyond the discipline to a greater extent than modernization theory, even at its zenith. To be sure, the latter had drawn substantially on the sociological literature, notably such figures as Max Weber, Marion Levy, Talcott Parsons and Edward Shils (Almond, 1960). To a much lesser degree, economics, anthropology and psychology also provided elements in the conceptual mix. At the same time, the incorporation of ideas from other disciplines was accomplished in considerable part through the process of redefining politics and political science with very broad strokes of the brush. In contrast, as Valenzuela remarked, dependency writings were more explicit in calling for 'a broad interdisciplinary perspective to explain the major themes of Latin American reality: economic underdevelopment, social inequality, political instability, and authoritarianism' (Valenzuela, 1988, p. 71).

The dependency literature insisted that the study of change required a comprehension of the global historical developmental process; an analytic focus on individual societies would not suffice. Thus, many studies began with extended historical analysis, as informed by economic, political and sociological data. Cardoso and Faletto (1969), for example, engaged at length in historical interpretation while progressively introducing large doses of economics as set within a political context. In this and subsequent works, Cardoso in particular stressed the socio-political dimension, which he himself called a 'historical-structural' approach. Other *dependentistas* also recognized the importance of historical factors in examining problems of underdevelopment. All this received greater impetus from the work emanating from a host of new social science research centres in Latin America (Graciarena and Franco, 1978).

In the long run, dependency was essentially an approach, a descriptive model rather than a theory *per se* (Cardoso, 1977). With the passing of time, it was subjected to increasingly abstruse definitional and semantic quibbling, only infrequently being tested by empirical research. And while this was taking place, another major perspective towards development arose in the form of corporatism. Drawing on the organic-state tradition, its exponents saw the Latin American tradition as linked to the Iberian, Thomistic view of the state. The political legacy was authoritarian, and the emphasis was on political community rather than the individual citizen. In more modern form, corporatism stood as an indigenous alternative to the presumably disruptive capitalist and socialist models:

> For its practitioners, who reject both modernization and dependency theory, corporatism provides a model of development that is genuinely Latin American. It is also a means of providing social solidarity and avoiding unrestrained individualism or class conflict in the face of the dislocations of modernity. (Klarén, 1986, p. 28)

None the less, it was also true that corporatist theorizing by the 1970s could be integrated into explanations of the emergence of modernizing authoritarianism. By this point, the dramatic shift of regime types in much of the hemisphere was providing further ammunition for the arsenal of those insisting upon the disjunction of Latin American studies from more universalistic comparativist concepts and theories.

Clearly, students of Latin American politics were then and today remain enduringly plagued and frustrated by the problems of political diversity. This is scarcely changed by the recent reintroduction and elaboration of cultural factors, which in the past have only too often tended to be treated indiscriminately as common to all the countries in question. Our task here is to consider and elucidate three principal contentions: first, that major 'theories' have not been as broadly applicable as some of their exponents would have it; secondly, that the introduction of cultural variables, if applied with care, may conceivably permit a modicum of generalization; and thirdly, that such cultural characteristics may help us in confronting endemic problems of comparability and conceptualization through middle-range theorizing about the politics of Latin America.

Before focusing on the rebirth of the culturalist perspective as applicable to Latin America, there is value in a summary review of important conceptual patternings which have emerged in the recent past. The first is that of bureaucratic-authoritarian (B-A) models, and the second relates to the variegated forms of the transition to democracy. This exercise will pave the way for subsequent attention to cultural influences.

Bureaucratic-authoritarianism and the Transition to Democracy

The malaise over modernization theory and liberal developmentalism became manifest with the attack of dependency theorists from both Latin America and the United States. The symbiosis between scholarship and politics was evident in the deterioration of party-based liberal democracies and the proliferation of military regimes. Events encouraged the observation that existing theoretical frameworks 'were inadequate to analyze the important role of the state in Latin America or to deal with the complex process by which the interactions between the state and organized societal groupings have been structured and restructured over time' (Malloy, 1977, p. ix). The emergence of bureaucratic-authoritarian thought was derived especially from the experience of the Southern Cone, where modernizing authoritarian regimes characterized by delayed dependent development took hold (O'Donnell, 1973).

O'Donnell's examination of Argentina and Brazil – especially the former – described a process in which economies moved beyond import-substitution to deepening industrialization, with populist forces controlled or eliminated through a repressive state apparatus. Technocratic elites operating in tandem with the armed forces would curb political participation while exercising centralized control of public policy. Generalizing beyond his original cases, O'Donnell contended that in contemporary South [not Latin] America, 'the higher and lower levels of modernization are associated with non-democratic political systems, while political democracies are found at the intermediate levels of modernization' (O'Donnell, 1973, p. 51). In subsequent writings the creator of B-A thought, while more restrained than many of his followers, none the less overgeneralized to the extent of suggesting the research potential of the B-A approach not only for Mexico but even to the Mediterranean experiences of Spain, Turkey and Greece (O'Donnell, 1978).

O'Donnell himself and a thoughtful band of comparativists examined his original formulations empirically, providing an instructive demonstration of B-A theory (Collier, 1979). The summary chapter by Collier provided a particularly polite but sharp critique. He questioned the contention that the crisis of import substitution had been a basic explanatory variable powerfully promoting authoritarianism in the late 1960s and thereafter. Looking towards a possible restoration of democratic regimes, he stressed the importance of recognizing 'that attempts to understand the prospects for democratization should be linked to attempts to explain this long-term cycle of change' (Collier, 1979, p. 394). Far from insensitive to critics, O'Donnell proceeded to reformulate and refine his conceptualization of Latin American politics. This proved especially constructive in an exchange with Remmer and Merkx, who summarized perhaps better than any other reviewers the strengths and problems in B-A theory.

They argued that the O'Donnell formulation had devoted inadequate attention to the presumed consolidation of B-A regimes. Furthermore, extension of the Southern Cone to distant nations – both American and non-hemispheric – reflected an inappropriate level of generalization from the specifics of the Southern Cone. For Remmer and Merkx, B-A theory demanded 'more systematic and empirically grounded comparisons among cases and consideration of a broader range of explanations of postcoup developments' (Remmer and Merkx, 1982, p. 35). O'Donnell's response further illuminated his elaboration of the bureaucratic-authoritarian impulse, as did his subsequent analysis of the Buenos Aires regime during 1966–73 (O'Donnell, 1982). In time, however, efforts to theorize broadly at the macro level gave way to the view that the B-A perspective was more descriptive of a type of regime than of a type of state (Lehmann, 1989).

As one critic put it, the B-A approach was relevant 'only to a limited number of cases and for only a very limited period of time, and therefore ... of little help in generating broad-gauged theory' (Seligson, 1990, pp. A49–50). And so, while B-A theory had been thought-provoking, it failed as a unidimensional explanation. The economic variable, while undeniable, was not uniformly applicable. The true universality of B-A applicability was seen increasingly with scepticism:

> The enduring quality of Latin American politics in this century may not be a particular form of regime, but rather the fact of change and the quality of politics in any regime which has only a short history and the prospect of a brief future. It is always possible that the cycles of varied types of regimes have come to an end. (Chalmers, 1977, p. 23)

Not only were there difficulties in extending B-A theory beyond the western hemisphere, as some ardent spokesmen proposed, but its very applicability in Latin America itself was limited.

Colombia's formalistic controlled democracy, for example, contradicted many aspects of the B-A argument. Neighbouring Venezuela, the strongest democracy of all the major Latin American states, also resisted, if it did not actually defy, bureaucratic-authoritarian tenets. Costa Rica constituted another exception; and even such late-developing states as the Dominican Republic, Ecuador and Peru seemed not to fall comfortably into the niches of B-A theory. Moreover, the decline of hemispheric authoritarianism, whether or not a transient phenomenon, powerfully nudged comparativists away from discussions of democratic breakdown, refocusing their attention instead on the proliferating array of newly democratizing nations.

Two major collaborative efforts marked comparativists' subsequent shift toward the analysis of democratization. The first was a seven-year undertaking involving three editors and nearly two dozen contributors (O'Donnell et al., 1986). In *Transitions from Authoritarian Rule*, the contributors adopted a broad-gauged definition of democracy consistent with relative disrespect toward liberal democracy, which was less highly valued than participatory forms of social and economic democracy. For example, in the closing paragraph of the entire work, O'Donnell and Schmitter contended that political democracy was the product less of unity and consensus than of stalemate. As they put it,

> Transition toward democracy is by no means a linear or a rational process. There is simply too much uncertainty about capabilities and too much suspicion about intentions for that. Only once the transition has passed ... can one expect political democracy to induce a more reliable awareness of convergent interests.   (O'Donnell et al., 1986, p. 72)

Transitions, then, employed an all-inclusive definition which called for a championing of social change.

Coming from a belief that critical theory should produce an altering of injustice and oppression, the editors and most of their contributors were evidently dissatisfied with practical institutional arrangements emphasizing accommodation and compromise. Negotiations among elites become undemocratic, while the legitimacy of elite–mass linkages are ignored or undervalued. Consequently, the study consistently went beyond questions of political liberalization to a position that also encompassed social equity and economic justice. As one critic put it, the editors of *Transitions* 'pay little heed to democracy as a coherent political system, ... are unhappy with the outcomes democracies produce, and consistently look beyond existing or likely democracies to better alternatives – presumably some form of socialism' (Levine, 1988, p. 393). Whether or not one accepted a broad or a less-inclusive definitional concept of democracy, the long-anticipated volume fell short of meaningful theory-building.

Neither did it build in cumulative fashion on its array of often outstanding case studies – presumably informed by, and committed to theoretical approaches discussed in lengthy sessions at the Woodrow Wilson Center prior to the actual writing of the manuscripts. In the final analysis, as another reviewer lamented, the ambitious undertaking failed to realize its initial intellectual promise, demonstrating among other qualities 'an unequivocal sense of haste' (Nef, 1988, p. 149). Not all of the difficulty, in short, lay with the question of the fashion in which democracy was conceptualized.

Somewhat more satisfactory theorizing about transitions to democracy was to come from the second major collaborative undertaking, *Democracy in Developing Countries*, which had originated with a December 1985 conference at Stanford (Diamond, Linz, and Lipset, 1988–90). In this instance, the view of democracy was more restricted than had been the case with *Transitions*. The editors proffered an unqualified belief that political democracy was in itself an acceptable concept.

They were insistent in separating issues of social and economic democracy from questions of government structure:

> Otherwise, the definitional criteria of democracy will be broadened and the empirical reality narrowed to a degree that may make study of the phenomena very difficult. In addition, unless the economic and social dimensions are kept conceptually distinct from the political, there is no way to analyze how variation on the political dimension is related to variation on the others. (Diamond et al., 1989, p. xvi)

Diamond and colleagues further underlined their concerns by identifying three essential, pre-eminently political conditions for their study of democracy: competition, participation and civil/political liberties. In all this they embraced not only political democracy but also the concept of stability as a critical dependent variable. This required examination of the persistence of democratic and other regimes over time, especially through periods of conflict. While the editors' final word about theory and concepts still awaits publication of the fourth and final volume of the work, which will attempt to pull together all the individual contributions, their basic effort would appear more modest, less all-encompassing and theoretically more constructive than that of *Transitions*.

In the final analysis, the editors of *Democracy in Developing Countries* saw the 1980s as a time for the development of 'a renewed and deeper appreciation for the democratic institutions that, with all their procedural messiness and sluggishness, nevertheless protect the integrity of the person and the freedoms of conscience and expression' (Diamond et al., 1989, p. x). Their undertaking provided substantial insight into a number of individual cases, including notably several from Latin America. At the same time, true generalization at the macro level did not produce startling revelations about the character of Latin American politics. Neither was there notable progress from other works which belonged to the 'democratic transitions' school.

In a three-country study based on the experiences of Costa Rica, Colombia and' Venezuela, John Peeler (1985) treated liberal democracy as masking an elitist concentration of power while popular participation was illusory. Structural accommodation between elites was seen as strengthening immobilism and shielding the socioeconomic status quo. At the same time, he was appropriately cautious in discussing democracy at the hemispheric level. More ambitious efforts concerning regime transition came from two compendia edited respectively by Malloy and Seligson (1987) and by Baloyra (1987). The former saw its country studies as leading toward two observations: first, wide diversity precluded the development of broad theories of democratic governance; and secondly, the linkage between recurring economic issues and regime shifts was not deterministic. Scholars should therefore concentrate on issues, problems and trends with which major political actors must contend. The editors provided support for the contention that the perils of broad theorizing about cross-national comparisons in Latin America were manifest.

At least implicitly, Baloyra presented the same message to comparativists in his *Comparing New Democracies* (1987). Describing democracy in political rather than social and economic terms, he differentiated the concept from the *process* of democratization, which involved implementation of the agenda of political transition on behalf of democracy. Baloyra's introduction provided a rigorous application of terminology – fortunately elaborated in a separate glossary – which was designed to sketch a model for the comparative and diachronic analyses of transition. The impact was heuristically sophisticated while, as he properly noted, theoretical problems remained which the 'democratic transitions' literature had not resolved. And at the fundamental preoccupation of our discussion, it is yet evident that systemic generalization at a universalistic level is inadequate. Whether the motivating impulse be bureaucratic-authoritarian or transitional-democratic, the effort to advance conceptualization and comparability in Latin America was found wanting. The framework for the next effort, then, became that of political culture, which was enjoying a second coming with political scientists.

The Political Culture Dimension

Comparativists' conspicuous interest in the theoretical potential of political culture has been described as 'one of the two still viable general approaches to political theory and explanation proposed since the early 1950s to replace the long-dominant formal legalism of the field' (Chilcote, 1981, p. 218). As early as 1952, Kroeber and Kluckhohn were able to review no fewer than 160 interpretations (Eckstein, 1988). The work of Edward A. Shils was influential, including his work as Chairman of the Comparative Study of New Nations, which began in 1959–60 with a grant from the Carnegie Corporation (Shils, 1961). Daniel Bell (1976) and Clifford Geertz (1973) were also prominent in putting forward cultural factors as decisive elements in the shaping of development.

The concept of political culture was generally linked to nations, thus representing in part a resurrection of hoary discussions of national character. For comparativists, it was applied at the outset almost exclusively to what would later be called the Third World, centring upon newly independent states – basically those in Asia and Africa. In due course the cultural dichotomy was transformed into distinctions between the so-called 'Western' and 'non-Western' states (Kahin et al., 1955). Pye later identified 17 distinctive characteristics of the non-Western political process (Pye, 1958), although questions about the breadth of such theoretical generalizations were later raised (Martz, 1966).

Cultural dimensions were incorporated into more empirically orientated research with publication of *The Civic Culture* (Almond and Verba, 1963). It probed public opinion in five nations as it related to the political symbols and beliefs that provided the backdrop for political action, while searching for the connection between political attitudes and regime types. Despite inevitable flaws, *The Civic Culture* constituted a dramatically innovative undertaking, one which drew explicit attention to the psychological dimension of politics. Third World specialists increasingly pursued the culturalist perspective, as in the notable case of the compendium *Political Culture and Political Development* (Pye and Verba, 1965). In time, however, comparativists increasingly challenged the cultural approach as being unduly classificatory and static. The justification of differences as being explicable solely on cultural grounds served as too easy a crutch, even though cultural influences were by no means irrelevant (Ward, 1974).

For at least two decades the concept of political culture continued to animate debate among political scientists. As a pair of French scholars aptly put it, 'Rarely has a concept been so frequently used and so often contended. The choice of the word "culture" denotes the concept's derivation and emphasizes how comparativists have followed a road opened by anthropology, sociology, and psychology' (Dogan and Pelassy, 1984, p. 58). The difficulty lay in the necessity of overcoming the analytic and scientific weaknesses embodied in prevailing applications of cultural elements. Huntington (1987, pp. 22–3) succinctly described the scientific *problematique* as 'tricky'; the cultural concept was 'easy (and also dangerous) to use because it is, in some senses, a residual category. If no other causes can plausibly explain significant differences between societies, it is inviting to attribute them to culture.' Consequently, he saw the concept as frustrating for the social scientist, running counter to the proclivity to generalize.

By the close of the 1980s, a renaissance in political culture studies was perceptible: less a commitment to deterministic explanation than a recognition that it constituted a valuable perspective. This vitality was accurately summarized by Wiarda in the following terms:

> In research project after research project over the past three decades focused on the developing nations, traditional political culture and institutions have proved to be remarkably long-lived and persistent. Rather than being swept aside by the tides of history, or consigned to history's ashcans, these institutions – whether in Asia, the Middle East, Africa, or Latin America – have repeatedly shown themselves to be flexible and accommodative, most often bending to change rather than being overwhelmed by it. (Wiarda, 1989, p. 194)

Three separate culturalist pieces have been published recently in the *American Political Science Review*; interestingly, none of the authors is regarded as a Third World specialist (Wildavsky, 1987; Eckstein, 1988; Inglehart, 1988). Debate was enlivened by an exchange between Wildavsky and Laitin (Laitin and Wildavsky, 1988). The case for renewed attention to political culture as a potent conceptual construct was stated firmly by Wildavsky in his American Political Science Association (APSA) presidential address:

Appraising the consequences of living lives of hierarchical subordination or of the purely voluntary association of egalitarian liberation or the self-regulation of individualistic cultures, at different times, on different continents, with different technologies, languages, and customs would be a remarkably productive research program. So would comparing cultures rather than countries or, put precisely, comparing countries by contrasting their combinations of cultures. (Wildavsky, 1987, p. 18)

Without extending the discussion to other cultural investigations which have recently appeared, suffice it to say that in the 1990s, any contemporary reassessment of comparative politics must embrace political culture as an important dimension. For Dogan and Pelassy, the concept of political culture has aged like good wine, reflecting the political beliefs and values prevailing in a nation at a given point in time: 'Because it filters perception, determines attitudes, and influences modalities of participation, culture is a major component of the political game' (Dogan and Pelassy, 1984, p. 58). Huntington, persuaded of the relevance of culture in explaining differing developmental patterns, has also argued that political culture offers an important means of improving links between area specialists and comparativists with developmental concerns. The culturalist approach becomes nearly indispensable for those seeking to explain the extent to which different countries have made different degrees of progress towards achieving the goals of development. 'Culture and its impact on development cry out for systematic and empirical comparative and longitudinal study by the scholars of political development' (Huntington, 1987, p. 28).

At this juncture we must resurrect our questioning of broad theorizing as having utility for comparative conceptualization in Latin America. For the record, it bears repeating that while area specialists have long been intrigued by the concept of political culture, relatively little empirical investigation has been reported over the past quarter-century or more. Robert Scott did contribute a chapter to the Pye and Verba (1965, pp. 330–96) collection but essentially limited his remarks to Mexico, for which he drew heavily on Almond and Verba (1963) data. Occasional regional overviews through the years have sometimes referred in qualitative terms to political culture, but customarily with a humanistic and literary flair (Moreno, 1969; Fitzgibbon and Fernandez, 1981). Among the more rigorous efforts was the author's investigation of Venezuela with Enrique Baloyra, although the concept of political culture itself was not the central preoccupation (Baloyra and Martz, 1977).

At least implicitly, then, the culturalist perspective on politics was largely set aside for some years by most Latin Americanists. Only a few were willing to examine the cultural component at length (Wiarda, 1981; Dealy, 1977). For most, however, qualitative analysis was presumably watered down by the diversity between and among states, while the availability of fresh raw data for political scientists and sociologists was limited. It is only with the present culturalist rebirth that Latin Americanist social scientists have begun to re-consider seriously the heuristic character of the approach.

Cultural Analyses and Latin American Politics

We have written elsewhere that those who elaborate presumably 'modern' analytic constructs 'without taking account of the legacy of past patterns of thought will but encourage generalizations and theoretical frameworks that become often incomplete or distorted reflections of reality' (Martz and Myers, 1983). We were speaking of Latin America, as was Wiarda, in observing that the region must come to grips with the reality of cultural continuity. It is true, to be sure, that political culture is not at present the sole explanatory variable, nor should it be. At the same time, it should not be under-valued, whatever the region of the world – whether predominantly industrialized or developing in character. There is no gainsaying the importance of historic cultural and intellectual traditions. The cultural dimension emphatically and incontrovertibly demands serious intellectual attention.

In looking more closely at the potential of cultural analyses of Latin American politics for the 1980s, then, it is incumbent upon us to consider briefly the most common criticisms of the culturalist approach raised in earlier years. Probably the most serious stressed the point that there were obvious cross-national differences in politi-cal behaviour that could not be accounted for by culture. In addition, there was concern that culturalist methodology was viewed as incapable of dealing with political change except in an *ad hoc* fashion. Advocates of the political culture approach necessarily mounted responses to such criticisms.

First, it was noted that never, from its very inception, was poli-tical culture intended to explain all differences in political behaviour. Even the most enthusiastic exponents further held that the approach was but one of several which were useful; thus it was sufficient that political culture might help to account for some, but not for all, such behavioural differences. Among the other likely avenues were those of rational choice theory, class analysis and institutional studies. As to the second basic point of criticism, culturalists began the effort to craft an explicit theory of change consistent with their more general culturalist assumptions. Indeed, it could well be that the ultimate fate of efforts to expand the predictive power of the political culture- approach – including its capacity to handle political change – might be dependent upon the willingness of researchers to test and to define its postulates through representative 'ethnographic' studies.

It is useful to remind ourselves of our basic concept in definitional terms. A recent overview of comparative politics phrased it in the following felicitous fashion:

> Political culture may then be said to regularly refer to the following elements: attitudes or conceptions of how things ought to be, values or preferences, belief systems or perceptions of how things are, cognition or knowledge and information, and feelings about political objects. (Mayer, 1989, p. 184)

Such a statement, consistent with others which could be cited, underlines the kinds of theoretical questions which are important. At least two emerge which will be mentioned here. First, the concept of political culture presupposes linkages between attitudes and regime types. Secondly, political culture is, as Eckstein has observed, the distinctive variable as to ways in which societies normally regulate social behaviour. To explore these more fully, then, and to examine the theoretical implications, hard on-the-ground empirical research becomes mandatory.

For illustrative purposes only, consider two ongoing projects: the first explores attitudinal comparisons between Costa Rica and Nicaragua; the second, a diachronic study of professional and technological elites in Venezuela. With the former, Booth and Seligson are seeking a culturalist explanation of Latin American democracy through exploration of the linkage between mass political culture and regime type in Costa Rica and Nicaragua. The co-authors have married rich historical analysis with a wealth of original attitudinal data. Their findings can be expected to provide further insights into the two-nation comparison, along with an elaboration of the potential for the culturalist perspective in theorizing about Latin American politics.

The Venezuelan inquiry, in which David Myers has joined me, explores unknown terrain in assessing the attitudes toward democracy held over time by an important sub-sector of Venezuelan elites, namely the professionals and technicians. Although comparable groups are increasingly influential in many of the Latin American states, there is a dearth of research on the subject. Our emphases have therefore been set within the context of middle-range theory as linked to the overarching culturalist perspective. This ethnographic study, drawing upon focus group interviews as well as a survey of public opinion, probes the attitudes of Venezuela's technological elite in providing support for the post-1958 democratic system. The research poses four principal questions, the answers to which will contribute along two dimensions to the debate over the value of political culture as a theoretical construct (Martz and Myers, 1991, 1994). Of the latter, the first profiles within a major Latin American country the political culture of a critical but previously unstudied group. The second dimension contributes to assessing the capacity of government to transform or to alter political culture.

Such transformation is viewed as using political power to engineer radically changed social and political structures and processes, and hence cultural patterns and themes. It relies upon power and control to alter the course of society and the polity. Culturalists hypothesize that reorientation is most feasible when society becomes temporarily formless, the time that follows destruction of the old order and precedes the consolidation of the new. This appears as a window of opportunity for transformation. Culturalist theory also hypothesizes that, as political culture recrystallizes, it will demonstrate a proclivity in the direction of new patterns. Theory suggests that the extent to which older, prior culture may survive is critical in determining the long-range impact of the transformation effort. If that culture emerges intact and unscathed, sheer inertia will incline mediating political orientations toward pre-revolutionary norms and away from those which are drastically different.

The point is not to engage in extended discussion of this particular project, but rather to illustrate both theoretical concerns and research possibilities. The relevance of scholarly inquiry at the middle level should not be minimized. For Latin Americanists, furthermore, it may well be that a less than hemispheric-wide data base is useful. Recall that O'Donnell drew initially upon the Argentine case, and then upon the Southern Cone experience. Regional diversity being what it is, the likelihood of applying B-A theory throughout the Americas was questionable from the outset. Subregional emphases may therefore prove more fruitful. For instance, the theoretical quest could be set within the Central American context. Inquiry might also be rewarded by theorizing about the states of Grancolombia – Venezuela, Colombia and Ecuador. Concepts and comparisons are clearly feasible when derived from defined sub-regions (Martz, 1990). There is a variety of other politico-cultural and geographic foci within the Americas which might readily be identified.

If the diversity of Latin America complicates or confounds broad theorizing at the highest macro level, then it may well be that investigations with middle-range theoretical potential should be the focus for the rising generation of students and scholars. This seems the implicit message of the Booth and Seligson, as well as the Martz and Myers undertakings. Moreover, there are indications that this may be occurring. As the reviving culturalist perspective continues to unfold, empirical inquiry along with theoretical reformulations are increasingly evident. All this testifies to the intellectual ferment among comparativists over the past decade and more. Theoretical sophistication has grown, with research stimulated and scholarly productivity increased. The effort to link empirical studies to broader trends in comparative politics has become self-conscious. At the same time, there has been a gradual if sometimes grudging admission that no single approach in itself can adequately pave the royal road to understanding.

It has become evident, for example, that recurring economic variables do not necessarily possess productive power as regards regime change. 'Rather, economic issues have mainly posed problems to be solved while limiting the options for solution' (Malloy, 1987, p. 237). Consequently, if some economic explanations disturbingly wanting, this is not to deny weaknesses in both institutional and cultural perspectives. At the same time, it is noteworthy that the two latter dimensions have not received extensive attention for some years. Only towards the close of the 1980s did scholarly interest revive. An obvious and unarguable observation accepted the potential of greater eclecticism and more synthetic theorizing. This led in turn to recognition of the value in linking economic, institutional and cultural factors. The prospect of less reductionist explanation, erected on multivariate socio-political analysis, could well provide a level of scientific insight which is currently lacking in theoretical efforts to dissect contemporary Latin American political reality. The culturalist perspective, in short, is now writ large on the research agenda of those who specialize in the region as it is more generally with comparativists in the final decade of the century (Martz, 1990).

In recalling our major points as stated at the beginning of this chapter, there is the belief that major theories have not served comparativists well and that, more importantly, intra- and inter-nation diversity mitigates against conceptual comparison. Further-more, the same condition prevails when the Americas provide the unit of analysis. We have argued that a concern with less grandiose theorizing, built upon solid empirical research, might well be fruit-ful as scholars proceed with the eternal quest for insight and for ultimate theoretical truths. Examples have been provided for the culturalist outlook, which has constituted a major focus of discus-sion. In the final analysis, as always, intellectual agility and audacity are prerequisites for genuine analytic comparison. For the Latin Americanist comparativists, there must be a commitment to linking area research with broader intellectual currents. If realism prevails, there should be an emphasis on middle-range theory, in which the culturalist approach promises to be fruitful in unleashing conceptual innovation and creativity.

References

Almond, Gabriel A. 1960: 'Introduction: A functional approach to com-parative politics'. In Gabriel A. Almond and James S. Coleman (eds), *The Politics of the Developing Areas*, Princeton, N.J.: Princeton University Press, pp. 3–65.

Almond, Gabriel A. and Verba, Sidney 1963: *The Civic Culture: political atti-tudes and democracy in five nations*. Princeton, N.J.: Princeton University Press.

Baloyra, Enrique A. (ed.) 1987: *Comparing New Democracies; transition and consolidation in Mediterranean Europe and the Southern Cone*. Boulder, Col.: Westview Press.

—— and Martz, John D. 1977: 'Culture, regionalism, and political opinion in Venezuela'. *Canadian Journal of Political Science*, 10(3): 527–73.

Bell, Daniel 1976: *The Cultural Contradictions of Capitalism*. New York: Basic Books.

Cardoso, Fernando Henrique 1977: 'The consumption of dependency theory in the United States'. *Latin American Research Review*, 12(3): 7–24.

—— and Faletto, Enzo 1969: *Dependencia y Desarrollo en América Latina*. Mexico: Siglo Veintiuno Editores.

Chalmers, Douglas 1977: 'The politicized state in Latin America'. In James M. Malloy (ed.), *Authoritarianism and Corporatism in Latin America*. Pittsburgh, Pa: University of Pittsburgh Press.

Chilcote, Ronald H. 1981: *Theories of Comparative Politics: the search for a paradigm*. Boulder, Col.: Westview Press.

Collier, David (ed.) 1979: *The New Authoritarianism in Latin America*. Princeton, N.J.: Princeton University Press.

Dealy, Glen Caudil 1977: *The Public Man: an interpretation of Latin American and other Catholic countries*. Amherst, Mass.: University of Massachusetts Press.

Diamond, Larry, Linz, Juan J. and Lipset, Seymour Martin 1988–90: *Democracy in Developing Countries*. Boulder, Col.: Lynne Rienner.

Dogan, Mattei and Pelassy, Dominique 1984: *How to Compare Nations: strategies in comparative politics*. Chatham, N.J.: Chatham House Publishers.

Eckstein, Harry 1988: 'A culturalist theory of political change'. *American Political Science Review*, 82(3): 787–804.

Fitzgibbon, Russell H. and Fernandez, Julio 1981: *Latin America: political culture and development*, 2nd edn. Englewood Cliffs, N.J.: Prentice-Hall.

Geertz, Clifford 1973: *The Interpretation of Cultures*. New York: Basic Books.

Gómez, Rosendo A. 1967: *The Study of Latin American Politics in University Programs in the United States*. Tucson, Tx: Institute of Government.

Graciarena, Jorge and Franco, Rolando 1978: 'Social Formations and Power Structures in Latin America'. *Current Sociology*, 26.

Huntington, Samuel P. 1987: 'The goals of development'. In Myron Weiner and Samuel P. Huntington (eds), *Understanding Political Development*, Boston, Mass.: Little, Brown.

Inglehart, Ronald 1988: 'The renaissance of political culture'. *American Political Science Review*, 82(4): 1204–30.

—— 1990: *Culture Change in Advanced Industrial Society*. Princeton, N.J.: Princeton University Press.

Kahin, George McT., Pauker, Guy J. and Pye, Lucian W. 1955: 'Comparative politics of non-Western countries'. *American Political Science Review*, 49(4): 1022–390.

Klarén, Peter F. 1986: 'Lost promise: explaining Latin American underdevelopment'. In Peter F. Klaren and Thomas J. Bossert (eds), *Promise of Development: theories of change in Latin America*, Boulder, Col.: Westview Press.

Kling, Merle 1964: 'The state of research on Latin America: political science'. In Charles Wagley (ed.), *Social Science Research on Latin America*, New York: Columbia University Press.

Laitin, David D. and Wildavsky, Aaron 1988: 'Political culture and political preferences' (exchange). *American Political Science Review*, 82(2): 589–97.

Lehmann, David 1989: 'A Latin American political scientist: Guillermo O'Donnell'. *Latin American Research Review*, 24(2): 187–200.

Levine, Daniel H. 1988: 'Paradigm lost: dependence to democracy'. *World Politics*, 50(3): 377–95.

Malloy, James M. (ed.) 1977: *Authoritarianism and Corporatism in Latin America*. Pittsburgh, Pa; University of Pittsburgh Press.

—— and Seligson, Mitchell A. (eds) 1987: *Authoritarians and Democrats: regime transition in Latin America*. Pittsburgh, Pa: University of Pittsburgh Press.

Martz, John D. 1966: 'The place of Latin America in the study of comparative politics'. *Journal of Politics*, 28(1).

—— 1971: 'Political science and Latin American politics: a discipline in search of a region'. *Latin American Research Review*, 6: 71–99.

—— 1990: 'Electoral campaigning and Latin American democracy in Grancolombia'. *Journal of Interamerican Studies and World Affairs*, 21(1): 17–45.

—— 1991: 'Bureaucratic authoritarianism, transitions to democracy, and the political culture dimension'. In Howard J. Wiarda (ed.), *New Directions in Comparative Politics*, 2nd edn, Boulder, Col.: Westview Press.

—— and Myers, David J. 1983: 'Understanding Latin American politics: analytic models and intellectual traditions'. *Polity*, 16(2): 214–42.

—— 1994: 'Political parties and technological elites: the professional community in Venezuelan politics'. *Latin American Research Review*, 29(1).

Mayer, Lawrence C. 1989: *Redefining Comparative Politics*. Newbury Park, Cal.: Sage Publications.

Moreno, Francisco Jose 1969: *Legitimacy and Stability in Latin America: a study of Chilean political culture*. New York: New York University Press.

Nef, Jorge 1968: 'The Trend toward democratization and redemocratization in Latin America: shadow and substance'. *Latin American Research Review*, 23(3): 131–53.

O'Donnell, Guillermo 1973: *Modernization and Bureaucratic-Authoritarianism: studies in South American politics*. Berkeley, Cal.: Institute of International Studies, University of California, Berkeley.

—— 1978: 'Reflections on the patterns of change in the bureaucratic-authoritarian state'. *Latin American Research Review*, 13(1): 3–39.

—— 1982: *1966–1973; El Estado Burocrático Autoritario; Triunfos, Derrotas y Crisis*. Buenos Aires: Editorial de Belgrano.

—— Schmitter, Philippe C. and Whitehead, Laurence (eds) 1986: *Transitions from Authoritarian Rule: prospects for democracy*. Baltimore, Md: Johns Hopkins University Press.

Peeler, John, 1985: *Latin American Democracies*. Chapel Hill, N.C.: University of North Carolina Press.

Pye, Lucian W. 1958: 'The non-Western political process'. *Journal of Politics*, 20(3): 468–86.

—— and Verba, Sidney (eds) 1965: *Political Culture and Political Development*. Princeton, N.J.: Princeton University Press.

Remmer, Karen L. and Merkx, Gilbert W. 1982: 'Bureaucratic-authoritarianism revisited'. *Latin American Research Review*, 17(2): 3–41.

Seligson, Mitchell A. 1990: 'Political culture and democratization in Latin America'. In James M. Malloy and Eduardo Gamarra (eds), *Latin American and Caribbean Contemporary Record*, vol. VII (1987–8), New York: Holmes & Meier.

Shils, Edward A. 1961: 'Mass society and its culture'. In Norman Jacobs (ed.), *Culture for the Millions*, New York: D. Van Nostrand.

Silvert, Kalman H. 1967: 'American academic ethics and social research abroad: the lesson of Project Camelot'. In Irving Louis Horowitz (ed.), *The Rise and Fall of Project Camelot: studies in the relationship between social science and practical politics*. Cambridge, Mass.: MIT Press.

Valenzuela, Arturo 1988: 'Political science and the study of Latin America'. In Christopher Mitchell (ed.), *Changing Perspectives in Latin American Studies: insights from six disciplines*, Stanford, Cal.: Stanford University Press.

Ward, Robert E. 1974: 'Culture and the comparative study of politics: or, The constipated dialectic'. *American Political Science Review*, 68(1): 190–201.

Wiarda, Howard J. 1981: *Corporatism and National Development in Latin America*. Boulder, Col.: Westview Press.

——1989: 'Political culture and national development'. *Fletcher Forum: a journal of studies in international affairs*, 13: 181–98.

Wildavsky, Aaron, 1987: 'Choosing preferences by constructing institutions: a cultural theory of preference formation'. *American Political Science Review*, 81(1): 3–21.

7

Asynchronic Comparisons

Weak States in Post-colonial Africa and Mediaeval Europe

Joshua B. Forrest

Introduction

I suggest a means of analysing states[1] at an initial stage of formation, in which institutions and administrative structures are generally
weak and porous, barely able to carry out their intended functions,
and where legal procedures and formal institutions do not guide
us to the loci of political events or political change. The point of
this analysis is to better understand what politics are about in weak
states and to develop a comparatively useful means of analysing such
states. In essence, weak states constitute hybrid regimes in which
power is shared by factionalized combinations of national elites
grouped according to bureaucratic unit, social class background,
region of origin, ethnicity or clientelism, often with the military
playing a crucial role in determining the particular leadership structure of these regimes. Politics in weak states are dominated by unbounded power struggles, while social forces wield great influence
on state organs, and ruling coalitions that stay in power rely heavily
on personal rule, patronage and force.

The comparative perspective I offer here is purposively asynchronic, skipping over or compressing time in order to bring states
with certain shared characteristics within a common analytic pur-
view.[2] I seek to highlight aspects or problems of these hybrid regimes
even though some of them – such as a number of those in mediaeval Europe – took hundreds of years to come into being, endured
for centuries and eventually became modernized states, while
others – that is, most of those in post-colonial Africa – were born
at one sudden historical moment (upon decolonization) and have

been in existence a comparatively short time, with the course of their institutional futures yet to be determined. The point of this asynchronic approach is to restimulate the truly comparative and analytical method within political science, not by formulating obtuse abstractions nor by overreaching in empirical depth but rather by drawing macro-level linkages among similar types of states sharing certain characteristics and difficulties. By doing so, I wish to suggest a means of better appreciating the intellectual and analytical value of research investigations across time and space.

Furthermore, in this chapter I seek to reaffirm an especially structural, behavioural and comparative approach to understanding politics in post-colonial Africa in particular. The failure of political system-building and the decline of state capacity in much of sub-Saharan Africa since independence suggests that African polities may *not* be experiencing 'development' or undergoing a stage of modernization. Thus, rather than teleologically focusing on the direction of Africa's political future, it may be more analytically profitable to examine comparatively the dynamics of state-building in independent Africa against those of states in formation more generally.

An asynchronic approach to the study of the weak states of post-colonial Africa reveals striking parallels with the fledgling states of mediaeval Europe. In both cases the state aspired to assert its power over its claimed national territory, but succeeded only in part and very superficially, often being forced to bend to the greater ground-level power of local elites, many of whom adeptly turned the state's penetration drive to their own advantage. While African and mediaeval European national leaders moved toward establishing a formal political system, politics actually revolved around unbridled competition among factions of political elites joined by personalistic, kin-based, ethnic, class, clientelist or regional ties. As the nature of this competition was unrestricted and was engaged in with little or no adherence to constitutional or legal rules, political outcomes were largely unpredictable, leadership coalitions at the national political centre in both mediaeval Europe and independent Africa changed frequently, the military played a large role in politics and violent efforts to overthrow the existing powerholders – contemporarily termed *coups d'etat* – were common. Also, because of the organizational fragility of government agencies, powerful social forces – usually barons in Europe, ethnic and clientelist groupings in Africa – were able to make their way into the heart of state power and assert their control over many official institutions and decision-making processes.

To be sure, the differences in historical contexts between mediaeval Europe and independent Africa are large and important, and do proscribe a more linear analogy. Class conflict played a much greater role in the European case and may have been crucial in the eventual realization of strong states (Skocpol, 1979). The most potent single opponent of many mediaeval state rulers was the Church, which has no exact equivalent in Africa, although other social forces have proved strong enough to counterpose successfully themselves to state policy. Many post-colonial African governments have a far more developed bureaucratic apparatus than any European government enjoyed in the pre-modern era. Also, mediaeval European state-builders were not imbued with the same conscious enthusiasm for a modernization agenda as their post-independence African counterparts. The borders of African countries do not correspond to their pre-colonial settings and dominant forms of social organization as closely as the borders of mediaeval European countries reflected a more natural circumference of the social agglomerations they enclosed.

Non the less, there are powerful analogies in historical context as well. Mediaeval Europe was relatively underdeveloped and disadvantaged in relation to other world civilizations and economies, such as the Byzantine, Islamic and Chinese empires; post-colonial Africa is similarly disadvantaged *vis-à-vis* the industrialized world. It is furthermore instructive to realize that both the early mediaeval European and post-colonial African states inherited political structures from collapsed imperiums: the Roman Empire in the case of Western Europe, and the British, French, Belgian and Portuguese colonial regimes in the case of Africa. In both cases, kings and other political leaders sought to preserve the public authority and government apparatus of the previous empire, but usually found that those political institutions and processes had not sufficiently taken root to make possible a successful continuity of state-building. Rather, regionalism was strengthened and local social units reasserted themselves, while governments increasingly failed to fulfil their developmentalist goals even as they were expanding in bureaucratic girth and diversity of functions (Strayer, 1971, pp. 341–8; Forrest, 1988, pp. 423–31).

States in mediaeval Europe and post-colonial Africa also shared a crisis of resource extraction, where a great portion of economic activities lay beyond the range of the central regime's extractive powers (Duby, 1968, p. 153; Hyden, 1980; Pletcher, 1986). Thus, for many of these regimes, a large portion of regional and local market-trading remained off-limits to national powerholders, despite their effort to obtain a larger share of surplus production through improved regulation, toll collection and taxation systems or reliance on feudal dues (Miller, 1976; Hart, 1982). Like many of the weak states of post-colonial Africa, revenues in mediaeval Europe were often collected in kind, so that the extent of public wealth in a given year depended on the amount of grain surpluses that were harvested, which in turn led to a condition of great financial precariousness for the centralized regime as a result of the frequent fluctuations in agricultural productivity. Consequently, the kingships of mid-to-late mediaeval Europe relied heavily on financing by Italian and Dutch bankers; the state bureaucracies of most of present-day Africa are similarly dependent on foreign aid and lending.

With this historical/comparative/methodological context, I wish to suggest that weak states, such as those of independent Africa and mediaeval Europe, share the following central features:

1 *inadequate administrative capacity* to achieve official goals;
2 a *low level of state penetration* due to the enduring power of local and intermediary authorities;
3 the dominance of *informal politics*, wherein the centre of politics lies outside the parameters of any formal political process or system, and is marked by the five following characteristics:

3.1 *personal ties* and personal rule;
3.2 *unbounded power struggles*, meaning that the components of state compete with one another essentially with few limits on their preferred type of political activity or strategy;
3.3 these power struggles occur among *factions* of familial clans, ethnic groupings, regionally based authorities, nepotistic cliques, personalistic networks, clientelist alliances, institutional agencies;
3.4 *social forces* are able to override institutional barriers and greatly affect the functioning and dynamics of intrastate politics;
3.5 the unbounded nature of politics means that *force* in general and *coups d'etat* in particular are common means of political change, and that those who monopolize the means of force, especially *military leaders*, are often at the centre of the state's political activities.

I propose that our understanding of states in the process of formation can be improved by focusing on the fact that they are able to achieve only a very low level of administrative capacity and political penetration. At the same time, politics within weak states may be considered informal and dominated by personal ties, unstructured power struggles, factionalism, the large impact of social forces on the government and the centrality of force, coups and the military. To be sure, administrative capacity and political penetration are not the sole criteria one may use to compare such hybrid regimes, and informal politics, as I define them, may not account for the entire range of what transpires politically in weak states. None the less, the following comparisons show that capacity and penetration do afford us two means of appreciating the limitations of governments and of national leaderships, and informal politics certainly characterize many states in formation, such as those of contemporary Africa and mediaeval Europe.

1   Inadequate Administrative Capacity to Achieve Official Goals

Weak states such as those of post-colonial Africa and mediaeval Europe lack the administrative capacity and trained personnel to carry out most official policies. To be sure, the sheer size and scope of official responsibility of African bureaucracies have expanded enormously since independence, with the number of personnel and of administrative agencies more than doubling in Nigeria, Kenya, Senegal, Ivory Coast and elsewhere in the first post-colonial decade and a half (Abernathy, 1983, p. 12). However, governmental institutions across the continent remain beset by organizational fragility and poorly trained bureaucrats, and are constrained by inadequate linkages with the elites of society and by fiscal limitations (Rothchild and Olorunsola, 1983, p. 7). Recent studies make clear that African states have proved unable to carry out policies within society consistently, to implement rules and regulations, or to institutionalize a system of state–society relations that would make possible the effective application of leaders' decisions (Rothchild, 1987). Bureaucrats have failed to co-ordinate the national, regional and local administrative systems, and this has contributed to the stagnation and paralysis of the machinery of government in much of sub-Saharan Africa (Hart, 1982, p. 102; Vengroff, 1985, p. 17). One indication of this is that the greater portion – commonly 70–80 per cent – of public budgets is spent on officials' salaries and on projects that essentially benefit only the political elites involved (Hart, 1982, pp. 306, 310).

Similarly, the government of Carolingian Europe (*c.* 687–987) expanded especially under Charlemagne (786–814). He increased

the number of his public servants, and this allowed him to further
sub-divide his palatial council into financial, judicial, ecclesiastical
and administrative departments, each of which directed a small
body of employees. None the less, these staff workers were not professionally trained and were too few in number to make it possible
for Charlemagne to impose his policies through his palatial bureaucracy (Folz, 1974). In the Holy Roman Empire of Otto I (936–73),
in the Norman-ruled Kingdom of Sicily (1070s to late 1200s), and
the English national monarchy of the ninth and tenth centuries,
centralized governments were forming and beginning to diversify
their administrative functions, but their sphere of governance was
extremely limited: they remained almost entirely dependent on regional officials, and had no power to enforce centrally made decisions
(Marongiu, 1970).

In the late mediaeval era, especially in England under Henry I
(1100–35) and Edward I (1272–1307), and in France under the
Angevins Philip Augustus (1180–1233) and Philip the Fair (1285–
1314) and then Charles VII (1422–61), it is certainly true that
complex and increasingly professional bureaucracies transformed
monarchical governments into powerful states. The development of
a professional chancery, an exchequer, an administrative council
(the *curia regis*, or king's court), and the centralized Royal Household in England and the loyal, salaried officials (*baillis*) with expanded financial judicial military and administrative functions in
France, immensely strengthened the overall power of these states by
the close of the fifteenth century (Strayer and Munro, 1959, pp.
278–83, 304, 371–5, 438–40). However, the coercive fiscal and
administrative apparatus of a government – for example with a
maximum of 12,000 employees in the French case to manage a
populace of 15–20 million people (a ratio of bureaucrats to national
population similar to many African states today) – remained inadequate to impose effectively a coherent official policy of any kind
except taxation (the figures are for the year 1500; Braudel, 1982,
p. 549). As in independent Africa, national leaders loudly proclaimed their authority over the local populace but lacked the infrastructural capacity to implement their policy decisions on a consistent
or effective basis.

2 Societal Barriers to Political Penetration

Concomitant with the effort to develop an effective administrative
capacity, states in post-colonial Africa and in mediaeval Europe

have pursued higher levels of political penetration than was heretofore possible by achieving firm bureaucratic control over regional and local authority structures. Through the process of political penetration, centralized national-level political and administrative elites sought to displace or dominate the micro-level nodules of power throughout their national territories and become the primary source of political authority. However, in Africa as in mediaeval Europe, states proved inadequate to the task of incorporating locally based groupings such as nobles, village elites or councils and ethnic social formations within a singular governmental hierarchy or bureaucratic grid.[3] To be sure, in both sets of countries, there were variations in the degree of penetration that was possible to be achieved, with, for example, central authorities in the geographically disparate and loosely joined Holy Roman Empire unable to aspire to the kind of penetrative control the king of England was at least able to take practical steps toward achieving. None the less, in all these cases non-governmental political and social units remained mostly independent of higher authorities, and regional rebellions commonly challenged the territorial jurisdiction of the state's authority.[4]

In Tanzania, Guinea-Bissau, and the Republic of Guinea (Conakry), village-level committees and party structures created by the ruling regime specifically to assure closer organizational ties between the national government and the countryside failed to achieve their mission of political penetration (Abrahams, 1985; Ergas, 1980; Forrest, 1992, pp. 51–3; Azarya and Chazan, 1987, pp. 106–31). In all three cases, these committees either became staffed by traditional village leaders who reflected the power structures of their communities or by relatively independent-minded local leaders determined to control their own micro-level political space. Zambian 'Village Productivity Committees' were perceived by villagers to conflict with their own economic interests and were uniformly rejected for that reason as well as because of poor management (Pottier, 1986, pp. 230–1). In post-colonial Ghana, political decentralization reached relatively extreme levels despite the efforts of several different regimes to reverse the trend, as peasant communities created or reaffirmed traditional forms of authority that bore little or no connection to national governmental or party units (Chazan, 1983, pp. 28, 39, 60–9).

In Cameroon by the late 1970s political and economic power in the rural areas had become largely dominated by localistic forces such as kin groups, village elders and traditional religious leaders (van der Geest, 1986). This is especially noteworthy in light of the fact that the countryside suffered a massive drive by state officials, including the president himself, to assure political penetration through the forced incorporation of historically significant social forces such as 'cadets' into the national bureaucratic framework (Bayart, 1979, pp. 179, 185, 217, 221–2, 238). While a centrally controlled administrative structure was successfully constructed at the very highest strata of provincial and district authority, this could not be duplicated at village level (Geschière, 1986, pp. 333–4). As a result, local-level decision-making remains independent of Cameroonian state authority and the vision of penetrative administrative power embraced by the ruling regime became in effect blocked.

On a more dramatic scale, the effort to extend the intrusive grasp of state power in Ethiopia, Angola, Liberia, Chad and Uganda helped to provoke violent, regionally based rebellions or secessionist movements in those countries that fundamentally destroyed the potential for national unity in all five cases for the forseeable future (on the origin of three of these conflicts see Young, 1983; Bienen, 1983, pp. 108–9; Thompson and Adloff, 1981; Decalo, 1980). Although it could be argued that outside intervention and other factors helped to fuel the respective rebellions, the state's centralizing, penetrative efforts were an important contribution to – and certainly proved unable to prevent – the fragmentation of government authority in these nations. By 1992, Eritrea had successfully seceded from Ethiopia, Angola had become decisively bifurcated into separate geo-political entities, while state power remains nominal in much of rural Uganda and Chad, and non-existent in almost all of Liberia.

The case of post-independence Zaire is particularly instructive. National leaders aimed to preserve the formal positions of traditionally legitimate village chiefs while instituting a centrally controlled rural administrative structure that would ensure a gradual reduction in the ability of chiefs to exert their authority (Callaghy, 1984, pp. 19, 53, 96–7). But this system proved largely unworkable, especially in regions with traditionally anti-centralist tendencies (such as Kivu and Shaba), due to the resilience of local leaders and their communities and to serious problems of administrative oversight. As a result, many rural policies assigned to region state functionaries were aborted, and the national government remained unable to render village leaders dependent on its bureaucratic authority.[5] In fact, by the early 1990s such policies had contributed to a severe crisis in national political legitimacy, a proliferation of regional rebellions and the disintegration of state power in most rural areas, with the survival prospects of Mobutu's hybrid regime appearing increasingly poor.

Like their post-colonial African counterparts, early and late mediaeval state-builders were intent on subordinating all privileged groups and independent areas within their nominal jurisdiction and incorporating them within a nascent administrative-politico framework, but were unable to overcome the resilience of localistic, regional baronial, religious or class-based social groups (Strayer, 1955, p. 198; Folz, 1974, pp. 102–6; Barraclough, 1976, pp. 58–61; Bloch, 1961, p. 416). It is true that Charlemagne created a corps of *missi dominici*, or royal envoys, who were sent out to supervise and inspect local governors to ensure that his orders were being followed; he established some 250 districts in Gaul, Italy and Germany; he appointed counts to rule each district who were not indigenous to that district, and who in turn appointed vicars or 'hundredmen' to rule the sub-divisions of each county. Also, twice a year he summoned a general assembly to gather together all the officials of the realm to consider political programmes and legislation; and he suppressed the peasant 'guilds' or 'brotherhoods'. None the less, this administrative apparatus was overstretched and practically ineffectual; the count had virtually no authority over the localities; the 'hundreds' were actually fully autonomous and self-governing; and the *missi dominici* had little power of enforcement and thus were effective only where local aristocracies were 'friendly' (Barraclough, 1976; Folz, 1974).

Later, in England, William the Conqueror (1066–87) extended royal authority through an especially systematic version of the Norman polity, with shires (counties) functioning as regional political units administered by a royal officer or 'shire reeve' (sheriff) (Hollister, 1982, pp. 14–17). Especially under Henry I, the Norman kings used this juridical system and relied on the income-generating Exchequer to extend their jurisdiction throughout the kingdom, reign reticent barons into their power nexus, and reduce the political distinctiveness of each district, so that by the 1200s most barons felt it necessary to push for their interests by working with the government and England had become the most unified country in the West (Strayer and Munro, 1959, pp. 109–11, 116–17; Painter, 1943, pp. 78–9). In France under St Louis (1226–70) and Philip the Fair (1285–1314), professional administrators (called *baillis*, as in England) ignored local tradition and worked hard to erode aristocratic privileges and extend royal authority. This effort at political penetration was pushed further with the subdivision of districts into viscounties headed by paid officials of the royal government (viscounts), who enjoyed strong judicial and administrative authority, and with the implementation of a system of itinerant royal inspectors known as *enquêteurs*, who represented local grievances and helped keep ambitious officials in line (Strayer, 1971, pp. 213–17; Strayer, 1971c; Hollister, 1982, pp. 262–4; Strayer and Munro, 1959, pp. 303–4).

None the less, centralized governments in this period, even the expanding apparatuses of France and England, held extremely limited power over their supposedly subordinate territories, for the feudal fiefdoms which predominated in the European countryside engendered an extreme degree of political fragmentation and local self-rule and presented powerful barriers to would-be state-builders (Figgis, 1970, pp. 233–5; Strayer and Munro, 1959, pp. 115–16; Strayer, 1971a). The breaking apart of the Holy Roman Empire and the proliferation of counties, duchies and ecclesiastical city-states precluded any effort at political penetration in Germany that the feeble empire might have aspired to (Hollister, 1982, pp. 235, 336). Nor was there a centralized power capable of extending its authority in Italy, which was divided among two Papal states and the northern city-states of Florence, Milan, Naples, Venice and Pisa, all of which warred frequently with one another (McGarry, 1976, p. 618). In England, despite the aforementioned gains in administrative power, the king was forced repeatedly to abide by the demands of the barony and often encountered rebellion when he did not. It was through two such revolts that the barons forced the abdications of Henry II and Richard II; they also established the dependency of the king on the barony for consultation through the Magna Carta of 1215 and through their role in Parliament. Furthermore, the above-discussed shire reeves were selected from the local gentry rather than from the centralized administration, and the procedures and customs of the shire court were rooted in the traditions of the locality rather than in royal mandates (Strayer and Munro, 1959, pp. 289, 293, 382–4, 429, 468–9, 479; Anderson, 1974, pp. 115–16; McGarry, 1976, pp. 109–10; Hollister, 1982, p. 242). As with the case of the Village Productivity Committees in Zambia, Revolutionary Local Powers in Guinea and village committees in Tanzania and Guinea-Bissau, so in mediaeval England local elites used the nascent politico-administrative system to obstruct national policy and consolidate their own rule based on local norms, thereby setting back the state's penetration effort.

Similarly in France at the time of Philip the Fair, each province, fiefdom and local principality had its own institutions, laws and customs that the central authorities could not override because the *baillis* and *enquêteur* systems were insufficient to the task. What little penetrative power the king was able to exercise was limited to the area between Paris and Orleans, known as the Île de France, and even there many petty barons remained wholly indifferent to royal law (Strayer and Munro, 1959, pp. 293, 300, 395; Strayer, 1971c, p. 50). Entire provinces, such as Flanders, Brittany, Guienne-Gascony and Burgundy, remained outside the reach of the monarchical state, the latter province violently seceding and becoming a powerful independent polity in the fifteenth century as the Burgundian aristocracy refused to submit to Valois rule (Hollister, 1982, pp. 332–3; McGarry, 1976, p. 445). Nor was an increase in monarchical bureaucratic staff size translated into a decrease in noble power; Philip IV's government needed to bargain constantly with local aristocrats and was ultimately dependent on their support for any of his policies to be effectively carried out. When he pushed the nobility too far, for example regarding taxation toward the end of his reign, they formed provincial leagues to counter the power of the monarchy. In 1315 these leagues forced the new king Louis X to issue a series of charters confirming their rights (Strayer and Munro, 1959, p. 427). The French state did not appreciably gain in strength as the remainder of the fourteenth century unfolded, for it continued to lack the administrative capacity to control localities in most of the country, and Charles VII (1422–61) was still obligated to bargain and negotiate with intermediary political powers (Anderson, 1974, p. 87).

Thus, mediaeval European states, like their post-independence African counterparts, built up their central administrations but lacked the bureaucratic power to overcome the varying localistic and social forces opposed to the state's predominance until at least the sixteenth century (ibid., p. 9). Warfare, rebellion and secession were mainstays of centre–periphery political relations in the weaker states of mediaeval Europe (Bloch, 1961, p. 409) as in large parts of post-colonial Africa. In both cases, those states which succeeded in implementing a generalized administrative structure found that locally based officials of the national government tended to use their positions to strengthen their local authority and to defend local traditions rather than dutifully integrating the local power structures into the bureaucratic interstices of the state. Thus, the drive to achieve nation-wide political sovereignty in mediaeval Europe and in independent Africa was held back by the continuing potency of locally orientated social forces; the resultant low degree of political penetration may be considered a central characteristic of weak states.

3 Informal Politics

In states which lack the infrastructural capacity to implement official policies and where governing institutions are unable to consistently, pervasively and effectively assert their authority over oppositional societal elements and over their territorial domain, 'politics' is really about *informal* dynamics among politically powerful people. Even though, in some cases, certain legal-parliamentary proceedings (as in Botswana and Zimbabwe), or customary feudal or Church-related obligations and religious sanctifications (as in many mediae-val European polities) may impose certain limitations on the scope of informal political action, the central determinants of political change and leadership succession are generally to be found in the informal political sector rather than within more clearly identifiable and visible formal political institutions and processes. Informal alliances, competition and conflicts among competing organizations, institutions, factions and individuals occur outside the parameters of the formal political/administrative/legal system. Bureaucratic agencies, national constitutions, parliamentary bodies, elections and plebiscites are all frequently manipulated, abused or ignored in order to assure the dominance of a particular ruler or ruling faction, while the 'real' politics of change and decision-making occur in the form of informal power struggles 'behind the scenes' among leading groups and politicians. The unstructured nature of politics at the summit of states in formation makes it especially propitious for the group or individual pursuit of higher office to occur apart from formal political systems and processes.

In such states, dominated by informal politics, success at political leadership in fact depends heavily on a given ruler's ability to construct personally based alliances. At the same time, the state becomes divided into fragmented power sections, with groups of leaders and officials involved in factional competition over the political and economic rewards of power-holding. Thus, politics at the national level mostly involves the formation of, changes within and power struggles among factions based on kinship, ethnicity, class, personal ties, regional backgrounds, clientelism and religion – with the armed forces serving as a crucial determinant of the outcome of this internal competition. State–society linkages tend to be fluid and informally established, which makes it possible for social forces to burrow into and dominate government institutions, further heightening the general political context of uncertainty and unpredictability within the state.

3.1 Personal ties and personal rule

The creation of personal ties is of central importance in understanding politics in weak states. Political success depends to a large
extent on the cultivation of personal linkages with secondary political actors and powerholders. For this reason, in mediaeval European
and post-independence African polities, elite networking became
a *modus vivendi* of statecraft, resulting in a blurring of the boundaries
of responsibilities assigned to officials because these informal power
networks cut across institutional borders and provoked administrators to carry out actions entirely outside their range of formal
duty. As the authority of the centralized state is fragmented, the
national elite must rely on the cultivation of loyalties and affections
within a network of mutually dependent personal relations (Dyson,
1980, p. 53).

In sub-Saharan Africa, heads of government, party officials and
cadres, ministers as well as middle-level functionaries often aspire
to construct alliances of power upon which they may consolidate
their domain of rule or advance in position. Jackson and Rosberg
argue that 'personal rule' represents, throughout post-independence
Africa,

> a distinctive type of institutionless polity ... [in which] the *formal*
> rules of the political game do not effectively govern the conduct of
> rulers and other political leaders in most places most of the time.
> (Jackson and Rosberg, 1982, pp. 8, 11; emphasis added)

The post-colonial African leader has been

> a personal ruler more than an institutional one; he [has] ruled by
> his ability and skill (as well as the abilities and skill of those he could
> convince to be his supporters), by his personal power and legiti-
> macy, and not solely by the title granted to him by the office he
> occupied and the constitution that defined it. ... If personal rulers
> are restrained, it is by the limits of their personal authority and
> power and by the authority and power of patrons, associates, clients,
> supporters, and – of course – rivals. ... the fact that it is ultimately
> dependent on persons rather than institutions is its essential vulner-
> ability. (Ibid., pp. 16, 19)

The high level of political flux has made it necessary for African
rulers to attempt to construct a 'political monopoly' so as to nullify the power and deflect the challenges of potential rivals (ibid.,
p. 52). What this means in practice is the employment of various

Machiavellian mechanisms that are activated specifically in order to out-wit rulers' actual or would-be competitors and to contain hostile power factions. Among the mechanisms most regularly utilized for this purpose are purges and rehabilitations, the manipulation of bureaucratic agencies, the amendment and rewriting of constitutions, and the holding of elections. The latter in particular have been carried out by a number of African presidents specifically in order to bolster support for their personal power networks. In Guinea-Bissau, as in Kenya, elections were implemented in order to strengthen the existing president, rather than to provide citizens with an opportunity to choose a new leadership (Forrest, 1987b; Barkan, 1987).

Reliance on personal ties in politics marked the first years of independence in Zaire, as well as the subsequent rise of 'Caeserism' in that country (Willame, 1970). Like Ahidjo in Cameroon, Banda of Malawi and other African leaders, as President Mobutu consolidated his regime in Zaire, there was 'a progressively more explicit personalization of the state', with Mobutu expanding the patrimonial nature of his rule and relying increasingly on

> an assemblage of courtiers doing the bidding of the presidential monarch. Access to high rank in all state agencies depended upon presidential favor; this was exercised by direct designation at the top levels, while presidential scrutiny and veto applied at intermediate levels. (Young and Turner, 1985, pp. 397, 399)

In the Middle Ages in Europe, similarly to independent Africa, loyalty was given to particular individuals or families rather than to the state as a political entity. It was a personal loyalty, but it was not wholly reliable: 'it was tested afresh every time there was a request or a demand for obedience' (Strayer, 1971b, p. 342). The personal nature of rulership meant that a king's strength and capacity for action depended almost entirely on the degree to which he could inspire devotion among his vassals (Barraclough, 1976, p. 61). Thus, for example, Emperor Otto I admitted that the difficulty in promulgating laws was that at least a few great men were absent from any given assembly, so that even though he, the emperor, was present, as was the majority of the leading chieftains, the fact that he had had no personal contact with the absent men meant that the law or policy could not be imposed (Bloch, 1961, p. 410).

The very basis of Carolingian political rule was informal, depending on kin alliances and the loyalty of friends and vassals (Hollister, 1982, pp. 83–4). The strength of Charlemagne rested largely on his ability to cultivate ties of personal loyalty and dependency through the power of his charisma and through the redistribution of land to leading aristocrats. Provincial officials obeyed royal commands largely out of devotion to the person of Charlemagne, for he had no other power to assert over them (ibid., p. 101). The personal nature of these ties is illustrated by the fact that the Carolingian government began to fall into disorder as soon as Charlemagne grew too feeble to travel in order to oversee personally the business of local mayoralties and to meet with his vassals in 808; the empire collapsed completely upon his death in 814 (Folz, 1974, pp. 91–2, 106–7).

In the southern Italian kingdoms of Naples and Sicily and in the city-states and numerous petty lordships (*signorie*) of the north, constant rivalries and mini-wars among factions of town-dwellers led to the rise of 'strong men ... sometimes as a result of a coup' (McGarry, 1976, p. 619). These *signori* (lords or despots), each with a large grouping of personal devotees, eventually ruled parts or all of the Italian city-states, the Medici, for example, ruling over Florence. The King of England, William of Normandy, was able to decide personally the fate of any legislative or legal issue under official discussion; those convicted of major crimes were at his personal mercy (Painter, 1943, p. 92). The personal role of Henry I was heightened as the procedures of the *curia* were conducted informally, its meetings were irregularly held and its records were incomplete (Strayer and Munro, 1959, p. 279) – a situation similar to many African ministries today, which helps to explain the easy intervention of African presidents in the affairs of government. King Henry III of England (1216–72) appointed friends and relatives to many positions in his administration. This aroused the jealousy of numerous barons and weakened his government (Strayer, 1955, p. 173).

The political business of Louis VI (1108–37) and Louis VIII (1223–6) was conducted through informal, *ad hoc* procedures, making it possible for those kings to remain involved in many government activities (Strayer, 1971c, p. 47). Philip the Fair, King of France (1285–1314), personally controlled and directed the workings of his government, assigning specific tasks to his councillors and intervening directly in any policy decision of interest to him (Strayer, 1971d, pp. 195–212) – very closely paralleling contemporary African presidencies such as those of Ahidjo of Cameroon and Mobutu of Zaire Even as late as the 1600s, the personal magnetism of the founder of the new Bourbon dynasty, Henry IV of France, was a key factor in the rise of Absolutist rule (Anderson, 1974, p. 94).

In England in 1625, Charles I was able to institute a more effective alliance between the state and the nobility not only through the strategic distribution of benefits but also through his close personal involvement in the functioning of the government (ibid., p. 139).

3.2 Unbounded power struggles

Because of the relative inattention to formal rules and political processes in weak states, these states are normally beset by an aura of covert and/or overt strife among contending political actors and factions. These struggles for power that occur among the state's component parts may be considered 'unbounded' in that the informal character of political relations sets few limits on the types of activities or methods of political change employed by national-level politicians. Mediaeval European kings and contemporary African presidents, as well as their challengers and rivals, have consequently used all manner of strategy to out-manoeuvre their respective opponents. These strategies range from personal lobbying, the dispensation of patronage and the alteration of constitutions or political bodies to arrests, imprisonment, torture, assassination and *coups d'état*.

The independent African state is largely composed of institutional interests, conflicting factions and contending leaders that openly or covertly struggle with one another for greater control over the centralized apparatuses of governance. As Claude Ake writes,

> political competition is without norms and unrestrained. ... this places a high premium on political power and makes the struggle for power Hobbesian. ... [B]ecause the power struggle is so intense, politics become an absorbing pursuit to the detriment of everything else. ... Those in power develop a seige mentality and see everything in terms of increasing their power. (Ake, 1985, p. 112)

In calling attention to the centrality of the 'nonformal political sector' in understanding the question of power in Africa, Chazan focuses her analysis of Ghanaian politics on the distribution of power throughout society, the formation and manipulation of power constellations within the state and between the state and society, and struggles for power at various levels of the polis (Chazan, 1983, pp. 8, 15, 378, 381).

Like many post-colonial African leaders, the authority of mediaeval European kings remained largely dependent on the outcome of internal struggles for power (Bendix, 1978, p. 4). National politics in the feudal period were marked by 'multiple zero sum struggles' among the component parts of the state (Brenner, 1986). As a result, 'the authority of any one king was always in jeopardy and had to be manifested continuously to remain effective' (Bendix, 1978, p. 4). Security of leadership depended on the extent of officials' personal loyalty to the king, but because such loyalty was often so difficult to secure, arbitrariness became a dominant feature of rulership (ibid., p. 220).

The lack of power consolidation that characterized the governments of kings meant that the more the ruler relied on other aristrocrats to carry out state functions, the less personal authority accrued to the king, as each state minister was able to expand his autonomy and his own resource base due to his control over his ministry's personnel and finances (ibid., pp. 4, 21, 220–2). Mediaeval autocracy was characterized by the king's personal initiation of governmental policy and by his effort to consolidate his rule, but bureaucratic infighting among powerful administrators and 'rival claims among members of the royal family' meant that they too formed part of the intra-state political process, with 'bloody turmoil' resulting when the administrative and resource autonomy of feudal retainers and of government ministers was challenged too strongly by the king (ibid., pp. 223, 524). The unbounded nature of political struggles allowed ruling cliques to employ any means to undo their rivals, so that, for example, the French King Philip IV and his government 'hood-winked public opinion [and] gained its ends through chicanery, slander, blackmail and brute force', while perjury, treachery, terror, torture and murder constituted the primary means of political change in late mediaeval Italy (Strayer and Munro, 1959, pp. 427, 522).

Thus, quests for power have led to virulent contests among leaders for the most prized positions in the states of mediaeval Europe and of Africa, and to various types of defences by rulers preoccupied (for good reasons) with constant challenges to their power. An account of the manifold cleavages and conflicts occurring among the principal state actors and their allies leads precisely to a study of unbounded power struggles among the various types of factions that comprise weak states.

3.3 Factional competition among familial clans, ethnic grouping, regional powers, nepotistic alliances, clientelist cliques and institutional agencies

In order to understand the dynamics of politics of states in formation, it is necessary to identify specific groups and individuals – government ministries, baronial groupings, ethnic units, personalistic factions, regionally based alliances – and to trace their particular role in the evolution of political conflicts occurring within the state. While it is true that factional power struggles are present in more or less incipient and, at times, overt form in the more stable and institutionalized systems of the present-day West and are an important part of the process of politics in the East (Heclo, 1977, p. 12; Seidman, 1980, p. 12; Crozier, 1964; Hough, 1971; Cocks, 1976), they constitute the very essence of intrastate politics in contemporary Africa, much as they did in mediaeval Europe.

In post-colonial Africa, as Bienen (1978, p. 40) points out, 'cliques, family circles, and factions have abounded in African one-party systems, including the so-called mobilization ones as well as the parties of notable or patron parties'. Young observes that independent African states have been increasingly marked by a generalized fragmentation, a multistranded division into independent 'institutional spheres' with their own particular interests. As a result, the state becomes 'a stage for ceaseless struggle among its component parts for the fleeting possession of its mythological unitary will' (Young and Turner, 1985, p. 20). Jackson and Rosberg argue forcefully that African politics are characterized by

> a personal or factional struggle to control the national government or to influence it ...; [by] internecine struggles of leaders and factions jockeying for positions of advantage and security within the regimes.
> (Jackson and Rosberg, 1982, pp. 1, 48)

Factional power struggles among groups devoted to one or another political leader seriously exacerbated the already heightening conflicts occurring within as well as between the government and the party in Guinea-Bissau. For both Presidents Luiz Cabral (1974–80) and Nino Vieira (1980-present), factional divisions raised the level of political uncertainty and helped result in the 1980 coup and in Vieira's 'purge' of the party (1981) and government (1982–3) (Forrest, 1987b). In Congo-Brazzaville, the civil service has been marked by 'clan loyalties' that gave rise to virulent 'internal competition within the public [sector]' (Lee, 1971, p. 43). Within the ruling party itself, 'the definition of political issues has been taken over by "clans"' who struggle amongst themselves for dominance (ibid., p. 45).

The case of the Cameroonian government provides an especially illustrative example of factional power struggles carried out through the various levels of the government and party hierarchies. Despite the fact that by the 1970s President Ahidjo had largely consolidated his personal control over the government bureaucracy, administrative

departments continued to engage in 'struggles for influence' within
the government (Bayar, 1979, pp. 226–7). Rivalries ensued among
the administrative branches over control of the *animation rural* programme, where *prefets* and *sous-prefets* virulently attempted to resist
the efforts at control by functionaries in the Ministry of Planning;
both these groups had to face separate challenges to their assertion
of territorial authority by the State Secretariat of Rural Development, the Ministry of Agriculture and Governors of Territorial
Administration. In a second example of inter-ministerial struggles
for influence, Bayart reports that the Ministry of Information and
Culture competed with the Ministry of Territorial Administration
for jurisdictional authority and for control over political matters.
In a third example, judiciary officials of common law courts and of
military tribunals similarly disputed their respective responsibilities
regarding legal matters (ibid.). It is not surprising that this complicated, intertwining compendium of competing factional interests
tends to produce a standoff of power undercutting the overall effectiveness of the government.

In much of Africa, institutional competition between the ruling
political party and the government is common and tends to involve
various levels and degrees of conflict. Factional battles between
government and party are enjoined over decision-making authority,
institutional autonomy or expansion, and budgetary increases, and
they tend to be much more unstructured, open-ended and of a
zero-sum nature than, for example, in present-day Eastern Europe
(Maquet, 1971, p. 120). This specifically means that officials' careers,
positions and power are more determined by their success at constructing personal coalitions of support than by job performance,
and it sets party and government leaders into competition with one
another for obtaining other officials' loyalty (Zolberg, 1966, p. 126).

In Guinea-Bissau, the government successfully strove to establish
dominance over the PAIGC (African Party for the Independence
of Guinea-Bissau and Cape Verde) during the 1974–80 period, only
to find itself increasingly subordinate to the regenerated party after
the 1980 coup (Forrest, 1987b). The socialist Party in Senegal is in
clear command of the government and has progressively consolidated
its power since Senghor assumed the presidency and out-manoeuvred
Prime Minister Mamadou Dia in their party-vs.-government and
personal battle for the political support of various state actors and
social elites. In Cameroon, while Ahidjo's success in consolidating
his personal control of both party and government has partially
mitigated the level of conflict between the two institutions, the fact
that the dominating social strata monopolize governmental positions

while the 'social juniors' are more closely connected to the National Cameroonian Union has perpetuated an underlying antagonism between party and government that at times does develop into virulent cadre–bureaucrat competition (Bayart, 1979, p. 273). Thus, the fluctuating and pliable nature of factional power struggles between ruling party and government has been at the centre of intrastate politics in many African countries.

Conflicts among ethnically organized factions have also divided, and further complicated, the terrain of intrastate politics across sub-Saharan Africa (see especially Horowitz, 1985). To take one example, in Guinea-Bissau between 1974 and 1980 President Luiz Cabral relied on members of his ethnic group, Cape Verdeans, in the party and government in order to strengthen his rule and allowed them to predominate at the middle and higher levels of both these institutions. This intensified the antagonism to Cape Verdeans already felt by other party members, especially Balanta, due to the collaborative role played by Cape Verdeans during colonial rule, and set the stage for the successful 1980 *coup d'état*, after which Cape Verdeans were ousted from all high-level positions of power. However, in the 1980–5 period, the post-coup leadership continued to shut the Balanta out of the highest-level posts, and consequently faced three (abortive) *coups d'état* by Balanta politicos and officers in that period (Forrest, 1987b).

Clearly, internal struggles for power among personalistic, institutional and ethnic factions within the state in a number of African nations are of an especially zero-sum nature. Factional conflict defines politics in countries throughout the continent, including those suffering from an especially fluid movement of power-holders and ruling coalitions, such as post-independence Guinea-Bissau and Mali, as well as more solidly entrenched regimes characterized by unitary presidential power, as in Cameroon and Zaire. In much of mediaeval Europe where states were taking form, politics were similarly characterized by factional disputation, which frequently led to political disintegration and a lack of development. In most of these states, factionalism generally took the form of confrontations among leading families, aristocratic groupings, regionalistic clusters and groups devoted to one or another personality.

The early Germanic states, which rose directly from the ashes of the Roman Empire, were marked by violent rivalries among factions of the nobility and ethnic groups such as Romans and Germans, Catholics and Arians (McGarry, 1976, p. 95). In Italy in the ninth and tenth centuries, three extended families and their supporters competed for control of the province of Lombardy, which was the political heart of the peninsula – the margraves and marquesses of Spoleto, the dukes and marquesses of Friuli, and the house of Tuscany – but none was able to hold power except briefly, as none was strong enough to dominate the other two (Barraclough, 1976, pp. 100–1). By the time of the High Middle Ages, the Italian city-states were divided into factions that competed with one another for control of particular neighbourhoods or of the city itself, despite extended efforts by some leading families to reach compromises on the form of political leadership. In Milan, for example, bitter struggles raged between the Torriani and Visconti, with the Torriani gaining the upper hand from 1237 to 1277 and the Visconti finally acceding to full municipal power in 1277 and holding it for nearly two centuries (McGarry, 1976, p. 621). In Florence, branches of the Guelph and Ghibelline families vied for supremacy; the Guelphs had established control by 1293, but the Medici wrested power away in 1421 and consolidated their rule despite a partially successful *coup d'état* on the part of the Pazzi family in 1478.

In fifteenth- and sixteenth-century Spain, fifteenth-century England, thirteenth-century France and mediaeval Russia, the ruling elite were divided among 'rank, function, ethnicity, legal status, family prestige, relationship to the royal house, place of residence, e.g. court versus provinces, and military skills', resulting in a high level of factional conflict (Lenski, 1966, p. 239). In England, for 19 years following the death of Henry I, his nephew Stephen of Blois struggled with Matilda of Anjou and her husband Geoffrey for control of the Anglo-Norman realm, with barons lining up on the side of one or other of these monarchical intrafamily rivals (Hollister, 1982, p. 246). As the state developed, a context of uncertainty was created by the barons in that (a) they allowed the king to set up and run his government, but made clear that they could step in and alter policy if it were in their interests to do so; and (b) they were divided among regional, familial and personalistic factions that intrigued constantly at the court (Strayer and Munro, 1959, p. 477). Indeed, factions of the nobility, each of which had access to a part of the royal government, vied with each other over who would receive the spoils of office by selling the government its supplies (ibid., p. 459). Factional power struggles within the government of Henry IV (1399–1413) made it necessary for the King to appoint new officials every time the baronial balance of power shifted. As a result, there were new chancellors in the Chancery less than every two years, and his Council members were replaced almost as often (ibid., p. 482) – a situation which starkly recalls the experience of many contemporary African presidents regarding their cabinets.

Factional conflict between the Beauforts, a branch of the Lan-castrians, and the Duke of Gloucester opened in the 1430s and lasted most of that century. Gloucester held the edge until 1441, when the Beauforts gained ascendancy and strengthened their power. This declined following the death of the Duke of Gloucester under sus-picious circumstances in 1447, five days after the Beauforts had arrested him (McGarry, 1976, p. 145). Murderous feuding greatly intensified when Henry VI became insane in 1453; two factions emerged, one headed by Queen Margaret and the other by Richard, Duke of York. This power struggle resulted in the War of the Roses, during which the barons fought hard 'to kill their rivals, and above all to be on the winning side' (Strayer and Munro, 1959, p. 493). In the 1480s, control of state power see-sawed between Richard of Gloucester and the Woodvilles, Richard at first winning Parliament's support, which declared him king (in 1483) and allowed him to imprison and apparently murder Edward V's two younger sons (McGarry, 1976, p. 585). Aristocratic factions continued to compete with one another within and outside Parliament throughout the reign of Henry VII, despite the advent of what some historians call Tudor Absolutism (Anderson, 1974, p. 118; McGarry, 1976, p. 585).

The predominance of factional unbounded power struggles in the mediaeval polity is also clear in the case of France. Intragovern-mental competition among the councillors of Philip the Fair (1285–1314) was rife, especially as no one minister was strong enough to dominate policy-making (Strayer, 1971d). Magnate feuding led to national fragmentation in the fourteenth century even greater than had existed in the thirteenth (Anderson, 1974, p. 86). The familial/regional power struggle between the Burgundians and the Armagnacs of Orleans over control of the French regency raged from 1392 throughout most of the fifteenth century, despite repeated efforts by the Parisian burgesses and by the Dauphin Charles to end the strife (Strayer and Munro, 1959, p. 483). From the late 1500s, three rival magnate lineages, each of differing regional origin – Guise, Montmorency and Bourbon – had developed a significant clientelist base within a section of the machinery of the state, and used that base and their portion of the state machinery to assert power over the others (Anderson, 1974, p. 91). Even under the regime of Louis XIII (1610–43), factions of the nobility proved able 'to weave their way into the pinnacles of state power' (ibid., p. 95) which was also true of the (first) Mazarin and (then) Colbert lobbies under Louis XIV (Braudel, 1982, p. 538).

Thus, states in formation tend to be divided into factional group-ings that compete with one another, without attention to rules or procedures. The unbounded nature of these conflicts means that outcomes are highly unpredictable and may result in a compromise (however temporary) between the leading contenders, total replacement of the ruling personnel, or the strengthening of a given regime. It is certainly the case that a high level of factional conflict pervades and dominates state politics in contemporary Africa as it did in mediaeval Europe.

3.4 Social forces and the state

Because the organizational boundaries of state institutions in Africa and in mediaeval Europe are and were weak and porous, many conflicts within society – among ethnic groups or social classes or clan/kin/clientelist agglomerations – seep into state organizations and help to divide national leaders into competitive factions. Especially at times of social crisis, state actors become 'immersed' in society-based struggles (Ake, 1985, p. 112), and formal institutions, such as parliaments, are unable to mediate these struggles. Thus, class, regional, factional, ethnic or familial forces with their roots located within society often transgress the institutional boundaries of the state precisely because those boundaries are so imprecise and poorly fortified, and proceed to manipulate the agencies and personnel of the state in a way that best secures their particularistic interests.

In parts of Africa, bargaining between state leaders and social elites reflects the working out of a 'hegemonical exchange' that takes place along informal channels (Rothchild, 1987). State leaders enter into reciprocal exchanges with regional and local elites and 'brokers for various ethnic sections' to secure their support (ibid.). This type of bargaining may be considered the primary mode of politics in Kenya (Barkan, 1987, p. 226; Lamb, 1974, pp. 110–31), and has typified the manner by which hybrid regimes were formed in Ghana, Sierra Leone and Zambia (Chazan, 1983; Rothchild, 1983, pp. 186–8; Keller, 1983, p. 264; Clapham, 1976). Similarly, patron–client politics predominate in a wide range of African nations, creating strong informal pressures on the allocation of government resources. These clientelist links help to personalize state–society interaction and encourage the formation of ethnic and kin-based power networks between national institutions and regional and local political actors (Hyden, 1983, p. 71). Presidents Ahidjo of Cameroon, Kenyatta of Kenya and Houphouet-Boigny of Ivory Coast became renowned for their construction of intensively personalized webs of clientelist support which linked village elites with district leaders, parliamentarians and high-level government bureaucrats (Barkan, 1987; Rothchild, 1983; Bayart, 1979).

Thus, informal linkages among elites in society and state leaders, between societal groupings and party or government or military factions, within ethnic groups, and between peasants and soldiers serve to connect those engaged in the pursuit of power within the state arena in Africa with certain sectors of the population located outside it. Rothchild has noted the degree to which contemporary African states have become interpenetrated by social units to the extent that state power depends largely on 'elite networking, coercion, and the distribution of resources within society' (Rothchild, 1987, p. 126). Chazan's work is especially effective in pointing the way towards a focus on power constellations linking state and society in contemporary Africa. She shows that specific groups based in society – traditional political units, subregional agglomerations, local geographic communities, professional and class-based organizations, ethnically defined groupings – have become 'politicized' in the post-independence period (Chazan, 1983, pp. 2, 6). This has led to the 'political engagement of society' and a 'dynamic interaction of Ghanaian polity and society' in that these various units are intimately connected to the organizations and alliances predominant in the state through factional, interest-based, patronage, personalistic and communal ties (ibid., 3, pp. 6–14).

The states of Europe in the Middle Ages were similarly penetrated by powerful social forces. In the Carolingian Empire, the ruling counts were recruited 'almost exclusively from the upper aristocracy, who were closely related to the royal family. They comprised several dozen great families bound to each other by marriage' (Folz, 1974, p. 104). In addition, ecclesiastical advisers enjoyed enormous influence within the Carolingian government, which greatly weakened the regimes of Louis the Pious (814–40) and of Louis the Stammerer (877–9) in particular (McGarry, 1976, p. 190). The circumstances of Hugh Capet's election in 987 as duke of 'France' clearly demonstrated the almost all-encompassing control of government by the nobility, for this exercise in electoral arbitrariness was carried out only because it allowed the feudal lords to shape directly the royal government and made clear that they could remove Capet at will (Strayer and Munro, 1959, p. 173). Later, the great rivalries among the noble families of Guise, Montmorency and Bourbon were brought directly into the French state and divided its institutions into three different patronage networks (Anderson, 1974, p. 48).

The barony of mediaeval England established its right to consultation and debate over royal policy, and the barons' personal contacts within the Exchequer and the king's courts allowed them to shape national policy directly, at times even to a greater extent than the ruling monarch (Strayer and Munro, 1959, p. 377). In the High Middle Ages, the powers of the English Parliament remained vague and its internal composition undefined and fluid. This enabled the barons to 'bargain discretely with the king in parliament for concessions in return for the granting of a special tax' (Hollister, 1982, p. 258). By the close of the fourteenth century, however, the baron-controlled Parliament had established 'almost complete control over taxation [and] great influence in legislation' (Strayer and Munro, 1959, p. 480). The power of the barony within the heart of the state can be seen in the fact that it was aristocratic factional struggles, played out in Parliament, which led to the deposition of two kings, Edward II in 1327 and Richard II in 1399 (Hollister, 1982, p. 329).

Thus, states in formation are partially penetrated by specific social forces that directly or indirectly help to navigate the direction of political change, decide how crises are resolved, and form part of the constellation of power supporting a given regime's rulers and/or its challengers. The above cases in Africa and in mediaeval Europe indicate the necessity of investigating these state–society connections in order to appreciate the full range of components in power coalitions at the summit of the national political arena. In weak states, it is important to identify junctures where ground-level groups themselves initiate their non-formal political participation, pressuring state leaders from below to act in certain ways or utilizing their connections to influence state groupings and factions so that they significantly affect power struggles within the state.

3.5 *The role of force in power politics:* coup d'état *and the military*

Many factional and personalistic power struggles within weak states involve essentially 'tactical' methods: the cajoling or convincing (through persuasion) of certain individuals behind the scenes; the building-up of a network of supporters through informal contacts and patronage; lobbying within local regions and with foreign powers for support for one's political programme. However, the unbounded nature of these tactical power struggles frequently leads to the use of force, which may involve attempted *coups d'état* by a section of, or the entire, armed forces, the imprisonment or execution of one's opponents for political reasons, the employment (in various ways) of armed security agents who are devoted to a particular leader or leadership group, or a leader's or group's mobilization of a specific social sector or region with the intent to stage a rebellion. The fact that violence is such a prominent part of politics in weak states and that government institutions are so fragile and porous means that: (a) the armed forces generally play a key role within the state; (b) military leaders commonly assume positions of political leadership; and (c) soldiers' connections with social forces may allow these social forces to penetrate and more strongly impact on the state.

Because the strongest concentration of physical power is in the armed forces, any leader requires 'the cooperation or at least the acquiescence of the military to remain in power' in a weak state, and, concomitantly, military intervention is a constant risk and a frequent occurrence (Jackson and Rosberg, 1982, p. 26). Army coups in post-colonial Africa are generally produced by a combination of threats to the corporate integrity of the military (interference in its internal affairs), the individual drive for power on the part of military leaders, and ethnic power imbalances either within the military or between the military and other state institutions (Decalo, 1976, pp. 14, 24; Gutteridge, 1975, p. 19; First, 1971, p. 20). It is certain that the *coup d'état* constitutes a central means of political change in many contemporary African states. Indeed, we may count 65 successful coups in sub-Saharan Africa up to mid-1985 (Welch, 1987, p. 191) and hundreds of near-coups.

The failure of former President Hamani Diori of Niger to effectively contain his rivals led directly to a successful *coup d'état* in 1974 (Higgot and Fuglestad, 1975, p. 387, as cited in Jackson and Rosberg, 1982, p. 53). In Uganda, former President Milton Obote's struggle for power with the Bugandan Kabaka (king), Sir Edward Mutesa, ended the Obote–Mutesa alliance that had served Obote effectively until 1964 and weakened the president's personal rule (Mazrui, 1975). In 1966, Obote forced the Kabaka of Buganda into exile and arrested five ministers in a move to strengthen his leadership and eliminate potential rivals from power (ibid., pp. 14–15). A plot from within the ruling Uganda People's Congress to oust Obote greatly raised the stakes of on-going leadership struggles. Rivals to Obote competed with him (and each other) for the loyalty of Uganda's military and security forces in individual bids for control of the centre of Ugandan political life that would culminate in General Idi Amin's successful coup of 1971 (ibid., pp. 17, 23).

Violent struggles for power have been played out even within the Marxist-Leninist state of Angola which, like Guinea-Bissau, obtained its independence from Portugal in a peasant-backed nationalist armed struggle but which has been – like Guinea-Bissau's PAIGC – marked by personal rivalries within the ruling MPLA

(Popular Movement for the liberation of Angola) (Jackson and Rosberg, 1982, pp. 61–2), including an abortive challenge for power by Nito Alves, the Minister of Interior (Marcum, 1978, p. 279). Twice, '[President] Neto's leadership was a focal point of controversy within a crippling, internal power struggle' (ibid., p. 197). Under Luiz Cabral's presidency in Guinea-Bissau, professionally undeserving presidential favourites were appointed to the officer corps while worthy military men were unfairly passed over for promotion in an effort to protect the civilian leadership from a potential military threat from restive barracks. As in Ghana in 1966 (Adekson, 1976) and Uganda in 1971 (Mazrui, 1975, p. 111), this attempt to secure the safety of the leadership by internal interference in the structure of the military provoked the exact response that the president had intended to prevent: a successful *coup d'état.*

Presidential efforts to circumscribe the powers of the army have many times been countered with violent military intervention, especially when combined with ethnic hostilities. The tacit Obote–Amin alliance of the mid-1960s gave way to a personal *mano-a-mano* between the two strongmen, with President Obote seeking to remove Amin from army influence by creating parallel command structures. In addition, Amin was upset over the dominance of Acholi and Langi troops and officers in the army. Similarly in Togo, the 1967 overthrow of President Grunitzky was a direct consequence of the president's effort to eliminate the power and influence of Colonel Eyadema, the 'strongman of Togo', and the November 1966 Ewe demonstrations in Lomé had helped to provide the background of ethnic discontent that augmented the likelihood of military intervention (Decalo, 1976, p. 20). 'Personality differences, competing ambitions, and corporate grievances also played a role in both the 1966 and 1972 coups in Ghana' (ibid., pp. 19–20). In Chad, the army moved against President Tombalbaye in 1975 'only after rumors started to circulate of further purges of their officer corps' (ibid., p. 21). In these cases, personal competition and efforts to supersede the corporate autonomy of the military for purposes of presidential power aggrandizement combined with factional and ethnic antagonisms to lead to intense intra-army discontent sufficient to provoke military intervention into the civilian political arena.

It is important to stress that military officers are often integrally involved with one or more sectors of the country's political elite and make definitive choices as to which individual leaders they support or oppose. Certainly, in Guinea-Bissau soldiers played key roles in disputes among top political leaders – especially in the power struggles between President Cabral and General Vieira (1978–80),

President Vieira and Prime Minister Victor Saude Maria (1981–4) and President Vieira and Colonel Paulo Correia (1982–5). These cases make clear the importance of overlapping ties among the military and civilian sectors and the extent to which the military is often involved in power struggles within the centralized political arena even though it may not itself be in power. At the same time, coups are 'more broadly ... an outcome of the military's interactions with social and ethnic groups' (Bienen, 1978, p. 5 and ch. 5).

Indeed, it is a striking aspect of post-colonial African politics that, whether independence was obtained through a peaceful transfer of power or as a consequence of guerrilla armed struggle, ethnic divisions within armies as well as between the military and other organs of state power often came to the fore and provided cause for large-scale grievances among many soldiers, politicians and unmobilized citizens. In the well-known cases of Nigeria, Chad and Uganda, soldiers coalesced into battalions or factions that were ethnically defined, eventually splitting into entirely separate units (Luckham, 1971; Mazrui, 1975). In Congo-Brazzaville, ethnic loyalties stood at the basis of intra-military cleavages and resulted directly in the attempted military coups of 1969 and 1970 (Lee, 1971, pp. 44–5). The ethno-factional divisions within the armed forces were clearly revealed in the army mutiny of June 1966, which was a consequence of discontent on the part of Kouyou soldiers, in the Lari-based plot of 1969, and in Lieutenant Kikanga's Lari/Bakongo attempted coup of March 1970 (ibid., pp. 42, 45–56).

Commonly, the formation of intra-army ethnic divisions coalesce between the officer corps, on the one hand, and the rank and file, on the other. This occurred in Nigeria, for example, where Ibo dominance in the officer corps exacerbated growing discontent among the Hausa-Fulani and Yoruba, both in the military as well as in society more generally, over the disproportionate numbers of Ibo within the country's leading political and economic institutions. It was a factor that eventually led to the July 1966 coup and to the internal break-up of the army in the following year (Welch, 1970, p. 28). However, it may also happen that ethnic animosities are provoked when a military marked by an officer corps predominantly from one ethnic group secures posts previously filled by civilian bureaucrats. In Guinea-Bissau, this occurred after Vieira was installed as president, when he appointed Balanta military men to the Revolutionary Council and to high government posts. This radically raised the level of expectation among the Balanta soldiers, whose demands for more-extensive promotions and other advantages eventually culminated in the attempted Balanta coup of 1985 (Forrest, 1987b).

Thus, coups and army leaders have been a central and integral part of the political landscape in the states of post-colonial Africa. Armies have served to connect state and society through the medium of ethnicity in a number of African countries. Through their connections in the armed forces, portions of society at times become integrated into struggles for power among the top political players, making it possible for political conflicts to bridge informally the organizational boundaries of state institutions. This has occurred in Congo-Brazzaville, Sierra Leone, Nigeria, Ghana, Benin and Burundi (see Pabanel, 1984; Bienen, 1983, p. 116; Bienen, 1978, p. 5 and ch. 5; Cox, 1976, pp. 12, 116; Welch and Smith, 1974, p. 246). In such cases, state–society linkages make possible the transmission of societally based divisions and power struggles to the pinnacle of state authority, fueling elite dissension and periodically helping to provoke *coups d'état*.

In the European states of the mediaeval period, actual military takeovers were not as common as in post-colonial Africa and many non-military regimes were long-lasting, but military commanders, the army and the use of force did figure predominantly. Indeed, 'like all successful monarchs of the early Middle Ages', Pepin II of Heristal (678–714) was an excellent general who defeated the Lombards in Italy, drove the Muslims from Aquitaine and quelled all dissent within the kingdom (Hollister, 1982, p. 88). His son Charles 'Martel' ('the Hammer'), was 'above all else a warrior-king', a superb military commander whose armies embarked on annual military campaigns and who led the Austrasian Frankish forces to victory over the Neustrians three times (in 716, 717 and 718), repulsed the Fisians, Saxons and Arabs, and subjected an expanded Frankland to his mayoralty (ibid.; and see McGarry, 1976, p. 137). The local mayors of the Carolingian Empire held on to power only by gathering around them large numbers of trained warriors (Hollister, 1982, p. 84).

Adelboro, whose political career typified the informal workings of mediaeval governance, was a leading citizen of Laon, the Carolingian capital, served as chancellor (chief notary) of Lothaire's Chancery, was bishop of Laon (from 977), counsellor to Hugh Capet and ecclesiastical leader of the province of Rheims. He played key 'behind-the-scenes' roles through a 60-year period (971–1031) spanning the regimes of Lothaire, Louis V, Hugh Capet, and Robert the Pious. He owed his positions almost entirely to personal and family connections and to princely favour. He was either the instigator or target of incessant plots, intrigues and conspiracies, all of which revolved around his personal relations with other members of the court and politically important noblemen. He became renowned for his dramatic capture of Lothaire's brother Charles of Lorraine in 991, which thereby removed the most potent threat to the power of Hugh Capet, but four years later carried out an abortive *coup d'état* in an effort to depose Capet and replace him with Charles's son (information in this paragraph is from Coolidge, 1965).

After 1415, when Charles VI of France went mad, his younger brother Duke Louis of Orleans and his uncles, especially Duke Philip the Bold of Burgundy, competed for control of the central government. This conflict intensified when Philip died and was succeeded by his son, John the Fearless, who hired assassins to kill Louis of Orleans (McGarry, 1976, p. 146). The Count of Armagnac replaced Duke Louis and held the Burgundians at bay between 1413 and 1418, when they rebounded with a general massacre of Armagnacs in Paris and then assumed control of the French state. Finally, Louis XI (1461–83), the Spider King, assumed the throne by the cunning use of wily diplomacy, trickery and bribery, and then used the same means to arrange the death of his most able opponent, Duke Charles the Bold of Burgundy, and to behead or otherwise murder his personal and factional rivals among the nobility (ibid., pp. 591–3, 519–20).

Internal state politics in mediaeval England sharply resembled the coup-laden political landscape of post-colonial Africa. The King of England was the greatest military leader of his people, and was the most adept at manipulating other military strongmen into supporting him (Tierney and Painter, 1978, pp. 175–6). At the same time, kings depended for their power on alliances with one or more baronial factions, as the nobility still provided the best-armed and best-trained cavalry (Strayer and Nunro, 1959, p. 385). Kings such as William the Conqueror and Henry II appointed their military followers to high political positions out of deference to their dependency on the armed aristocracy for support (Hollister, 1982, p. 243). Among other things, this ensured that the barons would retain control over royal military policy (Painter, 1943, p. 44). None the less, the fragile character of these alliances is indicated by the fact that of the nine kings who ruled between 1337 and 1485, six were deposed by a baronial *coup d'état* or revolt (Strayer, 1955, p. 204). Indeed, as in contemporary Africa so in mediaeval Europe, in a context of unbounded state politics militarily organized groupings and leaders often find the opportunity to play direct roles in national politics too tempting to resist.

Precisely because the armies of mediaeval England and France were comprised of companies raised by barons, monarchs were dependent on the support of these baronial warlords and had to find a place for them in their governments. At the same time, these companies of soldiers were commonly more loyal to their commander than they were to their king, which induced many baronial commanders to rebel against the king's authority by carrying out a *coup d'état* (ibid., p. 204) — a situation very similar to numerous post-colonial African polities. The large role played by the military in resolving inter-aristocratic disputes significantly defined European politics in the fourteenth and fifteenth centuries. As in independent Africa, the lack of attention to formal political rules or constitutional procedures allowed those with access to or command over the means of force to dominate or importantly affect politics within the state. In both independent Africa and mediaeval Europe, the connection of the army with social forces — barons in the European case and ethnic, clientelist or clan groups in the case of Africa — frequently secured a looming presence for those social forces at the centre of state power.

Conclusions

In this chapter I have sought to investigate the dynamics of politics and political change within weak states, focusing on an asynchronic comparison of the hybrid regimes of mediaeval Europe with those of post-colonial Africa. In doing so, I have identified three major aspects of politics in weak states. First, they are marked by an extremely low administrative capacity, in that states lack the infrastructure and trained personnel to implement official policies despite expanding the bureaucratic size of government agencies. Secondly, weak states are characterized by a very low level of political penetration, in that societal centres of power have been able to impede the state's drive to impose its authority throughout its claimed territory by (a) ignoring technically overstretched official agencies; or (b) using the state's territorial apparatus to serve the interests of local authorities; or (c) engaging in a sustained regional rebellion or secession. Thirdly, hybrid regimes such as those of independent Africa and mediaeval Europe are marked by what I call informal politics, wherein the turmoil of political interchange is in effect 'unbounded' by constitutional or legal constraints. In so far as one power block or alliance of elites succeeds in dominating their colleagues within the state, it is to a large extent a consequence of a given leader successfully developing *personal* ties and loyalties with a wide range and large number of supporters within the ruling power block. None the less, 'behind-the-scenes' or even overt struggles for power occur constantly among intrastate factions of familial clans, ethnic groupings, regionally based authorities, personalistic cliques, clientelist alliances and/or institutional agencies. These ongoing power struggles create a context of extreme instability and render political rulers highly vulnerable to challenges from within the regime itself.

At the same time, because of the infrastructural fragility of government institutions, the organizational boundaries of the state are often permeated by powerful social forces, such as groups of aristocrats in the case of mediaeval Europe or ethno-clientelist groupings in the case of post-independence Africa. Such groups are often able to affect strongly, even to dominate, the formulation of official policies and, when more than one faction of such groups penetrates the state, they bring their rivalries and feuding into the state, intensifying and heightening the level of intrastate political conflict. Finally, due to the unbounded nature of power struggles and the institutional weakness of hybrid regimes, the use of force is common and, because the means of force are concentrated in the army, soldiers are typically closely involved in politics, so that the *coup d'état* is one of the primary mechanisms of high-level political change.

This comparison of mediaeval European and post-colonial African regimes suggests that the political problems of independent African states are not unique but are shared among certain weak states operating within a number of structural and societal constraints. However, it is by no means clear that the historical trajectory of African polities may be confidently predicted; and it is in fact unlikely that they will pursue a similar path to that forged by the states of early modern Europe. At initial stages of state formation, internal political dynamics may eventually lead to greater infrastructural, administrative and penetrative power, or they may produce virtual or even total regime collapse, or they may lead dialectically to gains and losses of the regime's- power without achieving substantive state development over a period of centuries. At this moment, we can only indicate that Africa's weak states share some traits with other states in formation in various periods of history and geographical contexts – particularly those hybrid regimes emerging in Europe during the Middle Ages. Further analysis may well reveal additional parallels with weak states in Latin America and Asia at varying points in time.

Notes

I especially wish to thank Peter H. Merkl and his colleagues at the University of California, Santa Barbara, as well as Jim Pletcher, Kiren Chaudhry and Greg Noble for their very helpful suggestions and comments. I assume all responsibility for any errors.

1. I define 'the state' as that constellation of leaders, officials, political institutions, administrative agencies, military and police organizations that holds centralized political power in a given territorial domain.
2. In this paper I focus on the period of mediaeval European history stretching from the seventh to the fifteenth centuries. There are several references to slightly later dates which may be considered to fall within the Renaissance era.
3. Thomas M. Callaghy makes a superb comparison between post-colonial Zaire and late mediaeval/early modern France regarding political penetration in his *The State–Society Struggle: Zaire in Comparative Perspective*. Here, I seek to extend the train of that analysis to make possible a more general comparison between the majority of sub-Saharan African states and the states in formation of mediaeval Europe.
4. For a fuller discussion of political penetration in Africa see Joshua B. Forrest (1988), esp. pp. 427–31.
5. Callaghy (1984) pp. 15–17, 32–41, 60–5, 83–5, 136–7, 259–75, 344–5, 404–7. See also Young and Turner (1985) for further analysis.

References

Abernathy, David B. 1983: 'Bureaucratic growth and economic decline in sub-Saharan Africa'. Paper presented at African Studies Association 26th Annual Meeting, Boston, Mass., December 7–10.

Abrahams, R.G. (ed.) 1985: *Villagers, Villages and the State in Modern Tanzania*. Cambridge: Cambridge University Press, 1985.

Adekson, J. 'Bayo 1976: 'Army in a multi-ethnic society'. *Armed Forces and Society*, 2 (2): 251–72.

Ake, Claude 1985: 'The future of the state in Africa'. *International Political Science Review*, 6 (1): 105–14.

Anderson, Perry 1974: *Lineages of the Absolutist State*. London: New Left Books.

Author interviews 1983: With ex-minister of Guinea-Conakry and with expatriates in Senegal, October–November.

Azarya, Victor and Chazan, Naomi 1987: 'Disengagement from the state in Africa: reflections on the experience of Ghana and Guinea'. *Comparative Studies in Society and History*, 29(1): 106–31.

Barkan, Joel D. 1987: 'The electoral process and peasant–state relations in Kenya'. In Fred M. Hayward (ed.), *Elections in Africa*, Boulder, Col.: Westview Press, pp. 213–37.

Barraclough, Geoffrey 1976: *The Crucible of Europe: the ninth and tenth centuries in European history*. Berkeley, Cal.: University of California Press.

Bayart, Jean-François 1979: *L'État au Cameroun*. Paris: Presses de la Fondation Nationale des Sciences Politiques.

Bendix, Reinhard 1978: *Kings or People: power and the mandate to rule*. Berkeley, Cal.: University of California Press.

Bienen, Henry 1978: *Armies and Parties in Africa*. New York: Africana Publishing.

—— 1983: 'The state and ethnicity: integrative formulas in Africa'. In Rothchild and Olorunsola, 1983.

Bloch, Marc 1961: *Feudal Society*. London: Routledge & Kegan Paul.

Braudel, Fernand 1982: *Civilization and Capitalism, 15th–18th Century*, vol. 2. New York: Harper & Row.

Brenner, Robert 1986: 'What is the autonomy of the state?' Paper presented at University of Wisconsin, 28 October.

Callaghy, Thomas M. 1984: *The State–Society Struggle: Zaire in comparative perspective*. New York: Columbia University Press.

Chazan, Naomi 1983: *An Anatomy of Ghanaian Politics: managing political recession, 1969–1982*. Boulder, Col.: Westview Press.

Clapham, Christopher 1976: *Liberia and Sierra Leone*. Cambridge: Cambridge University Press.

Cocks, Paul 1976: 'The policy process and bureaucratic politics'. In Paul Cocks, Robert V. Daniels and Nancy Whittier Heer (eds), *The Dynamics of Soviet Politics*, Cambridge, Mass.: Harvard University Press, pp. 156–78.

Coolidge, Robert T. 1965: 'Adelboro, Bishop of Laon'. In William M. Bowsky (ed.), *Studies in Medieval and Renaissance History*, Lincoln, Neb.: University of Nebraska Press, pp. 3–51.

Cox, Thomas S. 1976: *Civil–Military Relations in Sierra Leone: a case-study of African soldiers in politics*. Cambridge, Mass.: Harvard University Press.

Crozier, Michel 1964: *The Bureaucratic Phenomenon*. Chicago, Ill.: University of Chicago Press.

Decalo, Samuel 1976: *Coups and Army Rule in Africa*. New Haven, Conn.: Yale University Press.

—— 1980: 'Chad: the roots of centre–periphery strife'. *African Affairs*, 79 (October).

Duby, Georges 1968: *Rural Economy and Country Life in the Medieval West*. Columbia, S.C.: University of South Carolina Press.

Dyson, Kenneth H.F. 1980: *The State Tradition in Western Europe*. New York: Oxford University Press.

Ergas, Zaki 1980: 'Why did the Ujamaa village policy fail?' *Journal of Modern African Studies*, 18: 387–410.

Figgis, Neville 1970: 'The lack of a state [in the Middle Ages]'. In Brian Tierney (ed.), *The Middle Ages*, vol. II: *Readings in Medieval History*, New York: Knopf.

First, Ruth 1971: *Power in Africa*. New York: Pantheon Books [Random House].

Folz, Robert 1974: 'Charlemagne and his Empire'. In Vaclav Murdoch and G.S. Couse, *Essays on the Reconstruction of Medieval History*, Montreal: McGill-Queen's University Press, pp. 90–107.

Forrest Joshua B. 1987a: 'State, peasantry and national power struggles in post-independence Guinea-Bissau'. Ph.D. thesis, University of Wisconsin-Madison.

—— 1987b: 'Guinea-Bissau since independence: a decade of domestic power struggle'. *Journal of Modern African Studies*, 25(1): 95–116.

—— 1988: 'The quest for state "hardness" in Africa'. *Comparative Politics*, 20(4): 423–42.

—— 1992: *Guinea-Bissau: power, conflict, and renewal in a West African nation.* Boulder, Col.: Westview Press.

Geest, S. van der 1986: 'Health care as politics? "Missed chances" in rural Cameroon'. *Cahiers du CEDAF*, 2–3–4: 241–59.

Gertzel, Cherry 1970: *The Politics of Independent Kenya.* Evanston, Ill.: Northwestern University Press.

Geschière, Peter 1986: 'Hegemonic regimes and popular protest: Bayart, Gramsci and the state in Cameroon'. *Cahiers du CEDAF*, 2–3–4: 333–4.

Gutteridge, W.F. 1975: *Military Regimes in Africa.* London: Methuen.

Hart, Keith 1982: *The Political Economy of West African Agriculture.* Cambridge: Cambridge University Press.

Heclo, Hugh 1977: *A Government of Strangers: executive politics in Washington.* Washington, D.C.

Higgot, Richard and Fuglestad, Finn 1975: 'The 1974 coup d'état in Niger: towards an explanation'. *Journal of Modern African Studies*, 12(3): 1982: 387.

Hollister, C. Warren 1982: *Medieval Europe.* New York: John Wiley.

Horowitz, Donald 1985: *Ethnic Groups in Conflict.* Berkeley, Cal.: University of California Press.

Hough, Jerry F. 1971: 'The party apparatchiki'. In H. Gordon Skilling and Franklyn Griffiths (eds), *Interest Groups in Soviet Politics*, Princeton, N.J.: Princeton University Press, pp. 47–92.

Hyden, Govan 1980: *Beyond Ujamaa in Tanzania.* Berkeley, Cal.: University of California Press.

—— 1983: 'Problems and prospects of state coherence'. In Rothchild and Olorunsola, 1983.

Jackson, Robert H. and Rosberg, Carl G. 1982: *Personal Rule in Black Africa.* Berkeley, Cal.: University of California Press.

Keller, Edmond J. 1983: 'The state, public policy and the mediation of ethnic conflict in Africa'. In Rothchild and Olorunsola, 1983, pp. 251–80.

Lamb, Geoff 1974: *Peasant Politics.* Lewes, Sussex: Julian Friedmann.

Lamb, G.B. 1977: 'Promoting agrarian change: penetration and response in Murang'a, Kenya'. In Lionel Cliffe, J.S. Coleman and M.R. Doornbos (eds), *Government and Rural Development in East Africa*, The Hague: Martinus Nijhoff.

Lee, J.M. 1971: 'Clan loyalties and socialist doctrine in the People's Republic of the Congo'. *World Today*, 27(1): 40–6.

Lenski, Gerhard E. 1966: *Power and Privilege: a theory of social stratification*. New York: McGraw-Hill.

Luckham, Robin 1971: *The Nigerian Military: a sociological analysis of authority and revolt, 1960–67*. Cambridge: Cambridge University Press.

Maquet, Jacques 1971: *Power and Society in Africa*. New York: MacGraw-Hill.

Marcum, John A. 1978: *The Angolan Revolution*, vol. II. Cambridge, Mass.: MIT Press.

Markakis, John 1989: 'Nationalities and the state in Ethiopia'. *Third World Quarterly*, 10(4): 118–30.

Marongiu, Antonio 1970: 'A model state in the Middle Ages: the Norman and Swabian Kingdom of Sicily'. In Brian Tierney (ed.), *The Middle Ages*, vol. I: *Readings in Medieval History*, New York: Knopf, pp. 238–47.

Mazrui, Ali A. 1975: *Soldiers and Kinsmen in Uganda: the making of a military ethnocracy*. Beverly Hills, Cal.: Sage Publications.

McGarry, David D. 1976: *Medieval History and Civilization*. New York: Macmillan.

Miller, Edward, 1976: 'Government economic policies and public finance, 1000–1500'. In Carlo M. Cipolla (ed.), *The Fontana Economic History of Europe*, vol. I: *The Middle Ages*, New York: Barnes & Noble, pp. 339–73.

Miller, Norman W. 1970: 'The Rural African Party: political participation in Tanzania'. *American Political Science Review*, 64(2): 1984.

Pabanel, Jean-Pierre 1984: *Les Coups d'état militaires en Afrique noire*. Paris: editions L'Harmattan.

Painter, Sidney 1943: *Studies in the History of the English Feudal. Barony*. Baltimore, Md: Johns Hopkins University Press.

Picard, Louis A. 1980: 'Socialism and the field administrator: decentralization in Tanzania'. *Comparative Politics*, 12: 439–57.

Pletcher, James R. 1986: 'The national, regional and household contexts of agricultural production in Eastern Province, Zambia'. In Yolanda Moses (ed.), *Proceedings of the African Agricultural Development Conference*, Pamona, Cal.: California State Polytechnic University, pp. 156–63.

Pottier, J. 1986: 'Food security, local administration and peripheral development in Northern Zambia'. *Cahiers du CEDAF*, 2: 230–1.

Rothchild, Donald 1983: 'Collective demands for improved distributions'. In Rothchild and Olorunsola.

—— 1987: 'Hegemony and state softness: some variations in elite response'. In Zaki Ergas (ed.), *The African State in Transition*, New York: St Martin's Press, pp. 117–48.

—— and Olorunsola, Victor A. 'Managing competing state and ethnic claims'. In Donald Rothchild and Victor A. Olorunsola (eds), *State Versus Ethnic Claims: African policy dilemmas*, Boulder, Col.: Westview Press, pp. 1–24.

Samoff, Joel 1979: 'The bureaucracy and the bourgeoisie: decentralization and class structure in Tanzania'. *Comparative Studies in Society and History*, 20: 30–62.

Seidman, H. 1980: *Politics, Position and Power: the dynamics of federal organization.* Oxford:

Skocpol, Theda 1979: *States and Social Revolutions.* Cambridge: Cambridge University Press.

Strayer, Joseph R. 1955: *Western Europe in the Middle Ages.* New York: Appleton-Century-Crofts.

—— 1971a: 'The development of feudal institutions'. In Strayer, *Medieval Statecraft and the Perspectives of History*, Princeton, N.J.: Princeton University Press, pp. 77–89.

—— 1971b: 'The historical experience of nation-building in Europe'. In Strayer, 1971a.

—— 1971c: 'Normandy and Languedoc'. In Strayer, 1971a, pp. 44–54.

—— 1971d: 'Philip the Fair: a constitutional king'. In Strayer, 1971a, pp. 195–212.

—— 1971e: 'Viscounts and viguiers under Philip the Fair'. In Strayer, 1971a, pp. 213–31.

—— and Munro, Dana C. 1959: *The Middle Ages, 395–1500.* New York: Appleton-Century-Crofts.

Thompson, Virginia and Adloff, Richard 1981: *Conflict in Chad.* Berkeley, Cal.: Institute of International Affairs.

Tierney, Brian and Painter, Sidney 1978: *Western Europe in the Middle Ages, 300–1475.* New York: Alfred Knopf.

Vengroff, Richard 1985: 'Decentralization and the implementation of rural development in Senegal: the role of rural councils'. Paper presented at 28th Annual Meeting, African Studies Association, New Orleans, 23–26 November.

Welch, Claude E. Jr 1987: 'The military and the state in Africa: problems of political transitions'. In Zaki Ergas (ed.). *The African State in Transition*, New York: St Martin's Press, pp. 191–215.

—— and Smith, Arthur K. 1974: *Military Role and Rule: perspectives on civil-military relations.* North Scituate, Mass.: Duxbury Press.

Willame, Jean-Claude 1970: 'Congo-Kinshasa: General Mobutu and two political generations'. In Claude E. Welch (ed.), *Soldier and State in Africa*, Evanston, Ill.: Northwestern University Press, pp. 124–51.

Young, Crawford 1983: 'Comparative claims to political sovereignty: Biafra, Katanga, Eritrea'. In Rothchild and Olorunsola, 1983, pp. 199–232.

—— and Turner, Thomas 1985: *The Decline of the Zairian State.* Madison, Wis.: University of Wisconsin Press.

Zolberg, Aristide R. 1966: *Creating Political Order: the party-states of West Africa.* Chicago, Ill: Rand McNally.

8

The Pendulum between Theory and Substance

Testing the Concepts of Legitimacy and Trust

MATTEI DOGAN

Legitimacy is the belief that the authority of a given country is entitled to issue commands which the citizens have an obligation to obey. Such a definition, inspired by Max Weber's theory of legitimacy, focuses on the key elements of entitlement and obligation.

The concept of legitimacy can be tested empirically by survey, research on confidence in institutions, trust of leaders and support for the regime. If people hold the opinion that existing institutions are appropriate or morally proper then those institutions are legitimate. Such a reference to opinion is clear in the widely known definition formulated by S.M. Lipset: 'the capacity of the system to engender and maintain the belief that the existing political institutions are the most appropriate for the society' (Lipset, 1959, p. 77). Juan Linz proposes a minimalist definition: 'the belief that in spite of shortcomings and failures, the political institutions are better than any others that might be established, and therefore can demand obedience' (Linz, 1988, p. 65).

Legitimacy is particularly important in democracies since the authority of the rulers depends ultimately on the support of at least a majority of the citizens. Such public support is considerably less important in non-democratic regimes. In dictatorships, while the granting of support or legitimacy may be an asset, it is not of primary importance because authority is based on force. The authoritarian regimes may not have legitimacy, but they need it. The subtitle of Michael Hudson's book *Arab Politics* is significant: *The search for legitimacy*. As he puts it,

> The central problem of government in the Arab World today is
> political legitimacy. Whether in power or in the opposition, Arab
> politicians must operate in a political environment in which the legi-
> timacy of rulers, regimes and the institutions is sporadic, and at best,
> scarce. ... assassinations, coups d'état and official repression, may
> in fact derive from the low legitimacy accorded to the political
> process. (Hudson, 1977, p. 2)

From Xenophon to Hume, philosophers already knew that the most
despotic ruler could not base his power exclusively on material
force.

Weber's typology of legitimacy is an essential aspect of his theory,
and it is this typology that I intend first to test empirically.

Obsolescence of the Classical Weberian Typology of Legitimacy

Max Weber's seminal typology of legitimacy has been meaningfully
applied in many historical studies: 'Since Weber, we have been
very busy putting the phenomenon into one or another of his three
boxes and charting the progress by which charismatic authority
becomes routinized into traditional authority which ... gives way in
turn to rational legal authority' (Schaar, 1981, p. 15).

Historically, traditional authority and charismatic power are rooted
in authoritarian regimes. They never appear in true democracies.
The implication is that some authoritarian regimes can be legitimate. Among the contemporary countries with rational-legal authority some are legitimate, particularly the pluralist democracies, but
most are not, above all the authoritarian regimes. Thus, the Weberian
typology does not cover directly the relationship between legitimacy
and democracy.

Throughout the centuries, until the American and French Revolutions, the governments of independent countries, with the exception of Switzerland, were based on traditional legitimacy. During
the nineteenth century all but two of the European countries were
ruled by monarchs. At the turn of the century Pope Leo XIII
proclaimed in his encyclical *Immortale Dei* that 'the authority of those
who govern derives from God's power and so has more than human
dignity'. But two decades later four emperors – one Catholic, one
Protestant, one Orthodox and one Muslim – fell almost simultaneously from their thrones, having lost their legitimacy. Today,
in the monarchies that still survive, the throne fills a symbolic,

mythical or ceremonial function, the most interesting case being the Japanese Emperor (Weber-Schäfer, 1986). Among the democratic regimes only in Spain and Belgium did the monarch have an opportunity to play, at certain moments, a political role – one that could have been also assumed by a president. True traditional legitimacy still exists for a significant part of the population in only a handful of countries (Morocco, Saudi Arabia, Nepal). Because the traditional dynastic legitimacy of divine right represents a vanishing form of authority, the Weberian typology is losing one of its 'boxes'. For the study of the contemporary world this type of legitimacy is statistically irrelevant.

Few words in the sociological literature have been as blessed as the word 'charisma'. Some scholars abuse it. Today the most frequent phenomenon is the personalization of power, which can take extreme forms such as the cult of personality or the engineering of political idolatry.

In the distant past charismatic leadership was always rooted in religious grounds, Moses, David and Muhammad being the archetypes. The concept of charisma, borrowed by Max Weber from the canonist Rudolph Sohn, has a religious connotation and for this reason is inappropriate for contemporary secularized societies, even if, as Luciano Cavalli (1981) emphasizes, it remains important as an 'ideal type' in historical studies.

The nineteenth century (1814–1918) offered few cases of charismatic leadership because Europe, as it was designated by Metternich after the fall of Napoleon, had been dominated by monarchs who embodied political legitimacy and who benefited from the accomplishments of heroes such as Garibaldi or of great statesmen such as Bismark, Disraeli and Gladstone.

The building of new nation-states after the Second World War in Asia and Africa saw the appearance of founding fathers, most of whom soon became armed prophets, political priests or plebiscitarian dictators; India was a clear exception. But this historical period of the emergence of new nation-states that idolized their founding fathers – Bourguiba being a notable example – has almost ended because there remain few nations that are deprived, as is Kurdistan, of independent status. Today, the most frequent phenomenon in Third World countries is authoritarian-bureaucratic rulership, in many cases of a military nature. These regimes born from *coups d'état* have a very low potentiality for legitimation.

The legitimacy of most leaders who were initially considered charismatic has been eroded. Biographical studies written after their fall or their death explain their successes not in terms of charisma but by taking into consideration a multiplicity of factors that reduce charisma to a congruence between the image of a personality and the aspirations of the masses – the best example being Nasser – or that interpret it as organized political religion. Yesterday's subjugation remains an historical fact, but it is necessary to stress that the degeneration of transient charismatic leadership into an idolatrous cult and tyrannical rule has been more frequent than the routinization of charisma into new institutions. For the twentieth century the notion of charisma is helpful only for a handfull of political leaders. Its application to a satrap such as Stalin or to a *commediante* such as Mussolini is misleading. The limited number of modern genuinely charismatic leaderships – Gandhi, Ataturk, Khomeini and a few others – makes the charismatic type of legitimacy a residual one.

At the dusk of the twentieth century there remains only one full 'box' in the Weberian typology: the legal-rational-bureaucratic legitimacy. A typology which in empirical research shrinks to such an extent is no longer fruitful. It becomes a inadequate tool, even though it remains a useful guide in historical sociology. The fact that we need several words to designate this single 'box' – legal-rational-bureaucratic – suggests that it is very heterogeneous, amalgamating many varieties.

In this amalgam we can distinguish at least four varieties. First, we have the advanced pluralist democracies accepted by most of their citizens as basically legitimate. Depending on the definition we adopt, we can count in 1991 between 30 and 35 advanced pluralist democracies that have enjoyed a substantial legitimacy for more than 20 years.

The second variety represents the so-called authoritarian bureaucratic systems (see Riggs, 1993, among others) where civil rights are partially respected and which have either civilian or military rulers. They may have some legitimacy in the eyes of part of the population. There is, obviously, a great diversity among these authoritarian regimes. The right question to ask is not whether or not they are legitimate but, avoiding such a dichotomy and using Easton's (1965) terminology, how much 'diffuse support' they enjoy.

The third variety includes dictatorial, tyrannical or totalitarian regimes rejected by the large majority of the population, even if it cannot denounce publicly such illegitimacy. Absence of revolt does not imply adhesion to the regime. Revolt is possible only in certain historical circumstances, when a regime is obliged to start a process of liberalization. In totalitarian regimes attempts to revolt can be suicidal. The Chinese communist establishment, by repressing the revolt in Tienanmen Square, wanted to stop the incipient liberal-ization movement. The number of *coups d'état* is the most visible measure of illegitimacy, for instance in Africa in the last three decades and earlier in Latin America. This criterion has been adopted by a number of scholars, but we should not assume that in a given country legitimacy exists simply because the regime is not openly contested.

The fourth variety refers to the countries 'where there is neither acceptance nor rejection of rulership' and for which 'discussion of legitimacy becomes meaningless' (Herz, 1978, p. 320). Most of these countrles are among the poorest in the world. In many rural areas of Africa and Asia, identified by the World Bank, and in the shantytowns of giant metropolises, the issue of legitimacy of the regime is absent from the minds of most people. Their poverty is not perceived as resulting from the behaviour of current rulers; it is attributed to some god or to nature. In these countries tyrants are often perceived as a fatality. Where violence is absent, legitimacy is not necessarily present. The concept of legitimacy is not adequate for perhaps one out of every four Third World countries.

This simple account shows that the majority of political regimes are deprived of legitimacy and consequently are not covered by the Weberian typology. Many other 'boxes' are needed: the quasi-legitimate type, the illegitimate type and so on.

Today it is more difficult than in the past to make clear-cut classifications, because the legitimacy of a regime can be based on more than one type of authority. American democracy is not based exclusively on the Constitution. How much rationality and how much tradition is there in contemporary Indian democracy? Max Weber has implicitly accepted this idea of mixed legitimacy by dis-cussing the dynamics of the process of legitimation and delegiti-mation. The ideal types that he constructed are antagonistic only in theory. In reality, all traditional systems have some features of legal-rational legitimacy: the Chinese emperors or the Russian tsars respected some of the rules of the game.

Briefly stated, the Weberian typology of legitimacy appears anachronistic in the contemporary world. It is no longer appropriate because only a few countries today have a traditional authority, while the charismatic phenomenon is extremely rare; Khomeini is the latest example. Two of the three 'boxes' of the Weberian typo-logy are, for the contemporary world, almost empty. In the third 'box' we have to lodge almost all independent nations – about 170 – mixing a wide variety of regimes. Weber's definition of legitimacy needs an updated reformulation by taking into consideration the neighbouring concepts of confidence, trust, popularity and effectiveness.

How Much Legitimacy?

There is not a single example of a country where the totality of the people consider the regime as fully legitimate. Legitimacy comes by degrees. Ranking regimes on an imaginary axis from the minimum to the maximum of legitimacy is a promising start for the comparative analysis of political systems. Many scholars have felt the need of such a comparison: 'Legitimacy runs the scale from complete acclaim to complete rejection ... ranging all the way from support, consent, compliance through decline, erosion and loss. In the case of conscious rejection we may speak of illegitimacy' (Herz, 1978, p. 320).

As Juan Linz (1988, p. 66) stresses: 'no political regime is legitimate for 100 per cent of the population, nor in all its commands, nor forever, and probably very few are totally illegitimate based on coercion'. Legitimacy never reaches unanimity; groups and individuals never recognize equally the authority of the political power. There are apathetic popular strata and rebellious sub-cultures, pacific dissidents and armed terrorists, and between them many who are only partially convinced by the pretensions to legitimacy claimed by the rulers. David Easton argues that the ratio of deviance to conformity as measured by violation of laws, the prevalence of violence, the size of dissident movements or the amount of money spent on security would provide indices of support (Easton, 1965, p. 163). But it is difficult in empirical research to measure 'violations of laws' or 'dissident movements'.

Opinion polls attempting to evaluate a regime's legitimacy measure things related to legitimacy more easily than legitimacy itself. For example, support for leaders and policies is easily measured by polls and may be related to a regime's legitimacy but none of these are real proof of legitimacy itself. Lack of support for a specific leader or policy does not mean a lack of overall legitimacy. In spite of all these difficulties it is possible to consider legitimacy as a trait of political systems which can be evaluated, and to say of a particular country that it has more or less legitimacy than another. Legitimacy is a concept that can be empirically tested.

A pertinent question has been asked several times in various countries, inviting people to choose between three statements reflecting the debate about legitimacy: (a) 'I accept overall the existing law, our present system of government and our society'; (b) 'I see many shortcomings in our present system, but I believe in a gradual improvement within the existing system of government'; (c) 'I completely reject the existing law, our present system of government and our society; the only solution is complete social change.' The first statement implies a strong faith in the legitimacy of the regime. The second, the belief that in spite of all its faults the existing regime is better than any other that could be conceived, and also the feeling that it could and should be improved. The third statement indicates that the current regime is considered illegitimate. In most democracies the proportion of people choosing the third statement in 1981 was very low: United States 9 per cent; Germany 3 per cent; Canada 7 per cent; Australia 10 per cent. In a few countries the proportion is relatively high: France 26 per cent; Britain 24 per cent and in one country, India, a level (41 per cent) which almost challenges the legitimacy of the system (Hastings and Hastings, 1982, p. 512). The absolute majority sees 'many shortcomings' and only a minority 'accepts overall' the system of government.

Theoretically, the lower the degree of legitimacy, the higher the amount of coercion. Therefore, in order to operationalize the concept of legitimacy it is advisable to take into consideration some indicators of coercion, such as the absence of human rights and civil liberties. These indicators are based on the evaluation of freedom of expression, of association, of demonstration, the degree of military intervention in the political arena, fair elections, freedom of religious institutions, independence of the judiciary, free competition among parties, absence of government terror, and so on. Raymond Gastil in his annual collection *Freedom in the World* (1980–9) has attempted in collaboration with many experts to rank countries according to these criteria. Such a ranking is very useful for the comparative analysis of legitimacy.

A high level of corruption is one of the clearest symptoms of delegitimation. The fall of political regimes is often preceded by generalized corruption, the most notable historical examples being the fall of the Chinese imperial dynasty, of the last shah of Iran, and of the Soviet *nomenklatura*. Multiple testimonies and dozens of books denounce institutionalized corruption at all levels of public administration in most African countries. When the judiciary is also contaminated there is no longer hope for the ordinary citizen. It is then that a crisis of legitimacy can be anticipated.

Pardoxically, the scandals which denounce corruption are not necessarily symptoms of delegitimation, because they can blow up only where there is freedom of speech. We may even say that a regime where scandals can blow up is not totally illegitimate. In some exceptional cases, the scandal may appear as an irrefutable test of democratic functioning of the system. The Dreyfus affair, the Watergate affair and the Irangate affair are superb monuments honouring the French and American democracies. Few countries have such a well-rooted democracy that it is able to correct political errors against the will of the army, or to oblige the president to resign. Italy is one of them: President Leone, involved in a corruption scandal, was obliged to relinquish his post.

Legitimacy of Regimes and Confidence in Institutions

The distinction between legitimacy of the regime and confidence in particular institutions or office-holders is needed for pluralist democracies. No institution can escape some criticism from some segment of society. Unanimity is a ridiculous pretension of totalitarian regimes.

A confusion is too often made beween the legitimacy of the regime and the legality of the government. In a democratic country the government is changed periodically and it is considered as legitimate precisely because there are formal rules regulating the replacement of one set of office-holders by another. Hostility towards the party in power is compatible with faith in the soundness of the democratic regime. Even an occasional violation of the constitutional rules by transient rulers does not challenge the legitimacy of the political system. What is lost then is confidence in specific institutions or trust in their officials.

The distinction between legitimacy and trust appears in the possible replies to a very simple question: 'Should a policeman be obeyed?' 'He should be obeyed because his order is right.' Such a reply implies legitimacy *and* trust. 'This particular policeman is wrong, and an appeal to a higher authority should be made, but for the moment he should be obeyed because he represents authority.' This second reply indicates legitimacy without trust. The police as an institution can be perceived as legitimate even if a particular policeman may not be trusted. If many policeman are corrupt or unnecessarily brutal, the police, as an institution, is mistrusted.

In many democracies presidents or prime ministers often receive a low score in the polls, their policies being disapproved of and even their personalities being questioned. The phenomenon appears with particular clarity in France, the United States, Britain and

Italy. But low popularity and lack of trust do not signify absence
of confidence in the presidency or the office of the prime minister
as an institution. When elected regularly, these officials have a
legitimate function even if they are unpopular as individuals.

The level of confidence in institutions should not be confused
with the proportion of people who approve or disapprove of the way
the government is handling various issues such as housing, employment, education, taxation, health services, pensions and so on.
Opinions on these issues fluctuate and are related to party preferences; they may change when parties in power alternate. A majority
of citizens could be dissatisfied with the way the government is
running the country, could think that the government's policies are
not fair to all concerned and find that its record is poor. Such
opinions do not challenge the legality of the government; they are
not directly related to the basic problem of confidence in institutions, but they do influence the extent of trust in the rulers. When
a majority of Canadians said in January 1985 that they had 'no
confidence' or only 'a little confidence' in the way the government
was handling the problem of unemployment were they expressing a
lack of confidence in the political regime itself or only a mistrust
of the current decision-makers? Other studies conducted in the
1980s leave no doubt that the majority of Canadians did not contest
the legitimacy of the regime and did manifest confidence in its institutions. Canada is taken here just as an example. This distinction
between issue-orientated opinion and faith in the wisdom of the
constitutional institutions should be applied to all advanced pluralist
democracies.

A democracy can always be improved; it is never perfect. The
diversity of opinions is inscribed in the logic of democracy. Some
people may be dissatisfied with the way in which the democratic
game is played: 'Criticism that a contemporary democratic state is
not democratic enough, or different concepts of democracy, are
difficult to handle in that the critics may still be supportive of democratic government in principle while finding the current regime
wanting' (Merkl, 1988, p. 23). Criticism of those who administer an
institution does not imply that the institution itself is seen as illegitimate. 'Trust might be an indicator of legitimacy, be derived
from it, and contribute to its reinforcement, but trust should not be
confused with legitimacy' (Linz, 1958, p. 66).

One of the most significant findings of survey research on legitimacy conducted during recent decades in Western pluralist democracies is of the persistent ubiquity of a significant part of the
citizenry that expresses limited or no confidence in some institutions

of the country and does not trust the leaders of these institutions, but does not contest the legitimacy of the political system itself.

To the question asked repeatedly in ten countries of the European Community since 1973: 'On the whole, are you very satisfied, fairly satisfied, not very satisfied or not at all satisfied with the way democracy works in our country?', the average proportion of people who were 'not at all satisfied', or 'not very satisfied' varied between 1973 and 1989 from 42 per cent to 49 per cent. These figures conceal important national differences: more than three-quarters of Italians compared with approximately one-fifth of West Germans (*Eurobarometer*, 1973–90). Yet, in all countries without exception, a strong majority admitted that 'everyone is free to criticize'.

One of the most suprising findings is the relatively high proportion of citizens who have no confidence in parliament ('not at all' or 'not very much'). From 11 democracies in 1981, only in West Germany did a majority express 'a great deal' or 'quite a lot' of confidence in this oldest of democratic institutions. In all the other countries only a minority showed confidence in parliament: about one-third in Italy, Belgium and Denmark (Hastings and Hastings, 1981, p. 554). Other surveys conducted in the 1970s and 1980s confirm that a persistent and significant proportion of people do not trust parliament, not even in Britain (Hastings and Hastings, 1984, p. 358). Other institutions such as the press or the trade unions are also mistrusted by the majority in all 12 countries of the European Community.

Mistrust of rulers ranks even higher than mistrust of institutions. People who advocated that parliament should play an important role in the functioning of the political system nevertheless confessed that they held most parliamentarians in low esteem.

The mistrust of the political class, or a part of it, is not attributed simply to inefficiency or incompetence. It has deeper roots: 'How would you rate the honesty and the ethical standards of the people in these different fields?' In Britain in November 1988, the percentage of adults who rated them 'low' or 'very low' was 32 per cent for Members of Parliament; 28 per cent for government ministers; 43 per cent for union leaders; and 58 per cent for journalists (Hastings and Hastings, 1988–9, pp. 276–7). These figures contrast with the relatively high rating for physicians, police officers, civil servants, university professors and engineers. Similar results had been registered in previous surveys, that conducted in March 1985 in particular. Britain is by no means an exceptional case; it serves here only as an illustration for the whole of Western Europe. In searching for a significant exception one may think of Switzerland first. Disappointing results. To the question: 'Identify all whom you trust, considering the institutions or organizations as a whole, and not individuals or groups of individuals (multiple answers allowed)', only a minority of Swiss responded that they trusted the House of Representatives (38 per cent); the Senate (36 per cent); the state government (36 per cent); the Churches (36 per cent) the Swiss Army (42 per cent); the courts (35 per cent); the press (13 per cent); the political parties (12 per cent). Only the federal government and the Supreme Court were trusted by the majority (Hastings and Hastings, 1983–4, pp. 309–10).

The levels of trust and confidence are no higher on the other side of the Atlantic. Every odd-numbered year between 1973 and 1983, and annually since 1984, the Gallup Poll has asked in a nationwide sampling how much confidence people have in each of ten different institutions. In the surveys conducted between 1973 and 1987 Congress was ranked sixth or seventh, after the Church, the army, the Supreme Court, the banks and the public schools. Nevertheless, Congress ranked higher than big business, television and organized labour, and at the same level as the newspapers (Gallup Report, 1973–87).

Invited by Gallup Poll in 1985 to evaluate the ethical standards and the honesty of each of 25 occupations from 'very high' to 'very low', senators received a lower ranking than 14 other occupations, and congressmen were ranked eighteenth. In 1988 the 'representatives of the people' inspired less esteem than building contractors, newspaper reporters and funeral directors, but more than car salesmen and real-estate agents (Gallup Report, 1988, pp. 238, 239). These two surveys confirmed the results of earlier polls.

At what level does a regime risk losing its legitimacy? Is there a warning point? Italy could serve here as a clinical case. Of all the European democracies, Italy is the one in which every year since 1973 we have found the highest portion of people who say they are 'not satisfied with the way democracy works'; for instance, in 1987 72 per cent of Italians said they were not satisfied, with only 26 per cent being 'very satisfied' or 'fairly satisfied'. In the 25 surveys taken between 1973 and 1990 a negative judgement was formulated by more than 70 per cent of Italian adults, and in only one survey (November 1987) by a lower proportion (67 per cent). Hundreds of books and articles, whether written by scholars, politicians or foreign observers have denounced all kinds of weaknesses, from corruption and clientelism to ministerial instability and 'partitocrazia'. At the time of the Cold War, journalists designated Italy as the 'sick man of the Atlantic Alliance'. Dozens of surveys in recent decades indicate that the Italians have severely criticized the regime and its political class in particular. Nevertheless, democracy is still alive and the legitimacy of the democratic regime is contested only by a small minority. Only its performance is at issue. Italians have been invited during each of the last 20 years by the *Eurobarometer* to choose from three statements: (a) 'The entire way our society is organized must be radically changed by revolutionary action'; (b) 'Our society must be gradually improved by reforms'; (c) 'Our society must be valiantly defended against all subversive forces'. During these two decades a large majority of Italians have constantly chosen 'reforms', implicitly admitting the legitimacy of the regime. A significant minority has chosen 'defence against subversion'. Those supporting 'revolutionary action', contesting implicitly the legitimacy of the regime, varied from 6 per cent to 10 per cent: only in two surveys, in 1976 and 1977, did the proportion reach 12 per cent (*Bollettino della Doxa* and *Eurobarometer*).

In several surveys conducted by the Institute Doxa, Italians have admitted by a large majority that 'it is better to have a mediocre parliament than no parliament at all'. In the same surveys they denounced 'the multiplicity of parties as the source of all ills' and recognized simultaneously 'that parties are indespensible in a free country'. Thus, although very cynical about their political system and requesting reforms, Italians did not contest the legitimacy of the democratic regime. Why should they? Italy has achieved impressive economic growth and social development, higher and more rapid than most European countries. 'The Italian State is sick' but Italian society is in good health. Many countervailing forces explain the equilibrium of Italian democracy.

Italy is an extreme case of a general phenomenon. Although not as high as in Italy, the proportion of people 'dissatisfied with the way democracy works' is significant in many European countries: in 1985, 43 per cent in Britain, 48 per cent in France, 38 per cent in the Netherlands, 45 per cent in Ireland. The average was 45 per cent for the ten countries of the European Community (*Eurobarometer*, June 1985, p. 7). In all these countries the legitimacy of the regime is not contested by the largest part of the population. The theoretical implication is that criticism, dissatisfaction, even protest, refer to the performance of the regime, not dIrectly to its legitimacy.

In their book *The Confidence Gap*, S.M. Lipset and W. Schneider (1983) have reached the same diagnosis. After analysing a large amount of American survey data, they ask: Is there a legitimacy crisis? They found that 'people lose faith in leaders much more easily than they lose confidence in the system ... the public has been growing increasingly critical of the performance of major institutions' (Lipset and Schneider, 1983, pp. 378–9). Their conclusion is 'that the decline of confidence has both real and superficial aspects. It is real because the American public is intensely dissatisfied with the performance of their institutions. It is also to some extent superficial because Americans have not yet reached the point of rejecting those institutions' (ibid., p. 384).

Substantial empirical evidence covering some 18 Western democracies obliges us to make clear distinctions between the legitimacy of the regime, confidence in institutions, and the popularity of or trust in rulers. In a democratic country, even if the number of dissatisfied people reaches a high level, as attested by opinion polls, and remains at this level for a long time while spreading to many important institutions, the legitimacy of the regime is not necessarily challenged, except in case of a disaster, economic, military or social. The democratic regime does not collapse because there is no better alternative to democracy than to reform it democratically. The virtue of democracy is that it provides a method for change, expressed in formal rules for the political game.

Political Legitimacy and Economic Effectiveness

Given the ever-increasing role of the state in economic matters, including its redistributive functions, the legitimacy of the regime is influenced in the long run by its economic efficiency. Juan Linz (1988, p. 66) goes so far as to ask: 'To what extent can one speak of the legitimacy of the political system as distinct from a socioeconomic system?' Discussing the dynamic between legitimacy and effectiveness, S.M. Lipset focuses, through his examples, on economic effectiveness, even if his definition is wider ranging. He defines effectiveness as the actual performance of the government or 'the extent to which the system satisfies the basic functions of government' (Lipset, 1959, p. 77). When faced with a crisis of effectiveness such as an economic depression, the stability of the regime depends to a large extent on the degree of legitimacy which it enjoys. H. Eckstein (1966) also stresses that legitimacy builds a reservoir of goodwill on which the authorities can draw in difficult times, and increases the willingness of the people to tolerate shortcomings of effectiveness.

The relationship between legitimacy and efficiency can be understood through an analysis of historical examples. The breakdown of democracy in Chile could be explained in large part by the economic failures, particularly the inflation rate (746 per cent in one year) (Valenzuela, 1978, p. 55). During the last years of the Weimar Republic the increase in the unemployment rate and of the vote for the extreme right were intimately related. During the Great Depression of the 1930s a major crisis in effectiveness severely weakened European as well as American economies. Many scholars, particularly S.M. Lipset, have contrasted the impact of the depression on the United States and Britain, which had high levels of legitimacy, with the effects on the political system in Germany and Austria, where legitimacy was low.

Temporary disapproval of the government by majorities does not indicate a legitimacy gap but, in the long run, economic failures could erode the legitimacy of a regime or at least the authority of some of its institutions. The Eastern colossus has collapsed, not because of a military defeat but because of a complete failure in effectivness. The speed of the breakdown of the communist system in 1989–90 in the Soviet Union and its European satellites demonstrates how the economic ineffectiveness of a regime can ruin its legitimacy over time.

Long-term effectiveness can give a regime the chance to build its legitimacy. The rulers of Singapore, South Korea and Taiwan have gained enough legitimacy through their economic success to enable them to organize relatively free elections. But the most famous examples are Japan and the German Federal Republic, where the democratic game was born, or implemented, during a foreign occupation in a climate of suspicion and scepticism. The economic miracle has raised these two regimes from a total absence of legitimacy and from national humiliation to the forefront of the most legitimate of pluralist democracies.

The strains on legitimacy and the loss of trust result in part from the difficulty of governing, of steering a society. There are two opposite kinds of ungovernability: either through doing too much and becoming overloaded with the demands of a very complex society, as in advanced democracies, called welfare states; or through not doing enough, because the state is economically too weak and lacks the resources required to improve society (except in the oil-exporting countries).

In advanced democracies the loss of confidence in institutions or rulers and the accompanying political criticism come from the fact that the rulers have to take decisions under the direct and permanent scrutiny of the public. In a legitimate regime the people have the right to criticize. In the authoritarian regimes of developing countries the rulers face different kinds of problems. Their weakness comes not from exessive demands, but from the meagre resources at their disposal.

The absence of significant vertical mobility coupled with pronounced social inequality can also erode the legitimacy of a regime in the long run. As a matter of fact, the Gini index of inequality is much lower in advanced and legitimate democracies than in authoritarian regimes. The causality of this relationship has been elucidated by several sociologists and economists.

The role of intellectuals in the legitimation and delegitimation processes has attracted the attention of many authors. When the intellectual elites are those who oppose the regime, its legitimcy seems more fragile. In China, in the spring of 1989, it was the most highly educated segment of society that protested. The students represented less than one per thousand in Chinese society, but they succeeded in shedding light on the illegitimacy of the regime. In a comparative analysis of the common factors in revolutionary movements in Puritan England, the United States at the time of Washington, France in 1789 and Russia in 1917, Crane Brinton stresses the importance of the intellectual ferment which subsequently led to the spread of new ideas to a large part of the population, engendering a crisis of legitimacy.

Other social strata have attracted attention in the theory of legitimacy, such as the working class in the Marxist analysis. The clergy has also played an important role, in the Protestant countries in the past and more recently through liberation theology in some Latin American countries. In the last three decades the army has been the most visible agent of delegitimation in dozens of devoloping countries. Today, many of the authoritarian regimes, particularly in Africa and Asia, are ruled not by civilians but by military officers.

Final Remarks

Survey research conducted in almost all pluralist democracies during recent decades has revealed a 'gap of confidence' in some major institutions and a relatively high level of mistrust of the political class. Expression of a lack of confidence in Institutions results very often from a lack of trust in the individuals who run them. The ubiquity of this phenomenon in advanced democracies raises important questions concerning the theory of representative democracy and the role of mediators in the party system.

Power, legitimacy, trust and effectiveness do not have identical meanings in London and Jakarta, in Washington and Cairo. The ambition to encapsulate these concepts in definitions of universal validity may be a sin of Western cultural ethnocentrism. There are nevertheless significant similarities within each class of countries. We observe the same trends among advanced pluralist democracies, even if the level of confidence and the speed with which it changes vary from country to country. For instance, the ranking of institutions according to the confidence they enjoy tends to be the same for 15 Western democracies. There are also striking similarities among the authoritarian regimes in their attempts to obtain some legitimacy.

In recent times we have witnessed a multiplication of forms of legitimation and delegitimation. Empirical research has shown that the concept of legitimacy has become infused with many other sociological concepts, so that today it is more difficult to discover it in a pure form. The search for crystal-clear legitimacy, expressed in ideal types, should be relinquished to the philosophers.

References

Brinton, Crane 1938: *The Anatomy of Revolution*. New York: W.W. Norton.

Cavalli, Luciano 1981: *Il Capo Carismatico*. Bologna: Il Mulino.

Citrin, Jack 1974: 'The political relevance of trust in government'. *American Political Science Review*, 68: 973–88.

Dogan, Mattei (ed.) 1988: *Comparing Pluralist Democracies: strains on legitimacy*. Boulder, Col.: Westview.

Doxa, *Bollettino della* 1946 to date. Milan: Istituto per l'Analisi dell'Opinione Pubblica.

Easton, David 1965: *A Systems Analysis of Political Life*. New York: John Wiley.

Eckstein, Harry 1966: *Division and Cohesion in Democracy*. Princeton, N.J.: Princeton University Press.

Eurobarometer: public opinion in the European Community 1971–90. Brussels: Commission of the European Community, issues 1–33.

Gallup Report 1973–90: Various issues on *Confidence in American Institutions*, and on *Honesty and Ethical Standards of Professions*.

Gastil, Raymond D. 1980–9: *Freedom in the World: political rights and civil liberties*, 6 vols. New York: Freedom House.

Harding, Stephen, Philips, David and Fogarty, Michael 1986: *Contrasting Values in Western Europe*. London: Macmillan.

Hastings, E.H. and Hastings, P.K. 1981–90: *Index to International Public Opinion*. Westport, Conn.: Greenwood Press.

Herz, John 1978: '*Legitimacy, can we retrieve it?*' *Comparative Politics*, 10: 317–43.

Hudson, Michael C. 1977: *Arab Politics: the search for legitimacy*. New Haven, Conn.: Yale University Press.

Linz, Juan 1988: 'Legitimacy of democracy and the socioeconomic system'. In M. Dogan, 1988, pp. 65–113.

Lipset, Seymour Martin 1959: 'Social conflict, legitimacy and democracy'. In his *Political Man: the social basis of politcs*, New York: Doubleday.

—— and Schneider, William, 1983: *The Confidence Gap: business, labor and government in the public mind*, rev. edn. Baltimore, Md: Johns Hopkins University Press.

Merkl, Peter H. 1988: 'Comparing legitimacy and values among advanced countries'. In Dogan, 1988, pp. 19–64.

Miller, Arthur H. 1974: 'Poiitical issues and trust in government, 1964–1970'. *American Political Science Review*, 68: 951–72.

Riggs, Fred W. 1993: 'Fragility of the Third World's regimes', *International Social Science Journal*, 136: 199–243.

Schaar, Arthur H. 1981: *Legitimacy in the Modern State*. New Brunswick, N.J.: Transaction Books.

Valenzuela, Arturo 1988: 'The move to a socialist society'. In Juan Linz and Alfred Stefan (eds), *The Breakdown of Democratic Regimes*, Baltimore, Md: Johns Hopkins University Press.

Weber-Schäfer, Peter 1986: 'Divine descent and sovereign rule: a case of legitimacy?' In Athanasios Moulakis (ed.), *Legitimacy*, Berlin: de Gruyter, pp. 87–95.

Table of Contents